PANTHER SOUP

PANTHER SOUP

A European Journey in War and Peace

JOHN GIMLETTE

HUTCHINSON
LONDON

First published by Hutchinson 2008

2 4 6 8 10 9 7 5 3 1

Grateful acknowledgement is made for permission to reproduce lines from the following:

Answered Prayers by Truman Capote by permission of Random House, Inc.

French Provincial Cooking by Elizabeth David by permission of Grub Street Publishing

Armageddon by Max Hastings by permission of Pan Macmillan, London.
Copyright © Max Hastings 2004

A Moveable Feast by Ernest Hemingway, published by Jonathan Cape & Scribner,
an imprint of Simon & Schuster Adult Publishing Group. Reprinted by permission of
The Random House Group Ltd & Scribner, an imprint of Simon & Schuster Adult Publishing Group.
Copyright © 1964 by Ernest Hemingway Ltd. Copyright renewed © 1992 by
John H. Hemingway, Patrick Hemingway and Gregory Hemingway

The Last Time I Saw Paris by Elliot Paul by permission of Eland/Sickle Moon

Some of the episodes in this book first appeared in a different form in
The Times and the *Sunday Telegraph*

Hutchinson
Random House, 20 Vauxhall Bridge Road,
London SW1V 2SA

www.rbooks.co.uk

Addresses for companies within The Random House Group Limited can be found at:
www.randomhouse.co.uk/offices.htm

The Random House Group Limited Reg. No. 954009

A CIP catalogue record for this book
is available from the British Library

ISBN 9780091921385 (hardback)
ISBN 9780091796730 (trade paperback)

The Random House Group Limited supports The Forest Stewardship Council (FSC),
the leading international forest certification organisation. All our titles that are printed on
Greenpeace approved FSC certified paper carry the FSC logo.
Our paper procurement policy can be found at:
www.rbooks.co.uk/environment

Mixed Sources
Product group from well-managed
forests and other controlled sources
FSC   www.fsc.org Cert no. TT-COC-2139
© 1996 Forest Stewardship Council

Typeset by Palimpsest Book Production Limited, Grangemouth, Stirlingshire
Printed and bound in Great Britain by
Clays Ltd, St Ives plc

To my father, Dr T.M.D. Gimlette

Contents

Illustrations

War memorials in Garmisch-Partenkirchen
German POWs
Josef Ratzinger, 1943 (*PA Photos*)
Manfred Rommel, aged 15 (*Courtesy of Manfred Rommel*)
Manfred Rommel, 2007
Olympic Stadium, Garmisch-Partenkirchen
US Army in the Alps (*US Army Photograph*)
The Leutasch Valley
Putnam Flint's father, 1906 (*Courtesy of Putnam Flint*)
Putnam Flint and his grandson
Putnam Flint with a marksman's *drillinger*
The Main Street, Innsbruck
Tirolean Austrians
Bruno Grossman, 2007
Bruno Grossman, 1945
The 'beach' at Oberhofen (inset: Putnam Flint)
The Oberhofen *Schützenfest* (inset: WW2 rifles & Alfred Kirchmair and his niece)
The summit of Hohe Munde
The Author on Hohe Munde
Putnam Flint as portrayed by a concentration camp survivor

Unless otherwise attributed, all photographs are from the author's collection. Every effort has been made to contact all copyright holders. The publishers will be glad to make good in any future editions any errors or omissions brought to their attention.

Line illustrations

All sketches are by the author

Maps

Acknowledgements

I would like to thank the following for their help with this book.

In France – Pascale Gautier-Keogh at the British Consulate, Marseille, Charles Allard, the Bentebackh brothers, Bernard Meyran (who now lives in the old Gestapo Headquarters, Marseille), Francine Huber of Lupstein, Mr Horace Thompson of the US Military Cemetery of St Avold, M. and Mme René Neu and Arsène Kirschner of Rohrbach-lès-Bitche, M. and Mme Arthur Steiner of Glasenberg, Alexandre Leininger, Mme Andrée Cuisse, and Pierre and Chantal Mazoyer of Bitche.

In Germany – Dr Manfred Rommel, Martin and Ester Keutner, Philipp Lepenies, Marc Rieppel, Dr Ann-Katrin Rupf, Dr and Mrs Johne, Linda Borchert (of the German National Tourist Office, London), York Beerman and Birgit Bliesener of Garmisch-Partenkirchen, and Alexandra Kern of the Hotel Aschenbrenner in Partenkirchen.

In Austria – Frau Gertl Schenk, Trude Harmer, Alfred Kirchmaier and Martha and Hermann Föger of Oberhofen, Veronika and Georg Haider of Gries im Sellrain, Heike Bruckner at the Oberhofen Alm, Wolfgang Kozák, Rudy Larcher, Johann Pfeifhofer, Rudolf Wille, Ulrich, Richard and Helmut Schlögl, and particularly Peter Schlögl for all his help and introductions in Innsbruck.

In the USA – Sim Smiley, Margi Flint, Lorraine Masone, Polly Whiteside, Jeff Bartley, Max Heller and Bill Warren (both formerly of A Company 824th TD) and the industrious team at Knopf, including Sonny Mehta, Diana Coglianese and Chip Kidd. But, perhaps above all others, my thanks go to Putnam Flint. Not only has he been a superb companion throughout many of the travels described in this book, he's also been unfailingly generous in sharing with me his memories and artefacts from the times that I've described. His frank and occasionally disturbing trips back into the past – not to mention his first return to the battlefield in six decades – were, I now realise, considerable acts of courage in themselves.

In England – Gilla Leigh, Sir Christopher Mallaby, Andre Chadwick, Patrick Chadwick, Sir Ewen Fergusson, Hugh Mainwaring, Caroline Hamilton, Nick Hills, Dickie Bannenberg, Gaëlle Richards, Christine Walker at *The Times*, Yvonne Constantinis for her logistical support, Carole Jobin, Nancy Wake, GM, Debbie Taylor, Maggie O'Sullivan at the *Sunday Telegraph*, Polly Cook (of the Austrian Tourist Board), Ann Noon (of Maison de la France), Gwen Kennedy, Francesca Montali-Woolaston, my agent Georgina Capel, and the team at Hutchinson, not least Tony Whittome and James Nightingale. I also extend my special thanks to my parents, Dr and Mrs T.M.D. Gimlette, for all their help and encouragement with this book, and to them, Melissa and Jonathan Taylor, Charles Thursby-Pelham and District Judge Alan Simons for their invaluable suggestions on the draft manuscript.

Sadly, there are three people whose contribution I am now too late to properly acknowledge. The first is Air Chief Marshal Sir Lewis Hodges. He died whilst I was writing this book. If I have understood anything of conditions in wartime Marseille it is thanks mainly to him.

The second person is Charlie Kennedy, who provided me with his own extraordinary first-hand account of the battle for Marseille. A generous and intensely modest man, Charlie always seemed to shrug off the plaudits although the truth is that few men have been so highly decorated by the government of France.

The third person is Kitora Bartley, who died in Maryland on 8 September 2007. She was born whilst her father, Putnam Flint, was serving in France in January 1945. Without her help and encouragement, her father would not have returned to the battlefield with me, and – without him – there would have been no book. Despite her long illness, her interest and enthusiasm for this project never faltered, and I shall miss her very much.

Finally, there's my wife, Jayne. As before, she's been a source of tireless inspiration and support, and, as an editor-in-residence, her comments and suggestions have proved indispensable. My gratitude therefore comes, as always, with all my love.

PANTHER SOUP

The Author's route through France, Germany and Austria

BELGIUM

GERMANY

LUXEMBOURG

Rhine

FRANCE

Mannheim
Heidelberg
Heilbronn
Bitche
VOSGES DU NORD
Lauterbourg
Saverne
Ulm
HAUT VOSGES
Strasbourg
Baccarat
ALSACE
Munich
LORRAINE
Epinal

Garmisch-
Partenkirchen
AUSTRIA
Innsbruck
Dijon

SWITZERLAND

Saône

Rhine

Rhône

ITALY
Lyon

Rhône

Avignon

Septèmes-les-Vallons
Marseille

Islands of
Ratonneau
and Pomegues
Les Calanques

N

0   50   100   150   200 km
0   50   100 mls

MEDITERRANEAN

Introduction

It's hard now to imagine the mire that Europe was by May 1945.

Years of war had left it smashed and sodden. In Germany, over three million homes had been lost, and another million in France. Sixty million Europeans had been uprooted or 10 per cent of the total population. Thousands of bridges were gone, not to mention schools, factories, mines, ports and farms. In many places, the simplest of utilities had ceased to exist, and people had reverted to conditions of primordial squalor. In Heidelberg, the citizenry were picking over the dump, and in Paris they were eating the pigeons again. Structures had vanished and so too had much of society. Nearly two-thirds of France's rolling stock had been stolen, and over a million of her citizens had spent the war in captivity.

Europeans will probably never forget how it all began. Six years earlier, German tanks had burst out of the Reich and fanned across the continent in *Flächenmarsch*, or formation drive. There was no stopping this great massed phalanx of armour, tanks to the fore and sides, as it ploughed across Europe. Everything before it was crushed and torched, and – in the tracks through the flattened corn – came the infantry and armoured cars. It's said that behind them came a stampede of riderless horses, like the wreckage of the Apocalypse. Europe was literally trampled to bits.

The Allies' response – some years later – was no less destructive. They'd produced four times as many tanks as the Axis powers, enough for a queue of armour 800 miles long. Then, for every ton of bombs the Germans dropped on Britain, the Allies unleashed 315 on Germany. By the end, they'd dropped 3.4 million tons, much of it as 'area bombing', the systematic wasting of cities, suburb by suburb. For every soldier the Allies killed on the battlefield, they killed at least two civilians. In the last six months of war alone, 275,000 tons of bombs fell on Germany's transport system, severing it from the outside world and making cavemen of its society.

Meanwhile, as the Russians hacked away at Germany's eastern flanks, the Anglo-Americans came in from the west. They brought with them over a quarter of a million vehicles, churning up the dirt. Once again, the countryside shuddered and reverted to mud. 'You get the feeling,' wrote one young US army captain, 'that the army is an immense flood pouring over the countryside tipped with violence at the crest and depositing flotsam in the backwaters.' In the last year alone, over 2.7 million Americans would come slogging through the muck.

Small wonder that, by the end, huge areas of the continent looked as if they'd been harrowed, or at least raked of life. In the fight for Germany, another 400,000 were killed and eight million made homeless. Many German towns appeared to have been pulverised, and the commentators of the day often wondered whether Germany would ever support civilisation again.

There were many oddities about these years of carnage. I have a mental picture of Christmas trees decorated with ribbons of anti-aircraft chaff, and of German postmen delivering mail to addresses under fire. The destruction was remarkable but so too were the lives that survived it. In this crucible, humankind seems to have found an intensity of feeling: whole lives lived in a day; love and joy snatched between weeks of boredom and terror; human spirit where nothing else was left. People have often told me that these were the worst moments of their life but also the best.

Sixty years on, there is much to misunderstand, and much that is richly bizarre. It's always struck me as strange how often the adversaries named their killing-machines after cats and other carnivores. The Americans had Wolverines and Hellcats whilst amongst the German *panzers* – or tanks – there were *Marder*, *Brummbären*, *Panther* and *Jagdtiger* (Pine Martens, Bears, Panthers and Hunting Tigers). Often, it was the fear of bigger predators – 'The Tiger Terror' – that determined the course of the battles. It's odd to think of the European chaos as the work of cats, a sort of feline stew, a *Panthersuppe*.

I've often wondered about the relationship between this wreckage and the places they've become. Can one still sense the boom and whine of battle? An enormous mobile 'city' of over two million Americans moved across the face of Europe, and yet what have they left behind? Does it feel as if the future of our world was forged here? Did it ever feel that way? What became of the people of these ruins? In the summer of 2004, and during the next two years, I decided to indulge my curiosity, and travel back through the war.

There were plenty of survivors to show me the way. During these travels, I would come across French and Algerian veterans, *résistants*, the children of the Blitzkrieg and the Hitler Youth, refugees, flak-gunners, battlefield farmers, German POWs, Austrian conscripts and a spy and an Allied pilot on the run. They had in common a sense of disbelief, a feeling that the past cannot have been as they remembered it, and a fear that they wouldn't be believed. Perhaps too they shared the anxiety of the *fin de siècle*, the need to preserve. Whatever it was, their memories would emerge with startling candour. I was constantly surprised by their revelations, whether it was the woman who loved fighting, the enemy's acts of humanity or – occasionally – the pointless cruelty of the Allies. *It must be told as it was*, they'd say.

But, through most of these travels, my guide – emotionally if not geographically – was an American, called Putnam Flint. In one sense, it seemed perfectly natural to make this journey with an American; after all, the liberation of Western Europe was largely an American enterprise.

In every other sense, however, the presence of an American made my travels seem even more exotic. All my adult life I've been drawn to Americans, with their determination to do the right thing, their sense of the possible and their talent for making it happen, but I've never truly understood them. At a superficial level, this is just a linguistic problem (Americans don't *bonk* or *slim*, and have no use for *bumph*, *crisps*, *plonk* or *Christmas crackers*) but – more profoundly – I realise there's truly a difference of perspective. As the tenants of an enormous space, Americans see no limit to human potential, whereas the British see only gaps and opportunities closing fast. Whilst the Americans might be guilty of overdoing things, the chances are we're doing nothing at all. Time too looks different to Americans. To them, history is awesome, whereas to us it's important. Perhaps that's why I enjoy being with them. To Americans, 'Liberty' actually means something whereas to us it's just a shop.

At the end of a star-spangled century it may be unfashionable to declare affection for Americans, but I'm not alone. Every year, the British spend over one and a half billion minutes on the phone to the USA, and there are over 45,000 flights between the two nations. Around 4.7 million Britons actually make the trip, some of them year after year. It's an affection that's partly cultural, partly genetic, and partly forged out of war. Of course, it wasn't always like this. Dr Johnson once said, 'I am willing to love all mankind except an American', a feeling he shared with a good few others, including Ruskin, Burton, Dickens, Wilde, Arnold and Trollope. But things have changed, and now the jibes are largely a matter of journalistic convention. Just as plenty of American writers insist that the British are all arrogant and phoney, so plenty of hacks over here portray America as all talk and no taste. Clearly, they can't have met men like Putnam Flint.

Flint and I had been introduced in London, over dinner with mutual friends. Our hostess was the Polar explorer, Caroline Hamilton, who Flint had met a year earlier on a cruise to Spitzbergen. This trip was in itself mildly surprising because Flint was now eighty-five, although he could have been younger. He told me he was a widower, and that he lived in Boston, Massachusetts, where he kept bees and blended his own sherry.

From the outset, I knew there was something special about this slight, rather elfin character, a sort of silvery impartiality. He spoke as if the only thing experience had ever taught him was that you can never learn enough. He was curious about everything and shocked by nothing, always courting uncertainty as if sensing only trouble in opinion. I now realise that, for much of Flint's life, such generosity of spirit had been an inspiration to others, most of them less fortunate than him. Some years on, I count myself amongst his vast – but now dwindling – coterie of friends, our friendship undaunted by the distance between us in years and miles.

During our first conversation, I stumbled into the war. Flint had begun to describe a much earlier visit to Europe, a remarkable journey that began in Marseille and ended in the Austrian Tyrol almost sixty years before. In all that time, he told me, he'd never spoken about it, and had never been back to the battlefields. Despite this, Flint was clearly an exceptional witness. His memory was like an archive of the senses, a repository of all the detail discarded by history. He could remember the sound of a bullet passing his ear, the smell of *Pfefferminz* schnapps and the taste of rabbit cooked with diesel, the feeling of tightness as the shells burst around him, and the jokes and the sex and terror.

Flint and I remained in touch by letter, and the following Spring he returned to London. The subject of the war often resurfaced, although never at Flint's instigation. He was always a reluctant historian. 'It was never like it is in the Hollywood movies,' he'd say. At other times, he'd declare that he had very little memory of the war, and then he'd go on to demonstrate that he had, and that it was probably the best of anyone I'd ever met. The dates and names of places had gone of course, but these, I realised, could all be recovered, by digging though the archives.

Some of Flint's happier memories were of those who'd travelled with him. He talked about his comrades as if he still saw them every day. They'd all been part of a large body of novice warriors known as The Tank Destroyers. By a curious coincidence of imagery, they too had adopted the big cat theme, and every man wore a panther on his sleeve. It was such a strong image that Flint and I would often refer to his unit as 'The Panthers' (although this was not, strictly speaking, a term much used at the time). But, whether feline or not, they were – as fellow-travellers – clearly unforgettable.

In the end, such an extraordinary journey emerged that it became the template for my own. I obtained Flint's battalion records from the National Archives in Washington DC, and began to join up the place-names on a map of Western Europe. A large knobbly 'J' appeared, upside-down across the face of the continent. This, I decided, would be the route of my journey through the end of the war. Only one question remained: would Flint come too, and lead me back along his road through the war?

For both of us, this presented a dilemma. For me, the issue was partly moral. Was it irresponsible to take Flint back to the battlefields of his youth? What emotional trauma might I inadvertently revive? And what would I do then? All this was something I'd have to discuss with him. Then there were the practical considerations. Was it feasible to take a man in his mid-eighties on such a long and uncertain journey? I had no idea then how strong Flint was. Nor was I entirely sure what such travels would reveal, or what to expect of Flint. Would his memory fail him, as he always predicted? Would he recognise anything of Europe restored? For months I was haunted by the image of us wandering aimlessly through a landscape of concrete and brand new homes, forlornly seeking the past.

As for Flint, his initial response was harder to gauge. When I eventually wrote to him, asking him to join me on my journey, I was met at first with several weeks of silence.

*

There have been Flints at almost every great moment of American history, mostly wishing they weren't.

The first Flints pitched up in New England on the eve of the English Civil War. It is sometimes rather ungenerously thought that they were Welsh robber barons but this has never bothered them. A sense of healthy impropriety has been passed down though the centuries and the Flints have always valued survival well above honour. In the twelve generations since their arrival in 1640, they have loyally adhered to the principles of self-preservation, though not always with success. Great-great-great-great-grandfather Flint was quick to join the rebels in 1775, and – though he ducked at Arlington – he was splattered at Stillwater. But Grandfather Horace and his brothers were harder to nail; Horace jumped marriages as if they were stricken ships, and then fled west and vanished; his brothers meanwhile bought their way out of the Civil War, by paying $300 to send a substitute. Then there was Uncle Billy, who sought self-preservation of a different kind, and traded his fortune for brandy before he too slithered from view.

In the last century, the Flints have flourished, now more baron than robber. But, although a hint of Welsh aristocracy had survived, they owed their good fortune not so much to blue blood as greenbacks. Cunning and inventive, they'd found themselves gratifyingly rich. They even acquired automobiles and a place amongst the Boston gentry. In their turn-of-the-century photographs, the Flints are depicted in gold braid and top hats, and riding camels round the Sphinx. Their friends now included the Pearys and Admiral Byrd, and Papa was appointed Deputy Chief of the New England FBI. Meanwhile, little Putnam Flint made his first appearance in the Boston Social Register in 1922, aged four. It was a promising start.

Such an exalted existence might well have continued like this but for the next Great American Moment. It was the Wall Street Crash of 1929. Once again, the Flints were paddling for survival. The servants were paid off and mother learnt to burn the pans. Oddly, hardship seemed to suit the young Flints and they happily shrugged off convention. Putnam and his brothers developed a taste for wine during prohibition, and knew every speakeasy. Once, they chartered an old wartime biplane and buzzed the Milton Town Hall, where their father was working. Even their sister, Fran, had become unnervingly feral. In later life, she'd become famous for her roadkill cookbooks, and – in widowhood – she'd have affairs with a Chilean and an African midget. She'd lived out west until she died, enjoying neither electricity nor plumbing.

The Thirties were full of great Flintian moments. In 1934, at the age of sixteen, Putnam and his brother, Vasmer, drove across the States in a Buick Roadster. Along the way, they slept in barns. Unsurprisingly, Putnam emerged from this Huckleberry adventure stronger than ever, and with an ancestral genius for survival. It would serve him well in years to come, amongst the ice and guns. Flint always claimed – rather modestly – that his greatest achievement of the Second World War was to have survived, along with all his men.

But let no one think a survivor's a shirker. During their eight months in the front line, six men of Flint's company were awarded Bronze Stars for their heroism, and one got a Silver Star. Of the Bronze Stars, two were awarded to men in Flint's platoon, one of them to Flint himself.

So when I asked him if he'd join me for part of my travels, his hesitation was unremarkable. His daughters told me that the battles of his past have never truly let him go, and have often reclaimed him at night. What happens when you turn your nightmares back into places, and your fears into forests? Do your demons burst into life? Or is it like the reassuring light of dawn? For weeks, Flint had wrestled with these thoughts but, in the end, his curiosity had triumphed, and he agreed, for the first time in sixty years to return to France.

John Gimlette
London 2007

Part 1 – Une Entrée Américaine

Sitting on my GI bed
My GI hat upon my head,
MY GI pants, my GI shoes,
Everything free, nothing to lose,
They issue everything we need,
Paper to write on, books to read,
Your belt, your shoes, your GI tie,
Everything free, nothing to buy.
You eat your food from GI plates,
Fill your needs at GI rates.
It's GI this and GI that,
GI haircut, GI hat,
GI razor, GI comb
GI wish that I were home

Panther Tracks, February 1945

Europe has what we do not yet have, a sense of the mysterious and inexorable limits of life, a sense, in a word, of tragedy. And we [Americans] have what they sorely need; a sense of life's possibilities.

James Baldwin

In America, everything goes and nothing matters. While in Europe, nothing goes and everything matters.

Philip Roth

The American army approaching Germany in the Fall of 1944 was in part a Children's Crusade.

Stephen Ambrose, *Citizen Soldiers*, 1998

This is how the world looked in the beginning, or perhaps how it will look in the end.

The air crackles with heat, and the sky is the colour of salt. It's an inert, waterless place, a series of eruptions blasted from the elements. My eyes sting with sea-smoke and ash. As I pick through the fissures and craters, I feel as if I'm scrambling through a petrified storm, great clouds of violet and magenta abruptly turned into rock. Nothing grows up here but sprigs of sea aster and sisal and fountains of dust. Way below, a volcanic sea cracks and sucks like blue glass burning. It is the ancient Mediterranean, in an adolescent mood.

This is the island of Pomègues, at the brittle end of the Frioul archipelago. From the cliffs, I can make out the knobbly, desiccated mountains of the Côte d'Azur, and, amongst them, the city of Marseille. Through all the smoke and vapours, it looks like Gomorrah, which is how most Frenchmen think of it. Forget it, said my friends in Paris, it's just a filthy port, full of whores.

Frioul has seldom seen hope welling up in the hearts of Frenchmen. Perhaps it's because – from a distance – the islands glow like bones, and turn the sea around them into liquid midnight. Or perhaps it's for all the hopes and promises that have foundered there. For centuries, it was a place of exile for criminals, revolutionaries, the mad and the diseased. Remarkably, I discover that the last hospital was only abandoned in the 1950s. Ossification has taken over so quickly that it now looks Pompeian. Rattoneau Island is covered in such ruins. Next-door Pomègues doesn't even have that.

The Marseillais still punish – or honour – their islands with isolation. I have Pomègues almost to myself. I clamber across the island and see no one except a group of Arab women swimming in a cove, and a very fat man. The women are fully clothed and hardly seem to notice the water around them. The fat man too seems very conscious of his clothes and walks as if he's wearing ermine and velvet. The oddest thing about it is that he's completely naked. Even the most sparing of places, it seems, can ease the harshness of reality.

After an hour, the island rises into a promontory and I'm attacked by *les gabians*. These foul, preternatural seabirds are the only creatures malicious enough to live up here, on this great, lifeless buttress. I begin to climb, under the snip and click of beaks and talons. The gabians have sown the aster with bones and shells, like a mortuary in the sky. Their vile pterodactyl chicks rasp at me from the ledges, and I can hear the bony scissors again, snipping at my ears.

Then I'm at the top, alone on an empty battlefield. It's like a landscape inside out, a great belly of eviscerated earth and rock. All around is the wreckage of an Armageddon, a vast fungal fortress system of shattered domes and concrete mushrooms, pillboxes, foxholes, giant gun emplacements, crumbling redans, rangefinders, embrasures and trenches ten feet deep. I find tiny, cement cells in the earth, like weird earth-borne fruits that have ripened and burst and turned to stone. Nothing has been spared the cataclysm. It's now a world of components and pieces; lumps of roadblock, bedsprings, a glittering carpet of glass, and fuel cans scattered like chaff. Obstinate chimneys nose their way up through the rubble and, in the cement, I see a date scratched with a stick: *1944.*

So, this bone-dry war village – *die Batterie von Pomègues* – flourished only momentarily before the bombs began to fall. It has flourished little since. These days the only colours erupting in the rubble are poppy reds and gassy clumps of lavatera. Few people come out here any more, to this rock so violently shunned. *Vive la Sodom*, says the graffiti.

Perhaps the aura of anxiety has never really lifted away. It's not hard to envisage the desperate battle that everyone knew would come, a short brutal flurry of rock, heat and dust. Amongst the sea-shells are bolts sheared, twisted steel, sleepers broken like matches, and armoured doors bent double in the blast. It's strange to think that these were liberating explosions – death to end tyranny, American bombs. And, of course, after the bombs came the ships, 880 of them on that first day of the Allied landings in southern France. 'The Other D-Day' had begun, exactly ten weeks after that to the north.

Had I been standing up here two months later – in October 1944 – I'd have seen them, still pouring down the Côte d'Azur; troopships, Liberty Ships, tugs, Blue Ribands, tankers, colliers and tramps. It must have seemed as though the whole of America was out there, ready to roll into Europe . . .

2

On 29 October 1944, it was the *Le Jeune*, steaming past. She had the look of a liner, a German liner, which is what she'd been until her capture. She was now a shadow of her former self, aged by blackout and wartime drab. On the quarterdeck was a tiny figure dressed in webbing and olive. It was Putnam Flint.

He'd remember this day with a degree of perplexity. It had been a curious voyage: the Straits of Gibraltar like a pair of gates; the tideless sea; Spain, looking empty; the water as blue as ink, and the storms that boiled up from nowhere and ripped off the davits. Then, at last, he'd got his first glimpse of France, these burnt crumbs scattered over the ocean.

Life had taken an uneven course up until now.

After his Buick adventures, Flint had briefly tussled with education. It was a hopeless struggle, which by 1938 had ended in expulsion. After that, he took a job in a glass factory, an experience that left him with nothing but a smattering of Polish. When war came in 1942, it had about it a hint of adventure. Flint was now faced with ancestral choices: whether to take to his heels like grandfather Horace, or to seek his salvation in khaki. With the future so thrillingly opaque, he opted for the army.

America was no wiser than Flint as to where the path led from here. Little thought had ever been given to the possibility of all-out war. In 1938, the regular army was about the size of a large town. Its big guns were mostly French, or antiques bolted to trucks. Her soldiers, meanwhile, looked as if they'd marched out of another era, with their gas capes and outsize bayonets.

'We were isolationist,' said Flint. 'Asleep at the switch.'

It was only with the Blitzkrieg that Washington woke up to the future. Rearmament began and – for the first time – the myriad units of the National Guard were gathered under federal control. But it was still an army that frightened no one. The British called the Americans 'our Italians', and – to the Germans – they were merely the 'ice-cream men'. Even the US veterans of this era have doubts about their own ferocity. To them, they were simply the 'Brown Shoe Army', a reminder that standardisation was still six years away, and the other side of a global conflict.

Leadership too was disconcertingly crusty. Often it was simply a matter of good schooling and admirable polo. Officers were still forbidden from carrying umbrellas because the Duke of Wellington had considered them offensive (except in the presence of ladies). Negroes, on the other hand, were excluded from all forms of military action, other than the wearily menial. It was thought they didn't have the moral fibre for the infantry, or sufficient co-ordination for the tanks. It says much for the America of that time that a German prisoner could eat in a Louisiana restaurant, whilst his Negro guards had to wait outside.

The process of shaping young Americans into soldiers was hardly edifying. Flint spent much of the next two years in the Deep South, being hauled from camp to camp. It was a sort of de-education, a numbing of initiative. Men had to perform Herculean feats of polishing and endless drill. There was jargon too, a soldierly babble of *sad sacks* (shirkers), *fart sacks* (sleeping bags), *pinks, peters* and *bang up* (trousers, penises and sex). Worse, every day was governed by *chickenshit*, which was the law of point-lessness. Whenever the army stopped to think, chickenshit kicked in. It required blankets to be folded in a particular way, and ties to be worn, even in combat. Chickenshit became a replacement for thought and even learning. Enlisted men were taught nothing about the dangers they'd face in the months to come: mines, trench foot, German weapons or enemy aircraft. It's a tribute to the remarkable adaptability of Americans that any of them survived at all – or that they persevered, rallied and ultimately triumphed.

Only two miracles happened in the chickenshit years. The first was that Flint married the granddaughter of a Native American. In their wedding photographs, Dorothy-Ann Smith is a woman of fierce beauty and Texan poise. As her ancestry wasn't fully appreciated in the Austin of 1943, people happily assumed she was aristocratic and probably French. Flint enjoyed the secrecy, and Dottie was always more lover than wife. Every morning and for the rest of her life, she'd begin the day by slip-ping naked into the garden, and plunging into the pool.

The other miracle was of a military nature. Somehow, amongst all the chickenshit and polish, the army had spotted cunning, and Flint was raised from the ranks. Even better, he was plucked from the infantry and resettled in armour, or the next-best thing. It was the 824th Tank Destroyers, a hotchpotch of gunners, tankers, volunteers, plunder, fallout and rejects. 'We were a bastard outfit,' says Flint proudly. Not that he cared. With the prospect of wheels, the war had begun to look promising. That summer, he grew a moustache, a flourish that's survived to this day.

The Tank Destroyers were the product of some feverish thinking.

Ever since 1862 and Antietam – the bloodiest day in American history – the army had been haunted by the prospect of casualties. It was constantly wrestling with the idea of how to get through wars both on top and intact. Men were expensive (Flint had cost almost $40,000 to train, nearly half the price of a tank) and yet surprisingly inefficient. Foot-soldiers only ever inflicted about a third of the enemy's casualties, and yet made up nine-tenths of American losses. The artillery, on the other hand, could inflict roughly the same damage, whilst accounting for only 2 per cent of the loss. The answer to the problems was therefore always the same: overwhelming firepower. Throw a storm at the enemy, and stay put until nothing stirs. This had become the mantra of American tactics.

The problem now was the breakthrough of tanks. Soldiers, or 'Doughs', were terrified of tanks, and *panzers* among doughs rendered artillery useless. Who would be there to staunch the flow of tanks? As the imagination faltered, the answer seemed obvious. Tank Destroyers would be like the rook in chess, a nimble reserve behind a line of pawns, ready to leap across the battlefield at the first sign of trouble. In reality, they lacked both leap and punch and thick enough walls. Such a lightweight concept was doomed even in blueprint. At almost the very moment that Flint was joining his battalion, General Patton was urging that the idea be abandoned.

He was studiously ignored. The War Department formed seventy-one battalions of Tank Destroyers, absorbing over 100,000 men. Over 5,000 of them would be killed in the frenzy to come, and many more injured. Only the infantry saw the Tank Destroyers for what they were: 'Can Openers', functional and piffling. Washington, on the other hand, saw the future in cats, dressing its wolves in panther's clothes. Every uniform carried the same uplifting emblem, of a giant cat enthusiastically munching a tank. Nor was it just uniforms. Panther fever was loose amongst war bonds, recruiting posters, newsreels, letterheads and kitsch. The Panthers even had their own growly motto: SEEK, STRIKE AND DESTROY. Flint hated such hubris.

'Huh,' he tutted, 'More like *Sneak, Peek and Retreat.*'

3

A dress rehearsal for the European Theatre was held, in Louisiana.

Most agree it was vintage farce. The part of Germany was played by a long, hot bog that swallowed up tanks. France too had lost all her buildings and was equally torrid. For several months, chaos settled over the swamps as nearly half a million Americans fought each other with fireworks and flags. Most of the time they were lost, and ended up smashing their way through their own reserves. It was worse at night, like a turkey shoot for the blind. Then the radios failed, followed by the boots, the underwear, the ammunition and the rations.

Some days, Flint simply borrowed a jeep and drove off the set. He'd continue driving until he reached Austin, several hundred miles to the west. These were the best moments of the mock-war, the real one still thousands of miles to the east. He and Dottie went touring in a Buick Opera Coupe, made love on the parade ground and picnicked at Barton Springs. Then, after several days, Flint would climb back into his jeep and hurtle back for the final chorus.

If the Panthers learnt anything from the Louisiana manoeuvres, it was the persistence of mud. That – and darkness – seemed to be the only certainties about the battle ahead. There was also the stark realisation that they might all be killed without firing a shot. Few knew what to expect. Sergeant Parham was the only one who'd ever known enemy fire (Panama '38), but it was not an experience he could humanely explain. 'I shot one right though his left ear,' he'd say, 'and it came out of his right.' The only other professional was Major Clint Smith, the battalion commander. He was a tall fleshless man from somewhere south-west, all chickenshit and razor-sharp dress tousers.

Everyone else felt much like Flint, overawed and out of place. The 824th were always an odd mix. Amongst almost 800 uprooted souls there were Cubans, Baptists, truckers, dockers, hucksters, accountants, cops, cheats, hunters, conscientious objectors (serving as medics), asthmatics, several athletes, countless adulterers, a couple known as 'The Rover Boys' and a Chinaman called Jung Chin. It was like a village in the ether, a community only in concept.

Flint was in B Company. Most of the others out there were Tennessee farmboys or savvy Jewish kids from New Jersey and Brooklyn. Even now, as Flint reels off their names, it sounds like the story of America: Pinzel,

Freiman, Finnegan, Doom, Captain Gleason the Meat Inspector, Loychik, Schroeder, 'Featherhead' Maclean (who dreamed of a bed), Grandma Gregory and Grandpapa Young, and the joker, Frankie Barone. Others would only find their names later – in the heat of the fight – men like 'Burp-Burp' Birdsey, 'High Burst' Bible and 'Stuka Joe' Sweet. And then, recalls Flint, there was a plumber from Pennsylvania, called George Hammel.

'Every time he got a shock, he'd yell, "JE-SUS CHRIST!! I mean . . ." We'd hear a lot of that.'

4

Few veterans will ever forget how this journey began.

The *Le Jeune* sailed from New York on 14 October 1944, with 15,000 men. It was like the voyage of Noah, rewritten by gremlins: one species, one sex, no doves and no explanation. No one had any idea where they were going, how long it would take, what they'd do when they got there, or when (if ever) they'd return. Only Flint was prepared for such a biblical collapse of reality. His God-fearing, teetotal mother-in-law had shrewdly deduced that fire and brimstone were almost at hand, and had sent him a case of Scotch. The twelve bottles were now on their way to war, packed in rifles and socks.

But this was no transport of delight. No sooner were they beyond Coney Island and out of the minefields than they began to zigzag across the Atlantic. Some way below the waterline, the 824th were stacked four bunks high, and as green as pears. Everything was rationed: space, light, fresh air and saltwater showers. The farmboys had never seen the sea before and were productively sick. For those that could eat, there were chow-lines the length of the ship, and discouraging confections of spam. To avert mutiny, the crew put on displays of anti-aircraft fire, and the men were made to act and box and learn simple French. Gambling was banned but became a micro-economy. Whole fortunes changed hands, along with houses and cars.

'I suppose,' said Flint, 'people felt a sense of abandonment.'

Some thought this journey would never end, let alone begin. Then, on the twelfth day, a great gateway appeared in the ocean and the *Le Jeune* sailed through, and they found themselves in the Med.

5

After Frioul, I called at an island of legendary improbability, known simply as If.

It was cooler now, and *les gabians* had called off their assault. I'd left Ratonneau with a wedding party that smelt of mussels and lacquer, and taken a ferry over the strait. The skipper had a uniform like an airline pilot and a boat like a bus. He told me that If was a royal rock, that it was Marseille's oldest foe, that it had its own green lizards, and that it was once the home of Europe's first rhino. All this on a slab no bigger than a good-sized ship.

'And the castle?'. I asked.

'We built it,' said the skipper, 'to protect us from ourselves.'

He dropped me off at the castle's dock.

'And now it's our own Alcatraz,' he added, '*sauf que un peu plus vieux.*'

As I climbed into the ramparts, I began to realise that If was possible. I spotted scaly green tails wriggling amongst the prickly pears, and gunports directed at home. I even found a copy of Albrecht Dürer's *Rhinocerus 1515*, a portrait of the vast armoured cabbage that had once visited If. Its story began as a fairy tale, a gift for the Pope from an Indian prince. But – after If – it was drowned and stuffed, only reaching Rome some years later, in a state of advanced upholstery.

Nor did I find much joy in the prison above. It still smelt of Renaissance widdle, and the doors were as thick as your neck. Every wall was gouged with the names of those damned, condemned, drowned, shot or hanged. The Château d'If hadn't been a castle for long, and had soon become a slammer. The first inmate arrived in 1580, and was strangled by the guards. Others were brought here for coining, usury, champerty, barratry, and other acts of general rascality (like failing to doff one's hat to the King). Most, however, were criminals of thought. Over 3,500 Protestants would add their names to the walls, along with heretics, reformers and some impertinent radicals. One, I observed, had spent the best part of 1848 hacking the word 'SOCIALISTE' into the stone.

'And this,' said the castle guide, 'is where the Count slept.'

Myth and suffering, it seems, have become richly entangled. Alexander Dumas wasn't the first to recognise that If was improbably daunting, but his tyrannical tale was easily the best. There are now twenty-seven film versions of *The Count of Monte Cristo*. It's a story that's been told so many times it's become almost true. If, too, has been transformed along the way, in substance, colour and size. *Blacker than the sea*, wrote Dumas, *blacker than the sky, rose like a phantom the giant of granite.*

Only the Germans had ever resisted such powerful myths. I noticed that they'd built their own little concrete nests around the cliffs. There were guns and lights too, bolted into the rock. It must have felt like a large unsinkable ship. But, when the gunners saw the Allied cruisers assembling out in the gulf, fantasy wisely gave in to discretion. They simply packed up and left, and the Château d'If was surrendered without so much as a squib.

It's ironic that the Americans should now find themselves steaming past If.

To men like Pinzel, Finnegan and Doom, the Old World was always an uncomfortable thought. It was the primeval stew from which their ancestors had emerged before flopping gratefully on to American shores. Getting away from Europe was a hereditary commitment – like Evolution or Progress – and the further away one was, the better it felt. For generations, Americans had given thanks for the vast amount of geography between their past and the present.

Now they were heading back there, passing If. This tuft of rock was – and perhaps still is – the epitome of everything Americans dread about Europe. Here were all the things their ancestors had feared, and from which they'd eventually fled. If was like the Old World in summary: petty, pompous, monarchical, despotic, dark, poky and small.

6

Arriving in Marseille is like falling through several layers of history and ending up just short of the present.

I always enjoy this journey. From a distance, the coastline looks much as it did to its earliest settlers, the Phocaeans. I can see great haunches of limestone ribbed with forest, an inlet and grizzled woods along the shore. The Phocaeans realised that such a magnificently blue country was wasted on the savages that lived here, trading in horses and daughters. So they swapped the inlet for a promise of marriage and ended up with a swarthy girl and the city of Massalia.

More centuries fly by, and the foothills are covered in pantiles and villas. People say it's like Rome, but even more sensual and pink. It's been a good place to be a Roman but not so good for the Christians. In the harbour mouth I can see the place where St Stephen was supposedly ground up between two millstones.

Millennia pass, and I'm among forts and guns. The villas have grown shadows and turned into tenements, and the inlet is now a rectangle paved in stone the colour of barley. There's a feeling that this is no longer enough for the Door to the Orient, and so a dockyard appears around the headland. It will be called La Joliette, inspired by London, cut from bluestone and built by the army. It will be a fortified machine for the enrichment of France.

It's 1866 and La Joliette is complete. I'm now among dizzying parallel lines of gantries and steel, and the sky is purple with rock. There are seven storeys of caves, and roads right up through the roof. The guards tell me it was *une vaste chaîne de transit*. Whole cargoes were swallowed up in elevators, lifted, ramped, passed from chain to belt, unwrapped, counted, bagged, knotted, boxed, winched, dangled and dropped into waiting trucks. Even the floors are made of rock, secure against rats, fire and the British.

But the stevedores have long gone, and this is now a bastion of cafés and suits.

'*La Joliette en farce*,' say the guards.

I feel I've almost reached the present, and descend to the quays. Down here, the armoured doors are spotted with holes, melted by gunfire. I push through, half expecting to find myself amongst clippers and brigs. Instead, there's nothing but a huddle of Algerian ferries, and empty docks as far as the eye can see.

A whole generation of quays have come and gone since that violent summer. Now, once again, it's a wilderness of old water, and cranes folded in rust. Although Marseille is still Europe's third port, trade is no longer a matter of boats. Instead, great steel cities float in and attach themselves to the shore. For a few days, the skyline is transformed by these huge, oily suburbs and then they lurch away, distended with Peugeots and plonk.

So now the quays are empty again. In 1944, they'd almost vanished for good. First came the American 'Fly Boys', ploughing the docks and much of the town. Over 2,000 Marseillais had died in these raids, always a dampener on the liberation to come. Then the Nazis, sensing that the

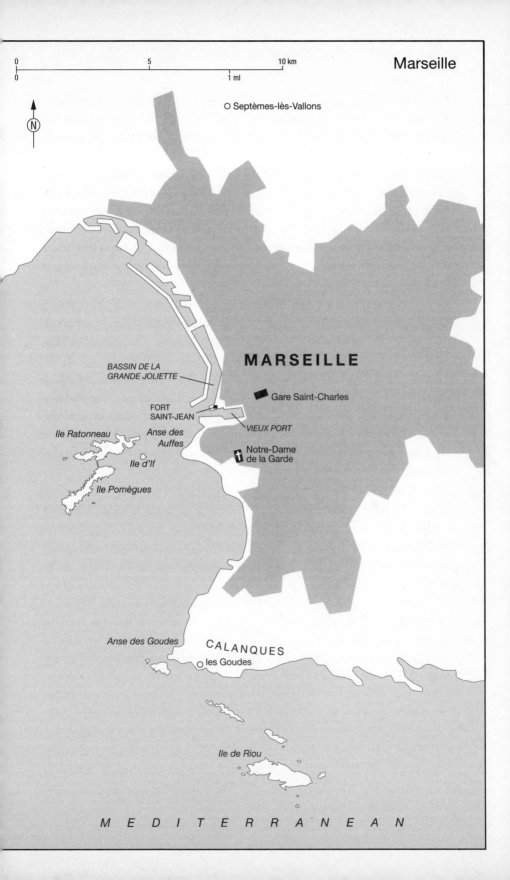

game was up, had reduced the basins to a soup of wrecks. They'd scuttled 176 ships, blown up the wharves and torched the rest. Even by the time the *Le Jeune* arrived, two months later, there was still nowhere to berth. Soldiers were tottering ashore on planks, lashed from hulk to hulk.

After their spam-flavoured fug, the Panthers would've been grateful to land anywhere. Except Marseille. Few Americans had ever seen such devastation or such passion so pointlessly spent. 'It was our first view of the ravages of war,' wrote Flint later. 'Destroyed buildings, some with putrefying dead. There is no description of this smell.'

If they were expecting a ticker-tape welcome, they were much mistaken. The cheers for the liberators had long dispersed. The Marseillais, never easy with uniforms, now regarded their new guests with candid disdain. To them, *les Fridolins,* or Krauts, had simply been replaced, with *les Ricains.* Even the new workforce, recruited to clear the docks, seethed with contempt: they refused to work in the rain, on Sundays, Mondays and during siesta. When the Americans tried to use Italian POWs, this merely caused a riot. Such hostility puzzled the new US authority, Civil Affairs. 'Misconceptions of American ideas and policies,' they reported, 'are starting to cascade.' As so often in France, food was at the heart of this discontent. Right now, there was none. The city was starving.

So, the Panthers arrived to a ragged reception. A great, grey crowd had formed, up in the docks. It was a welcome of sorts – from the nefarious, the desperate and the underfed. Civil Affairs described their new charges as 'the dregs of six continents, the flotsam of many races'. To such a swarm, the Americans looked extravagantly green. Little hands were soon amongst them, plundering half-tracks and prising off lids. It was the first time Flint had ever seen Frenchmen, an impression he'd never forget.

'We often had to shoot over their heads, just to keep them out of our stores.'

These were inauspicious first shots: the liberators loosing off at the freed.

Part 2 – La Soupe Marseillaise

Marseille is one of the most debauched towns in France. It is astonishing the quantity of whores. They are impudenter and bolder than in any other town.

Marmaduke William Constable-Maxwell, 1784

If you are interested in how the other half of the world lives, a trip through old Marseilles – by daylight – cannot fail to thrill, but it is not wise to venture into this district at night unless dressed like a stevedore and well-armed . . . The dregs of the world are here unsifted. It is Port Said, Shanghai, Barcelona and Sydney combined. Now that San Francisco has reformed, Marseilles is the world's wickedest port.

A Guide to the Gay World of France from Deauville to Monte Carlo, 1929.

Marseille is incorrigibly optimistic. That is its nature. It believes intensely in itself.

Sisley Huddleston, Mediterranean Blue, 1948

7

Hell, it seems, knoweth no fury quite like Marseille.

This often worried me, as I prepared for my visit. The city appeared to be in a state of advanced perdition. A sense of ancient doom even seemed to well up out of the map. Amongst the clutter, I could see Lazarus, Sleepless Cove, Dragon, the Reformed, the Prophet and the Abandoned. No one seemed to want to go there. Eurostar stopped just short of the city, and even the most unfrilly airlines had kept away. In the guidebooks, it was a place to be endured not enjoyed. Only one hotel had more than three stars, and there were no proper museums, boutiques, Disneylands or intelligible works of art. This was odd, considering it was the oldest and most spacious city in France.

For Marseille, I realised had always been like this, suffering years of catastrophe and then being doggedly spurned. Each century seems to have brought bigger and ever more lavish disasters. To begin with, it was merely leprosy but then came fires, Barbarians and plagues. The disease of 1720 brought half the city out in boils (and the dead lay on the quay for the next three weeks). Union with France had brought more ships, but not calm. Marseille would have its own revolution, its own Terror and its own nihilistic commune. France would respond to these upheavals with withering force, reducing the city to nothing. Once, it even lost its name for a while, surviving only as *La Ville sans Nom*.

France still blamed Marseille for most things. I trawled through my old French friends for some sign of affection. They were all horrified that I wanted to go there. Most warned me about the hookers, but there were also pickpockets, con-men, extremists, junkies, and a vast underworld known as *le milieu*. In fact, little good had ever come of the Marseillais. The only things they'd been famous for were football (at which they cheated), soap (which they never used) and the National Anthem (which was actually Alsatian). Like all southerners, they were lazy and feckless and always on strike. There didn't seem to be any government, just a kleptocracy which – every now and then – was swept off to jail. These days, most people were either on benefits or heroin, or some sort of jihad.

'Be careful,' I was told, 'Marseille's like a bomb.'

French writers have been equally unforgiving. Several compare Marseille to a whore. André Suarès even suggests it looks like one, taking us on a gynaecological tour. Gabriel Audisio was more poetic, portraying an artless city, the melting pot of humankind. Others describe it as loud, mysterious, gobby, anarchic, singular and bloody. Even Axel Toursky, who had his own theatre there, warns that it's lethally weird. 'No one understands Marseille,' he wrote in 1950, 'You either ignore it or you like it. And if you like it, you've had it.'

8

It's hardly surprising Flint and his men were over-awed by Marseille. A city that was – at the best of times – zany now tottered at the edge of reason.

War had inverted everything. The nights had turned into days, and the days were haunted by nightlife. Children had become adults, and adults urchins. Trade had been replaced by theft, and sewage now spewed through the streets. The battle had finished and yet the fighting continued. Gunfire crackled across the city, as peace returned, and the oppressed rose up to hunt the defeated. No one knew who was fighting whom in this drive-by war. Somehow, thousands of Nazi *collabos* had simply merged back into the shadows, and rumour was seldom embellished with fact. For a time, the *milieu* became the law. Meanwhile, the *collabos* became the *milieu*, until they too took charge, and set out in the hunt for themselves.

To the Americans, Marseille was an eerie city and its people grotesque. They'd never seen so much green and blue hair before, or such public displays of piss. Nor had they ever seen money-changers, charcoal-burning cars, squat toilets, baguettes, Berbers, Bretons or bidets. It was like a freak show for the chronically unhygienic. Then there were the stragglers, the runts of every military outfit from Cloud Cuckoo Land to Timbuktu. They didn't seem to be part of this war, in all their feathers and sashes, turbans, daggers and leggings. The Panthers began to wonder if it was all a bad dream, an illusion caused by too long at sea. Only the noise was real, but it was meaningless prattle. They assumed no one spoke English, even the countess who'd invited them all to tea.

'Ma'am,' ventured one of the boys, 'I'd like to fuck you.'

'A nice wish,' she replied sweetly, 'rather crudely expressed.'

No one had anything except time. Flint remembered how the barber spent hours cutting his hair, standing back between each artful snip. At least he had work. Many resorted to begging (and every soldier had his own flock of waifs, like seagulls after a trawler). Others sold what they had, and then traded in virtue. Sex became feverishly cheap. Even now, Flint is troubled by this, the sight of women swapping themselves for cigarettes and beans. It puzzles him too that he could still buy presents for Dorothy, exquisite silk lingerie in a city that was starving to death.

I realised that, if I was to try and understand Marseille, I'd have to travel alone. Although Flint would return, he was never keen. He'll there-fore only reappear in this story when it's time to move on and leave Marseille behind. That's when we'll find him, standing on the quayside, looking as astonished now as he did then.

9

I stayed first in the docklands, at a hotel the wrong end of an empire.

It had been handsome once, beneath the streaks of wiring and soot. I could even make out limestone and ironwork and some fancy nymphs. The balconies, it seems, had fallen off at about the time of Suez, followed shortly afterwards by the corbels and most of the shutters. The owner, Fumel, hardly seemed to notice. The hotel's decomposition was nothing compared to the collapse of trade. Once, he said, we were full every night, with stokers and sailors, off all the best liners.

'*Ethiopiens, Martiniquais, Sénégalais . . .*'

It was a crisis that called for plenty of sleep. Every time I went through the lobby, I'd find Fumel flat out on the couch. I think he liked me at first, and found me exotic. But the enthusiasm soon waned, when I kept turning up in his sleep. Or perhaps this was just the way of the Marsellais. In the city of arrivals, it was only arriving that mattered. Being, staying and departing were inferior states. It was the same everywhere: greetings were flamboyant, protracted and noisy, whereas a farewell could be said with a nod. In the meantime, it was Service with a Shrug. By the third day, Fumel couldn't even manage a grunt, before rolling over and going back to sleep.

He never went upstairs, leaving me to find my own way. It was diffi-cult in the dark, like clambering through an upturned ship. My cabin was a sort of seabed blue and had a television attached to the ceiling. Sunlight never seemed to reach these parts although at night a green, neon glow leaked in through the cracks. I'd lie awake for hours, listening for sounds of life, but I never heard much except Fumel snoring down in the hall. No other guests checked in.

It wasn't just the hotel that I had to myself. The Rue Mazenod had been almost abandoned, except by the pigeons. Each morning, they appeared in the windows of the tenement opposite and flopped lazily into the street. Few people ever ventured down here, except an African wizard called Monsieur Mohammed, and children trying to steal cars. From the lobby, I could see them darting from handle to handle and then scurrying off in a wail of alarms. Monsieur Mohammed was in less of a hurry, and told me he could cure anything from envy to Aids.

'*Je suis un homme de Dieu,*' he'd say, leaving me with a card and a holy number to call.

Next door was a house full of motorbike scrap, and beyond that, a football bar. I often went there at dusk. If Marcel Pagnol had still been alive, I'm sure he'd have been there too, borrowing stories for *Manon des Sources*. Everyone's lives seemed so colourfully poignant, and yet far too guttural to understand. My own notes of these evenings capture something of this, and read like a stream of cognac. *Les chiens nous gouvernent! Liberté!* My wife was drowned in a vat of fish. *Un chat est un chat.* All agreed that there'd soon be a war. One of them even remembered the last war in the docks.

I asked what happened, but he just smiled.

'We hear,' he said, 'that the British danced, as they were bombed.'

By day, I climbed up through the layers of the *quartier*. It rose steeply, like a carbonised forest; great avenues of limestone, blackened pools, stumps of burnt-out car, flyovers, cobbles, and washing the colour of ash. This was as bleak as Marseille ever got, draining Provence of its brilliance. I've seldom felt more alone, or more remote. It was like a *film noir* ticking away at a few frames per second. Perhaps the lethargy that had taken such hold of Fumel was now seeping upwards through the streets.

'The place is dead,' he'd say, '*un quartier mort.*'

There were, however, occasional signs of life, usually a spasm of protest. Even here, it seemed, the Marseillais couldn't resist a good revolt. Sometimes it was a moment of private insurrection, an inexplicable rage or a surge of rum. Once, I saw a man weaving along the rue de Forbin, ahead of the cars. I don't suppose he could remember why he was angry but the traffic still slowed to the speed of a drunk. Other protests were more ambitious, involving placards, banners, anarchists, housewives, toddlers and the Communist Party. These little uprisings happened almost weekly, lashing out at everything from the EU to abortion. Oddly, the most violent of all was a march against parking meters.

'*Y'aura révolution!*' roared the crowd. '*Non aux horodateurs!*'

Although appealing, most people were too immersed in crime to bother with protest. Delinquency was almost a matter of pride. Even those who didn't participate seemed to spend their time dreaming of crime. It was the talk of the football bar, and gangster *raï* was the theme tune of *quartier* life. *Milieu* mythology seemed to get everywhere, with its spectral hitmen and a godfather known as *Le Vrai Monsieur*. You couldn't even get in a taxi without it blasting off like a getaway car. Most of the time, it was hard to know where the fantasy stopped and the hoods began. Certainly, back in the Fifties, Marseille was the world's biggest producer of heroin. But where were the *milieu* now? Only Fumel seemed to know.

'All gone,' he said. 'Gone to Nice. Why would they hang around *here*?'

Crime, then, had lost some of its glamour but none of its grip. On a typical day, the police reported that they'd smashed a vice ring, recovered eight tonnes of stolen cigarettes, and arrested two girls for killing a pervert. Perhaps, in some ways, crime had become more democratic, more evenly spread amongst the Marseillais. I was only ever threatened once. A gang of *voyous* – or louts – caught me taking pictures on their patch and chased me away under a hail of sticks. The ringleader was probably no older than ten.

10

Three streets up, crime and protest had once been briefly united.

The bars hadn't changed much in seventy years. Some were Corsican, but others, like La Sirène, were less specifically shifty. They were heartless places, just somewhere to sit as the liquor hit home. The one that worried me most was La Joliette, which always looked so coldly violent, stripped down to the zinc and tiles. In the Thirties this was a battleground – for votes, favours and dope. Mostly, these were primitive clashes, fought with trumpets, chairs, stink-bombs and whistles. But occasionally someone would flick off the catch and spray the place with gunfire. To the old boys in the Football Bar, this was the beginning of a gold-toothed age.

'Marseille-Chicago!' they squealed. '*Le milieu* ruled!'

Certainly, city politics had a new sound, in the casual chatter of guns. But the figure to emerge from the smoke and glass was hardly Al Capone. It was Simon Sabiani, a one-eyed Corsican haberdasher, who fought duels and never slept. Sabiani had always been in the wrong place at the wrong time, as he was the evening at Verdun when a bullet had smashed through his face. The experience had left him with a split-second fuse, and a permanent scowl. He made up for his lopsided look with charm and – where charm failed – there was always his persuasive enforcer, a convict called Signor Carbone.

What followed wasn't exactly politics. Sabiani tended to drift through ideologies, guided mostly by clients. Initially, he was elected as a Communist but then he spotted the Fascists, and denounced the Reds as 'parasites encrusted in human flesh'. It was a canny move, on the eve of German expansion. After this, Sabiani's accession became almost a parody of Hitler's, a pantomime of screaming and goonish brown outfits.

Little good ever came of this time. Probably the best moment was the day a new eatery appeared, called Pizzaria Etienne. Fumel told me it was still going strong, down on the southern side of the canton.

'It's the best anywhere,' he said. 'The beautiful taste of the poor.'

II

I've often thought about Fumel's words, since that evening at Etienne's.

For men like him, I now realise that food is a resort, a bit like sleep. It's almost a world of its own, a sensual landscape existing in parallel to misfortune. Escape is everywhere. Even in the vilest corner of the city you can find a *curiosité de bouche*, a moment of goat's cheese and fennel, perhaps, or fresh peppers and garlic, rosemary, olives and thyme. A man can be poor and yet, in the garden of his senses, he's happy.

Foreigners have long recognised this. There's even a line about it in *The Wind in the Willows*. 'Why, sometimes I dream of the shellfish of Marseilles,' says Water Rat, 'and wake up crying.' Before long, Marseille's gift for pleasure was being exported. M.F.K. Fisher took it back to the States, and Elizabeth David brought it to the stodgy tables of Britain. It was called Mediterranean Cuisine but most of it began here in the soot, the product of solace.

Nowhere said all this better than the Pizzaria Etienne. The upper floors were derelict and crumbling into the street. I almost missed it in the dark, and it didn't begin to feel like a restaurant until I was deep inside, amongst whitewashed arches and waiters in trainers. Around the walls were pictures of Sixties film stars, but nowadays everyone got the same extravagant welcome. The waitress knew the people on the next table, and showered them with kisses before patting them into place.

It wasn't long before the evening began to bloom. I have a happy vision of myself, throwing back rosé and working through dish after dish of exquisite sensations: warmth, zest, tomato-cool, crust, cheese, chilli, bitterness, sweetness and lemon, and then tiny squid in a fiery sauce. There was no need to order; the waitress just brought whatever was fresh. As she put the dishes before me, she announced them, like a long procession of outlandish guests.

'*Gigot d'agneau aux herbes!*'

'*Banon* dressed in chestnut leaves!'

'Ravioli stuffed with his wild mushrooms!'

'*Tarte Provençal!*'

It was midnight before I lurched back to my rotting hotel. Fumel was right: I'd caught a glimpse of beauty. Perhaps it was a turning-point, or perhaps it was just the wine? As I tottered along, I decided it was probably just Marseillais contentment, the happy state of food.

12

Over the headland was *le Vieux Port*, famous for its bluster and slaves.

From the promontory, I could look down across the whole of the ancient basin. No wonder it was once thought the centre of the world. It was like a room full of sea or an enormous box of light. To the ambitious Phocaeans, who'd believed almost anything possible, this was an encouraging sight. Long before Rome, they'd sailed off to Africa and Britain and other improbable places. Even their lies were spectacular.

I wasn't sorry to be leaving the docks and crossing the hump to the port. It was like walking from a restless night into a promising dawn. Colour and sound returned, dabs of ochre at first but then blasts of yellow and aquamarine. The basin itself was packed with thousands of yachts, all clinking and fluttering like a flock of tall, metallic birds. None of them ever seemed to go anywhere. After a while, I decided they probably couldn't, and were merely an ornamental foreground to the lives on the harbour wall.

Over the days to come, I'd spend hours on this great limestone rim. After the shadowy tenements, it felt like an affirmation of the senses, a cacophony of fish and sirens, whistles, drunks, Ferraris, sunlight and *raï*. Sometimes I walked but often I just sat, enjoying the experience of sensory overload. I imagine that half of Marseille felt the same. Every morning, people drifted down out of the hills, just to gather on the edge of their magnificent liquid piazza.

Each day began with a fish market. They say that every day has begun like this for the last twenty-six centuries, and it's still as bloody as ever. I had no idea that the Mediterranean contained such ogres, enormous creatures covered in fins and spikes. One fisherman told me that Marseille even had its own scorpion fish, and showed me a thing like a gin trap with wings. But best of all were the fishwives, who drove old post office vans and were exquisitely dainty in their lipstick and blusher.

'*Du vivant au prix du mort!*' they'd shout. (The living, at the price of the dead!)

Further along, people would settle down around the harbour wall. To many, it was just a place to live, as it had been for centuries. Originally, the inhabitants of these stones were galley slaves – mostly Muslims and Huguenots – and by day they'd been allowed out of the Arsenal to take up a trade on the wall. They'd made an unnerving spectacle, each chained by the foot and naked except for a red bonnet and canvas drawers. Although, by the mid-eighteenth century, this slavery was over, its routines had somehow remained.

Up on the wall, there was virtually nothing people wouldn't do in public: arguing, chiding, teeth-cleaning, sewing, embracing, kissing, peeing, rolling pastry, practising the flute or sleeping. In such an opaque city, this was surprising. I sometimes felt I'd found the glass quarter, a few acres of translucent lives. It was even divided into its own sectors, succinctly defined by race. The Algerians lived over on the west quay, along with the Peruvians (in all their feathers and pipes) and the Berbers; next to them were the Kosovans and some gypsies in pinstripe suits; further east were the sub-Saharan Africans, living in the debris of the fish market and trading in watches and snails; the French, meanwhile, had the Quai de Rive Neve and the best of the sun. Over here, even the slums had become unnervingly chic and were known as *les lofts*.

*

Some had no sector, no loft and no home at all. One of these was a pedlar called Charles, who sold knots and lived on a nest of beer cans and string. I often sat near him, watching as he weaved his Turk's Heads, Pineapples and Monkey's Fists. With his stoop and his burnt back and ragged shorts, he looked like the last of the harbour's slaves. At some stage during his wanderings he'd picked up some English, and now this and his string were all he had left.

'I'm just a Professional Drunkard,' he'd say, 'and a Philosopher of Knots.'

I enjoyed Charles's Gordian view of the world, with its 4,000 knots. Each one was the antithesis of his life, a beginning and end linked by beautiful, orderly patterns. He said Britain was a paradise of knots, which I assumed was flattery and offered to buy him some beer.

He smiled. 'Ah, another drunkard? Are you a professional too?'

'Just a beginner.'

He was happy with this, and so we spent the rest of the afternoon sitting on the wall, dangling our legs and drinking beer. We talked about living in the open, and Marseille, or, as Charles called it, the City Underground. Trying to understand its intentions, he said, was like trying to see in the dark

'We even have a terrible game called Marseille chess.'

It was like ordinary chess, he said, except that each player could take two moves, as long as the first wasn't check. The effect on the game was catastrophic, stripping it of strategy, intellect, set pieces, masterstrokes and finesse. Instead, it became a sort of chequered punch-up; and it was impossible to see anything beyond the next move.

'And the winner,' said Charles, 'is always the man who lives by his wits.'

This was an intriguing thought as I tottered away, up Canebière. Few streets have ever held such promise, or been so badly let down.

13

Canebière begins with sea monsters and a poem, and ends with a chauffeur shot through the throat.

From the port, it looked like the gateway to France, an enormous portal of cherubs and columns. Almost everything about it suggested a glorious path ahead, all clumped in acanthus and draped in laurels. Beyond, I could see classical flummery fading into the distance; a stock exchange in the shape of a senate, and the front of the Hôtel Louvre et Paix supported by four voluptuous nymphs. To my surprise, this entire tableau was lit by monsters, every lamp in the grip of an enormous fish.

I'm not the first to have crossed into Canebière with a sense of heightened expectation. For centuries, people have blithely assumed that good would somehow come of it all. According to legend, Canebière led to the end of the earth, and even Conrad was given to some fancy ideas. 'For me,' he wrote, 'it has always been a street leading into the unknown.' The only hint that all was not as it seemed was a sign bearing a line from the poet, Vitour Gelou: '*Is birth worth it if one should completely die?*'

Sure enough, two blocks up, the glory faltered. The stockbrokers had gone, and the nymphs looked as if they'd just clambered out of the coal. Most of the great boutiques, which had provided cut-glass service through the Steamer Age, had now either vanished or were trading in crossbows and samurai swords. Meanwhile, the Louvre et Paix had become a department store, offering a stark range of clothes in ghoulish Soviet colours. According to a plaque, Mark Twain had once stayed here, amongst the socks and pants.

No one seemed to like Canebière any more, even those who lived on the street. The drunks were always shouting at the buildings, and peeing on the doors. Some were anarchists, who wore combat gear and daubed every wall '*Non à une Europe militarisée*'. I don't suppose even this was an outcome they wanted, as it would have left them with almost nothing to wear. In fact, nobody seemed very sure of their unhappiness. One group appeared to have taken against shoes, and another only ever drank sparkling wine. The only man who wasn't drunk thought he was a dog and spent all day on the corner of Rue Papère, barking at the traffic. Disappointment, it seems, takes many and varied forms.

But worse things can happen on Canebière.

Perhaps the very worst is to be assassinated, which is exactly what happened to the King of Yugoslavia on 9 October 1934. Again, a promising outing was soon in ruins. The King had done well in France, finding plenty of allies in his fight against Fascists. The drive down Canebière was supposed to have been a glorious moment, an affirmation of civilised values amongst all the nymphs and fish. Every moment was caught on camera – the first time, as it happens, that an assassination had ever been filmed.

In the flickering pictures, there's pomp and glory until two blocks in. Then, when the car passes the Bourse, there's smoke, and the shot that tears away the driver's throat. As his lifeless body flops on to the brake, the car stops and an assassin jumps aboard to kill the King. Everyone dies in the seconds that follow: the driver, the King, and the assassin who is slashed to the ground by cavalry swords.

There's little disagreement as to what happened next. Canebière became first a mob, which tore the assassin apart, and then a stampede. Amongst those fleeing the sabres and guns was a young New Zealander, reporting for a Parisian paper. 'Marseille crowds are never very orderly,' she later wrote, 'but let someone loose with a gun and they become more dangerous than the person with the gun.' As a foreigner, she was a suspect and was pursued by the police into the bar of the Louvre et Paix. But, it seems, in Nancy Wake they'd met their match.

'No Marseille *flic*,' she'd say, 'was going to out-shout me.'

It wasn't long before the police realised they weren't looking for pretty girls or Kiwis but Croatian Fascists. The ringleader, Ante Pavelic, was traced to Italy but Mussolini refused to hand him over. Eventually, the French courts sentenced him to death *in absentia* but he'd survive another twenty years. Then, in 1957, the Serbs found him in Buenos Aires, and he too was hacked to the ground.

Marseille, meanwhile, has never forgotten the outrage on Canebière. There are memorials all over the city, to the 'King who died for peace'. For France, this was a Sarajevo moment, the shot that started the war. Only Sabiani and his whelping Fascists remained in denial. They said it was the *Sûreté Nationale* who'd staged the killing but no one believed them. Instead, the world was subjected to the weird spectacle of the radical Third Republic tumbling into alliances with monarchies, aristocracies and Americans. It was an autumnal time, as the political colours of Europe began to change.

Everyone's life was changed that day, including the Kiwi's. Nancy Wake would never forget her first trip down Canebière, nor would it be her last. In fact, her life became so entangled with Marseille that she even married into the *milieu*. But this, I discovered, was merely the beginning of her story, an adventure from which she'd emerge as a courier, *résistante*, saboteur, and the most highly decorated woman of the Second World

War. Even better, I discovered that she was still alive, at ninety-three, and that she lived only a few miles from me, on Richmond Hill.

One day, one of those beautiful spring days that London excels in, I went over there to find out where the road had taken her, after Canebière.

14

In all her pearls and silk, Nancy never looked as though she'd killed a man with her bare hands.

She was always immaculate, and energetically hard to place. Despite the wheelchair and a memory ravaged by time, there was a certain defiance about her, which seemed to veer from suspicion to pride. I've often wondered whether, as we get older, we become more of ourselves or less. Nancy managed both. The first time we met, she seemed guarded – at least, initially – and quiet, and yet she was wearing a scarlet jacket, cream blouse and silver shoes, with a gold-sequined handbag and bright red nails. She looked like an ageing actress, simultaneously exuberant, grand, opaque and diminished.

That first visit, we went to a pub, with her Australian lawyer, Debbie Taylor. It was a day like any other in Nancy's extraordinary life, an odd mixture of gentility and open revolt. She seemed to like the pub at first, and the promise of a convivial lunch, but then she scowled when she saw the menu, everything balsamic and drizzled in oil. I was surprised how much this annoyed her but, in the end, she settled for a plate of chips, a fairy cake and two gin-and-tonics.

'When we weren't fighting,' she said, suddenly, 'we were *drinking*!'

As the afternoon wore on, more snatches of the past emerged, like clips off the studio floor. She remembered the raids, the dogs, losing her jewellery under gunfire, and the American she'd dragged over the Pyrenees. She loved the war, the guerrillas and the fighting and even remembered the words of a coded song, 'The moonlight lit upon her tit, Oh Jesus Christ Almighty . . .' But there was anger too, loosed off in volleys at officials, Nazis, the War Department, and a homosexual known as Rake. It was almost as if the war was still there, crackling away, and she'd hardly noticed the last sixty years. Even the secrecy, it seemed, had survived the decades.

'I'm sure,' said Debbie, later, 'that Nancy only ever tells half the story.'

But, even as a story half told, it was a breathless tale. Over the years, it's emerged as an autobiography, two biographies, a Hollywood script and numerous citations for courage. The story is never quite the same (the strangled sentry is sometimes there, sometimes not). But, through it all, a pattern emerges, of a life on the run. It begins in Wellington, New Zealand in 1912, with a child who's part-Maori by birth. Then two years later the infant and her parents jump out of their lives and go to Australia, where Nancy will live until she's sixteen, and old enough to run away herself. Somehow she drifts round the world, via San Francisco and New York, fetching up in Paris in 1932, where she'll live as a reporter for the next seven years.

Nancy never seems to appear in the stories of her own life. She's an ethereal character, always one step ahead of her improbable, corporate self. There are lovers in Paris, flatmates who marry gangsters, parties with Mistinguett and Josephine Baker and assignments amongst Viennese Nazis. But emotionally Nancy isn't in these scenes, having long slipped away. Whether in love, war, friendship, marriage or death, she's unreachable. She even shrugs off her name as she moves from plot to plot, so that – by the end – she's a whole cast of caricatures. To the Marseillais, she was Madame Fiocca; to her husband, Nanny; to friends, Gert; to the secret services, Madame Andrée; across the radio net, Hélène; to comrades, Ducky; to the Gestapo, the White Mouse; and to the post-war world, Mrs Forward. Only now is she back where she began, as Nancy Wake.

I asked her about Marseille but got only half the story again. She said that, strangely enough, she'd never been afraid in the city. In fact, she'd soon caught her eye on a charmer, and by 1939 she'd moved south to join him. Henri was fourteen years her senior, and born of the notorious Fioccas.

'They *hated* me!' she shrugged. 'Said I took him away!'

In her memoirs, Henri is an 'industrialist' but the devil is there, in the detail. He could 'arrange things at the Town Hall', dealt in scrap, and had 'a reputation with the girls'. There was always plenty of cash, and Nancy talked of this time as the Champagne years, although when I found their old flat (on Rue Daumier) it seemed surprisingly modest. During the war Henri wore suits of fine English cloth, looted from a wreck down on the docks. These were glorious days, in their way.

'I even cooked a bouillabaisse once,' said Nancy, 'for Maurice Chevalier.'

15

Nothing exercises the imagination of this city quite like bouillabaisse.

I'd never come across a soup so ambitious. People said it was a love potion, an emetic, a tonic, an aphrodisiac, both a stimulant and a sedative, and a cure for most things, including autumn and discontent. The saffron was supposed to induce the calm so vital to Marseille, whilst the eels gave a man endurance and vigour. Then there was the scorpion fish, an unassuming creature on a plate of his own but a riot of taste amongst his friends, the John Dorys, weavers and crabs. I was also told what it cost, and worked out that – drop for drop – Love Soup was almost four times the price of Scotch.

Unsurprisingly, there were plenty of imitators and lashings of fraud. Around the Old Port I was offered almost every variant of bouillabaisse except the real thing: frozen, vegetarian, microscopic and fishless. I even consulted the government's list of accredited soup-makers, but most were booked up, weeks ahead. Perhaps the whole city was addicted to this seafood potion, alternately calm and priapic?

Eventually, I found a soup shop out at Vallon des Auffes, a tiny fishing cove like a crack in the cliffs. The waiters made a great fuss about the sincerity of their fish, and paraded the ingredients before me. It was a repulsive sight, like a tray of giant insects and slugs. As I was introduced to each creature in turn, and then the potatoes, I began to wonder if bouillabaisse wasn't just some old fishermen's joke. What better way of selling off the freaks and runts that turn up in your nets? It was a concoction assembled entirely from the unwanted and the grotesque, which of course is much how the world sees Marseille. In bouillabaisse, it seems, the Marseillais were simply enjoying a little symmetry and a lot of money.

Fascinatingly, it tasted even worse than it looked. A yolky *rouille*, saffron and a good boiling had done nothing to improve the ingredients. The fish remained resolutely lukewarm and bland, and now bobbed around in a thick orange gloop. Even worse was the persistent insecty crunch. It was like eating tomato soup with sprats, whipped cream and the occasional locust. How could anyone feel amorous sluicing that lot away? Love Soup must be one of the most overrated dishes in the world, alongside *foie gras*, bird's nest soup and fish and chips. It was impossible to keep it down without a lingering sense of regret. In fact, I didn't think nausea could get any worse than this – until the waiter reappeared with dessert. It was a marshmallow and a flute of lemon cream.

16

Halfway down the Vieux Port was the town hall, where Nancy was married.

It was already one of my favourite buildings in the city. Somehow this lanky pink palace had survived almost four centuries of revolutions, communes, foreign invasions, Mediterranean tantrums and the occasional riot. Across the front of the building there was hardly a stone unfrilled, and even the podgy face of the King had been restored to its niche. Everything about it seemed to defy time, and occasionally understanding. In its statues, for example, France is depicted as an armed beauty, sportingly naked from the navel up. Who was *that* supposed to impress?

I often ducked inside, out of the heat and light. Whilst the exterior had looked vaguely wiggy and regal, inside it was splendidly languid. Neither sound nor air penetrated its great lime-green chambers and halls, and I usually had the place to myself. Somewhere amongst all the marble and silk I could hear a leaking tap. No one seemed bothered. Although almost one in ten of this province's workers were civil servants, they were conspicuously discreet. The only *fonctionnaires* I ever saw at the *hôtel de ville* were a concierge (who chased me away from the leaking tap), an apprentice carpenter chipping tiny particles off a hinge, and his master, asleep in a chair.

Around the walls of the marriage hall were paintings of cavaliers, all under-exerting themselves with exemplary flourish. This is where Nancy and Henri were married on 30 November 1939. It was an unforgettable occasion, she told me, all those Fioccas sitting down to plates of sea-urchins and salted Norman lamb.

'Did they behave?' I asked.

'Oh yes,' she said. 'I'd spiked the wine with a few bottles of brandy.'

Nowhere had better symbolised the torpor of Marseille at that time.

The city seemed to run on graft and grog. Sabiani was always up near the front, trading votes for jobs and engaging more and more Corsicans on an empty purse. Every now and then the city would announce ambitious financial pogroms but – several years later – there'd be even more *fonctionnaires*, and a civil service more spectral than ever. The politicians meanwhile were drinking their way into power, drowning debate with their *vins d'honneur*. 'Alcoholism reigns in the city hall,' ran one contemporary report. 'All you meet on the stairs are deputies sleeping off the electoral drinking and counsellors dead drunk from champagne.'

It wasn't just Marseille. Throughout the Thirties, France had been working herself into a state of nervous collapse. She'd realised – too late – that she hadn't won the Great War, and that no one had. Almost one and a half million Frenchmen had been killed and another million left unable to work. By 1939, she had the oldest population in Europe, and was almost running on empty. Poverty was followed by waves of xenophobia and lassitude. There was still a huge army but it lacked the old ideals of the republic, and the civil service was demoralised, resentful and powerless.

Few people had any prospect of anything except slow defeat. There was even a new verb, which became the byword for survival: *te débrouiller* (to get oneself out of the soup). Most Frenchmen became accomplished *débrouillards*, except the politicians. Each government made the same mistake, chopping its own head off and then running around madly for a while before toppling into obscurity. One government, in 1929, even tried to sell off the army's rifles. Five years later, another administration was evacuating the Ruhr, planning an invasion of Germany and carpet-bombing the Saharan tribes. France began to spiral into inertia. The World Trade Fair of 1937, held in Paris, was one of the first ever to be described as 'shoddy', and the only people to take it seriously were the German secret service, who saw it as a good opportunity to map out the land.

Somehow, the French government deluded themselves into thinking the Nazis could be kept out with a wall. Between 1929 and 1935 France spent over 5 billion francs on the greatest folly the world has ever known: the Maginot Line. In theory, France's eastern frontier would be impenetrable. In reality, it was a stupendous human endeavour of virtually no use at all: 22 large fortresses, 50 Alpine forts, 401 casemates, 100 kilometres of tunnels and several gaping holes – known as Saarland, Switzerland and Belgium.

But the Maginot Line wasn't just about keeping the Germans out. It was also to keep the nineteenth century in. France was still obsessed with an idyll, an image of itself as Catholic, bucolic and patrician. It needed protecting, by barriers if necessary. The concrete and casements were merely figments of this Chinese Wall mentality.

But not all Frenchmen agreed. Some weren't so sure that France could be saved by walls, or that the enemy was on the outside. One such person was 'The Hero of Verdun', Marshal Pétain, now the ambassador to Madrid. Pétain had fallen for the idea that, whereas victory would mean certain revolution, defeat might come as a saviour. There were plenty who shared his perspective, and so – by 1939 – France, in the words of one commentator, was 'like a princess in her castle, almost willing the barbarian to come in and ravish her'. When, later that year, the wine harvest failed, many Frenchmen saw this as an ominous sign that the time had come. '*Nous sommes en pleine pagaille*,' they'd say. 'We're in the soup.'

17

To get a better view of the city's defeat, I moved hotels, staying on the hill above Canebière.

By now, I'd worked up an unhealthy affection for Marseille. It horrified me how easily I'd adapted to the sound of sirens and the smell of dust and pee. Worse, I felt disconcertingly at ease amongst its cheery, foul-mouthed, fish-faced citizens and was delighted to find myself so studiously ignored. I was free to wander anywhere, following little alleys until they turned into courtyards or fantasy fountains of dolphins and Negro slaves. It was impossible not to enjoy it all, even the brash and cheap. I loved the hand-painted cars, the streets of lime trees, the voluptuous plasterwork, the elaborate displays of dogs, and the flea markets with all their war-clubs and clogs. I loved too the way that – during the day – the city worked itself into a frenzy of heat and litter, and then – each morning – opened the fire hydrants and washed it all away.

HAVE A DREAM, invited the graffiti, or *How will you breathe this summer?*

I realised I was probably a century too late to enjoy it all at its best. The great hotels of the railway age were now all in retirement or ruins: the Normandie was covered in kung fu posters; the Nouialle, where Wagner had stayed, was now an office block; and the Hôtel Splendid had been overrun by *fonctionnaires* (all brutally oblivious to its laurelled ceilings and twiddly pillars). At the top of the hill was the station itself, St-Charles. It was a sort of palace for those in a state of arrival, with friezes and statues, and an enormous imperial staircase sweeping down into the heart of the town. The statues here were the most fanciful of all: *Asie* and *Afrique* sprawled out like two lascivious sluts, ripe for colonisation.

Only the boarding-houses had survived, and so I stayed at the Duc Hôtel. It was a spartan place with squat toilets and a memorable role in the history of anarchy. In January 1905, one of France's greatest ever political agitators, Louise Michel had died in the room just below mine. I often imagined that she was still down there, or at least in the plumbing. It grumbled and ranted all night. Sometimes it was joined by a hiss from the taps, or an anarchic, rattling door. I did what I could to placate such restlessness, wedging the windows with socks and tightening up the taps, but these were persistent ghosts. Matters came to a head one day at dawn when the curtains flew off the wall, admitting an early view of the rooftops and a blast of the mistral.

This would, I suppose, have been as good a place as any to watch the bombs trickling on to Marseille. On 1 June 1940 people had stood here, just like me, watching in utter amazement as the Germans attacked from the sky.

France had always expected this war, and yet was bewildered when it happened. As before, an air of unreality pervaded almost everything she did. The army was sent claret instead of tanks, and then went underground, allowing the Germans to drive round the sides. Desperate for heroes, Marshal Pétain was recalled from Madrid and installed in power. It didn't seem to matter that it was twenty-three years since Verdun, or that he was now eighty-four and kept nodding off. France would be saved by '*Philippe le gaga*'.

Marseille, too, had its role to play in the *drôle de guerre*, the funny war. Its citizens were told to paint their light bulbs blue and fill their attics with sand. The *fonctionnaires*, never popular, became the enemy within, arresting anyone without a gas mask. Conscription too was keenly enforced, although there weren't enough guns to go round. Even Sabiani swallowed his ideological pride, and joined up for a while. Henri Fiocca was also enlisted, and was marched off to Alsace in some moth-eaten puttees and an enormous greatcoat that came right down to the ground. Before he left, he took the precaution of buying Nancy an ambulance, in which she followed, a safe distance behind.

The enemy, on the other hand, saw nothing funny about the war ahead. As Europe weakened, Hitler was viciously blunt. 'Our opponents are like little worms,' he told his commanders. 'What matters, in starting and waging war, is not righteousness but victory! Close your hearts to pity!

Proceed brutally.' A few months later, the first bombs were bursting on La Joliette and 400 dockers were burnt alive or torn to bits. Ten days later, the Italians joined the war, and followed it up with a raid of their own. They were as earnest as the Nazis but not as accurate. To the delight of the Marseillais, *les macaronis* dropped their bombs wide, landing them amongst their allies, the *Sabianistes*.

That, paltry as it seems, was the end of good fortune. No Frenchman who witnessed this time will ever forget the shock of what happened next. People have often told me that it was a defining moment of their lives, the end of certainty and the upheaval of values. One moment this great and wonderful country was a leading power in the world, the next it was a carcass, being sawn up like a tree. During the six, wild weeks of Blitzkrieg France had simply buckled and collapsed; 90,000 of her soldiers had been killed, 200,000 wounded and another one and a half million carted off into captivity. 'I cried for days,' wrote Nancy later, as she tried to make sense of it all. No one, it seems, could explain this catastrophe – although Pétain would try. France, he decided, had been ruined by over-indulgence, the breakdown of family life, alcohol, syphilis and journalism. With views like that, he'd soon find friends on the German side.

For Marseille, the Battle of France didn't end with a boom, but an old man's voice. Pétain's message of surrender was broadcast down Canebière and throughout the squares. You can probably still find the wires that delivered defeat, amongst a tangle of others. In his ancient, stentorian croak, Pétain told Marseille of the honour he'd saved and the honour to come. It was a hard message to follow, but no one opposed him. Even America went along with Pétain, believing that only he was capable of uniting France. Britain merely despaired. At the last minute, she'd offered France the prospect of union, but Pétain had rejected it as being like 'marriage with a corpse'. 'Better to be a Nazi province,' added one of his ministers; 'at least we know what that means'.

Six weeks later, France wasn't even a province. It was stripped of its democracy, its economy and its finances, and then it was divided. Berlin asserted direct rule over two-thirds of the country, including Paris, and the rest was left to Pétain. He was installed in Vichy, and given notional control over the navy, a pipsqueak army, the rump of the empire, and the sleepy south. As far as the Nazis were concerned, he was merely a puppet, in charge of their vacation land and the unspeakable sore called Marseille. On 31 July 1940, all contact between the two portions was severed: movement was prohibited, telephone wires cut, and the post was stopped at the border.

Meanwhile, the threat of partition had prompted the greatest migration since the Middle Ages. Over ten million people had fled into this dwindling corner of France. During those last weeks, the road south was a rackety snake of car horns, whinnying horses, engines, brakes and tears. Foreigners had marvelled at what the French thought worthy of salvage and had heaped on top of their cars: mattresses, quilts, pillows, feather dusters and linen. 'It was,' wrote one observer, 'a peculiar sadistic irony of Fate, to have turned the most *petit-bourgeois*, fussy, stay-at-home people in the world into a nation of tramps.' Somewhere amongst them was Nancy Wake, grinding through the gears. Eventually, the ambulance had died and was abandoned, and Nancy – like Henri – would have to beg her way home to Marseille.

The city had undergone a transformation of sorts. It was no longer the gate to hell, or Asia or anywhere else, but a destination in itself. The Great Migration had brought with it an exotic tide of tramps: writers, artists, Jews, communists, German anti-Nazis, Weimar politicians, and Alsatians dodging the draft. Some wrote, some drank, and some merely contemplated the persecution ahead.

18

Marseille is still a city of refugees. It hardly bears thinking, the number of citizens reared on trauma.

I often found myself trying to read people's faces for some hint of the past. It wasn't difficult to work out who was from where. Marseille is like an enormous Venn diagram of trouble, its victims only ever interlocking at the margins. Most people up on the hills were Corsicans, on the run from poverty and feuds. Amongst them were pockets of Armenians (23,000), Italians (100,000), Spaniards (15,000) and Greeks, all the fallout from genocide in its varying forms. More recently, there'd been an influx of Balkan outcasts, but they still wandered from sector to sector, undefined by the city. They often turned up in the most surprising places. Once, I even came across an Albanian couple in the Tunisian souk, fighting tooth and nail over a weeping child.

Of all the refugees, however, the Algerians were easily the most obvious. This was partly because they were so effusive, probably the most engaging people I've ever met. I'd hardly been in the Algerian Quarter a day before I became part of the scene and was being cuffed and patted wherever I went (*'Al-salam alaykum!'*). These great public displays of affection had even survived my anarchic hotel, the Duc. The owners, the Bentebackh brothers, were impeccably kind, and showed me their entire family history, which began with a call to arms in 1939.

But the Algerians weren't just genial, they were also conspicuous. Almost 130,000 had fled here in the Sixties. Now, they owned not only the Duc, but most of the street and much of the hill. I imagined it reminded them of the Algiers they'd left, with its cafés and hookah pipes, skullcaps, hilal, and the scrape of violins. This seemed a reasonable idea when I looked at the map and saw Algiers a short hop over the Med, and Paris way off to the north. But the Bentebackhs were politely appalled.

'We'd go back tomorrow,' they said, 'but we can't.'

The others felt much the same. Drugs, persistent prostitutes and brutal *flics* made them feel awkward and dislocated. But it wasn't just this. The North Africans also realised that they themselves were a source of the city's reproach. Once again there was talk of *sales métèques*, or foreign scum. Even though there were nearly six million Muslims in France, they'd never felt nearer the edge. It was impossible, they said, to improve themselves and climb aboard the *ascenseur social*. Marseille was no exception to the hostility, and was always showering its bigots with votes. Occasionally, the politicians made a play for Muslim support, with promises of a mosque, but it was never a pledge they intended to keep. 'I have no objection to the building of a mosque,' Mayor Gaudin once said, 'as long as it's in Marrakesh.' For most Algerians, life in Marseille was a constant taunt, a reminder of just how savage their old lives had been, before they'd given them up.

At least they now had homes. Three streets down, on Cours Belsunce, were the tribesmen who'd drifted off the Sahara. Whatever traumas had driven them north, they were doggedly nomadic. The men had long beards and turbans and wore scraps of military drab, whilst their women rifled the bins. A few had set up trades, on sheets of cardboard, but most just sat. These were light, transient lives, with everything packed into sacks: umbrellas, silvery kettles, and sets of drums. Once again, I found myself searching faces for some hint of the lives they'd known, but there was nothing there. The looks I got back were distant, noncommittal and remote. The nomads had simply wandered out of their past. Marseille had seldom experienced such a collapse of pride.

Once, however, there was a time when the entire city faltered. It was over sixty years ago, during the rule of Vichy.

19

Pétain had no idea what to do with France, except make everything smaller.

Over the four years of his rule, the nation shrank almost to nothing. She'd already lost her strength, and soon there'd be little left of her spirit. Her confidence dwindled, her great ideals deflated, and even the old cries of the revolution ('*Liberté! Egalité! Fraternité!*') were reduced to the wincingly mumsy ('*Travail, Famille, Patrie*'). Political life was cropped and pruned, and so were consensus, wine production, free speech, cubism and sex. It was almost as if Pétain wanted his country to slip out of sight, or revert to a village. Perhaps then the Germans wouldn't notice it, and would never again come crashing out of the woods. Pétain may have been a collaborator but he was first and foremost a fool.

With each pruning, the Pétainistes declared more honour saved. Unlike the Nazis, they were snivellingly parochial and often saintly in thought. Over-indulgence was one of the first of the evils they sought to trim, and, in Marseille, the bars were shut for three days a week. But almost everyone shrivelled under the old man's rule. Prostitutes were sent to internment camps, and the exposure of legs was banned. NO MORE SHORTS! said the signs at the beach. NO MORE WOMEN DISGUISED AS MEN! Abortion became an offence punishable with hard labour for life, and married women were forbidden to work. Within months of the new gerontocracy, France was moving along at a rheumatoid pace.

In this piffling condition, France was obligingly compliant. Although Pétain was never truly Nazi, he never opposed them either. Until 1942, Hitler was able to manage the whole of France on a garrison no greater than the Parisian police, some 30,000 men. Marseille itself became a puppet show of the Reich. There were grotesque acts of censorship, and the Pétainistes squawked their policies round the schools, with pamphlets like *Le Communisme contre Dieu*. Sabiani even sought volunteers to go off and help his allies, although this was mostly a failure. The first contingent of 'guest workers' comprised a few police informers, a trapeze artist and a prostitute. It was even worse when he sent a military force to the Eastern Front. The *Légion des Voluntaires Français* got no further than Smolensk, where it froze to the ground and was viciously lopped and crisped by an enemy far more driven and wild. After that, it was some while before the Germans began recruiting again. (A few years later, the *SS Sturmbrigade* set up an office on Canebière, but – like me – all they ever found were drifters, petty criminals and the colourfully insane.)

'Dark days indeed,' said Nancy. 'We all felt so defeated and small.'

There was little light relief under the Pax Swasticana except once, when the sirens went off by mistake. Everyone stopped and looked up wistfully, reminded of the good old days of the war.

While France cut itself to size, the Nazis carried off the surplus. 'The real profiteers of this war are *ourselves*,' announced Hitler, 'and out of it we shall come bursting with fat!'

It wasn't simply a question of skimming off the cream: France was almost gnawed to the bone. Hitler ordered her to make 'reparations' at the rate of 40 million francs a day, all paid in food, at an exchange rate set by Berlin. It was plunder on an industrial scale. During their occupation, the Nazis stole around two million bottles of champagne, vast quantities of cheese from Normandy, whole herds of Burgundy cattle, wheat from the Île de France, and – each year – over 320 million bottles of wine. Even Eastern Europe, which was supposed to be the breadbasket of the Reich, couldn't produce a feast like this. It all left Germany's new Head of Economic Affairs, Hermann Goering, drooling with greed. 'Fatty' (as the other Nazis called him) was always mixing policy with pudding. 'France,' he wrote, 'is fattened with such good food that it's *shameful . . .*'

Officially, the business of looting fell to the Armistice Commission. It wasn't exactly a dignified task. *Transform yourselves*, urged Goering, *into a pack of hunting dogs!* In Marseille, their mission was so ambitious and grand that they moved on to Canebière and took over the whole of the Louvre et Paix. This infuriated Nancy, who still made a point of talking loudly in English in the American Bar. There was nothing the Germans could do; Marseille was not yet theirs.

'Fascist bastards,' she told me, 'I can never forgive them.'

The commission's looting didn't stop, of course, at food. Marseille was stripped of its buses, its cars (which were supposedly needed in the invasion of England), its bronze statues (which were melted down for guns), and most of its horses. By the end, half a million of France's horses were trotted away, along with three-quarters of her iron ore, half her aluminium and much of her coal. For the first time in their history, it was no longer possible for Germans to describe a bon viveur as they had before: *er lebt wie Gott in Frankreich* (he lives like God in France).

God had never lived in Marseille, and kept well clear in the Vichy years. It was a dark, lifeless place, bereft of both morals and pleasure. The electricity failed, and at night the gas burned only weakly and blue. There were few trains and no taxis, and the only way of getting around was on weird contraptions made of scrap: bicycles with cork tyres and cars fitted with ovens. Theft became a candid pursuit, especially in the context of food. All the city's pigeons disappeared, and so did the limpets, the crabs and Nancy's dog. Although there were rigorous curfews, these just made the city feel eerie rather than safe. For a while, a few of the tarts came down from occupied Paris but they didn't stay long, and were soon smuggled home. The only good news came in December 1941, when America joined the war, but there was still a general feeling that worse was to come. *Everybody*, said one of the old boys at the Football Bar, was plotting *something*.

'Usually, a way to get out.'

20

Now the trains were running again, and the *gare* was back in full swing.

If Marseille is ever threatened by a deluge, taxonomists would do well to rescue the station as a sample of species that once lived in the city. It even looked like an ark, stuck on top of the hill. Inside, it was a dense spectacle of caricatures, like all my encounters assembled as one. There were pedlars, Berber tribesmen, jugglers, paratroopers with gleaming black guns, sailors, bankers, pickpockets, a man with a barrow of oysters, *fonctionnaires*, jackdaw girls with their hair scraped back all glossy and black, Monsieur Mohammed (again), dozens of spivs and a mad old woman who was charging people to look at her snake, which was made of wood. The only real clues to the date were the TGVs, which occasionally nosed their way up to the *quais*. They were an impressive reminder that St-Charles was still part of our century, and still firmly anchored to earth.

Of all those who came swaggering off the trains, easily the most striking were the legionnaires. I'd been told they had their base nearby, out in Aubagne, and, like everyone who's ever been a schoolboy, I was gripped from the start. Descriptions of the French Foreign Legion have always seemed so superbly appalling; men who called themselves *les morts vivants*, who prayed at the severed wooden hand of Capitaine Danjou, and who thought nothing of changing their names and marching off to fight for, well, whatever was going. Now, here I was amongst them, every one a Popeye, ready to die for his képi. Peter the knot-smith told me they'd even got their own dismal recruiting song, called 'The Black Pudding.'

Together with our sorrows, we forget that death
So seldom forgets us, the Legion.

It wasn't a jingle that would've tempted me, but at least the chorus was jolly. 'There's sausage, there's sausage, there's sausage for us/ But none for the Belgians because they're a bunch of shirkers' (*tire-au-culs*). Perhaps, after all, I'd got the Legion wrong. There were even more surprises in close-up. I noticed that *les légionnaires* were very well ironed and always wore their kit a size too small. It wasn't quite what I'd had in mind, all those years of the Living Dead.

From time to time, the *gare* had disgorged the odd celebrity legion-naire. Amongst them were Cole Porter, the King of Serbia, the expressionist Ernst Jünger, Prince Napoleon and the American poet Alan Seeger (who was sent to the Somme, and famously foretold his own punch-line in 'I have a Rendezvous with Death'). But the most curious of all was a shambling Hungarian, who seemed to be doing a tour of Europe's jails. During his travels, he'd divested himself of all his money, his nationality, his girlfriend, his communism ('the worst farce in the world') and most of his clothes. By the time he got to Marseille, on 15 August 1940, he was wearing an Algerian tunic, puttees, outsize boots and a cherry-red tarbush finished off with a silver sickle moon. Somehow, he'd discovered that the best way to disappear in France was to become conspicuous, and had traded his name and joined the Legion. To the Vichy, he was a Swiss nobody, called Albert Dubert. To the rest of the world, he was the writer and philosopher, Arthur Koestler.

He stopped only once as he tripped down town. Outside the Normandie he ran into some old German friends, ministers of the defeated Weimar Republic. They were as astonished as him by this chance encounter.

'*What,*' they said, 'is this fancy dress?'

'*Why,*' he replied, 'are you not on the run?'

They told him something would turn up in the end, but Koestler was not convinced (and within a year they were dead). 'Their individual fate,' he later wrote, 'reflected that of their nation – the tragedy of credulity and illusion.'

After a thoughtful tea, Koestler was back on his way. He was heading down to the fort in the harbour mouth, and so I decided to follow.

21

The Fort Saint-Jean had taken several centuries to build, a few hours to prime, and a split second to burst like a broken dam. The outlines of this catastrophic explosion (the Germans' last hurrah) were still owned by the army: three ramparts, a chunk of barracks, two and a half towers and a crater. Inside, there wasn't much to see. Everything was a chiselled lime-stone pink, and draped in shadows. Otherwise, several tons of explosives had done a thorough job of scouring it of detail. The violence of the blast had been so intense that even the window bars were splayed and bent like haywire. On the other side of the crater, I could see into the opened belly of the barracks: a row of attenuated cells, a chapel, a tower like a fifteenth-century ballistic missile and the commandant's wife eating an enormous salad. She ate very slowly like a rabbit, and was a model of contentment in her broken home.

Koestler, by contrast, was rather less than happy in his lumpy abode and was always planning escape. Eventually, he crept on to a ship, which carried him away, past If and Frioul ('The last outposts of continental France, sleeping under stars in her enormous, dishonoured nakedness, humiliated, wretched and beloved'). After adventures in Algeria and Lisbon, he eventually ended up in London, where once again he was thrown in jail. He spent the first three months of 1941 in Pentonville, mostly in the dark (it was thought he might use his light to signal to the enemy). But, despite the gloom, Koestler managed to secure a publisher's advance and a typewriter, and tapped out his first book in English, an autobiography called *Scum of the Earth*. It was the beginning of a remarkable literary life, all the more remarkable for its conclusion. Despite the suffering of his youth, Koestler decided that a life in pain was not a life worth living, and so when – in 1983 – the doctors told him that his pain was terminal, he took a fistful of colourful pills and brought it all to an end.

The oddest thing about Koestler's time in Saint-Jean is that it was all so emphatically British. Every dormitory in the fort was packed with solicitors, crofters, pilots, old chums from school, Geordies and chaps from the City. For Koestler, it was an odd introduction to the cranks who'd become his compatriots. The British were noisy and kept demanding salt and beer, and played football with artichoke heads, wrote cheques and kept accounts at the local shops. But, although they made light of their stay, they too were the flotsam of defeat. Some were remnants of the Highland Division, who'd continued fighting after Dunkirk. Others were stragglers and airmen, who'd all thought they'd get back home by heading for Vichy. But Pétain had honoured only his promise to Hitler, and so the British were interned.

I spent weeks trying to find a survivor of the British sojourn, and eventually found one, in Kent. It was Air Chief Marshal Sir Lewis Hodges, a man who'd risen to such spectacular heights within the RAF aristocracy ('C-in-C, Allied Forces Central Europe, 1973–76' according to *Who's Who*) that at first I felt rather loath to intrude. But these feelings of vertigo soon subsided, when I rang his home and spoke to his wife. I suddenly had a happy image of us all enjoying the garden together, sipping tea and poring over the pictures (which was much how it turned out). Two days later, I was chuntering down through the hops and wheat, off to pay them a visit. 'Bob has lots to show you,' Lady Hodges had said, 'although his memory's not the same since he had his stroke.'

The Hodges lived in a large white house, in which the war continued in pictures and silver. There were little shiny bombers swooping along the mantelpiece, Hampdens up the wall, Wellingtons lumbering out of the place-settings and a dense livery of crowns and wings across everything else. Sir Lewis was out in the conservatory, in a fawn cardigan and comfortably settled in his chair for the day. Lady Hodges, on the other hand, seemed to soar between several rooms at once, gathering up the things for tea. She was surprisingly agile at eighty, and told me later that she'd had her own war. While Bob was kicking artichokes round Marseille, she was in Gosport, stripping down gunboats and up to her earrings in grease.

'What *exactly* do you want to know?' said Sir Lewis.

Air Chief Marshal Sir Lewis Hodges.

It was well-practised suspicion, but it soon wore off. When Sir Lewis realised that all I was after was a stroll through the past, he relaxed and his uneven scowl became an uneven grin. Life at his altitude had been challenging and hard but, in his jagged memories of Saint-Jean, he was unable to resist the richly absurd. Soon the stories were breaking loose and tripping up in giggles, and albums and forgeries began to sprawl across the table. Out of the corner of my eye, I could see a large ginger cat out in the paddock, and when it saw us, absorbed in our huddle, it crossed the lawn and pressed its nose against the glass.

Sir Lewis began with the pictures. 'This is my Hampden, and the crew under my command. We were on our way back from a raid on Stettin . . . Look, here's the date: *9th September 1940*. Somehow or other we lost our way . . .'

Lady Hodges enjoyed this story, and was soon steering it along.

'Thought you were in Cornwall . . .'

'. . . And *actually* we were in Brittany . . .'

'. . . Then you ran into enemy fire . . .'

'. . . So I ordered the crew to bale out, and landed the plane in a field.'

'Did the others get away?' I asked.

'No, they were all captured – except the rear-gunner, Sergeant Wyatt, who'd not heard my order to bail out, and was still in the tail. He and I were the only ones to get away. We kicked off our flying boots, couldn't walk in them, and sent a pigeon back to England,' he chuckled. 'Imagine that! We had a *pigeon* in our plane!'

'. . . More tea, John? Must let the cat in.'

'. . . And somehow,' continued Sir Lewis, 'we got hold of clothes and shoes.'

There was then a snapshot of the escapees, dressed as improbable Gascons.

'A few days later, we were arrested, trying to cross the Pyrenees.'

After that, Hodges and Wyatt were escorted across Vichy France, united with the runaway Scots, and all ended up in Saint-Jean. It wasn't incarceration exactly but it wasn't freedom either. The displaced Britons were allowed to leave the fort, buy drinks, rummage around for food and even take digs in the town. In their pictures, they might easily be on holiday, the young men, knitted together and grinning: Garrow and Fitch who escaped, Treacy the Irishman (who also got away and was later killed on a raid), Wilkins, Murchie and Hodges. 'We were a team.'

Most days were spent trying to break out of their stifling holiday. Sir Lewis had kept every jot and scribble of these threadbare escapades: forged passes and counterfeit money; charge sheets and committals to prison; a *laissez-passer* printed with an old potato; a child's *cahier*, with each twist and squeak of the tale set out in great loops of pencil; letters of congratulation, and telegrams from those they'd left behind.

'My first attempt was a failure,' said Sir Lewis. 'Tried to stow away on an Algerian steamer and was caught on the docks in Oran. They sent me back to Marseille, where I stood trial at the Palais de Justice for breach of parole. I even had a lawyer called Maître Something . . . But they wouldn't let me back to the fort. I spent Christmas in the prisons of Chave and St-Pierre (where I shared a cell with three criminals). They were terrible places, with almost nothing to eat . . .'

We found the diary entry for Christmas Day 1940: *What a mess to be in.*

'If it's any consolation,' I told Sir Lewis, 'both prisons have gone.' The massive, star-shaped St-Pierre had been crushed and replaced with an ugly school, and Chave had been encased in smoked glass and swallowed up by a clinic. Sir Lewis didn't know whether to be pleased or not, that so brutal a part of his life had almost vanished.

'But, at least,' I asked, 'you did *eventually* get away?'

'Sure,' he said modestly, 'there were a lot of people trying to help.'

'And how did you come across them?'

'Well, we met an extraordinary woman in Basso's Bar, down on the old port. She was very brave and indiscreet, and her name was Nancy Wake.'

22

Although Basso's had gone, the port at dusk was still a place of indeterminate fate. It was often busier in the evening than during the day, as people assembled for the ethereal circus around the quays. Often nothing happened, but there was always the feeling it *might*. Many times I joined this hopeful audience, settling down in one of the bars or taking a seat on the wall. The whole place was a masterpiece of expectation, like an enormous stage awaiting the arrival of angels, perhaps, or mounted hordes. Everything glowed with a delicate, antique light, and yet the air squealed with excitement, or, more probably, swallows.

For a few, anticipation wasn't enough, and they were always probing at chance. The pickpockets patted their way through the crowds, and the Africans cast their lines in the oily water below. Occasionally, whores came tottering down from St-Ferréol or Paradis, hoping to gather any lusty strays. It all added to the spectacle, and the sense of something about to happen. Most people would have been happy with a sunset but – for others – there was always the prospect of a wallet, or uninhibited sex or just a jar of sprats.

Not everyone was happy to share the suspense. The whores were often hissed at and pelted with names. Once, one of them was chased down the quay by a gang of suited thugs, and she came clattering into my bar. 'What's up?' I said, and a huge head of lacquer and pins came level with mine. For a moment her gaze froze, and then she decided she could survive without me and that I had no place in the minutes to come. *'Va te la mettre, copain,'* she murmured, *'et melez-vous de vos affaires.'* (Go fuck yourself, pal, and mind your own business.)

Up on the sunny French quays, aspirations were more delicately expressed, if just as crude. The Bar de la Marine was a perfect example of fisherman's chic. I once spent a whole evening there, watching the yachtsmen at the art of seduction. I've no idea whether the French are as good at sex as they say, but they're certainly handy in the preliminary hustings. Unlike us English, they seem to strike a better balance between being impressively earnest and amusingly drunk. One man even seemed to be making progress with two women at once, a consummate skill in a city where all options are open.

The women too played an enjoyable role in my plonk-fuelled studies. Staring is no crime in Marseille, unlike turning away or ignoring a person's gender. The harbour wall, meanwhile, was like a carnival of womankind, each woman demanding at least a cursory look. It was all there: beauty, dignity, neglect, surgery, improbability and disaster. In the end, I reached the unsteady conclusion that the older women were more attractive than the younger ones, who often looked shapeless and spare. Perhaps the world is getting uglier? Or perhaps this only happens in France? Anywhere else, women seem to emerge from youth and assume that their looks are forfeit. Not France. Here, every woman knows that her look has yet to be *earned*.

As darkness fell, I walked back towards the wilder quays of love. By now, most people had gone home, leaving only the promise of trouble. Occasionally there was genuine bloodshed – fighting tarts, or drunks slugging it out in the bars – but usually it was just the persistent rumour of riot.

I often felt that these rumours began where they should have ended, with an army-in-waiting called the CRS. By day, *les Compagnies Républicaines de Sécurité* (as they're officially known) were always slouching round the port but at night they became edgy and tense. Nothing lends France the feeling of turmoil quite like the CRS. With all their clubs, plated helmets and armoured shins, they looked both impenetrable and dim-wittedly cruel (which, I was told, they generally were). They also kept sixteen coaches round the back of the port, and at the first whiff of protest they set off like a giant caterpillar, wailing through the city. If there wasn't a riot when they left, there was by the time they got there.

I soon began to despise the CRS, almost as much as did the Marseillais. I often saw the words *CRS Mort* daubed across walls (or anything standing still), and – in their presence – people became pointedly sullen, as if the CRS were an occupying force or a bout of bad weather. This was odd considering *les Compagnies* had emerged from the old communist militias who'd flushed out the last of the Nazis. People even taunted them with comparison ('CRS-SS!' they'd shout). Clearly, the CRS were no longer the shining knights. Somewhere along the line, they'd adopted their enemy's taste for black, and its brutal manners to boot. For myself, I despised the CRS because they'd waved their clubs at my camera. It left me feeling that French democracy was not perhaps in the gentlest of hands.

One night, I met Charles the knot-man picking his way through the armour. He knew exactly what the CRS stood for: '*Connards, Racistes et Salopards*' (Pillocks, Racists and Absolute Sods).

It was on a night like this that the pilots met up with Nancy, in Basso's. It would be a pivotal moment in the lives of all.

For Hodges and his friends, it meant escape and a chance to rejoin the war. To begin with, there were dinners at the Fioccas' flat, and a first taste of wine ('We'd never really tried it up until then,' said Sir Lewis). Then there were the false uniforms and forgeries, and the boys were handed from friend to friend until they ended up in Spain. Amongst Sir Lewis's papers was a letter from Nancy, dated 25 May 1941. In it, she wishes him well on the last leg, and in the bombing raids ahead. 'All I ask,' she writes, 'is that you drop an extra one for me.'

For her, the encounter at Basso's was a point of no return. By conferring with Germany's enemies, she'd committed an act of *terrorisme*. She could now be arrested at any time, and then beaten perhaps, or kicked to a pulp before being hanged. None of this deterred her, nor did the fact that the Vichy police commissioner lived in the flat below. Nancy had found a vocation, a channel for her restlessness and her constant urge for action. She became a *convoyeur* (or courier), at first, running cash and radios up and down the coast, and then a smuggler of men.

Nancy's resistance might have continued at this level if the Germans hadn't revoked the treaty and burst into the south. Alarmed by Allied successes in North Africa, Hitler had decided to take direct control of the Mediterranean coast. Sweeping Pétain aside, he ordered his troops into the so-called 'Free Zone', and on 12 November 1942 Marseille was occupied by foreign troops for the first time since 1815. In the newsreels of this time, there are ugly hummocks of armour all the way from the station, down Canebière to the port. Most Marseillais had never seen a German before, and regarded them with complete disbelief. The soldiers returned their stares with complete disgust. During the next twenty-one months the city would descend from hunger and mild contempt to outright treachery and hate. In the violence that followed, Nancy would lose everything she'd ever had, including her flat, her life in Marseille and the exuberant M. Fiocca.

'Poor Henri,' said Sir Lewis sadly, as he tucked his pictures away.

23

I often found myself touring the old haunts of *Marseille allemande*.

All around me, the hotels had fallen under German control. The navy took over the Louvre et Paix (replacing the hated Armistice Commission) and the *Wehrmacht* had settled down in the sumptuous Hôtel Nouialle. Meanwhile, the regional commander, General von Fischer – after a lavish attack of *folies des grandeurs* – had moved next door, into the Hôtel Splendid. Soon he was spouting orders across his surly domain. First, the signposts turned yellow, and then Saturday was cancelled and a six-day week began. Fishing was banned, for a while, and so were sailing, photography and the use of English words, like *grill room*, *lavatory* and *five o'clock tea*. From now on, Anglo-Saxons had to be referred to as *Anglo-Américains*, and it was forbidden to make any reference at all to Alsace-Lorraine, the cost of the occupation, Austria, Poland or Yugoslavia. Even the word *vandalisme* was outlawed, because it suggested that mindless destruction had originated with the Germans, or that at least they enjoyed it the most.

All down my street, the cafés had turned field-grey. The Brasserie du Chapitre, which still seemed to smell of greasy boots and gunpowder coffee, became a snug for the troops, or a *Soldatenheim*. The locals were unsure what to make of their conquerors at first, and called them the *doryphores* (or potato beetles). The Germans all seemed to have long, ponderous titles like *Sonderführer* (Task Force Leader) or *Oberverwaltungsräte* (Senior War Administration Official), and – compared to the locals – their own women were baggy and grey. To the Nazis, these girls were the Blitz Chicks (*Blitzmädel*) but to the Marseillais they were nothing less than mousy, and were called *les souris grises*. The men, on the other hand, were impeccable, and always paid their bills. They bought scent and knickers for their girlfriends, and toured the town as if they were on holiday with rifles. Unsurprisingly, this worried the *résistance*, and one of their first slogans was: REMEMBER, THESE PEOPLE ARE NOT TOURISTS.

Co-operation with the enemy was never great, although – sixty years on – it still vexed the city. It was thought that only about one per cent of Marseillais collaborated with Germans (which was about the same as the number that took up arms in resistance). For most *collabos*, like the waiters and whores, it was merely a matter of keeping afloat. Even those who became more intricately involved often did so out of necessity. As the war dragged on and the shortages bit, more and more women yielded to the invader, a phenomenon known as *la collaboration horizontale*. But it was usually the same women: the poor, the hungry and bleakly opportunistic. Of the sixty-five women prosecuted after the war for *débauche* or *rapports intimes*, a quarter were chambermaids from the hotels up on this hill.

Collaboration had taken a more sinister turn round the corner, on Canebière. Somewhere, amongst the drifts of soot and dust, Sabiani had set up an office for his Fascists, who became the party in power. There was no memorial to this place and – even during the months of Sabiani rule – the Marseillais were always tossing grenades into the lobby or trying to wreck it with bombs. This was the rotten core of collaboration in Marseille, and had ruled according to a simple, lumpy creed: Vichy had been weak, Hitler was a peacemaker and the arch-unifier, and Britain would not come to the rescue as London was already in ruins. For their muscle, not only could the Fascists rely on the *Wehrmacht,* but there was also a large and boisterous French militia, known as *La Milice.* They were unnaturally vicious, as their oath would suggest: 'I swear to fight against democracy, against Gaullist insurrection and against Jewish leprosy.'

'I've known *miliciens,*' said Nancy, 'who have been just as violent as the most savage Gestapo agent.'

With power assured, the city was run by the gangs on the Cours Belsunce. I've often wondered whether, in its state of tribal squalor, the street was still paying the price of its cruelty and greed. Under Sabiani's patronage, the gangsters set themselves up as the *Comité pour la Paix Sociale,* otherwise known as 'The German Police'. They established their den in the Hotel Californie (which has long since crumbled away) and rode shotgun round the town. Ostensibly, they were after people offensive to the regime (like Jews, Gaullists and Anglophiles), and would drag them back to the Californie. In practice, they were also doing what gangsters always do: extortion, pimping, racketeering and every variant of theft. Amongst those wrongly arrested by them, and deported (never to return), was a man denounced by his neighbours because he'd had the 'nicest vegetable garden', and another denounced by his daughter when he'd tried to prevent her turning their home into a brothel. Naturally, no one was deported until they'd been relieved of their possessions and spattered around the hotel. 'Did you see how I hit him?' one of the hoods was heard to say. 'He'll be pissing blood for a week, that poor bugger.'

The Germans watched all this with grim satisfaction. Once again, the French were policing themselves. It was almost as if they'd been invaded from within, or as if the Nazis were merely incidental to their self-reproach. With complicity assured, the occupiers could even start on some ambitious plans of their own. They'd begin with Le Panier, the slum on the promontory between the old port and the new. It was this area that disgusted them more than anything else, and the architect of the horror to come was one Karl Oberg, *Polizeiführer* to the French Gestapo.

'Marseille is Europe's cancer,' he told Hitler, 'and Europe cannot survive until Marseille has been purified.'

24

When I first climbed up to Le Panier, I had a sudden feeling that – like the proverbial cat – curiosity would eventually get the better of me and that this was a prowl too far. The streets narrowed and buckled, and the sky became merely a crack in the shadowy firmament of washing and walls. Most of the lanes were so narrow that, once, fish could only be carried up here on poles, and the high street was barely the width of a cart. Others were too steep even for carts, and looked like river beds tumbling off the hill. One even ended in a cliff, and if I peered over the edge I could see the Old Port and sunlight way below.

As I clambered upwards, I realised that Le Panier had worked hard to earn its name, the Basket. It was a dense lattice of lanes and chutes, criss-crossed with conduits, sewers, alleys, bolt-holes, and rat-runs that led even deeper into the dark. Perhaps long ago, someone had pulled a loose thread and the normal warp and weft of the hill had tightened into this compacted knot of life. Even history had become rather dense and knotty up here. According to the inscriptions, all manner of people had been tangled up amongst the poor, including Napoleon, Casanova, the painter Puget, and a convent of nuns who'd cut off their noses to frighten off any Saracen raiders.

Life was still compact, and people were still spilling out of their homes. There were tiny orange squares full of children, and a pump where water was once bought by the jug. Most of the elderly had moved their chairs on to the street, and would watch me pass as if I was the television or a tropical fish. I was surprised how many people wore slippers, and decided that's how we'd all become if we were packed as close as hens. Le Panier made up only one per cent of the city's sprawl, and yet – not long ago – over 50,000 people lived there (or one in fourteen of the Marseillais). It was often called 'Le Petit Naples', although Italians were only part of the tale. Stacked in amongst them were Africans, gypsies, Armenians, and even a band of long-lost Cossacks.

Naturally, it was a place of legendary depravity. '*Leis fillos de Lorette,*' went an old saying, '*pouedon pas coucher soulettos.*' (The girls on Lorrette just can't sleep alone.) In fact, for centuries the entire slum had been maddened by the itch. There was once a time when the chairs on the street were not for the old but for those on the game. The Rue Lanternerie was like a sex market at the bottom of a geological fault. Somewhere in there, a sailor could have found every stunt he'd ever dreamed of (and a few he'd not thought possible). It was said that the *filles de joie* here were amongst the most obliging and unrepentant in the world, and that – occasionally – the odd rake still wandered up here, in the hope that nothing had changed. But the girls had long gone, and so had the brothels: Madame Sphinx, Chez Aline and Le Chat Noir. The only things left were the little old ladies, the Rue des Repenties and a surfeit of ugly convents.

At the crest of the hill I stopped to contemplate my survival, and realised that I'd been wrong. Le Panier was not as satanic as either I'd imagined or it had threatened. Although it was still defiantly foxy in parts, the tales of depravity had, it seemed, lingered long into gentrification. Whatever restlessness this place had known had gone, and the itch had been subdued. Now everything had a pastel glow, and the shops sold soap and gifts in scented paper. Perhaps it was different on the other side, I wondered, and began to descend to the port.

I didn't get far, before coming to a halt in complete disbelief. At the far end of the Place de Lenche, the quarter suddenly stopped. The other half of Le Panier had simply vanished, completely scraped off the hill. All that remained was a void, a few concrete towers and a plaque to those who'd died.

Le Panier wasn't the Nazis' only attempt at town planning, but it was easily their most savage. Despite the fact that it was no more than a miserable ghetto of refugees, it was referred to in Berlin, rather mystically, as the *Kasbah Marseillais*. Seldom has fantasy ever got such a grip on reality. It seems Reichsführer Himmler allowed himself to be taken in by Oberg's reports (despite the fact that the *Polizeiführer* had a head like a tree stump and a wit to match). Oberg's version of Le Panier had been teeming with spies and gun-runners, and he'd predicted that wild gangs of bandits would soon be breaking free and screaming up through France. Alarmed, Himmler had demanded a '*radikale Lösung*', or radical solution, a clear indication of the atrocity required. At least in Oberg he had a man he could rely on to do something catastrophically futile.

Oberg was seen grinning in the scenes that followed, and plodding around in his herringbone coat. He called his plan Operation Sultan (which had a nice Johnny-foreigner ring), and summoned his photographers to watch it unfold.

Their album, published as *Der Blick des Besatzers* (The Occupiers' View), is still sold in Marseille, and I was often offered a copy. It's a ghostly work, a glimpse into neighbourhoods lost, and into faces burnt or buried almost two generations ago. Every moment is there: the fixed bayonets and the SS troops at the end of the street; stringy, knob-jointed hands clasping a bundle of clothes, and wide, disbelieving eyes; the Milice in their leather jackets – proud to be here – and the narrow alleys, empty now and grey with shame. During the night of 23 January 1943, over 25,000 people awoke to the sound of breaking doors, and were ordered out of Le Panier. Women were given no time to dress, and the sick and old were poked along and prodded into trucks. They are last seen leaving Marseille in cattle wagons, wondering whether this was just the end of a nightmare or the beginning of another. Of the 804 Jews arrested, not a single one survived. As for the rest, they were dispersed, deported or enslaved, and few of them ever returned.

Oberg's party piece, however, was yet to come. Over the next two weeks his sappers packed the empty *quartier* with dynamite, and looted what they could. Then, on 1 February 1943, with both the press and populace assembled on the quays, the charges were detonated and Le Panier disappeared under a thunderous cumulonimbus of dust. For hours afterwards it rained sand, and then there was quiet. A total of 1,924 buildings had been destroyed, along with thousands of homes. All that was left was a swathe of rubble, and a desert of grit and junk stretching from the headland right to the heart of the town.

The next day there was a different mood about Marseille. From now on, the Germans could expect little courtesy. The tourists were misdirected and misunderstood, and found their drinks knocked over and ink stains on their clothes. Flowers appeared at the memorial to the Yugoslavian king, and in the cinema people coughed and laughed through the German news. Meanwhile, the underground press denounced the 'Nazi bandits' and their 'valets from Vichy', and exhorted the city to fight. *'Ralliez à notre cause!'* it implored. *'Défendez-vous par tous les moyens!'*

But only a few took up the call to arms. The Marseillais had got used to Vichy, and feared reprisals, or worse, civil war. Perhaps, too, many felt that the daily hardship of occupation was little worse than the deprivation they'd always known. This only changed later, when the Germans started extracting slaves – two labourers in exchange for every POW held (a con known as *la Relève*, or the Relief). After that, the trickle became a flow. Many headed straight out to the Maquis, to live Robin Hood lives in the scrub. But a few stayed behind. The Corsicans made the best *résistants*, with their law of silence and a background in feuds. At least one assassin from the *milieu* was awarded the Légion d'honneur, and, on their best day ever, they appeared from nowhere and shot up the Hôtel Splendid.

After Le Panier, one of those to answer the call was Nancy Wake. Until then, her resistance had been merely an inconvenience to the enemy, but now it was about to become wholeheartedly bloody.

'It was decided I'd leave for England,' she said, 'as soon as I could.'

25

There were still pockets of resistance all over the city.

Most of these were safe houses, as ordinary now as they were supposed to be then: the Mission, Nancy's flat, and Dr Rodocanachi's house on the Rue Roux de Brignoles. This last place, I discovered, was a tall, elegant building divided into clinics and flats. It had cream shutters, well-scrubbed stonework, and gutters in matching taupe. From June 1941 until February 1943, it had been the terminus for an escape line that stretched from here to Madrid. The doctor's house was also once the site of a kangaroo court. It was an odd trial, with an unhappy ending that had a lot to do with the gutters.

The accused was a British deserter called Cole, who was known to have betrayed the line. Whilst the *résistants* deliberated on how to dispose of his case (the doctor favoured insulin and a dip in the dock), Cole jumped out of the bathroom window and slithered down the drainpipe. This sturdy pipe would cost many lives, by delivering him safely to earth. Free again, Cole hadn't stopped running until he'd reached the Gestapo, where he sang off the names down the Line. Dr Rodocanachi was shot, the Australian agent in Perpignan was beheaded and countless others simply vanished for good (Cole meanwhile continued to sing until the end of the war, when he was traced to Paris by MI9, and died in a blaze of gunfire).

As always, there was no plaque to mark this sorry tale. Instead, the doctor's house had been overwhelmed by the squat next door. It was called Golgotha, '*un collectif antipsychiatrie*'. One of the squatters came out to talk to me, and told me that We are all Abnormal although, as an anti-psychiatrist, he couldn't explain what this meant. Across his front door was a splash of mad, yellow letters: LE TRAVAIL TUE, it said, WORK KILLS. Heroes, it seems, didn't live here any more.

After Cole, the *résistants* were more wary and had acquired a dungeon, under the café where I sometimes had my lunch. The Bar le Petit Pucet was just next to my hotel, and was, I imagine, as hospitable now as it had been then. Perhaps the biggest difference was that these days the owner was Algerian and all his meat was halal. After copious *salaams* and *Insha Allahs*, he'd sit me down and feed me on *boeuf* and plonk until I could eat no more. It wasn't good food but I liked him and I liked his dusty bar. There was football straight from Africa, and Christmas decorations from about 1972. The only relic of the *résistance* days was a dark and whiskery clock, which – every now and then – rattled bronchitically, but never got much beyond a quarter to three.

One day, I asked the owner about the cellar and the *résistance*.

'Yes, it's all still there,' he said. 'Paintings and all.'

'*Paintings?*'

He shrugged. 'The soldiers must have done them. Come, I'll show you.'

He led me down through a tiny trap door set in the floor of the bar.

'There,' he said, as he swung his torch around: 'the Art of the Resistance!'

In the yellowy murk, I could see playing cards scattered across a stone floor, crates of furry bottles and curious shapes up in the vaults: vines, dancing figures and a Negro bent double with chains. It wasn't much more than graffiti but at least it was the Art of the Resistance, or the men they sought to save. For several months, Le Petit Poucet had been a clearing-house for fugitives: escapees, patriots and airmen who'd filtered down the Line. Each man was questioned here, and those found to be lying were shot through the back of the head and dumped in a ravine. As for the rest, they were returned to the Line.

I asked the owner if these men ever came back.

'We had some last year,' he said. 'Almost killed themselves on the stairs.'

'And what about the old *patron*?'

He shook his head. 'They said the Germans took him away, and he was never seen again.'

Le travail tue, as the anti-psychiatrists would say.

Nancy also took off for England, by passing down the Line.

It was a tumultuous journey. With a price on her head, and her bra full of Henri's cash, it took her months to get across France. She escaped from custody twice, slept in sheep pens, caught scabies, lost her shoes, made six attempts at the Pyrenees, and was machine-gunned as she jumped from a moving train. But she made it, and arrived in London in June 1943. One of the first things she did was to have dinner at Quaglino's, and then lunch with Lewis Hodges, who'd also made it home.

'I was,' said Nancy, 'in seventh heaven.'

But she didn't stay long, and was soon back in the fight. Six months later she parachuted into the Auvergne, wearing two revolvers and a camel-hair coat. As with so much of Nancy's life, her account of this war is richly surreal. Everyone has a cartoon name (Judex, Gaspard, Bazooka and the Macaroni Man) and the *résistants* try to rob her at first, and then make her *Chef du Parachutage*. London sends her Sten guns and lipstick, gelignite and packets of Brooke Bond Tea. The Americans meanwhile send two advisers, each in chocolate cavalry boots and without a word of French. At night, Nancy wears pink satin pyjamas, and – if the battle restarts – she fights in them too. There's also a twenty-ninth birthday party in an abandoned château, and gifts from all the guerrillas: ice-cream spoons from the French, etchings from the Americans, wild flowers from the penniless Spanish, and linen from a beautiful colonel, who will lose his legs. For Nancy, these are happy times, in their way.

'I want my ashes scattered there,' she told me, 'up in the Montluçon hills.'

But, however she tells this tale, it was still war and dismally cruel. The Germans sent more than 22,000 SS troops up on to the plateau. They weren't ordinary soldiers, but fanatics and 'Mongols' – or Russians – men who made collections of fingers and ears, and nailed their victims up in the trees. It was a dirty, restless struggle, in which wounds were swabbed with cognac, and prisoners usually shot. Nancy often found herself driving – or pedalling – hundreds of miles for a transmitter, and being blasted again from the air. Contact with London was sporadic, and air-drops dependent on luck. The bazookas arrived the day the Germans attacked, and Nancy was still reading the instructions when the first of her missiles hit home.

Gradually, by August 1944, the enemy began to melt away. The Maquis followed them into the valleys, and for a while the killing went on. The headquarters of the Gestapo in Montluçon were wrecked with grenades, and then there were raids on factories, trucks and retreating columns. Nancy is vague now about the role she played, and uncertainty swirls around her again. Perhaps the detail doesn't matter any more, whether she fought with her gun or her voice, or even her own bare hands.

I asked her if she had any regrets.

'Yes,' she said, quietly, 'Henri. I wish I'd never left him behind.'

On the day Vichy fell, she got her first news of him for over a year.

'He'd been arrested by the Germans, and sent to Rue Paradis.'

26

Despite its saintly name, the Rue Paradis plunged through a broad range of moral possibilities before vanishing from sight. It began with *les bars américains* and prostitutes, soared through the boutiques and money-lenders, picked up a few quirky Tibetan institutes, dipped into the obstetric quarter, and then plummeted through guns, hosiery, fortune-tellers and a bakery, before disappearing off to the sea. It was here, amongst the pastries and glaze, that the Gestapo had set up their home.

'They had the big house round the back,' said the baker.

'Best villa in the area,' said his wife. 'Huge private gardens . . .'

'You don't know *what's* buried in there!'

I could see they enjoyed their patter, and had often said it before.

'Can I get inside?' I asked.

They shrugged. 'It's just flats now.'

'I'll show you,' said one of the customers, 'I live in there.'

My new host was an enormous man in his forties, who swung along with an awkward angular gait. He said his name was Bernard, and that he'd been a paratrooper until five years ago, when he'd ended his career in a tree. 'Avoid trees,' he advised, 'and never jump at night.' His hair was silvery and his face minutely abraded and worn, as if his descent through the twigs had not only broken his back but had polished him up like a coin.

We passed a handsome block of apartments, and turned into his drive. 'That's where the *milice* lived,' said Bernard.

He unlocked his gates. 'And this is where the dirty work happened.'

Ahead of us was a large Italianate house and all that remained of its well-tamed woods. Penury and concrete shops had closed in on the villa, shrinking the garden to a few stands of cherry, some succulents and an old, lonely palm. The house, on the other hand, was still a mish-mash of grand ideas. Size was important to the original design but so was ornament, and it had ended up with too much of each. It looked like a cliff, wearing a balcony, an Etruscan frieze and a Chinese hat. All it had ever needed was an owner of grandiose intention (and not too much taste), which is what it got, in 1942. Rolf Mühler had taught French before the war, and was as surprised as anyone to find that his ugly, unbridled views were bouncing him upwards through the ranks of the secret police. Number 425 was a handsome reward for all his spleen.

'It became the Gestapo's regional bureau,' said Bernard, lurching through the shrunken forest. He stopped at a tiny pink farmhouse, now almost hidden in a clump of cherry. 'The guardhouse,' he said. 'They kept the riff-raff out of the house.'

The foliage ended in gravel and a doorway down to the basement. Bernard fumbled with some keys, winced and then admitted us into the cool. It was a pleasant set of rooms, the past banished by bright rugs, Indonesian furniture and abstract art. I could see a kettle squashed flat like foil, and a tailor's dummy wearing a képi and medals. The coincidence of suffering was unsettling – and compelling: the Gestapo basement, the deformed sculptures, and the man broken by gravity, and tortured every day. Bernard must have read my thoughts, at least in part.

'Only a few people were interrogated here,' he said, absently.

From upstairs, we could hear footsteps in Mühler's old house.

'Just the *special* cases,' said Bernard.

But, in all I'd read, there was nothing special about the interrogation team. Mühler recruited people who were callous, amoral and dependent. They were all criminals. There was Antoine the Boxer, who could break people up with his fists, and Palmieri the Jew-hunter, who liked spiffy

black suits and drove around in a Citroën *traction avant*, peddling chocolates and fancy liqueurs. Then there was a jewel thief called La Belle
Rouse, and Gaston Daveau, a mechanic who was so savage that even the
Gestapo found him revolting. La Belle Rousse was his mistress for a while,
until he caught her astride one of the sergeants and put a bullet through
her head. After that, the Gestapo had him crated up and sent to
Sachsenhausen, from whence he never returned.

Mühler's lieutenant was a drifter from Saxony, called Dunker. He was
an inept swindler but a talented linguist. Between spells in prison, there
was always a home for him at Rue Paradis. His special talent was in raising
informers, or 'getting the crows to sing'. He and his mistress, Blanche di
Meglio, made quite an occasion of torture, with Blanche serving the titbits
and drinks, while her lover applied his tools. They made a lively if unusual
couple – until Blanche tried to kill him, and was herself broken up and
sent to the camps to die.

'I'm no angel,' Dunker later told the Allies, 'but it was no party either.'

Party or not, none of them did well when the canapés stopped. Dunker
was tried in 1947, and was still snarling away in flawless French ('*Vive
l'Allegmagne! A mort la France!*') when a volley of bullets hit him smack
in the chest. Palmieri was also shot, but not before he'd diddled the SS,
sold their supplies and offered himself to the Allies. The Boxer was the
only one to die fighting (or at least driving his car through an ambush,
in Aix). Mühler alone survived, did twenty years' hard labour, and ended
his days running a drink shop in Mannheim.

'Bastards,' said Bernard to his salon, as if the ghosts were still lurking
there.

Perhaps the most one could say about them is that they were productive. During their twenty-one months in Marseille, thousands were
deported, making a small but ugly contribution to the total tally (the
Nazis deported over 80,000 Frenchmen, of whom only a quarter returned.
A further 39,000 were executed). In Marseille, the Gestapo killed at least
eighty-two people, a few of them here beneath the villa. Amongst them
were Dr Rodocanachi (after whom the side-street was named) and, of
course, poor Henri Fiocca.

Nancy always seemed to know she'd never see Henri again, and says
he appeared in a dream on the night he died. He was arrested in May
1943, when Nancy was already in Spain. For the next five months the
Gestapo worked on him, trying to tease out the story of the missing

White Mouse. Henri was pounded, stripped, pierced, dunked, cajoled, tricked and then beaten again. I imagine they were all there at the finale: Gaston and La Belle Rousse, Dunker, Blanche with her titbits, and Antoine thrashing about with those big purple fists. By the beginning of October, Henri was vomiting soil, and a few days later he died. His body was never recovered, but nor was his silence forgotten. He now has his own back-street behind the Bourse, called the Rue Henri Fiocca.

Grief had an odd effect on Nancy. Instead of wrecking her, or leaving her marooned, it merely set her adrift. After the war, there was nothing to keep her in Marseille (the Gestapo women had stripped her flat, and the Fioccas wanted her gone), and so she bobbed around, feeling aimless in the peace. For a while she lived in Paris (where she fought the waiters), and then Australia (where she fought an election) and then, in 1951, she returned to Whitehall where she wrote a guide to surviving behind enemy lines.

Then she remarried, and there was happiness for a time, or at least nostalgia suspended. Her husband had been a prisoner of war, and perhaps he shared her fear of standing still. The couple drifted from England to Malta and then back to Australia, where Nancy became a champion of veterans' rights, and resisted all awards. It was only when her husband died that she felt herself adrift again, and started wandering back to the war. She sold her medals and, in 2001, she returned to London and booked into her wartime haunt, the Stafford Hotel. Now all she wanted was the years to fall away, and the story to start again.

It's surprising the life that had welled up from the past. Old comrades had reappeared – airmen, couriers and saboteurs – and visited Nancy in her new military residence, the Star and Garter Home, which is where I met them, when she turned ninety-three. None of them thought their lives the least remarkable. 'The war was just something that happened,' I was told by an elderly widow in lilac and pearls. She'd weighed only six stone six when the Red Army found her, in a camp at the end of the war.

Fame too had attended Nancy's return. There'd been radio interviews, features, birthday cards from the President of France, ceremonies, more awards and a visit from Prince Charles (who'd finally paid off her bills, or so it was said). She'd even made a trip to Number 10, although she was surprised to find that they didn't keep gin, and that Mrs Blair greeted her guests in a pair of odd shoes. People often assumed that Nancy was the inspiration for *Charlotte Gray*, and were endlessly curious about her fantasy lover. Such whimsy also tended to stir up the cranks, who'd laid down a siege of demands – for visits and autographs and even locks of her hair. Not that Nancy minded the attention. 'I've got nothing else to do.'

Nowadays, she said, she spent most of her time reading and watching the box. Her big hope was that one day Jonny Wilkinson would come trotting off the rugby field and gather her up in his arms. She liked him almost as much as she loathed James Bond. 'I hate all that violence,' she said, 'it's so depressing.'

'And what about the books?' I asked.

There was only *Anne of Green Gables*, read time and time again.

'It's a beautiful story,' she said. 'Nothing ever goes wrong.'

27

The Marseillais often said that, when a thing was spent or bust, it had gone away to Goudes. It hadn't far to go. When I looked at the map, I could see Goudes off down the coast, snagged on a point like a claw. Beyond it there was nothing: Marseille ended, and so did the roads, rivers, beaches and names. All that remained was a scribble of inlets, officially known as Les Calanques (or the Creeks) but often referred to as *le bout du monde*. This made perfect sense: if, as people believed, the world begins with the sea, so must it end in land. Even the Nazis had been troubled by such apocalyptic thoughts. With the Allies massing for the attack, they'd closed off the coast in 1944 and sent an army to the end of the road.

There was still a rich folklore on the theme of nothing. Most people agreed that Les Calanques were devoid of life. On the bus to les Goudes, one of the passengers told me there was not a drop to drink beyond Cap Croisette, that there were over fifty wrecks scattered through the creeks and that the scrub burned so fiercely it caused the fire trucks to melt. I didn't really believe any of this until I saw a pack of dark shaggy islands forming in the sea, and the skyline started filling with rock. The gentle hills of the suburbs had suddenly boiled themselves into an exorbitant fortress of molten limestone slashed with silver and splintery crags. Perhaps this really was the ragged edge of the earth? The bus seemed to think so, and came to a halt in a cleft. It had no intention of tempting extinction, and continuing on to Goudes.

'What now?' I asked my ghoulish friend.

'You walk,' he said. 'Either along the coast road, or over the mountain.'

I chose the mountain, and clambered up between two vast cathedrals of rock. It felt odd to be alone again, breathing pine and myrtle, and with the path so close to my face. For a while, all I could hear were the stones trickling off my boots and into the valley below, but then I was on the top, and in the roar of the mistral. It had been an industrious sculptor, blasting out fins and armour and an eye the size of a hangar. From up here, Les Calanques looked like a slumbering litter of dinosaur pups. I was surprised that anything had survived such a reptilian regime, but it had: the End of the World is flecked with poppies, and smells of fresh sweet herbs.

After the Col du Bres, the path began to wriggle down towards the shore. Ravines turned to creeks, and then to sea-water, brilliantly blue like flashes of static through the rock. After an hour I was back down, amongst stiff clumps of sisal and sea aster, and brilliant chandeliers of white-petalled candles. Along the way I found an old bullet, a nest of tiny white bones, and the stub of the road from Marseille. This promising sign of humanity had even sprouted a village, called Callelongue, where I bought a pizza made with ewe's milk cheese.

Around the headland in les Goudes, I ran into the first of the German defences. The hill above the village was still crusted in concrete and lumps of steel. It was like the grey, crumbling skin of a long-dead monster, all tangled and matted with plaits of barbed wire. Parts of it had collapsed under its own weight, but most of it still gaped and moaned in the breeze. I could see bunkers, mess-halls, godless crypts and even parts of a half-eaten stove. Across one wall someone had daubed HITLER POUR 1000 ANS, which, in a structural sense, was probably true. People will ponder these fatuous ruins for as long as we've pondered the Pyramids, equally puzzled by the link between effort and purpose. And, like the Pyramids, it was all built by slaves – 16,000 recruited in Marseille alone.

Les Goudes had recovered well, next to its fossilised foe. Once again there were dainty *pointus* bobbing around the harbour, and fishermen looking cheerfully antique. Despite its spectacularly well-toothed setting, few people ever ventured out here, so the villagers had it all to themselves. Some had even spread out along the coast road, living in the pill-boxes on Hole Creek and Monkey Cove. These bunkers made curious homes, with balconies and awnings across the slits. At least one had become a restaurant, which was like eating lunch inside a very large pebble.

The concrete carried on like this, back to the edge of Marseille.

Only the waiting had ended. In his New Year broadcast of 1944, Hitler had acknowledged that his war was in crisis. Later, he sacrificed the 244th Division to defend Marseille, knowing that the city's loss would be a terrible blow. Sabiani alone predicted Nazi victory. He saw the skies full of wonder weapons from V1 to V9, and told the Marseillais that – unless they rallied to the Fascist cause – they'd all end up down the mines. It was only when the Allies appeared on the horizon that he lost heart, loaded his *dependiti, parenti* and *amici* into trucks and fled up the Rhône. Along the way, they were picked off by the *résistance* and shredded by American planes. 'Jews and gangsters!' declared Sabiani, as he scuttled out of range.

In the last scenes of French Fascism, there was little pity. Sabiani and the remnants of the Milice eventually reached Germany, and sanctuary of sorts. But it didn't last. Most of them died from being forgotten. Their families were interned but not fed (sixty French children starved to death at Siessen). The last 10,000 *miliciens*, on the other hand, were sworn into the SS, tattooed, and thrown against Marshal Zhukov's tanks. Most had barely overcome their surprise before they were ground into the dirt. Sabiani would need all his cunning just to disappear, which is what he did, at least for now.

Meanwhile, on the Concrete Riviera, the waiting had ended but not with bombs. On 15 August 1944, a stupendous force of over 60,000 Americans and 100,000 North Africans had landed further up the coast, away from the big guns, in the Gulf of St-Tropez. It was a peculiar army; amongst them were the Free French ('A rag and bobtail lot', according to their Allies), paratroopers borrowed from the British, and a regiment of Japanese-Americans. The overall commander, a veteran of Utah beach called Admiral Moon, was so certain they'd fail that he killed himself five days before. Anticipating failure was the only error he'd made in a flawless plan. Within a month his army would advance 400 miles, capturing 57,000 Germans, at a cost of only 7,000 casualties. It was a rout to be remembered as 'The Champagne Campaign'.

Wherever the troops landed they left a trail of abandoned gas masks, and were soon pounding through the hills. People say they made a different noise to the Germans; instead of the crunch of jackboots, there was the squeak of thick rubber soles. On the fourth day, the Free French peeled away and drove west around the back of the wilderness of Les Calanques. The German bombardiers hadn't expected the invaders to emerge from the rock, and with their guns all trained on the sea, gave up the cape with hardly a fight. The old bullet I'd found was probably all that was left of the battle.

After the End of the World, the Marseillais had risen in open revolt. The Free French paused at the edge of the city, gathered their strength, and then poured down Canebière.

28

I once met an English soldier who was with the French when they burst into the city.

Charlie Kennedy had spent his life being in the wrong place at the wrong time. It was supposed to have been the life of a Middlesex grocer's boy, mixing teas and slicing ham. Instead, he'd been buffeted from country to country, had fought alongside fierce African tribesmen, had done hundreds of jobs, had never earned a bean, and now had cancer, a titanium knee and the Légion d'honneur. None of this surprised Charlie, who thought it perfectly normal to live in a state of upheaval. He hadn't even finished up where he'd begun, but now lived in an old council house in Harlow, with some busy little armchairs and carpets the colour of autumn. The only constant in his life was Gwen, his wife, who'd been with him the day he set out for the desert.

'We married on embarkation leave,' she told me, ruffling his hair: '1941.'

Charlie smiled as if Gwen was all he'd ever wanted, and more than he'd ever deserved. Even in the army, Charlie's flair for displacement was as vigorous as ever. Just by standing in the wrong place or joining the wrong queue, Charlie could find himself bouncing off to another unit. He was constantly changing cap badges and battlefields: a spell with the Middlesex, then the Rifles, then the Service Corps, Cairo, Naples, Monte Casino and Pompeii. Eventually he ended up with a liaison unit, fighting for the French. Even then, his life seemed to veer from the sublime to the colourfully outlandish. His comrades were always colonial troops; first, the Tahitian marines ('Friendly'); then an Algerian division ('very nice'); and then the Moroccan Mountain Division ('Tough').

'I made friends with all of them,' he said, unabashed by his remarkable fate.

'What language did you speak?' I asked.

'A little French,' said Charlie, 'and I learnt Arabic in Italy.'

He'd even kept a diary like a grocer's ledger: lists of friends, addresses, ships travelled on, mileages, dates, and comrades killed. Amongst the crumbling pages was a photograph of Charlie in his baggy uniform, arms around an American friend with strong pearly teeth, and an Algerian in a Middlesex beret. 'He didn't have a hat,' said Charlie, 'so I gave him mine.'

Charlie flicked through the years with only mild surprise. War is often absurd, but there are always grades of anomaly. He recalled how the French fought with astonishing courage, and yet travelled with a *bordel militaire de campagne* and despised a night in the open. He remembered too the bluish coffee called *la soupe*, the summary justice, and a huge vat of Tunisian wine that it'd taken his comrades a week to drink. It was only when they reached the bottom that they found a dead New Zealander, pickling in the dregs.

His memories of Marseille were more fragmented, like the battle itself. Explosions flared and puttered like flickering candles along the coast; scuttled ships, ammunition dumps and Fort Saint-Jean. It was beautiful weather, like a holiday in a deserted city. The citizens vanished underground and the gunners fought duels in the streets. More fighting erupted across the roofs of La Joliette, on the station's magnificent stairs and in vicious flurries around the centre. There was no front line, merely the deafening seconds of conflict and then blind confusion. On one occasion, Charlie was arrested by an enemy patrol, and then released when he addressed them in English. Another time, a German armoured car appeared in front of him and then vanished in a cloud of shrapnel and smoke. By night he slept in the open, and by day he crept through the shadows. At some stage, he found two wounded comrades screaming in pain and still taking hits. Charlie drove them to safety, through the crackling streets.

'And that,' said Gwen, 'is why they gave him the Croix de Guerre.'

Charlie grinned shyly. 'What *else* could I have done?'

On the third day, the Germans withdrew to the hill of Notre Dame de la Garde. It was a perfect last resort, like a cowled head that watches over the city. From here, they could drop great leisurely blooms of orange on to almost every quarter, and make the streets bubble and spit under squalls of fire. The Algerian *tirailleurs* were sent to prise the enemy away, and with them went Charlie.

'We got behind a tank,' he said, 'a Sherman called the *Jeanne d'Arc*. We thought it would be safer there. But then we came under fire and it was too warm for us so we let it go.'

'Did it make it?'

Charlie frowned. 'I don't know. I think it was hit.'

Always bad news for a Sherman; the Germans called them Tommy cookers.

'Yes,' said Charlie, 'they brewed up pretty quick.'

The *Jeanne d'Arc*
Marseille.

In seeking salvation in Notre Dame de la Garde, the Germans were only doing what the Marseillais had done for centuries. It's said that this hilltop has been a place of prayer and supplication since Roman times, when the *sacerdos* would flip-flop up the hill to bathe his knife in blood. Paganism received a further flourish in 1870 when the basilica was added, all slim and striped like a pillar of candy. On top of this unlikely confection is a vast golden Virgin, now the Goddess of Good Fortune, carrying a baby the size of a small plump elephant. To give an idea of what a colossus this infant is, it's a five-foot journey around his wrist. If the Virgin were ever to lose her battle with gravity, she'd not only obliterate the car park but would crash her way through several neighbourhoods before blocking off the port.

The Marseillais have repaid such improbability with devoted surrealism. These days, the basilica is like a repository of catastrophe kitsch. People still bring the Virgin gifts in gratitude for her intervention: men who think they've drowned bring bits of their boats; firemen bring pools of molten fire trucks; soldiers bring helmets snagged with holes; and there's a whole room full of crutches, lifebuoys, false limbs and broken skis. Around the walls are paintings that celebrate not so much the moment of salvation as the seconds before: the moment trains crash; bombs trickling on to the city; a child swooping out of an attic; or a man tumbling under a coach. Amongst all of this are tablets recalling the city's plagues, riots and fires and – for some reason – Drogba's number 11 football shirt from Olympique de Marseille. All carry the same message: *Merci Bonne Mère*.

The Virgin had been less indulgent with her German defenders. Perhaps she was French after all. The last moments of this struggle are still gouged into the walls, savage chunks bitten from the masonry, and a ditty of holes round the door. On 26 August 1944, the Virgin was freed by Muslim soldiers, men of the *3ème Regiment Tirailleurs Algériens*. I noticed that they'd also left gifts for her, laying helmets and Red Crescent banners amongst all the *ex-votos*.

As I clambered down the hill I came across an armoured tomb that I felt I knew. It was the *Jeanne d'Arc*, with her tracks restored, fresh paint and a marble plaque. Charlie was right; she'd been hit and had brewed up quick, and her innards had melted away.

'I didn't feel much by then,' said Charlie, 'just surprised to be alive.'

29

The North Africans who liberated Marseille still inhabit the city, less now in body than spirit. But even this was surprising, given the absence of any acknowledgement of their role, yet alone a monument. The nearest Marseille got to a war museum was a shop on Rue de Papillon, stacked to the ceiling with ancient rifles and képis. It was a museum because old Madame Peris kept the prices just high enough to ensure that nothing was ever taken away.

The North African story had largely survived by word of mouth. Most of the Arabs in my street seemed to have had relatives who'd played their part in the city's redemption. The café owner downstairs said his uncle had chopped his way from here to Berchtesgaden, and was one of the first into Hitler's den. These were often stories of exuberant detail. 'The Algerians had a lucky sheep!' said the patron. 'A giant ram!' Meanwhile, my landlord told me his grandfather had been with the Zouaves for five years. 'His was a continual struggle,' he said (and it finally ended down a mine in Metz in 1955, under a downpour of coal). All that was left of soldier Bentebackh was a turban-badge bearing a Panther's head. Even the Arabs, it seems, saw it all as a war of cats.

Occasionally, I met the veterans themselves, or people who claimed as much. I was always wary of confessions of bravado in Marseille; if everyone was as warlike as they said they were, the whole city would be on the march (I once met a Vietnamese who'd sewn some ludicrous epaulettes on to his linen suit and was passing himself off as a *légion-naire*. 'Which legion?' I wondered, 'The Ruritanian? Or Brobdingnag?'). But there was one man, a tramp, who made a more convincing claim than others. He was a disconcerting sight: snaggle-toothed, dressed in rotting green drill and with a face like cherry-red leather. On the back of his hand was a dark wrinkly crescent, the outline dispersing now as if created from smoke. From the lining of his cap he produced an old snapshot he'd stolen; it depicted happy Germans, marching through Paris.

'I killed *dozens* of them,' he clacked, 'and now I don't get a centime!'

The killing was easy to believe. Charlie had warned me about the ferocity of colonial troops. 'They hated shellfire,' he told me, 'but they were fearless when it came to a fight. Sometimes, it seemed as if they wanted to fight the war with knives.' The Moroccans were the most alarming of all; many kept collections of ears, and the Goums took their warfare so seriously that they even brought their own women, hapless creatures raised for fornication from the age of twelve. But, at least with the Goums, the locals were spared. The Algerians had a reputation for rape on a Soviet scale. Charlie said he'd never forget the sight of the Zouaves tearing a girl apart and then, when they'd finished, deftly cutting her throat.

'What *could* I do?' he implored. 'They'd have killed me too. And besides, we depended on them for our lives.'

In the face of such a determined foe, the battle had simply collapsed. The Moroccans were far inland before the Allied cruisers had even finished pounding the shore. There were few Germans to be found. On 28 August, General Schaeffer surrendered Marseille, and the last of his army abandoned Provence and fled up the Rhône.

Meanwhile, as the Arabs picked up the stragglers, the Marseillais turned on themselves. The *épuration*, or Purge, was an exercise in self-mutilation that began with slaughter and has haunted France ever since. It followed a familiar pattern, like the Terror of 1789 – random, opportunistic and pseudo-judicial. Some even see it as just another stage in the old *guerre franco-française*, the struggle between the ruling elite (white, monarchical and Catholic) and the revolutionary Left (anti-clerical, urban and now anti-American). There's no sign that the conflict will ever abate. Occasionally, it erupts spectacularly – like 1968 – but otherwise it's simply the backdrop against which the French live. The riots are merely biannuals that bloom like fiery weeds and then shrivel away.

The Purge began honestly enough with its colourful violence. Sabiani's flat on Rue Fauchier was ripped apart, and the plaque to his son (who'd been killed in Russia) was smashed. The enemy's signs were also torn down and their women were shorn. On Canebière, the Fascists' office was enthusiastically slashed and plundered, and then daubed with the words 'Property disinfected'. Later, the newspapers printed the names of suspected *collaborateurs*, and bodies started to appear, dumped at the cemetery gates. The killing had begun all over again. Gangsters became *faux policiers*, and enjoyed a new era of uniformed crime. Even the *résistants*, the FFI, had become unmanageably feral, and were given the order to hand in their guns.

For a while, the fate of many lay in the hands of the *Comités d'épuration*. Even Robespierre would have admired them for their chilling aversion to justice. They were merely courts of revenge. It was no better when the civil courts resumed control. As most of the judges had once sworn oaths to Pétain, they now used their powers as an expression of enthusiastic loyalty and commitment to the restored republic. In Marseille, 166 people were shot, and 67 were given life imprisonment. Even the most petty *collabo* could expect up to ten years in jail, although military men could commute their term for a sweltering spell in Hanoi.

It was much the same all over France. Amongst those accused were Edith Piaf and Maurice Chevalier (for performing on German radio) and Georges Simenon, creator of Inspector Maigret (for making a German film). Even Arletty, who'd long since been forgiven for being a whore, and who'd starred – unforgettably – in *Les Enfants du Paradis*, was jailed for several months for sleeping with a German (it could have been worse; most people thought she'd had her breasts cut off). 'My heart is French,' she'd said in her defence, 'but my ass belongs to the world.' Meanwhile, over 2,000 people were sentenced to death, including Pétain. In his case, de Gaulle wisely intervened. There was nothing to be gained from putting an old man of ninety before the firing squad. Instead he was sent to the Island of Yeu. There he remained until he was no longer coherent, dying shortly after his release in 1951.

Even now there's a nagging feeling that the *épuration* was not about justice at all. Often, Vichy officials simply merged back into the establishment, leaving their minions to take the heat. For the rest of the twentieth century, the ruling elite would simply close in around its guilty past. President Chirac was the first president to acknowledge that France had played any role in the Nazi design. Meanwhile, his predecessor, François Mitterrand, enjoyed perpetual immunity from all forms of gossip (the story of his time as a Vichy official, *Le Grand Secret*, was banned for the rest of his life). Even worse was the head of the Parisian police; despite the fact that Maurice Papon had overseen the deportation of the Jews from Gironde, it didn't occur to anyone to bring him to book until 1999.

The chaos of Marseille – the dump of bodies and the shots in the night – was probably no worse than anywhere else. But the effect on its American liberators was unsettling. Had good triumphed over evil? Who was who in the purgatory of liberation? And what was there to save?

Two months into the chaos, on 29 October 1944, there was a new face on the dock. It was 01824846 Second Lieutenant Flint, a touch bilious, a little perplexed, armed with whisky and ready to serve.

30

Almost exactly sixty years later, Flint joined me in Marseille, arriving with the same degree of perplexity, a fraction of the Scotch and a grandson called Jeff. Emerging from the airport, they both looked awkward and overdressed, as if they'd arrived too early or in the wrong place. Jeff had never been to Europe before, or eaten an olive or spoken French. He was about the same age as Flint had been when he'd stepped ashore, and probably felt much the same. They'd even looked alike: slight, vaguely auburn, light-footed and furrowed with curiosity and interest.

'Very excited to be here,' said Jeff, although he didn't seem sure.

It was hard to know what they thought of the journey to come, up through France and Germany and into the Alps. Flint was wearing an olive-green suit, a bush hat and a pair of enormous boots, each with a tread like a tractor. Perhaps, in his mind, Europe was just as he'd left it, bosky, ruptured and dire. That night we all stood on the harbour wall and I could almost feel the horrors, ebbing away. After a long silence, it was Flint who broke the spell.

'I didn't know it was all so *grand*. It felt very different then . . .'

Such understatement and generosity was typical of Flint. Looking back, I couldn't have wished for a better guide to the campaigns ahead. Although he was wizened and whitened with time, he was youthfully optimistic and still found much that amazed him after eighty-six years. I often felt as if I was travelling with a much younger man, an idealist trapped under layers of age. Humankind may be in a piteous state, he seemed to say, but it should never be despised. Flint was endlessly indulgent, almost mischievously so. When – later that night – a junkie tried to wrestle him into a wall, Flint wagged him away with a freckly finger. 'If you want to be a pickpocket,' he said, 'you'll have to do better than that.' The boy must have thought he'd had some bad skunk, and, with his eyes popping, fled back into the night.

For Flint, it still felt odd to be back. The French were as puzzling as ever, with their cobbles and public holidays, and the way they got through the day without bacon and eggs. Nothing was quite as he expected, often because it wasn't as odd as he'd imagined. He was astonished to find ships again – afloat in the port – and when he saw all the punks asleep with their hounds, he thought we'd arrived in some sort of market for dogs. Only an American could have assumed that the French had become so quaintly bucolic. Like so many of his countrymen, Flint had long believed that France had a flair for nothing except defeat.

'They were never grateful,' he said. 'I don't think they wanted us here.'

Jeff was equally bemused, but harder to read. Although I became very fond of him, it would have taken months to work out what he felt. Jeff was everything an American was not supposed to be: shy, averse to controversy, and acutely sensitive to the mood of others, even those he didn't understand. If he had a passion, it was in the smoothly whirring world of machines, particularly racing bikes. He wore biking clothes and a biking visor (always an exotic touch amongst the well-groomed French). He even worked in a bike shop, and would admire bikes in the way that some people look at horses or food. Of course, he had his moods – like everyone else – but on the surface nothing would change. Jeff simply disappeared inside himself. In fact, he'd made quite an art of disappearing, and had once cycled off 3,280 miles across the States. It took him eighty days, of which he spent forty with his great-aunt in Wisconsin, in her house without water or lights. 'We ate squirrels, whatever died on the road,' he said. 'Squirrel's good, a whole load better than lynx.'

'What happened from here?' I asked Flint.

'We marched to the staging area, eleven miles up in the hills.'

There was no question of Flint walking the route all over again, but I did it myself a few months later.

'What about the gear?' I'd asked him. 'What happened to that?'

'I got mine on a truck, but the men had to carry their own.'

The baggage of 1944 was so much more impressive than now. Each man carried up to 80 lb. of kit, everything he'd need for the struggle ahead: rifle, cartridges, horseshoe roll, a suit of olive drabs, a sweater, two pairs of socks, a change of underwear, helmet and liner, knitted cap, woollen gloves, an 'Elgin' watch, canteen, mess kit, toilet articles, some K-rations, a box of matches stamped STOP HITLER, a 'Tex Mex' GI condom, and a tactless army read like *The Fireside Book of Verse*.

By contrast, all I had was a notebook, a baguette and a lump of cheese. It was a pitiful tribute to the sea-green troops who'd staggered out of the docks. Marseille's war had ended but theirs was about to begin.

31

Just as my arrival had seemed like a journey into the present, so the road from Marseille seemed like a journey into the past. As I left the port and headed north, the docks and railways fell away, along with the depots and mills. Sometimes they fell away completely, leaving only a bonfire or a smatter of tufted asphalt. Time had weighed heavily on St-Mauront, and the suburb of Arenc was blackened and blank. But, as the road climbed, older villages began to emerge from the weeds. These were enjoyable places, usually built round ancient farms, with great petals of lilac paint flaking off the doors. In the first village, I found an old leather holster on the pavement, which made me feel that the Americans were just up ahead, dropping military litter.

When he saw me loitering over this refuse, an old man came over and stabbed a thick grey finger into my chest. He had eyes the colour of meat, a beard down to his belly and a trolley full of cardboard and rags. 'What's going on?' he rumbled. 'What are you doing?'

I explained that I was on my way to Septèmes, to the old American camp.

'*Putain!*' he said. 'Fuck me! That's some way . . .'

I asked him if he knew it at all.

'Me? Why would I go up there? It's just a load of rocks.'

This was not an inviting thought but at least the views got better. Long terracotta viaducts looped from ravine to ravine, and ornamental trees appeared at the side of the road, well-coiffed firs and coppiced limes. Each of the villages now had its own square with a pâtisserie, a priest on a bicycle and a bar with beads hanging over the door. In one place, I found a shop for dogs and a hammam that promised '*Les Charmes d'Orient*'.

It was textbook France but, after ten hours on the go, the Americans had found it outlandishly weird. The entire hillside was in darkness by the time they got here, except for the dirty little fires where the men warmed their hands. Worse, the sky still shuddered and whined with planes, although whose no one knew. All night great lazy chains of tracer floated upwards into the clouds. Occasionally, trucks would burst out of the darkness, as blind as boulders as they thundered downhill. Eventually, one of them smashed into a platoon under the Saint Antoine viaduct, smearing two soldiers down the road. Somewhere, someone will think their great-uncle died a hero's death, instead of ground up under American tyres less than a day into France.

It took me several hours to get to the ridge above the edge of the city. From here, I could look back across a shimmering sprawl of gravel and glass. Far over to the east, I could see the Cité Radieuse, rising from the clutter like a concrete tooth. In 1946, Le Corbusier had promised to harness technology to peace instead of war, and to give the city 'a machine for living'. I remember going there once, and wandering around through the streets in the sky. I half imagined that these great two-laned corridors had names like Place de la Concrete or Rue de Linoleum, but the inhabitants seemed happy enough. One floor had been almost entirely colonised by architects as if they could somehow absorb the genius. I found it harder to enjoy, perhaps because it reminded me of too many places that it's inspired: the sink estates of the Sixties, slums from here to Bombay, and the gigantic dentistry of Soviet Europe. The locals, I discovered, called it *La Maison du Fada*, or The House of the Raving Mad.

A touch of this fada-ism had even broken out on the ridge. Several mute, featureless towers now loomed over the edge. From time to time, I could see things detach themselves from the concrete – fruit peelings perhaps, or the odd lump of chair – and flutter down to earth. Even in the names of these places, there was never much hope: La Bigotte or Les Abattoirs. The problem for Le Corbusier was that peace never really came, only refugees. Each successive wave brought more poverty and a hatred of the wave before; Algerians, then the *pied-noirs* who'd ruled them, then moderates, extremists and another wave of the poor (when, some months later, the Interior Minister, Nicolas Sarkozy, himself an immigrant, suggested that the 'scum' should be evicted, the estates erupted and – across France – some 4,000 cars were torched). Le Corbusier's concept was not so much a Machine for Living as a Machine to be Endured.

This would have been a sad end to Marseille, except that it wasn't quite the end. As so often with this city, at the moment when you think you despise it, it produces something wonderful and you love it all over again. Suddenly, the last remnants of the suburbs parted and I found myself amongst windmills and luxuriant clumps of sycamore and ash. The road now climbed up through paddocks of cow parsley and poppies, and a stream appeared, playing its way through the boulders. At the sight of such tranquillity many of the Americans had simply fallen out of line, and waded into the grass and slept.

My own march ended on a knoll of Aleppo pines, overlooking a wide, flat dip called le Plan-de-Campagne. There, I was joined by an old farmer, called Monsieur Pelat, who'd spent all his life on the knoll, wrestling vegetables from its bright red grit. He had a large bristly head and hands as jagged as rocks. At the top of his hill we stood on the edge of a network of holes, which looked like a warren for burrowing dragons. Monsieur Pelat told me it was all that remained of an SS camp. 'They used to go on raids as far as the Var,' he said. 'You know what? They once burnt down an entire village! *Imaginez! Même l'école et les poulets!*'

He was only twelve when the SS had settled at the top of the knoll.

'It was probably the only time my father ever beat me,' he said.

'Why?'

'I went into their camp and stole a few things. Bread mostly, but also a beautiful bazooka. "You'll get us all killed," said father, and that's why I was beaten.'

But in the end it was the Germans who died, atomised in a storm of shells that rolled in from the sea. Only the locals survived, hidden in tunnels and mines.

'And so the Americans took over the camp?'

'No, not here. This hill was wrecked, and stank of the dead.'

'And so they settled on the Plan-de-Campagne?'

'Exactly,' said Monsieur Pelat. 'As far as the eye can see.'

It was an awesome thought, and for a few moments we both stood, staring over the plain, as if the Seventh Army were still out there, engines turning, ready to roar up the Rhône.

Part 3 – Picnics on the Rhône

Everything ends this way in France – everything. Weddings, chris-tenings, duels, burials, swindlings, diplomatic affairs – everything is a pretext for a good dinner.

Jean Anouilh

The rapidity of the Rhone is, in great measure, owing to its being confined within steep banks on each side. These are formed almost through its whole course, by a double chain of mountains, which rise with an abrupt ascent from both banks of the river.

Tobias Smollett, *Travels through France and Italy*, 1766

La destinée des nations dépend de la manière dont elles se nourrissent.
(The fate of nations depends on how they eat.)

Brillat-Savarin

32

What should have happened next is a beautiful journey. Provence is danger-ously magnificent. The mountains are as keen as knives, and the soil's the colour of blood. Rivers never seem to meander here, but boil through the stones, and the trees are as hard as iron and knotted by the wind. You only have to gaze upwards from the Plan-de-Campagne and there's St-Victoire, a crag so brutally alluring that Cézanne couldn't stop painting it, and gave us more than sixty different versions. He even visited it on the day he caught a chill in 1906, and died on the walk back home. Poor Cézanne, he wasn't the first great artist to bring us news of Provence, but was the first to die of its beauty.

Humans here have an apologetic role, their fields diminished by the grandeur and their houses begged from the rock. The land won't be hurried but patience is rewarded. From this huge shattered landscape come some of the most exquisite tastes in the world: peppers, wild herbs, garlic, olives from trees over a thousand years old, aubergines, and tomatoes ripened in cruelty and sweetened by the sun. Little has changed for centuries. There have always been vines here, and pigs there, and onions on the plain above Septèmes.

Indeed, it was even a bed of onions the week 30,000 Americans arrived and trampled through the furrows. Then came the rain, swirling mud and onions together and transforming the landscape into a glutinous, bright-red soup.

33

Despite his gluey memories, Flint was determined to see 'Delta Base Section' again, and so we took a train to Septèmes, and ambled up to the plain. The onions, I noticed, had not returned, but had been replaced by *garrigue*, a waist-high fuzz of thyme and stumpy oaks.

It worried Flint how little he recognised. Gone were the huge anti-aircraft guns of his dreams, the tank-traps and the sea of sodden tents. Perhaps what worried him most was that so substantial a part of his memory could simply vanish, leaving nothing but the crimson and stones. I could almost sense him struggling with the years that had gone, trying to discern the shape of the past, and to summon back the cold. 'Everything you owned was wet,' he said absently, and shivered.

That first night, they didn't arrive until after midnight, and flopped wearily on to the sludge, where they ate their rations raw. The men were then dispersed in pairs across the plateau – in case of attack – and made to dig slit-trenches in the gravel and glue. 'It's the rockiest soil in the world,' said Flint, scuffing a boot in the hard-baked clay, 'including Texas.' After several hours' digging, the paired men then clipped their ponchos or 'halves' together to make a tent. It may have kept the rain off, but it did nothing to stop the rich colours of Provence seeping up from below.

'Then, once set up,' said Flint, 'I gave my first order in Europe: "All NCOs to my tent."' This was a Flintian moment: the triumph of cunning over a gruelling ordeal. As the men assembled, mutinous with cold, Flint produced a bottle of Scotch, and made them toast their own fortune and sluice away the mud. It was a well-timed gesture, and the beginning of loyalties that have survived ever since.

But that, it seems, was all that had survived. Unlike their enemy, the Americans had fought the war without concrete, and had disappeared without a trace. Or perhaps the last little bits of the camp had been swallowed up by the mud? I noticed that in the middle of the plateau there was a now a vast retail park, the biggest around, according to local lore. An American concept astride a great American midden heap? It was no surprise the place had thrived.

The Panthers had spent three cold, sticky weeks up on the plain. Life slowed to a trudge, as if time had become sympathetically viscous. The men rehearsed the war in slow motion, their listless manoeuvres engulfed in the goo. Once again, chicken ruled, and the days went by in a series of tasks, each energetically futile: forming parades, guarding huge immovable objects, and polishing stuff that was then trailed through the mud. Even Flint was caught up in the drudgery of chores. Unlike the British Army, batmen were forbidden; it was considered inappropriate to make servants of enlisted men.

'There was no them and us with the men,' said Flint. 'You eat, sleep and poop together.'

All soldiers should, however, unnerve their commanders a little, and Flint's were no exception. An outsider might even have wondered whose side they were on. Of the fifty-six men under Flint's command (1st Platoon, B Company, 824th TD), over a third spoke German. But this, said Flint, was no reflection on their loyalty; they were just brought up on Brooklyn

Yiddish ('and a few dreadful adjectives') or in the Teutonic wilds of Tennessee. According to the historian, Stephen Ambrose, such abundant German was not even particularly unusual on the Western Front, a conflict he depicted as a clash of the cousins. Both the Supreme Commander (Eisenhower) and the commander of the forces in the south (General Devers) had German-speaking grandparents, and many men had German relatives even closer than that. To some, speaking German would be useful in the battles to come, but mostly it was just a source of mischief. Sammy Piltch, for example, became adept at chatting up *Fräuleins* in Yiddish, and Corporal Konitzer was always winning over local girls, and offering his spares to Flint.

'For a bit of *therapeutic adultery,* he'd say. Cheeky devil.'

Others were mischievous enough, even in English. Flint remembered them as if they were still here, camping all around: his platoon sergeant, Joe Harrison ('a wonderful man'), his driver, Walter Kinzel, who was older than the rest and could bluff his way through hell, and Miah Levinson, who gave lectures on the finer points of sexual intercourse. Then there was Sergeant O'Moore, who wrote love poems for the regimental magazine, and Herminio Cardona, a Cuban bigamist, who'd only enlisted to keep one step ahead of the law. But perhaps Flint's favourite was his gunner, George Nowicki, from College Point, New York. In a former life he'd been a furniture restorer but it never troubled him, the transition to destroyer.

'A great gunner,' said Flint: 'never missed a shot.'

It was as much as Flint could do to keep his men in grog. Most of the time, they bought it off the farmers who wandered into their wargames ('Two quarts of wine for a packet of smokes,' according to Monsieur Pelat). But there was never enough to take the edge off the cold. So, one night, Flint took a tapered twig and a five-gallon can and drove back down to the marshalling yards. There, he found a tanker of Algerian *pinard*, put a bullet through the side, drained off a can, and tapped his plug in the hole. Even the mud and rain were forgotten that night. 'I don't know how we drank it,' said Flint. 'It wasn't even *vin ordinaire.*'

But despite their hardened palates, few Panthers felt ready for war. Even the reappearance of their equipment only made them feel cumbersome. Each platoon was reunited with a truck, two jeeps, four piffling guns and four clumsy, grunting half-tracks, at best a set of hippos on wheels. The 824th had never felt less like the army's pincers, and more like its excess luggage.

The great torpor of November 1944 soon began to tell in the American advance. As the vast juggernaut smashed its way up the Rhône, its rear wheels seemed to falter in Marseille, and sink into the mire. Theft was draining the army of strength. This wasn't merely the loss of a little Algerian *pinard*; almost 20 per cent of the supplies landed were being stolen. At one point, gasoline was disappearing in such industrial quantities it even threatened the advance. But it wasn't just gas: whole convoys were disappearing, along with soap, spam, nylons, cigarettes, morphine and whisky. It's surprising what an army needs, just to make it move.

But then, suddenly, on 21 November, the wheels freed, and the order came to go.

34

Flint's second excursion up the Rhône valley was rather less complicated than his first. We decided to cover the 357 miles to Dijon by train. This time, there were no lice inspections, no air guards, no brain-juddering rides through clouds of ash, no emergency hospitals, no evacuation points, no cocked machine-guns or olive drabs (with 'full field steel'), no radio silence, no obliteration of identity, no orders in the event of attack ('Continue to travel'), no convoy guides, no rations and no hurry. There wasn't even a Peter Parade to sully our departure.

'What's a *Peter Parade*?' said Jeff.

Flint tried to recall exactly how it went. 'Every man had to line up, wearing just a raincoat. He then had to milk his penis, and, if it wept, he had VD.'

'Wow,' muttered Jeff, blanching at the thought.

Our journey seemed so much less involved than that before. We could hear almost nothing through the layers of laminate and metal. Our train didn't even seem connected to the landscape, but merely wriggled through it with a hiss. A great green river of snow-melt tumbled past as silently as silk, and elaborate outcrops of crimson lunged at the windows and then vanished in a blur. If modern travel continues like this, becoming ever more imperceptible to the senses, it'll end up no more than a series of destinations linked by coloured lights.

Of course, French trains weren't always so serene. In August 1944, the US Air Force came churning up the valley, incinerating 30 locomotives, 263 carriages, and some 1,400 vehicles packed along the road. The last time Flint passed this way, hulks of blackened flesh and metal stretched from here to Dijon, almost half the length of France.

It was reassuring now to find the greens restored and the cinders gone.

'It would make a great bike track,' said Jeff.

Did he always judge a place like that, according to its bumps and dirt?

'Sure,' he said, 'it's the first thing I think of wherever I go.'

'It reminds me of Texas,' said Flint happily, and fell asleep.

He didn't sleep long. Forty-five minutes later – and a day ahead of the Panthers – we pulled into Avignon, where we unwisely decided to pause.

35

Avignon has been hated in many different languages for almost seven hundred years. Plutarch said it was 'a sewer where all the filth of the universe has gathered'. The Vatican has been harsher still, blaming it for 'The Babylonian Captivity', a century of papal exile and gluttony, beginning in 1309 (at the election of Clement VI, it's said, the revellers ate 1,023 roasted sheep and 60,000 tarts). Even modern guidebooks are surprisingly sparse in their praise: Avignon is 'crowded', occasionally 'monstrous' and famous mostly for the revolting habits of cardinals who've long since gone. The best thing about it is that it's surrounded by a three-mile wall. This may not keep the tourists out, but at least it keeps Avignon in.

I can't imagine why I'd suggested we stop there. I'd barely got to the end of the main street before realising that the critics were right, and that Avignon was in the grip of its Babylonian urges. There were sex shops down every alley, police in thick padded gloves, and windows full of ludicrous clothes with names like Getaway and Circle. Does a woman wearing several hundred euros-worth of latex feel pampered, or merely pornographic? Everything was like this, either sensual or imponderable, or just extravagantly futile. An absurd little plastic train trundled visitors round the town although there wasn't much to see. I felt sure the statues were drunk, and the beggars here had huskies and beautiful Mohicans, or faces painted up like clowns. Even the famous Pont d'Avignon seemed more pointless than I'd imagined, and was down to its last few arches. I remember a little Japanese girl studying it thoughtfully, wondering why anyone had bothered with the song. Meanwhile, her father took pictures of the pigeons.

I had a terrible feeling that my American friends would think I liked all this, although they were far too generous to say so. Jeff even agreed to come with me into the Palais des Papes, a selfless act on his part. No one better exemplified the New World's enthusiasm for the innovative (New Frontiers, New York, New Deals and New World Orders) and its suspicion of all things old. I repaid his courtesy with probably the most grotesque (and certainly the largest) Gothic palace in the world. Almost everything about it seemed to cause a shrinking of the human spirit: the dizzying parabolas of stone, the interconnecting chasms, the ghostly whiff of pestilence and the perverts leering out of the corbels. At one point, we even found a crusty human skull with a crossbow bolt through its eye. To any decent American, the *palais* is proof beyond doubt that the best thing about the past is that it's over.

It didn't surprise me that the world still detested Avignon, especially during its festival. It's one of the few occasions in the French calendar when Left and Right unite, in a cacophony of jeers. That year was the fifty-ninth Arts Festival, a lavishly over-ripe occasion that waddled along on a government grant of almost €10 million. Productions included *A Beautiful Child/I apologise* (naked prepubescent girls lie in a coffin for an hour), *Either the Well was Deep* (loud bursts of electronic pain), and *After/Before* (a panel of people answer the same question for forty minutes). Every year, such shows are enthusiastically booed, and walking out has become a rite of summer. I was sorry to have missed it. 'You may think,' reported *Le Figaro*, 'that you've reached the lowest point in mediocrity, pretentiousness and confusion but – no – there's always something worse.' Perhaps *L'Humanité* had found it, or at least a case of ancestral vice. According to its arts correspondent, the prevailing mood of Avignon was a 'triumphant sense of masturbatory autism'.

Even our hotel seemed to be somehow tainted by such self-indulgence. It was evangelically spartan and yet sumptuously priced. The more you paid, the less you got; or at least you got a bigger bit of nothing. Almost every surface was either white or slathered in varnish, except the hall, which was booby-trapped with plants. No sooner had we arrived than Flint caught his foot in a yucca and began to topple into the greenery. But as he lost height, he managed to lash out and grab a few creepers and armchairs, slowing his trajectory to a more stately pace. 'Shoot', he said softly, but the receptionist didn't seem at all concerned. It was obviously quite common here to find an eighty-six-year old, face-down in the lobby, buried in cushions and peat.

I'd been warned about places like this. In his grumbling masterpiece, *Travels through France and Italy* (1766), Tobias Smollett takes us on a surly tour of the region's inns. It's a bowel-tangling read, like a guide to the world of indifference. Smollett's hotels are filthy, the laundry maids casually trim the lace off his handkerchiefs, and the publicans airily rob him. Even worse is the privy, or Temple of Cloacina: 'The French who frequented her house, instead of using the seat, left their offerings on the floor . . . this is a degree of beastliness which would appear detestable even in the capital of North Britain'. But there was nothing to be done; the hoteliers were beyond reform. 'If you chastise them with sword, cane or horse-whip,' wrote Smollett, 'they will either disappear entirely, and leave you without resource; or they will find the means to take vengeance by over-turning your carriage.'

This extract was of some comfort as we made our way back to the station the following day. I enjoyed the idea of Smollett marching before us, lashing out at the *Avignois* with his enormous whip, scattering fops and receptionists, the pretentious, the thieving laundry girls and the chronically auto-erotic.

36

Back on the railway, France unfolded like a series of gardens, each more lush than the last. The great Cézanne reds of Provence gave way to a corridor of rocky arbours, followed by orchards, the herbaceous flanks of the Drôme, a valley of watery allotments, and then the steep green terraces of the upper Rhône. The only constant was the river itself, foaming along, hackles raised, as wide as man can shout. It was scenery that baffled my American friends. It seemed to remind them of so many places, but none a perfect match.

'Texas,' said Flint.

'Or the Carolinas?' ventured Jeff.

'Maybe. Or Montana!'

'With a bit of West Virginia . . .'

'Sure. Or Arizona . . .'

Perhaps it really was like that, a bit of everywhere all at once. It had never occurred to me how compact France was. In just three hours, we'd been through a dozen landscapes, and were halfway across the country.

'*Half*-way?' said Jeff, looking around, as if he'd been shut in a tiny room.

He didn't mean to be unkind, but America just doesn't work like this. Unlike France, it's infinitesimal, changing only imperceptibly even after hours on the road. It never seems to close in around the traveller, but always rolls out in front. The United States could swallow up seventeen Frances and still have room for two Belgiums. What's more, the American countryside is seldom a garden. More often than not, man's grip on the land can look decidedly parlous. Tornadoes, earthquakes, cougars, grizzlies, and floods the size of Wales are just part of the scenery – and make France look deceptively cute. Jeff didn't even have the words to describe such serenity but tended to think of it in terms of *ranges*, *swamps* and *drives*. As for the network of footpaths now latticed across the slopes of the Rhône, he'd never seen anything quite so quaintly medieval. America was cruel to feet, and had rushed straight to the age of the engine.

'I guess there's a lot of time here,' said Flint, 'crammed in a pretty small space.'

And a lot of wine too. The Côtes du Rhône were so densely contoured with terraces they looked like a map that had sprung to life. This was gardening at its most extreme; every inch of the valley walls had been ploughed, staked, wired, planted, pruned and picked. More than a million Frenchmen toil away in the wineries, producing a billion gallons a year, a sizeable proportion of the world's total. I was once told that the viticulture had been given its biggest lift in the Great War, when France promised every soldier his litre a day. It was a Faustian contract, and now the devil's exacting his price. These days, drinking kills more Frenchmen every year than cars and warfare put together.

Flint gazed up at the vines as if he hadn't noticed them in 1944.

'We came through here so fast,' he said, 'we didn't even stop for a pee.'

It was the second great American invasion of the Côtes du Rhône. The first was an invasion of tiny American lice, called phylloxera, with American appetites and a fondness for roots. By 1914, they'd eaten their way through France, and the only solution was to graft the old vines on to lice-resistant roots. It was a further dent to French pride to discover that these too were American.

This was quite a thought as we peered out, over the *côtes*.

'French to the naked eye,' grinned Flint, 'but American under the surface.'

During the second invasion, France was keen to avoid another American insult. The French commander, General de Lattre, saw to it that the Americans advanced up the east bank, where the grapes didn't matter, while his own troops took the western side. 'Whatever you do,' he told them, on the eve of liberation, 'DON'T CRUSH THE VINES.' In despair, the Americans watched as their allies tiptoed through the Burgundies and Beaujolais. As the grapes got better and better, so the advance got slower and slower, and the Germans got away.

This was a serious failure. Army Group B was now one of the best-preserved units of the German Army. By the time Flint came careering up the valley two months later, it was well dug in, only a hundred miles ahead. 'Of course, we didn't know that then,' he said. 'As soldiers, you never get to see the bigger picture.'

It was all they could do to keep their eyes on the road, as the Rhône streaked past in a blur.

37

For centuries, this journey has threatened the lives of tourists, or at least their dignity.

In one of the earliest accounts, a Lincolnshire lawyer called Fynes Moryson (1566–1629) loses most of his clothes. Ambushed by highwaymen, he's robbed of his food, his money and much of his finery, including his bonnet. His tormentors, he says, replace it with another, 'a deepe greasie French hat'. With nothing else to drink from, the little lawyer then uses the hat as a cup, making a soup of water and crumbs. 'I thought I'd never eaten better brewesse,' he noted ruefully, 'but three days of sicknesse of vomiting and loosenesse made me repent of this intemperance.'

Smollett, on the other hand, maintains his continence, but his trip of 1763 is still splendidly miserable. The old quack is a heart-sinking sight as he travels up the Rhône, wearing – as he puts it – 'a grey morning frock under a wide great coat, a bob wig without powder, a very large laced hat, and a meagre wrinkled, discontented countenance'. Travel-writers don't come like that any more, nor do they write with such waspish feelings for everything foreign. That's a shame because *Travels through*

France was an instant success, and caught the mood of the time. France, according to England's Paymaster-General, was 'a dunghill, not fit for gentlemen to live in'.

Smollett hates the Rhône, and finds plenty to make him unhappy. Killer mules attack his horses with incredible fury, and at least three times a day his axles catch fire. The French are consistently revolting, and have eaten all the dogs and all the songbirds. On Fridays – or 'meagre days' – they eat seagulls, which the French church has reclassified as a kind of fish. Smollett buys a blunderbuss to keep the locals at bay but this only attracts an even bigger crowd, eager to admire his *petit canon*. The only way he can make progress is by firing it over their heads. Meanwhile, the river disgusts him, and he suspects it's a source of malevolent vapours. It's not even good for navigation. Boats are carried downstream 'with great velocity', and often get smashed to bits on the Pont d'Esprit. Boats going upstream have to be towed by oxen, with their drivers sitting up between their horns.

Amongst those careering downstream is an arch-enemy of Smollett's, another writer called Captain Thicknesse. He's much better company, and loves France. He and Laurence Sterne are always mocking Smollett (whom they call 'Smelfungus') and his grumpy travels. Unlike Smollett, Thicknesse is boisterous, colourful and even a little American. In 1735, at the age of sixteen, he'd emigrated to Savannah, Georgia, where he'd chronicled the sexual adventures of the Wesley brothers and learnt to eat like an Indian (squirrels, and venison dipped in honey). At one stage, he'd almost married a 'squaw' but then he'd had a sudden vision of his mother, and fled back to England. Years later, he declared that the experience of living amongst savages reminded him of France.

So it was that, in 1775, we find Thicknesse plunging down the Rhône with his carriage lashed to a raft. He's not alone but has with him his household, which looks like a company of strolling players. There's Mrs Thicknesse, who breaks into song at the least encouragement, and her daughters, who accompany her on their fiddles and lutes. Mrs Thicknesse also has with her a parakeet, which she believes is the soul of a departed lover, and which either flies along above the raft, or nestles in her bosom or dangles upside down from her tippet. Then there's a spaniel, Callee the horse ('a little touched in the wind'), and Jocko the Monkey, who rides postilion, and is wearing jackboots, a scarlet jacket laced with silver, and a tricorn hat with a ponytail stuck on the back. Thicknesse too is splendidly attired, for he's wearing the full dress uniform of a captain in Colonel Jeffries's Marines. Not unnaturally, the French are astonished by the sight of the Thicknesse family, and whole towns are brought to a standstill as the raft comes hurtling past.

After Lyons, the Rhône veers away to the Alps, and the northbound traveller must follow the Saône. It's a beautiful calm, green ribbon of water, galleried with *châteaux* and vines. 'It is this placid appearance,' writes Smollett, 'that tempts so many people to bathe in it at Lions, where a good many of them are drowned . . .'

Somehow, pleasure survives Smollett, and there are still little boats bobbing around on the river. Thicknesse finds ferries amongst them, sculled by strong, pretty girls who make him blush. He asks one of them, 'How do you earn your bread in winter?' '*En l'hiver,*' she winks, '*j'ai un autre talent.*' Thicknesse glows with admiration: 'I could not refrain from giving her a double fee as I thought there was something due to her winter as well as her summer abilities.'

But there's also darkness ahead. At Chalons, where the road north peels away from the river, the Thicknesse family come across a bandit family dangling from a gibbet. There are nine members of the strangled family, 'a man, his wife and their seven children who had lived many years by robbery and murder'. Nor is banditry merely a family affair. Wolves have driven the Burgundians from their ancient ducal capital, Auxerre. Packs of these creatures would continue to terrorise the vineyards right up until the time the Americans arrived. It was said that, in times of famine, they ate the rotten grapes off the vine, got howling drunk and then made for the towns, looking for a fight.

38

Flint always enjoyed these accounts. Perhaps they confirmed everything Americans think about France: that the nation's a relic, and that the French are untrustworthy, coquettish and hick. It's different for the British; we've learnt by a process of proximity that the French are – increasingly – just a southern version of ourselves. One in ten of us even goes there every year, a feat we no longer regard as exotic. Not so the Americans. Between them and the French there's still – in every sense – an ocean.

But if the Americans think France is effete and tuckered out, the French are hardly adoring. They tend to think of America as a large unruly teenager, even after several hundred years. To them, Americans become quickly boring, foist their intimacy on those around them, enjoy everything superficially and understand nothing in depth. 'Whoever wants to know the hearts and minds of America,' wrote Jacques Barzun, 'had better learn baseball.' Even the words *à l'américaine* (American-style), *américanisation*, and *bar américain* are invariably said with a perceptible sneer. When anything is said 'to become Americanised' (*s'américaniser*), this usually implies that it won't be quite the thing it was before.

It's a relationship rich in misunderstanding. The great American smile makes the French feel patronised and their response is usually boorish. Americans resent this incivility, and so relations falter. Almost every encounter seems to activate old anxieties: French fears of being insignificant, and American fears of being unpopular. These days, the Americans even have websites, like *www.fuckfrance.com*, dedicated to this suspicion of all things French. Meanwhile, in France, after twelve years as president, Jacques Chirac declared: 'I have constant problems with the Americans, who always want to impose their point of view.'

Looking back, there have been few moments in the Franco-American *entente* that were ever truly *cordiale*. This is surprising, given that it started so well. American independence was won with French bullets, and France was the first country to recognise the infant state. When the Marquis de Lafayette was wounded at Brandywine, there was even the prospect of an enduring alliance. But it was only a case of Mine Enemy's Enemy. Besides, the political system that *le marquis* stood for would have appalled the founding fathers – as did the revolution that followed. These days, the name Lafayette sounds more like a memorial to friendship, than the promise of good days ahead.

For Flint, of course, the mutual distrust was a product of the war. France hadn't enjoyed the experience of four million Americans on an armed break. As the historian Antony Beevor wisely deduces, American skins were too thick, and French too thin; the GIs were too ardent for French girls, and US business too ardent for its markets. After years of moral rationing, the sudden reappearance of free enterprise was just too much. France and America found new reasons to call each other names.

But, I suppose, there's more to it than simply economics and a bit of hanky-panky. Perhaps it's significant that, in both countries, there's a strong hint of 'exceptionalism', the belief that one's own nation has been somehow chosen above all others. For Americans, this idea began with Jefferson and the Unitarians, but the French are no less keen. De Gaulle used to tell everyone that 'France is the light of the world. Her genius lights the Universe.' President Mitterrand solemnly took up the theme in his inaugural speech of 1981. 'A just and generous France,' he said, 'can light the path of Mankind.' The problem for the exceptionalists is that there's never room for two.

What's more, apart from this shared belief that they're each unique, there's almost no coincidence of ambition or ideas. To outsiders, Frenchness can often look like the antithesis of Americanism. They're like two equal and opposite concepts, repelling each other in almost every dimension. France is vociferously secular, America insidiously evangelical. France is divided up by class, America by race. The French have only contempt for politicians, the Americans only unreasonable expectations. For the French, culture is duty, for the Americans it's pleasure.

Even work is differently perceived. The Americans feel ennobled by work, the French enslaved. In France, it's even considered poor form to ask someone what they do, whereas Americans often feel that what they do is what defines them. Engineers might even have their achievements printed on their calling cards, as Flint does ('*1955 – First Automatic Batter Mixer with Viscosity Control*'). The French, on the other hand, mock themselves for their aversion to work. In 2004, *Bonjour Paresse* ('Hello Laziness, or Why Hard Work Doesn't Pay') became a bestseller. 'France,' says its author, Corinne Maier, 'is a country where no one does a damn thing.' But the French aren't lazy, they merely aspire not to work. They think American attitudes to employment are barbarous, and the working breakfast crass. They also enjoy dozens of holidays and long weekends, and often join them together with *ponts*, or bridges, as if what lies between is cold and unwelcome or even hazardous to pleasure.

I sometimes wondered how Jeff, as a young American, felt about France. If his questions were anything to go by, the place was still thrillingly medieval. 'Have the French got bagels yet?' he'd say. 'What about avocados?' He was also fascinated by the curious plumbing, and *priorité à droite* (and the idea that a main highway could be brought to a halt by a mule emerging from a cart track). But there were also surprises, and sheer delight at the sight of a hover mower, which he'd never seen before. 'What's *that?*' he'd gasp, as if he'd spotted a flying saucer on a lead.

His curiosity was endlessly aroused, but what did he think of the French?

'Cool,' he said: 'they got the best concrete bike grounds in the world.'

It wasn't quite the image France was after, but at least there were signs of a thaw.

39

That afternoon we arrived in Dijon, the capital of mustard and the straining girth.

I was delighted to be in a city that thought of nothing but food. Dijon has given us more dishes – hams, mustards and cheeses – than almost anywhere else in the world. The entire city groaned with pleasure. Everywhere, there were little fruits carved into ancient gateways, and drinking fountains to refresh the palate. Almost everything looked edible, including our hotel with its chocolate beams, walnut furniture and salmon-coloured walls. Even the old cathedral gargoyles seemed to dangle over the street, wondering what delight was coming next. In a popular poster, the Burgundian is depicted as a well-padded monk sating himself on meat and pastries whilst being straddled by a wench. Clearly, to live *à la Bourguignonne* is to enjoy a life of red wine and cream, and to die aged forty-two under someone else's wife.

It was impossible not to enjoy all this. Dijon was everything I love about France: discerning, appreciative, beautifully detailed and yet always faintly reckless. Even Smollett warmed to Dijon, although he said it was a 'venerable old city'. Thicknesse got a harder deal; he was brought here to see a public execution (although he'd paid to see a coronation in Rheims). Before the condemned man was hanged, he'd had all his limbs shattered with a large blunt cleaver.

That's typical of Dijon, to be so meticulous. Here, there were shops that sold only corkscrews or only cheese. Vegetables were scrubbed and polished and sorted by size. Spices too were elaborately sorted, arranged in strength from astronomic down to zero. *Moutarde* of course was a matter of even subtler distinctions, and enjoyed a street to itself. It was all there, including mustards made with strawberries and others mixed with curry.

Nowhere but France could people be quite so serious about what they put in their mouth. The Dijonais were sniffers, tasters and prodders. I got the feeling they'd cross town for the perfect *gougère* (a cheese best eaten warm, with a spoon). As for bread, it had to be still smoking, like a gun. The idea of eating crusts baked yesterday was considered slightly vile.

At seven, everyone began to drift towards the food, and so we followed the flow. That night, we ate snails stewed in Chablis and shallots, saddle of hare cooked in red wine, veal kidneys, apple tart, and a slab of *gougère*, all washed down with several bottles of burgundy and a globe or two of brandy. It wasn't an easy night after that, dreams haunted by monks and hummocks of pulsing cheese. I suppose it was just sleep *à la Bourguignonne* (except without the wench).

I don't know what my companions made of this fastidious gluttony. For Jeff food was merely fuel, and he often spoke about it as if he was on a public relations drive for pizza. Flint, on the other hand, appeared to enjoy the food, although he found the pageantry of French cuisine obsessional and vain. He was always far more likely to worry about whether there were *enough* beans rather than whether they were polished. It's sometimes said that – when it comes to food – the French care only about quality, the Americans quantity, and the English table manners. I've an uneasy feeling this may be true. Perhaps in matters of food, we're merely the people our ancestors were: either cavaliers or puritans or something in between.

Next to our hotel there was an old man, living up to his neck in the war. Michou sold battlefield scrap: rusty bayonets, safe-conduct passes, German helmets, anything left behind. It was surprising how recent the war looked in his parchment hands. I noticed that Roosevelt's instructions to the Germans on how to surrender were still bundled up in rubber bands.

'I remember the day they left,' said Michou: '10 September 1944!'

The next day, the Americans from Normandy were united with those from the south. The *Wehrmacht* was in poor shape here, said Michou. The soldiers were mostly Ukrainian, who shot their officers and then gave themselves up.

'So, she saved us again!' cackled Michou. 'The Black Virgin!'

I remembered her from Dijon cathedral: a primitive effigy, armless and charred.

'She's been looking after us for a thousand years!'

'And then came the Americans?'

'Bless them, yes, in their beautiful trucks.'

He said they camped in the park and ate like kings.

Using Flint's old battalion maps, we made our way back to the camp. In the American version of Dijon, there were strange military suburbs with names like Reno and Miami. We found the park at the end of a long row of mansions, near the forgotten neighbourhood of Tulsa. It was a cool green place, inhabited only by Grecian nymphs, coaxed from voluptuous marble. Once, an entire division had slept here, beneath the chestnut trees.

'Nine *thousand* men,' whistled Flint, peering into the shadows. But it had all gone – bivouacs, kitchens and trucks full of doughnuts and cheese. Michou, on the other hand, said the *Dijonais* had never forgotten the Americans and their life-giving food. It was a beautiful tale of cupboard love.

Presumably, it was the other way round with the Germans.

'How did you all get on?' I asked, but Michou merely laughed.

'*Ventre affamé n'a pas d'oreille.*' A hungry stomach has no ears.

40

From Dijon, we hired a car to take us up to the Front. This was always going to be an ordeal for me, because I loathe cars. As far as I'm concerned, it's hard to think of another inanimate object that can be quite so wilful and sly. Ours was no exception. It was called something like *le Missile*, and yet it had all the grace of a bread van. Whenever I thought I'd got it under control, its on-board computer would come up with some amusing deceit. *Rapid loss of pressure in front right tyre*, it would flash. *Stop immediately*. In those rare moments when I wasn't lying in the verge, gaping upwards into the chassis, I was grinding along with the handbrake on, or bunny-hopping into the hills. Somehow, I managed to convince myself that the car simply didn't like me, and that a squabble had developed. Whilst I tried to kick it northwards, it tried to buck me off.

Jeff watched these transactions with extraordinary tact. 'You might want to change gear,' he'd say, or 'If you want to do *that*, we'll probably lose the transmission.' Eventually, he agreed to take over the driving, a role in which he was mercifully happy. Jeff loved technology. He obviously thought about it most of the time. I must have made a useless companion, so technologically inert. Just when he'd thought of something interesting, he'd find himself slap up against my ignorance. 'What proportion of British cars are diesel?' he'd ask. 'Do you have shops to convert cars from left-hand drive to right? Do you use the same keyboards as the French?' I hadn't got a clue.

But what Jeff loved most of all was cars, especially Volkswagens. Often, when he saw them on the road, he'd shout out their names, as if they were passing friends. *Combo! Westy! Synchro!* But the real prize was an old purple Caravelle, which he spotted languishing in rust and incontinent of fluids. To Jeff, this was worth a photo, and a crawl under the wheels. A few minutes later he emerged, covered in flakes of ancient crankcase. 'People think I'm mad,' he grinned.

Flint wasn't so sure. 'Respect for machines probably won us the war.'

'*Respect?* How?'

'We never stopped moving. If the machine broke, we just said "Fuck it" and fixed it with a bit of haywire. The French and Germans didn't do that. They always left it for someone else. I guess we just knew our machines.'

Even the Missile was happy in American hands, and was soon throbbing along, intercontinental once again.

After this change of driver, the horizon steadied. For a while, it glowed with wheat but then the land began to swell and bulge into slopes of meadowland and oak. Everything seemed bigger up here: big cattle, giant dogs, enormous children weaned on beef, hydrangeas the size of trees, and villages carved out of bright red rock. Even the names sounded mildly outlandish, like search engines or bizarre diseases suffered by rabbits: Darney, Vannexy, Nomexy and Dombrot.

Flint said little as we neared the old front lines. Occasionally, a name would prompt some atavistic remark ('Ah, Contrexville!' he'd say. 'That's where father's mineral water came from'). Another time, a little French tank with rubber tracks wandered into the road, and then squeaked off into the bushes. 'Quieter than ours,' said Flint, but that was all.

Perhaps this, as then, was the moment he'd dreaded, confronting the uncertainty of what lay ahead. On 23 November 1944, Flint and the Panthers had driven all day, 145 miles from Dijon, right to the rim of the battle. Many veterans have written eloquently about those last few hours of calm. They describe a diminished world, still deaf with shock and blind with disbelief; villages look abandoned, their roofs open to the rain; the survivors produce garlands of flowers but their eyes are red and raw; everywhere there are blackened tanks, like shipwrecks in the uncut wheat; a young German is pulled from a cellar, and the farmers kill him like a fox; a local boy paddles the troops across a river, and takes a fatal shot through the liver; then the Russians appear, pulling off their German uniforms and offering themselves to the French. For men like Flint, this journey goes on for ever, an unforgettable foretaste of things to come.

There were still bitter reminders of the battles that had smashed through here. Along the way, we passed through Épinal, the final resting place for over 5,000 American dead, and then the turning for Saint-Dié. It's said that the monks of Saint-Dié were the first to use the term 'America', in 1507, or at least the first to commit it to a map. Maybe this infuriated the Germans because, when they left, they dynamited the cathedral and torched the town before heading for the Vosges.

A vast, impenetrable obstacle lay ahead. As the American troops vanished amongst the trees, even their commander was rendered obscure. 'Since the beginning of the military history of Europe,' wrote General Brooks, 'to force a successful passage of the Vosges Mountains has been considered by military experts an operation offering such small prospects for success as to forestall consideration of such effort.'

For a while at least, the war had disappeared, deep into the forest.

41

Few places devour quite so much light as the Vosges.

From a distance, it looked like an impending storm, which, in a way, it was. Ahead of us, the day seemed to shrink under deep black shrouds of granite and forest. It had been raining here for almost 300 million years, or ever since these great slobs of mountain first heaved themselves out of the sea. For a while, the Vosges massif had stood as high as the Alps, before it collapsed into its shadows. The first humans to live here were always climbing up to the light, to plead with the sun-god, Bel. Today, their stunted peaks, the Belchen or *Ballons*, stand as proof (if proof were needed) that geology has no ears. After thousands of years, *les Vosgiens* have learnt to live with the dark.

For two days, we drove through this dripping, tangled gloom. Night never seemed to lift from the forest, but was simply diluted by dawn. It was beautiful in an uneasy, primeval way. Although it was still summer elsewhere, everything was veiled in cold, pale mist, and the earth was clammy and black. Even the foliage was beautifully ominous: great wet clumps of anemones, deadly nightshade, musk mallow, scabious and yellow wort. Once, I thought I saw a dead wolf by the side of the road, but when I turned to look again, there was nothing there but forest.

We stayed overnight in Baccarat, a town of Hansels and Gretels. It had an onion-domed church, a police station made of fudge, and a row of little cottages burrowed into the town walls, like homes for giant rabbits. The last time Flint was here a panzer division had just moved out, but otherwise little had changed. We may even have met the same old ladies and fallen into the same potholes. That night, we ate at the Hôtel d'Agriculture, an improbable name so deep in the forest. The food however was surprisingly fresh, even if everything else was stolidly ancient and lacy. The waitress looked as if she'd just emerged from a hundred years of sleep, and the piped music was so faint it sounded like *Aida* sung by a chorus of flies. This same great sleep had also overwhelmed our hotel, which had no name, no guests and no staff. The only person we ever saw was a little pixie, who turned up covered in jewels and demanded payment in cash.

'Must be money laundering,' said Jeff.

The only person who's ever truly understood the Vosges is Bernard Newman, an eccentric Englishman whose mother was Alsatian. He was up here for the bloody artillery battles of 1918, walked across the massif in 1929 and then returned twenty years later, on a bicycle called 'George the Fourth'. Perhaps Newman understood the Vosges because he had something of the forest about him. During his life he wrote more than sixty books, mostly about the paranormal, UFOs and murders involving lesbians and tennis. His first book was about a group of scientists who fake an alien landing in order to unite the Cold War factions. It was a plot so similar to the Rothwell incident (when the U.S. military supposedly faked an extraterrestial incursion) it was often read as a warning to the Americans that Newman knew exactly what they were doing. The *New York Times*, on the other hand, said he'd been a German spy, and there may have been something in this. Certainly, there always seemed more to his Russian rambles than idle curiosity.

But here in the Vosges Newman found a place commensurate with his own sense of the bizarre. *Les Vosgiens* were always gratifyingly foresty and weird. During his travels Newman met a gypsy, who tried to force him into marriage, and a farmer who'd trained his cats to flush the fields of mice. But best of all were the *Schlitteurs*, who used to ride the mountains on sledges loaded with logs. They hoped their feet would act as brakes – but if these ever failed them they'd plummet very rapidly into the darkness and disappear for good.

There was always a sinister side to Newman's tales, and the Vosges was perfect for his purpose. 'This was no setting for fairy stories,' he wrote, 'but legends of witches and devils could easily be credited.' *Les Vosgiens* were tormented by superstition, and every mountain had its spirits and sacrificial stones. Newman discovered that even women who died in childbirth were allowed no rest. They were buried in their shoes, so they could find their children and suckle them in death.

42

The battle for the Vosges would be vicious and dark. 'It was,' said Flint, 'a terrible place to fight.'

Nobody could decide which was worse, the rain or the Germans. A man could either rot where he was, or take his chances with an enemy he couldn't see. The forest floor was littered with *Schuh*-mines, each just enough to shred a man's leg or rip away his foot. As the shells came through the tree-tops, they burst, filling the air with white-hot metal and blades of sharpened wood. It horrified the medics, the damage trees could do: arms lopped, faces flailed away, and splintered larch driven deep into muscles and bowel. Suddenly the war wasn't looking as easy as it had before. There was no more talk of the Champagne Campaign.

By the time Flint arrived, the Americans were almost three weeks into the forest. Already the casualties were mounting. Most of the men were beginning to wonder if they were ready for this war. The equipment which had seemed so smart in training, now looked shoddy in the field; the tommy guns were clumsy, the binoculars useless and the tent-poles snapped; the men had also discovered that their combat jackets had a give-away sheen, and that their ammunition smoked and drew returning fire. It was not an encouraging start.

It would be no better for the Tank Destroyers. In the forest, the half-track, or 'M3', was just a ponderous, lumbering bucket. Never great at rapid response, in the Vosges it hardly responded at all. The battlefield was just too cluttered for fancy flanking moves, like 'rooking' and pincer manoeuvres. Besides, the Germans could always hear the M3 grinding towards them, and if there was any element of surprise it was merely mild surprise at the sight of anything so clumsy. Everywhere it went, the half-track was greeted with a shower of shells. Inside, the crew were completely unprotected from the shrapnel and the blaze of lethal splinters. Flint hated it. 'To make any contribution at all, we had to dig our guns in and wait for the enemy to come to us. It was not an effective deployment.'

The enemy never came. Instead, they were playing a lethal game of Kill and Run, fighting backwards towards stronger positions. It ought to have been Cat and Mouse, because the Americans had twenty times as many tanks and planes, but the Germans made unconvincing mice. In November 1944, Hitler still had ten million armed men at his disposal. As to his army, it was disciplined, experienced, bound together by five years of *Kameradschaft*, well equipped, determined, bloody and brutal. After the rigours of Russia, fighting the Americans seemed easy, a picnic in the Vosges.

Meanwhile, the Americans were appalled to discover that the mouse still roared. To a people so congenitally proportionate and democratic, the German commitment was horrifying. Even at this stage, two out of three German prisoners still believed that Hitler would prevail. Mostly, the Reich could rely on their self-delusion but – if that failed – there was always terror. During the course of the war, more than 15,000 German soldiers were executed, with 44,000 being sent for trial in October 1944 alone. But, whether through love or fear, the psychological advantage was always theirs. For as long as this war would last, Americans like Flint were taunted by a single thought: that they were merely enthusiastic amateurs, whilst the enemy was professional.

Firepower, they realised, was the only way to bring sense to this battle. For almost a month, the mountains boomed and shuddered, and the Americans punched their way up through the woods. Then, on 25 November, there was a lull and they found themselves high on a ridge. Below them, on the other side, was a wide fertile plain of woods and vineyards, and ancient fortified farms.

It was Alsace, a beautiful troubled land that would eventually cost the Americans a winter, four months' advance and 16,000 lives.

Part 4 – Alsatian Crackers

Whilst travelling in Alsace, that is full of these war memories and heavy with suspicion for the future, it is impossible not to long in all sincerity that the statesmen of Europe will in this generation carry through some means of terminating this deep-seated feud between the Teuton and the Gaul.

B.S. Townroe, *A Wayfarer in Alsace*, 1926

Ne parlez pas trop d'Alsace Lorraine; c'est une création des Allemands. Il n'y a pas d'Alsace Lorraine. Il y a l'Alsace et il y a la Lorraine.

André Maurois, *Les Bourgeois de Witzheim*

Both France and Germany are fond of quoting the parable of the Prodigal son. It is not very apt; Alsace is no prodigal; not even a son. Alsace is the fatted calf – which, you will recall, was slain. The occasion was doubtless great, but nonetheless unpleasant for the calf.

Bernard Newman, *The Sisters Alsace-Lorraine*, 1950

To know an Alsatian is to know a rugged, self-reliant individual. They seek little of the glamour of life.

The 824th TD Battalion newspaper, *Panther Tracks*, 11 February 1945

It was an Alsatian figure, comfortably filled out with good solid country food.

Jeanne Gosse, *Alsatian Vignettes*, 1946

43

I once met a woman in Alsace whose father had lost his thumb near Moscow.

'Shot clean off!' she said, waving an imaginary stump.

She blamed everyone for this outrage, and for the destruction of her farm.

'Where were the French when we needed them?'

'But surely,' I said, 'it was the Germans who took him there?'

'Sure, they were wicked too! And then the Americans bombed us to bits!'

She started digging again, turning over the soil.

A thought occurred to me. 'Who did you *want* to win?'

'What did we care?' she snorted. 'We just wanted it all to end!'

She described a relentless war, three armies in less than four years.

'Everyone always wants this land,' she said, 'but no one ever wants us.'

44

Alsace is quiet today, quieter than it's been for centuries. I now realise that, for most of its history, it's felt vulnerable, and those around it jumpy. Even in its odd Teutonic-Latin name there's more than a hint of upheaval: *Ali Saz*, 'The Place of the Others'. Once, the very word was synonymous with chaos and disorder (in seventeenth-century London, *Alsatia* was a lawless enclave, inhabited by bandits and thieves). For now, however, the turmoil has simmered down, although much confusion remains. These days, we're unsure whether the Alsatians are French-thinking Germans or German-speaking Frenchmen. They, of course, think they're neither, but a rule unto themselves.

'We're Alsatian first,' they say, '*then* French! And then European . . .'

Few places have seen such warfare. Alsace has featured in almost every great war Europe's ever had, and has often been the cause. The Germans claim they've been invaded twenty-three times by the French, always from Alsace. The Swedish and Hungarians, on the other hand, descended on the place 'like a swarm of locusts' during The Thirty Years War (1618–48), and destroyed it so comprehensively that in one region only seven men survived. Napoleon thought that such fighting made great soldiers of its natives, and recruited more generals in Alsace than in any

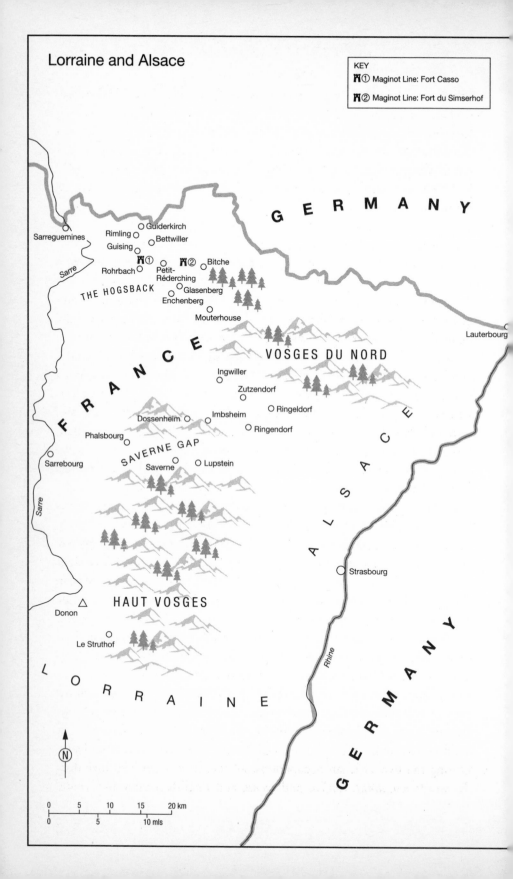

Lorraine and Alsace

KEY

🏰① Maginot Line: Fort Casso

🏰② Maginot Line: Fort du Simserhof

GERMANY

Sarreguemines

Sarre

Rimling
Guiderkirch
Bettwiller
Guising
🏰① Rohrbach
🏰② Bitche
Petit-Réderching
Glasenberg
Enchenberg

THE HOGSBACK

Mouterhouse

FRANCE

Lauterbourg

VOSGES DU NORD

Ingwiller
Zutzendorf
Ringeldorf
Dossenheim
Imbsheim
Ringendorf
Phalsbourg

ALSACE

Sarrebourg

SAVERNE GAP

Saverne
Lupstein

Sarre

Strasbourg

HAUT VOSGES

△ Donon

Le Struthof

Rhine

LORRAINE

GERMANY

N

GERMANY

0   5   10   15   20 km
0   5   10 mls

other part of France. 'Leave these good folk to speak their dialect,' he declared, 'and they will wield their sabre with the might of a French forearm.'

Meanwhile, in the last hundred and thirty years, Alsace has changed hands four times, taking a pasting on each occasion. Some villages barely had time to resurrect themselves before they were levelled again. Alsace is built on the rubble of its past.

All this makes for ugly history and a curious map.

Perched on the eastern shoulder of France, Alsace looks a tempting prize. Invaders see only the alluring flatlands of the Rhine, and the defenders only the ramparts of the Vosges. Bounded by mountains and giant rivers, no other region of France is so clearly and topographically defined. Poetically, if not politically, it often feels like Middle Earth.

Wars and insurrection have left the map strewn with star-forts, castles and casemates. The biggest of these were added within living memory, a vast concrete folly looping over the plain. But the story of its people is written in its place-names. With each fresh bout of disorder, the old names were obliterated or new ones grafted into the chaos. It's all there: French, German, *Francique*, *Alsacien*, Latin, *platt*, pixie, babble and boar.

But, of course, it's not only the names that have changed. The Alsatians have spent most of their history on the hoof, a population in a permanent state of flux and flight. It's hard to say when this human ping-pong began. Some think it was the French invasion of 1648. Others go back earlier. All, however, agree that the German occupation of 1870 was by far the worst, bringing with it 300,000 settlers. For the next forty-eight years Alsace, or *Elsass Lothringen* as it was called, was run like an African colony by petty officials known as the *Schwobs*. Then, when Berlin's rule came to a violent end in 1918, most of the settlers were on the road again. The same thing happened in 1940, when the Germans reappeared. This time, half a million Alsatians fled for France, to be replaced with thousands of ersatz Germans, who were actually from Romania.

A curious language has survived the wars. France has long since resigned itself to *Elsässich*, although it still regards it as the patois of the elves. 'The farmers speak to their cows in dialect,' reports *Le Figaro*, 'and to their children in French.' The authorities haven't always been so indulgent. During the two German occupations, all French was banned, including the words *restaurant*, *coiffeur* and *menu*, and English became the second language in Alsatian schools. A shopkeeper could be fined for using the French term *liquidation totale* (sale), instead of the German *Totale Liquidation*. Many people were even encouraged to Germanise their names, and then – with liberation – to change them back again.

None of this has done anything to endear the Alsatians to government. Years of *Schwob*-rule have made them eagerly defiant. Even now, Paris suspects them of disloyalty, and perhaps it's right. Although theirs is the smallest region of France, the last 1.7 million Alsatians are still refreshingly awkward. They hate nothing more than being spoken to in German or being encouraged to be French. If ever they feel they're not getting their way, a rash of red paint appears across bridges and public buildings: ELSASS AUTONOMIE! But, of course, the Alsatians don't really want independence. These days, nothing suits them better than being neither one thing nor the other.

Ambivalence, it seems, stalks every aspect of Alsatian life. I don't suppose I'll ever know what makes them tick, and there were few clues in all I'd read. Their women were once famous amongst Grand Tourists for being the ugliest in Europe, and the national hero is a miserable troglodyte called *Hans in Schnocken Loch* ('Johnny of Mosquito Hovel'). Although their gifts to the world seem useful enough (glazed pottery, elementary education, baby clinics and the Statue of Liberty), Bernard Newman describes his kinsmen as solid and superstitious, the sort of people who'd sleep with an onion to cure their pains. As for the most famous Alsatians – Alfred Dreyfus, Albert Schweitzer and the Arsenal manager, Arsène Wenger – they'd little in common, except that they'd all left Alsace.

The struggles and durability of Alsatians have tempted some odd comparisons. In 1926, a British guidebook noted: 'The Alsatian is in certain aspects akin to the Irishman. He is usually "agin" the government; he is somewhat obstinate, with a vein of rather malicious wit, and he possesses great independence and initiative.' Strangely, the Alsatians have often enjoyed this analogy. According to Newman, one Strasbourg professor even thought the Alsatians were so Irish that the Irish didn't count.

'The Alsatians,' he declared, 'are the Irish of Western Europe.'

45

We crossed the ridge of the Vosges. Over on the other side, we came across a place like hell, created by the Nazis with all their genius for cruelty.

It had always been a forbidding landscape. All summer, the Haut Vosges smoulders with damp, and in winter it blazes with cold. The ridge is pocked with graves and trenches from the Great War, and the bones of its defenders are gathered in stupendous ossuaries of up to 12,000 souls. There's no open space in this deathly world, no spare light and no relief from rain and snow. The highest point on the ridge is nothing more than a featureless tombstone of granite, called the Col du Donon. Once, notes Newman wryly, this was the Jerusalem of Druids.

Here, on the Alsatian side, the shadows seemed even deeper than before, with the clouds lapping into the forest. As our car climbed through ever darker shrouds of sycamore and ash, a collective gloom seemed to seep amongst us. Flint shuddered, as much from cold as recollection. Occasionally, we'd come across tiny farms made of hammered tin and stone the colour of beef. It was still a bitter life for those that lived up here, with their mop-haired cattle and huge cages full of dogs. Once, I saw an old woman picking mushrooms but, when we waved, she scowled, as if we were merely the portents of more rain to come.

Up nearer the ridge there was no view, except the soggy, grey sky below. Once, we stopped and waded out through the long wet strands of goat's beard and sorrel. Flint had never been up here before, and had often wondered what went on. Now he looked around with renewed surprise. How could such a small country have so much of nothing? Ahead of us, a great wilderness rolled off into the mist, broken only by ghostly ski trails and old quarry workings like giant red wounds in the rock. It was so quiet I could almost hear the blood in my ears. The only sound we ever heard was a scream, the long thin wail of an eagle.

Les Vosgiens have long-believed that their mountains are haunted. Sometimes it's merely the *houtata*, a mischievous forest spirit that hides valuables and plays jokes on foolish wives. At other times, it may be the Devil himself, who, spurned by an Alsatian beauty, now returns to the forest as a stallion, intent on his lustful revenge. Or perhaps it's a more ethereal spirit, like the *schlabi*, who's often thought of as 'the evil shade of night'. Like an undertaker conjured from gas, the *schlabi* wafts through the forest, seizing the sinful and dragging them down through the forest floor. There they remain for ever, imprisoned in the earth. *Les Vosgiens*, says Newman, still hear the *schlabi's* victims screaming up through the roots.

Ghosts, screaming soil and a world with no view. The mountainside was perfect for the Nazi purpose. In September 1940, a detachment of criminals was marched up to the ridge to dig the foundations for Natzwiller-Struthof. It would be the only concentration camp ever built in mainland France.

Struthof is an enduring monument to the tyranny of nothing.

The terraces carved by the convicts are just as they left them, gaping over the void. It's like an amphitheatre without a stage, the greatest show that never was. You'll *see* nothing, it seems to say, and you'll *be* nothing. This concept of nothingness was one the Nazis had worked hard to develop. Long before anyone else, they'd realised that to disappear was far worse than to die. Death created martyrs, whereas disappearance created uncertainty and fear. 'The only weapon to deal with terror is terror,' said Hitler, and that – at Struthof – is what inmates got. Here, as elsewhere, political prisoners simply vanished, stripped of everything except a number. With their aptitude for tragedy, the Germans had even given them a fancy name, borrowed from Goethe. They'd be the *Nacht und Nebel*, (the night and fog). Here one moment, nothing the next.

In this great empty panorama, the paraphernalia of imprisonment looks like an afterthought, the detail added in pencil: electric fences, spindly charcoal gates and great drifts of black barbed wire. Most of the huts were burnt down long ago, leaving nothing but their ghostly outlines in the dull red gravel. Each rectangle has a sorry tale to tell; here was Block 1, the 'Shot Hut', for those too sick to work, and due for a jab of Phenol; here, the *Schonungbedürftig*, or Rest Hut, where the doctors would dig out a man's kidneys or inject him with detergent, and then enjoy the details of his lingering death. For much of the camp's existence, more than 3,000 people lived up here in the tiers, although it was only built for half that number. Towards the end, as Nazi rule shrank into this last benighted corner of France, the population rose to 7,000, and the inmates were stacked three to a bed.

Ironically, the most persistent remnants of Struthof are the watchtowers, set back around the edge of the empty tiers. They are unadorned structures, like garden sheds on wooden skirts. It had been a brutal regime, slavery organised as an exacting science. Every inmate was rigorously classified – homosexual, *blöd* (or imbecile), political, conscientious objector, convict, gypsy or Jew – with a coloured symbol sewn into his clothes. The prisoners even had highfalutin titles – like *Lagerältester* and *Blockältester*

– so that, by compliance, they could clamber upwards through the skinny ranks of the camp. Only the criminals excelled at this, rising to the rank of *Kapo*, or *Kameradpolizei*. In this position, they had their own whips and rosters, and could be expected to kick a man to death. That was the beauty of this system, that the condemned imprisoned themselves.

Life was lived to a chorus of sirens and dogs. Every day began at four, with a pointless parade, up here on the tiers. For hours, the inmates stood under the freezing glare of arc lights while they were counted, detailed, shuffled and kicked, time and time again. If anyone faltered they were beaten, and if they didn't work they were starved. At Christmas, they were treated to the spectacle of a public strangulation, and were made to file past – *Mützen ab* (caps off) – as the victims slowly died. 'We marched past like automatons,' wrote one inmate, Dr Ragot, 'unconcerned, our eyes vague, mostly thinking of the soup that was waiting for us, and going cold in our mess tins.'

Those who survived Struthof often say their worst fear was of mental collapse, or the destruction of the spirit. To lose one's mind, they say, was to lose the only thing the Nazis couldn't readily take away. It was a constant struggle, and food played a curious role. Naturally, being no more than a flap of old bread or a pint of watery soup, it became mostly an obsession. But it also corrupted, and divided men of common fate. An inmate would think nothing of dishing out the thinnest soup to his comrades while saving the richer sediment for himself. It appalled men like Léon Boutbien, who'd once been a doctor, how frail human dignity could become. He was still reeling from the horror of it all when, years later, he wrote:

> Imagine a man who, all of a sudden, is no longer human, but has become a monstrous animal, hitherto unknown to zoological classification; he's reduced to a digestive tube; he's become a puppet made of bones, a walking skeleton – cachectic, wandering, haggard and hallucinated; such was the disintegrated man who died of hunger and cold, who talked of nothing else but food, and who dreamt of biscuits stolen from a dog in his kennel.

At the far end of the terraces, we came across the crematorium block, a slate-grey hut with a steel furnace. Inside, there was a pile of shoes by the door, as if the inmates had just gone off to take a bath. They say a band played whenever the furnace glowed, giving death a musical touch so lacking in life. Nobody knows how many people died here. Three thousand? Perhaps ten. ZONE DE SILENCE, say the signs, RESPECTEZ CE LIEU.

Some distance away, through the trees, were the remains of the gas chambers. Although Struthof wasn't built as an extermination camp, it wasn't long before nothingness became annihilation. The first to die in here were gassed at the request of the Professor Hirt of the Department of Anatomy at Strasbourg University. He'd asked for unmarked corpses for his populous collection, and Himmler found him eighty-seven suitable Jews, who were sent to Struthof to be prepared for science. The gas chambers were hastily arranged using the ice-house of an old hotel. The task went without hitch and, years later, the *Kommandant* – a dim-witted thug called Josef Kramer – even admitted that he himself had mixed the gas. 'I felt no emotion when performing these acts,' he told the judges. 'That's just the way I was brought up.'

But the real killing was not here but in the quarries.

As we drove away across the red, mutilated ridge, it was impossible not to get a sense of the scale of this atrocity. The entire mountain looked as if it had been flogged and gouged, with enormous chunks torn from its sides. Occasionally, we came across the great steel wagons which the slaves had dragged, laden with granite. Much of the stone had been used in the building of Nuremberg, now emerging as a gruesome feat of neo-baroque. The SS even had their own company – Deutsche Erd und Steinwerke GmbH – to turn blood into money. Killing was merely part of their design; men shot or crushed, beaten to death, killed by dogs or run over the edge. It was an enterprise thought of as *Vernichtung durch Arbeit*, or 'Extermination by Work'.

There was no great liberation up here. By the time the Americans had clambered on to the ridge, the camp was empty. Ten days earlier, on 16 November 1944, the last of the inmates were marched down the mountain in their clogs, and taken to the station. Those too weak to walk were dispatched with a *Nackenschuss* (a bullet to the neck), and the rest were shunted off to Dachau. Struthof meanwhile had ceased to exist, and the Americans found exactly what the SS had wanted them to find, which, of course, was nothing.

Flint hated Struthof and our return to the ridge. The mist and barbed wire seemed to summon up the worst of his past. I tried to encourage him. 'But this is what you fought for, isn't it?' I said.

He looked unconvinced. 'Revenge was never part of the deal.'

Perhaps too there was a lingering sense of disbelief. 'Germany should be *ashamed* of this,' he said, as if we'd discovered something he'd never thought was true. Like so many Americans, Flint had taken a long time to come to terms with the possibility that civilisation had become so vile. When the first journalists arrived at Struthof, sent by the *New York Times*, in December 1945, they too were sceptical. Even though they were shown the hooks from which the gas victims were suspended, they tended to report the story with an air of detachment, as if it was all too bad to be true. It would be several months before American soldiers learnt the full horror of the Holocaust.

In the meantime, they still had to fight their way off the ridge and out on to the plain.

46

From here, the ridge ripples northwards until it plunges into the cleft that divides the Haut Vosges from the lower mountains of the Vosges du Nord.

It took us all morning to descend through the forest and into the cleft. Occasionally, we came across wild horses – lumpy, inconsolable creatures covered in scars and with manes like oily flames. They still panicked at the sound of engines, and, whenever they heard us coming they crashed off through the trees. The only people we ever saw were the *bûcherons*, now hauling their logs on sixteen-wheelers, instead of suicidal sledges. I spoke to one once. He said he wasn't surprised to see Americans back in his forest. 'We get a lot of old prisoners too,' he said. 'They always cry when they come up here.'

Lower down, the air warmed and great clumps of saxifrage and willowherb swelled out of the shadows. At some point, we stopped for a wheel of cheese, which we shared with a magpie, his eyes as black as tacks. Flint rallied at the taste of cheese. 'Perfect,' he said, and then closed his eyes until we reached the cleft.

There, he awoke suddenly, startled by the reappearance of day. The cleft was wide here but, away to the east, we could see that it narrowed like a funnel. At the far end was a chink through the Vosges – the Saverne

Gap – which looked like a door in a sky full of trees. Throughout history, whoever has controlled this attenuated passage has held the key to Alsace. They've all been this way: the Romans, the Alemani, the English in the twelfth century, the Armagnacs in the fifteenth, and then the Thirty Years War, scouring the plains of every whimper of life. Since then, the fighting has flared and raged almost every fifty years: and the valley is still littered with violence: tanks on plinths, and towns with ugly military names, like Xouaxange, Phalsbourg, Fleisheim and Bust.

We stopped briefly at Sarrebourg, a town still mildly jubilant. No one, it seemed, could believe the long interval of peace, and every street was drenched in colour and truffled in ornament. There were stone monkeys and chocolate rabbits, and almost half the inhabitants were statues, most of which were naked. Abundance and nudity were, I suppose, some consolation after all that war, or at least they disguised the fact that there was nothing very old. Even Marc Chagall had added to this polychromatic binge, by designing a window for the chapel in the square. His *Tree of Life* is more explosion than tree, an eruption of cobalt and reds. Although it was hard to find much depth in this design, no one was more entitled to his moment of pointlessness than Chagall. His war had been starkly surreal. After the experience of eating Varian Fry's goldfish in Marseille, he'd fled to America, a land he'd never understood, and there his young wife died. Like Sarrebourg, he had a lot to remember and a lot to forget.

According to his records, this is where Flint's platoon linked up with The 45th.

'Hardened veterans,' he said, 'A sight to behold . . .'

Wherever they went, the 45th Infantry Division made a lasting impression. They were the rump of the old Oklahoma National Guard, and started the war with a swastika on their shoulder patch. Changing it to a thunderbird was probably the only concession they'd ever made. They were unambiguously tough – the survivors of both Africa and the Vosges, and the first unit to use napalm in Europe (it was intended for the Japanese). 'Battle is the most magnificent competition in which a human being can indulge,' General Patton once told them. 'Remember, in a fist fight, the attacker wins! Attack ruthlessly, rapidly, viciously and without rest . . .' Perhaps some of the men had had these words in mind the day they'd machine-gunned their captives on the Comiso airfield in 1943. Patton was suspended for a while but the fight went on. During this war, the Thunderbirds would participate in eight campaigns, mount four amphibious landings, and capture 126,000 Germans and several cities, including Nuremberg and Munich. In fact, the fighting has never really stopped, and on the internet I can still see them, blasting their way through Iraq.

'Whipcord tough,' winced Flint, as if describing a painful affliction.

To men like him, who'd yet to fire a shot in anger (and who'd never seen the enemy), the Thunderbirds gave pause for thought. In their appearance, it was possible to see oneself in the months to come: lean, frayed, sunburnt, hollow-eyed and tattooed with grit and smoke – assuming, of course, that one survived. Ever since the first shudder of shells, the men had been preoccupied by the idea of staying alive, and now Flint sought out an old veteran ('a weathered Master-Sergeant') and asked for his advice.

'He was pleased,' said Flint, 'to find a green lieutenant that had the brains and the humility to ask. His few words were probably the most significant of all my battle training. I remember him saying, "If you want to bring your troops home, then do foot reconnaissance before you move your men and that heavy noisy equipment". I followed that advice and, yes, we all came home.'

Ahead of them, the Thunderbirds had already punched through the end of the valley, and the Panthers followed. It's a vertiginous ride, the road to Saverne. From the air it must look like baby scribble. For a while, it trails in the groove of the valley, but then it scrawls uphill, flails around in the switchbacks, passes through a tiny aperture and curls off into the open. Even Goethe, not best known for his civil engineering, found words in praise of the road. It was, he said, 'an unthinkable labour. Built in snaking curves over the most dreadful rocks . . .'

Passing though the Saverne Gap still feels like walking on stage. The curtains part, and the landscape lights up with promise. Ahead lies a deep, green and purple landscape, fringed by German hills to the north and the Rhine far to the east. Alsatians often blame this view for tempting the first of the French invasions, in 1648. 'Ah!' said Louis XIV greedily, as he peered through the gap, '*Quel beau jardin!*'

But this wasn't Flint's first thought as he passed this way, on 27 November 1944. Ahead of him lay an anti-garden; cattle scattered – frozen and broken – on the soil, woods ablaze, and the sky weeping oil.

47

'I remember my men,' said Flint 'but I don't remember *this*.'

Ahead of us unfurled the Alsatian plain, repaired and whole. Flint was confused by its integrity and the restoration of structure and colour. It was like watching someone getting younger, or paper turning back into trees. In the winter of 1944 the reduction of Alsace had seemed so complete that no one had ever imagined it would flourish again. Now, none of it made sense – the plump flanks of corn and mustard, the reds and violets, the rich purple soil, and the buzzards lazily suspended in the haze. Byron once described this land as 'a blending of beauties' and only a local writer, René Schikele, knew better. It was, he said, 'a heavenly garden of pain'.

We drove north, along the escarpment of the Low Vosges and around the western edge of the plain. Occasionally, we spotted little villages, tucked defensively into the hill. They reminded me of the villages that come with train-sets, all half-timbered and mullioned and spotlessly medieval. At the edge of one, called Dossenheim, we stopped in a pear orchard and got out to stroll through the greenish-golden light. Flint had been here before, on 27 November 1944. As he wrote in his letter home: –

> My platoon was the first to be committed to action . . . We came in to an area high on a hill near a town. The noisy half-tracks are left behind – we don't want to announce our position. We used the jeeps to haul the heavy guns moving quietly into position, and wait and wait. Finally, daylight comes and we can see an abandoned German tank and a charming little village. The infantry checks out the village – no enemy there – and we hook up the guns to the half-tracks and gallantly move into the town.

It was a moment of relief rather than triumph. With barely a German in sight, it appeared that the plain had fallen to the Allies. That night, throughout the division, there was beer and peanuts. *Germany next!* they cheered. It occurred to no one that the Germans were merely abandoning the indefensible, and clearing some space for the kill.

Below us, on the plain, an enormous army had assembled.

It was like a wheeled city, with great green suburbs rolling off to the

Front. In this sector alone there were 250,000 men, or fifteen divisions, spread along an 84-mile line that wriggled from Strasbourg to Saarbrucken. Along the line, to the north and south, were more armies, creating an unbroken front from the Mediterranean to the English Channel and comprising 73 divisions. Of these, 43 were American, with a total population four times the size of San Francisco, at around two million men. Every day, another 5,000 Americans arrived at the front, and so – by February 1945 – there'd be almost 2.7 million of them, moving in a straggly line across the face of Europe.

But it wasn't just a city in length. It also had depth. The battle formation reads like the plans for a huge restless conurbation, many miles across. It's still possible, using old maps, to tour the neighbourhoods of the military mind. Although the hardware's gone, the lines survive, and so too do the great imaginary suburbs. Amongst the arrows and symbols one can see whole districts on the move, wandering villages and mobile 'streets'. Looked at as a whole, the city is an *army group,* but it divides into two *armies,* French to the south and American to the north. The American army is then divided into two *corps,* each of which splits into three *divisions,* which in turn divides into three *regiments.* Each regiment (comprising roughly 3,000 men), then subdivides into four *battalions,* which are like the villages of military life. Each is split into three *companies,* known rather sparsely as A, B or C. Within each company there are three or four *platoons,* made up of *sections* of just a few men each. Flint's position therefore places him very precisely in the battle order, like an address: Platoon Commander, First Platoon, B Company, 824th Tank Destroyer Battalion, attached to 397th Infantry Regiment, seconded to the 45th Infantry Division, Seven Army, Sixth Army Group, Alsace.

It was a city that wanted for nothing. Although it was fringed with violence to the west, life was often unnaturally routine. Along the entire Western Front, seldom were more than 300,000 men exposed to direct fire at any given time. For everyone else, their city was like any other, apart from being on the move. There were workshops, hospitals, travelling movie theatres, post offices, 'rest centers', taprooms, portable bathing facilities, doughnut units (run by girls from the American Red Cross), mobile money-changers, film processors and kitchens on wheels. Each day began with a rush hour, or a communal slosh through the mud. Amongst those slithering to work were typists (off to maul the placenames), policemen, historians, clerks (who entered every shell in their ledgers), psychological warfare consultants, and a team of public relations men who toured the front scrounging stories for the public back home.

Each battalion even had its own newspaper. There were twenty-seven regimental newspapers in the 100th Division alone. Flint's men had *Panther Tracks*, twelve mimeographed sheets that emerged every week like a bundle of smog. Across each issue were the words THIS PAPER MUST NOT FALL INTO ENEMY HANDS and a banner depicting a set of tracks trailing off to Berlin. Although it was censored, it was full of soldierly chatter. There were titbits of gossip, poems, birth announcements and the 'straight dope' – advice about mines and booby traps, or new weapons (like the plastic bazooka) or 'What to Expect in Germany'. But also, quite unwittingly, *Panther Tracks* was a barometer of crisis. One could always tell things were bad when it was down to three sheets, or printed with surgical spirit.

It's hard now to imagine the power exuded by this city camped across the plain. Its elders could do almost anything they wanted. They could make the hinterlands boil with bombs, jam the Germans with electronic counter-measures, or call up the best showmen of the day (Bob Hope, Josephine Baker, Marlene Dietrich, Jack Benny and Larry Adler all called by, at various times). They even had artificial moonlight which could turn night back into day, and a crew of cleaners, called the 'Field Hygiene Services', for mopping up the dead.

The weakness of the American front was that it had to be fed. Its appetite was stupendous. A long line of trucks now snaked 330 miles from the Channel ports to the front, bringing everything from shower units to gasoline and crackers. Even then supply couldn't meet demand. Every day, the Allied armies got through 700 tons of shells, and the Germans (who needed only 200) joked that there was an American shell for every one of them. This, they said, is how a rich man fights his war. In Normandy alone, the US army had distributed over 124 million maps, and now – each day – it was losing 1,200 small arms and 5,000 tyres. In the last few months of 1944, over 13 million jerry cans went missing, which is why – these days – almost every French farm has one of its own.

For most soldiers, supply was a mystery, always too much or too little. They called the suppliers the Department of Sex and Rhythm, and would taunt them with cowardly names like the Canteen Commandos or the Chairborne Division. 'We always had one man in the line,' joked Flint, 'for every five bringing up the Coca-Cola.' But it was no joke in the foxholes up at the front. Vital supplies of winter clothes, blankets and antifreeze had yet to arrive, or were still bobbing around off Cherbourg waiting for a berth. Some new divisions even had to be diverted to England, due to the failure of supply.

Down on the plain, the great city came to a halt. Unable to sate its appetite, it was unable to advance. The great thrust for Berlin had faltered right here in this purple soil, hungry and overweight. It was obvious that nothing would move until after the snows, and so the generals gallantly called this halt 'The Winter Guard'. But the Germans had another name for it. To them, it seemed the Americans were too bloated to finish the job, and that their attack was more bean feast than Blitzkrieg. Why were the *Amis* giving them a chance to get home and rebuild their divisions? For the Germans, this break had come not a moment too soon.

To them, it would be known, now and for ever, as 'The Miracle in the West'.

48

After several days in the Vosges, Jeff drove us out on to the plain, towards the violent rim of the front.

It was rich farmland, a brilliant brocade of cabbages and mustard. As soon as the road hit the flat, it shrugged off its fences and hedges and swooped off through the great estates. Here, every manor house was a little red castle, with vast ornamental gates like the entrance to a city. Nowadays, the chatelaine is as likely to be a lawyer in Strasbourg as a master of onions and pears. But it still felt like land worth dying for. Occasionally, we caught a glimpse of Christ, arms outstretched in the corn. I often wondered what powerful spiritual urges had planted him there, and what he would have said. 'Here lieth 20,000 bumpkins (*rustauds*),' perhaps, 'slashed to bits in the great revolt of 1525'?

'Or, "This way to Jerusalem",' suggested Flint.

'Or "Thanks for all the cabbage",' said Jeff.

That evening, and for the next few days, we toured the villages of the old front line. Often they seemed like collections of castles, the streets like sandstone gorges topped with timber ramparts. Everything was drenched in wealth, which in Alsace means lilac and chocolate and pink. Even the dovecotes looked like miniature palaces, and most of the fortress-farms had their own theatrical courtyards, with cattle in the lower stalls, and families, dogs and plaster angels living in the cloisters above. In the middle of each courtyard, centre stage, was a magnificent dunghill, usually the size of a whale.

Flint could remember the smell of these places long after he'd forgotten their names. We revisited each of the villages in which he was billeted in December 1944 – Ringendorf, Ringeldorf, Zutzendorf and Ingwiller – but the names meant little. Even then, they'd hardly mattered; soldiers slept at grid references, the hills were merely numbers (determined by their height), and the villages just words to be scrambled up in typing. As far as Flint was concerned, the names had long gone, whilst the dunghills had lingered on.

'Think of the *bacteria*,' he said, thoughtfully. 'Perhaps they get used to it . . .'

Modern life had intruded only gently on these scenes. Each village still had its water trough with a dragon-head pump, and a fire station no more than a shed, and – every day – a tart-seller rumbled up the street, sounding her horn and announcing her pies. Even the storks were back. Alsatians believe that they bring luck, and that a house will never catch fire with a stork on the roof. We often saw them up in the churches and towers, perched on a dump of twigs and feathers and Rhineland frogs. With their bald heads, black gowns and round shoulders, they looked like lawyers waiting for a judgment. Perhaps they *would* have been lawyers if only they'd had voices. Instead they had to clack their beaks, which only made them crosser still. They'd hated the war, and for almost fifty years they'd stayed away.

49

The writer, Maurois, warns that the Alsatians can be 'gruff and surly' but we needn't have worried. There were even signs of contentment in Lupstein, the village where we stayed. Every morning the *Lupsteiners* got up and drove to Germany where they filled their pockets with German salaries and then trundled home, barely touched by tax. It was all a welcome distraction from the stress of being Alsatian. They didn't even worry any more about the Protestants in the next village ('There's been a lot of wars . . .', they said), or the fact that there were still 10,000 medieval rebels stacked up in the churchyard waiting to be buried.

'They were from the *Bundschuh*,' said farmer Wendling. The Clog League.

His wife nodded. 'They say the fields turned red from here to Saverne . . .'

The Wendlings had spotted us looking aghast, and were now peering out of their yard. Although Lupstein was another street of manor houses, they were the only people who still kept cows. Everyone else had traded them in for BMWs and got themselves out of the muck. But there was something refreshingly obstinate about the Wendlings. It was obvious their pride and joy was their manure heap, and Madame Wendling wore skirts and leather leggings, and had a dog with eyes like a fish and paws as big as a bear's.

Jeff waved a camera at her. 'Can I take your picture?'

'Certainly not,' she said, 'I'm far too old for that.'

She was surprised that Jeff and Flint had come all the way from the States.

'I've only ever been as far as Heidelberg, unless you count Corfu.'

The experience of travel had convinced her that, although there was life beyond Lupstein, it wasn't worth the effort. She was even more surprised to discover that Flint was on his second visit in sixty years. Although she wasn't old enough to remember the last time the Americans were here in strength, she knew the stories. Now she stood back and surveyed Flint fondly, as if he were an ancient tractor.

'You've lived in troubled times,' she said. *Une époque agitée.*

We stayed at the house of Madame Huber, three gateways down the street. It was an enormous place, like a galleon that had somehow sailed up over the plain. I could make out entire oak trees baked into the bulwarks of clay and straw and wisps of animal hair. Higher up, amongst the gables and raising plates, it was a masterpiece of whittling and detail. There were symbols to ward off evil, sheaves of corn, marriage plaques, the diamond shapes of female fertility and the interlocking curls of sexual love. Madame Huber said the man who built it, in 1780, had fathered lots of babies and had always slept with his newborns, as snug as muffins in the parlour. Some of his furniture had even survived, painted in ox-blood and potato juice, and fitted into the panels.

Jeff frowned at all the wood. 'How are your termites in Europe?'

Madame Huber looked puzzled. The idea that something small and unhygienic could eat your house was entirely alien to the Alsatian mind. Housework was almost a matter of religious conviction. Our little hobbitty rooms had been scrubbed to a saintly sheen, and the sheets cracked like communion cloth when I clambered into bed. But still Madame Huber fretted that things were not as they once had been. 'Not long ago,' she said, 'we used to gather up everything we didn't need and take it down to the church, and there we'd pile it up in the shape of Judas Iscariot and set it all on fire.'

Flint was happy to be back amongst such orderliness, even though it was harder now to climb a tree to bed. Perhaps he should have found himself a cellar, as he had in the war. *Panther Tracks* once carried a story about a little girl who'd shown the men down to the cellar, just as the shelling began. Once they were all safely underground, she bid them all good-night and went upstairs to bed.

Stoicism like this had mystified the Americans. Many of the soldiers had never come across a people quite so strange, and, before long, there was a flourishing souvenir trade. All down the line the half-tracks started filling up with silverware, lace, knives, fowling guns, coins and wooden clogs. In every village the clog-maker was swamped with orders, although each pair took only half an hour to carve. Everyone bought some, including Flint. One of the sergeants even bought thirty-nine pairs, had a few painted up with the names of his buddies, and sent the rest back to Brooklyn.

But the reserve and impassivity still intrigued the Americans. Most suspected that behind the silence there was pain, but the story was never very clear. 'Years of this strife,' reported *Panther Tracks*, 'have hardened these people to the rigors of war. Outwardly, they appear immune to hardships and the total destruction that has been inflicted upon them.' As to what was going on inwardly, no one would know for several decades. Even now, people are only gradually beginning to realise what wartime meant for the benighted Alsatians. 'It set brother against brother,' said Madame Huber, as though speaking for them all.

The Nazis began with a referendum, to make the Alsatians feel as if they'd invaded themselves. Against a background of threats and disqualification, an improbable 95 per cent of the electorate voted to be German. At a stroke, the old German colonies of 1870 – Alsace and the Moselle region of Lorraine – were gobbled up into a fantasy called the *Deutsche Volksgemeinschaft*, the Germanic Community. This meant that, suddenly, the *Alsacien-Mosellans* acquired the rights and duties of Germans, a sure sign that they were about to become cannon fodder in the Nazi design.

Don't worry, Berlin assured them. 'If we ever need you, we'll have lost the war anyway.'

Within the year, the Germans were back, demanding their pound of flesh. That was the deal, wasn't it? Between 1942 and 1944, over 140,000 Alsatians were marched off into the army. Some went willingly, and even joined the SS *'Das Reich'* Division. But, for most, military service was a matter of compulsion and they'd be known for ever as *les malgré-nous*, or 'We, the Unwilling'. It wasn't long before they discovered they were hated, both at home and abroad. The Germans never trusted them on the Western Front (because they thought they'd desert) and so they went to Russia, where both sides treated them as traitors. Over 40,000 were killed, usually up front or clearing mines, and another 40,000 simply disappeared. Almost every household in Alsace has its tales of relatives lost in Russia, or a death notice that begins with the words *'Gefallen für Führer, Volk und Vaterland . . .'*

During our travels in Alsace we met several men who remembered this time, and who I promised not to name. It was not so much fear they felt, as outright shame. Alsace had simply crumbled away in those years, with no ideas of its own. One man remembered how every school day began with a chorus of *'Es lebe unser Führer!'* (Long live the Führer!) and a song about *Saint Empire*. Another recalled the summer camps of the Hitler Youth, a time of sausages and violence. Every night, they jumped through huge bonfires shouting *'Heilig Deutschland!'* ('Holy Germany!') and sang of the day when they'd march off to Russia.

There was a choice, they said, but it was no less shameful. *'Aller se battre en Russie, ou disparaître dans la clandestinité'* ('Get killed in Russia, or vanish underground'). No one liked to remember the days spent living like a rat. One man said he and his brothers had spent eighteen months hiding in the forest, only returning to the farm by night. Another said he'd known a man who'd lived in a well. 'And my uncle would jump in the wardrobe when *les traquants* [trackers] appeared. He'd always have a grenade in each hand, ready to blow!' He explained that few people survived a visit from *les traquants*, at least with ears and fingers intact. They were the last of Vlassov's men – a Russian army that had defected to the Nazis – and were trigger-happy, hungry for booty and eager to please. I recognised them as the men who'd hunted Nancy Wake, known then as *les Mongols*.

'By the end, they were hunting anyone,' said the fugitive. 'Sending them off to the factories and putting them to work.'

'Even young girls,' said the old Hitler youth, 'as long as they were strong.'

Alsace, they all agreed, had never been the same again. By the time the Americans arrived, one in fifty Alsatians was either dead or missing. Lists of those killed would be posted in shop windows for the next five years, and the last 20,000 prisoners didn't get back from Russia until 1955. Even then, they were traitors. To this day, *les malgré-nous* are the shame of Alsace, denied medals and pensions and public office.

Liberation, on the other hand, received only a cautious welcome. People dreaded a return to French rule, and the recriminations that would follow. 'We didn't want to be French,' said the fugitive, 'we just wanted to be Alsatian.' At least the war had settled one issue: never again would they vote to be German.

As for the Americans, the response was cool. The Alsatians could see that Uncle Sam had a tenuous grip on the land. One false move and the Nazis would be spewing out of the hills, and reimplanted in their lives.

50

Beyond Ringeldorf, the plain seemed to sink, and then rise again, into the German forests to the north. We followed the platoon east then west and north, as it sought to make contact with the enemy. The battle felt more immediate here, and – from a cornfield on the slope – we could peer across, into the enemy's old positions along a distant strip of pine-blue hills. Flint spent ages, staring out over the grasslands. Perhaps he could still see men out there, crawling into the earth. In this war, there'd been no trenches on the Western Front, merely foxholes, dug – or chipped – from the frozen soil. It meant that men had simply vanished into the ground, leaving the landscape as empty then as it appears today.

'I think this,' said Flint, 'is where we took our first hits.'

And so began the Panthers' duel, under a rain of shells and sleet.

To some, this was a beautiful battlefield, even then. They listened in awe as huge volleys of shells, known as 'freight cars', trundled over their heads and off into German lines. For a few, there was even something magical about this wintry, polyphonic scene. One of the women driving ambulances for the French, Anita Leslie, who was Irish (with an American mother), wrote:

The ice cracked, and in the air sounded the whistle of German shells and the fluttering, feathery laughter of our own shells that faded as they hurtled eastward. In the cold air you could hear the rattle of machine guns and the short crack of rifles . . . Even rifle bullets have their baby whistle.

But – for most – the beauty was harder to see. If it wasn't pouring shells, it was pouring rain. That winter was one of the wettest on record, and – as November turned to December – the rain turned to sleet. Mildew bloomed across leather and webbing, and the new machines began to rust. It was impossible to keep warm. The men were still dressed for a war in the South of France, not the frosty plains of Alsace. Occasionally, they managed to dry themselves around evil home-made braziers – a drum of earth, soaked in diesel and stirred to the consistency of porridge. But, from now on, there was always a constant background snivel of colds and flu, and even the simplest military operations slowed to the pace of the sludge.

The men had never felt more alone than out in this mire. The air force had disappeared, grounded by fog for all but five days in December. Tanks too were useless in the slush. 'They had very narrow treads,' said Flint, 'and were easily bogged down.' Often, they were more of a danger to the men around than the enemy up front. The sight of a comrade crushed in the tracks was so spectacularly diagrammatic that few could believe what they'd seen. 'To me, it was one of the worst things I went through,' wrote another veteran. 'This poor bastard had graduated from high school in June, was drafted, took basic training, shipped overseas, had thirty seconds of combat and was killed.'

It was better for the Panthers than for the Joes up front. At least Flint's men lived beyond the constant pitter-patter of small arms fire. Occasionally, their guns were tiptoed up to the front like giant snipers, to pick off a bunker or cover a road. But the rest of the time they were held back in defence. Like GIs all down the line, they bore their duties without conviction, and without complaint. The Tennessee farmboys even managed to attain a sense of normality amongst all the muck and barns at the rear. Leahy and Miller took in pigs and chickens and even the battalion mail clerk managed to deliver a calf. It was different for the Brooklyn boys. To them, agriculture was almost as alarming as war.

The incoming shells were harder to get used to. The locals called them *arrivées*, as if they too were trains. Even a far-off barrage was perturbing at first. Some men never got attuned to distance and heard only thousands of tons of hardware piling into the landscape. Others thought of it merely as traffic, usually going the other way.

'If it's yours, it's yours,' they'd say.

But it was quite another matter when the shells started landing close. Then, it was impossible to ignore the sheer concussive force of the explosion. Survivors of these onslaughts often say it feels as if the air opens to admit the shell, and then slams shut behind. It's so deafening you hear nothing, but the pressure changes and you squeeze your eyes shut to stop them popping out of their sockets. Then there's silence, and the air crackles with sparks and sizzling chunks of metal. 'You never hear the shrapnel that hits you,' wrote another veteran. 'The first realisation is that your senses start telling your brain that your body has been injured. Sometimes you are not precisely sure where the injury is located ...'

The Panthers were caught in just such a squall on 1 December 1944. Flint's men were spared but, alongside them, A Company weren't so lucky. They'd already lost two men the day before, and now the trees burst and the sky caved in. A hail of giant splinters tore through the ranks, ripping up faces and hands. 'Shrapnel went everywhere,' reads the official report.

'That's a lot to get used to?' I ventured.

'Hell, yes,' said Flint. 'It was years before I could properly relax.'

51

The taste of this time had survived better than any other memory of Flint's.

He was still haunted by the dank, dead porkiness of spam. Even the very mention of it was enough to elicit a pasty, grey pallor. After the Atlantic voyage, Flint had hoped he'd seen the end of spam, and, for a while, this seemed almost possible. From the forward kitchens came a succession of textures: boiled, stringy, lumpy, gritty and mush. There was nothing delicate about this food but at least it was the artefact of cooks. Such people held remarkable power in this flavourless society. Chief amongst them was Sergeant MacLean, who despised approval and resented flattery. 'Don't give me that line of bullshit,' he'd say, 'and think I'm going to give you more gruel because I'm NOT!'

But, as they neared the front, the kitchens fell back, and it was soon spam without end. Every ration pack came with another brick of pasted pork, and there was spam for Advent and spam in the Christmas mail. The men hated it and called it 'Armoured Pig' and the coffee 'Java'. Occasionally, however, this diet would be reinvigorated by the farmboys, who'd come back with rabbits killed in the booby traps or a deer they'd shot in the forest. On those nights there'd be 'Shit and Shingle', a feast of biscuits and mangled meat. Better still were the days when they shot an 'enemy lamb' and got Cardena the Cuban to roast it, seeded with garlic and dripping with fat.

But treats like this were always the exception. Most of the time it was piggy paste, Hershey bars and powdered lemonade. It's a great tribute to the American digestive system that so many young men got through this war without either mutiny or pandemic constipation. Some even managed to joke about their bland, lacklustre regime.

'Meatless days,' they'd say, 'and boneless nights.'

It was always better for those with a billet in the village.

One night we ate in Dettwiller, a few miles back from the old front line. It was an odd restaurant, run by a pair of horse-faced twins who refused to speak anything but English and *Elsässich*. From the ceilings dangled tools and ploughs, bedpans, gnomes and bits of car. I half wondered if the place hadn't once been blown up, and reassembled inside out. Jeff had never seen so much ironmongery reflected in his soup, but Flint was less surprised. Although the Panthers had been puzzled by the Alsatians, they were always delighted by the food that appeared wherever they happened to stop.

'*Schmeckt gut! Schmeckt gut!*' said Flint, as he smacked his lips.

These were probably the happiest moments of his return to Alsace, old terrors banished, or displaced by food. The dinner we ordered was Brueghelesque, a country banquet of pigs' knuckles, cabbage pickled in coriander and cloves, smoked shoulder-blades, duck, tiny papery pastries filled with almonds and raisins, huge bowls of cherries, apples as big as babies' heads, a bottle of Gewürztraminer ('strong enough to make a priest forget his vows,' according to the twins) and a large clay pot called a 'house of burning cream'. It was the sort of feast to make heaven of any winter, and even the wizardly Bernard Newman had been reduced to grunts of Christian praise. 'I have described Alsace,' he wrote, 'as a gastronomic paradise.'

In all the tastes and flavours of the evening, Flint found a piece of the past he thought he'd lost. At first, recollection came slowly ('This is where I had the best mashed potato I've ever eaten') but soon the memories were gushing free. He remembered *Baeckoffe* – a stew made with layers of smuggled meat and cooked with dandelions and sorrel – and *Hasepfeffer* or jugged hare, and a rampant sausage called Mother's Pride. Then, he was back amongst the farmers and their wives, in all their clogs and aprons and black silk bows. They called him *Herr Oberleutnant Flint* and lavished on him peppermint schnapps, made in their illegal stills.

'Was it good?' I asked.

'*Sehr köstlich*,' Flint growled. 'Quite delicious, and – at 200 per cent proof – the best antifreeze money could buy.'

52

Throughout early December 1944, the front line creaked and yawed. Everyone knew that something was about to go, but no one knew when or where. It felt like stalemate in a long, iced-up game of chess. Perhaps nothing would ever move, and the great green city would grow foundations and roads? Meanwhile, the life expectancy of a junior officer fell to just six weeks. The Winter Guard had become a deadly wait.

At some stage during this lull, Flint was given a forty-eight-hour pass. This was a valuable prize, one that could be won, earned, gifted and forfeit. It entitled a man to two days away from the shelling, and a train ride up to Paris. Every week, *Panther Tracks* ran wild reports of the spectacle ahead. Paris has never looked more feral than in those grainy sheets. The city is in the grip of *zig-zig*, there's limitless liquor and everybody seems to be dressed in fur and painted up like dolls.

'Fancy another trip?' I asked Flint.

He thought about this for a while, and shook his head.

'No,' he said. 'It was a terrible experience. I never want to go there again.'

Part 5 – La Sauce Parisienne

Good Americans, when they die, go to Paris.

Thomas Gold Appleton

Lunch kills half of Paris, supper the other half.

Montesquieu

Without the new antibiotics Paris would be rotten with VD. Absolutely rotten with it.

Fabienne Jamet, *Palace of Sweet Sin*, 1977

If you are lucky enough to have lived in Paris as a young man, then wherever you go for the rest of your life, it stays with you, for Paris is a moveable feast

Ernest Hemingway, *A Moveable Feast*, 1964

A seething madhouse of drunks, semi-drunks, quarter drunks, and sober maniacs . . . It was a silly useless life and I have missed every day since.

Harold Stearns, *The Street I Know*

53

Five months later, I found myself alone on adultery night in a jazz club on Huchette.

Strictly speaking, it was always adultery night at Le Caveau. Although musicians came and went, so too did vows, promises and good intentions. With all its roving eyes and wandering hands, the place was like a carnival of knowledge. It was perfect for this purpose: hot, vaulted, subterranean and dark. In all the times I ever went there (my room was only ten yards away), I never saw anyone who wasn't about some libidinous, underground scheme. Some nights it seemed as if every roué in the Latin Quarter was there, extending his extra-marital estate.

It was always the same people I saw: louche, improbable characters drawn from Lautrec, solemnly lustful and dancing in hats. After a while, I even got to know their names. The men called each other things like Zippo, Popeye and *L'égout* (The Drain). The women, on the other hand, always sounded like lingerie – Lala, Secret, Geneviève and Délice – names all lacily frivolous and no doubt easily discarded. Although I never spoke to them, it was obvious they were married, and were seeking a moment of conspiracy and not a mate for life. Occasionally, they even managed to concentrate on the Dixie, though their hands were always somewhere else.

I did however speak to Zippo once, when he came and sat at my table. He was a tiny, bald man with little flames of red hair licking up from his ears. Although his accent was strong, I think I got the essence of his life: *échangisme, clubs de rencontres* and the endless thrill of the chase. He told me that, in France, the orgasm is known as the *Le Petit Mort.* 'Because that's the end,' he said, '*la fin de la chasse.*'

'And you're always hunting?'

'Of course!' he said. 'It keeps me out of trouble.'

Zippo, I soon realised, was not unusual in this city. In the old days, almost every self-respecting Parisian kept a *cinq à sept,* a floozy to fill the time between the end of work and going home. Now, it seems, '5–7' is just his weekly tally, and he works them round the clock. 'Polygamy', Zippo would say, 'is the opposite of monotony', and many would agree. It's now thought that more than three million Frenchmen are into swinging, and there are over 400 swinging clubs and a whole shelf of swinging magazines.

Zippo didn't stay for long, and was soon back in the fray. I noticed that the woman he'd been stalking, a fizzy blonde of at least fifty-five, had tired of his inattention and had heaved herself off on to someone else. Even the little hunter was surprised by this, and stood around looking fidgety and spare. That night, it seems, the rate of *échange* was too fast even for Zippo.

54

The English have long been in awe of the Frenchman's flair for infidelity. We've never understood why the French aren't more proprietary about their other half, and why a spouse seems so much a person to be displayed, lent and mutually enjoyed. Even presidents are at it. How could Madame Mitterrand stand there at her husband's grave, shoulder to shoulder with his lover? Much English ink is spilt on the subject, whilst Paris hardly gives it a thought.

For centuries, we've been trying to make sense of it all. But to understand it is one thing, and to participate another. English travellers have long been warned of the dangers of dabbling in seduction. The experience of Thomas Dixon stands as a warning to us all. In 1717, he found himself in a carriage with Madame de Polignac, and – in his words – 'could not forbear putting his hand where some women would not let him'. She, however, responded enthusiastically by handling his 'arms', only to find the equipment 'not fit for present service'. Enraged, she beat him heartily and hurled him out of the coach, warning him 'never to attack a young handsome woman as she was when his ammunition was spent'.

This was an enjoyable thought, as I sat in my corner, watching Zippo try to pick up a scent. After a while he gave up, returned to the table and flopped into a chair.

'What about you?' he asked. 'Looking for anything in particular?'

'Yes, actually, I am,' I said. 'Some Americans.'

'*Americans?*' spluttered Zippo.

'Well, ghosts, really. They used to drink here, a long, long time ago.'

55

Zippo hadn't found what he was looking for that night, and nor had I.

But, whilst he'd missed his chance by a couple of minutes, I'd missed mine by almost eighty years.

It's hard now to believe that Le Caveau had ever been a hang-out for genius. These days, with its drunken Dixie, its Zippos and its lumpy stone walls, it's unlikely to inspire anything much, beyond basic primal urges. But, had I been here in the Twenties – when this was the Hôtel du Caveau – I'd have found myself amongst some of the greatest names in the American arts. They were all here: James Thurber, e.e cummings, Duke Ellington, Helena Rubinstein, Gertrude Stein (and her lover, Alice Toklas), Louis Armstrong and Josephine Baker, famous for wearing only a string of bananas. I might even have seen Scott Fitzgerald working up a little tragedy, or Ernest Hemingway smashing through the doors. It's hard to say which would have been more disconcerting, the Caveau of 1927 or the Caveau of today.

It seems the place has always been mildly subversive. Most of the Americans were here to see a surrealist from Boston, called Elliot Paul. Along with his friends Picasso, Miró and Man Ray, Paul had set up an anarchical review, called *Transition*, which he ran from the hotel. Nowhere was better suited to their cause. Once a fortnight the waiter, a Serb called Georges, tried to cut his own throat, and the only other guest was an elderly Greek-American called Mary, who survived on prostitution and Dubonnet. Each night, Mary and the cook sang 'The Missouri Waltz', and a few bawdy songs 'consisting mostly of gestures'. I realise now that if anything has survived of the old Caveau it's probably this music and Man Ray's insatiable lust.

Life for the Americans in Paris was beautifully haphazard, which is probably why they liked it. No other city in the world has nurtured quite so much American genius, and that without even trying. Disorder and dysfunction, it seems, was at the very heart of American success. Hemingway drank, Scott Fitzgerald worried about the size of his penis, Gertrude Stein spent hours wandering though her own consciousness artfully obliterating grammar (another surrealist, Wyndham Lewis, thought her work an 'infantile, dull-witted stutter') and Toklas dreamed up cookies made with hash. Even Elliot Paul said he only discovered the Rue de la Huchette because he met a prostitute aged seventeen and followed her back home. On the other hand, his account of eight years lived on this street, *The Last Time I Saw Paris*, is one of the most endearing and luminous travelogues ever written. 'Most of the men and women of the Rue de la Huchette were active, if unproductive,' he begins. 'They sold food and produce, shelter, sex and refreshment, or scribbled in large ledgers . . .'

The American artists' curiosity about Paris was limitless. Ezra Pound and e.e. cummings spent much of the early Twenties here; Gertrude Stein never went home, and is buried in Père Lachaise. Josephine Baker declared that the city had – like her bananas – entwined her ('*J'ai deux amours,*' she said, '*mon pays et Paris*'), and it too became her home. Hemingway also found plenty to entwine him, and stayed from 1921 to 1929. Sometimes, it seems, the American literati admired the place almost as much as their fellow countrymen despised the rest of France.

It's always been the other way round for the British. For some reason, we seem to descend on the city like low cloud, a constant drizzle of discontent. Most of the time the complaints are pretty ordinary: dog poo; coffee like creosote; homicidal waiters (and drivers), and antiquated plumbing. At other times the anxiety is more general, a suspicion that Paris is somehow playing a nasty trick. Britons often think it's capricious, and that its architecture is pompous. We enjoy only the fact that Haussmann's layout was designed to discourage rioting, and that, at any moment, an army might appear and flush the Parisians away.

That's not how I see Paris, although it's far from perfect. To me, it's the most beautifully contrived city in the world and should've been a template for everywhere else: compact, leafy, residential and ornate. The worst bits, I've always felt, are simply over-loved – kitsch running riot along Rivoli, or the Sacré-Coeur like a festival of tat. What's surprising is how much the British have contributed to all of this; even in 1786, we were spending over £1 million a year in Paris. These days, it's several hundred times this, as – each year – one in six of us makes the trip across the Channel.

More remarkable still, the moaning has never stopped. Worst of all are the British literati. Even as long ago as 1608, the best thing the travel writer Coryate could think of to say about Paris was that it had some 'nice looking gallows'. A century on, Hazlitt declared all Parisians to be 'whiffling, skittish, snappish, volatile, and inconsequential', and Romney said that the cleverest of them all was a monkey at the Louvre. Even Thicknesse, writing in 1776, declared Paris to be the 'least agreeable place I have seen in France'. After that, it was fair game for a massive literary assault. Almost everyone's had a go, from Dickens through to Orwell. Even the great writers of our own age have little good to say. Jan Morris thinks Paris is too harmonious and lacks the natural chaos of our time, and Clive James always finds plenty to mock (the *bateau-mouche* is 'a boat that looks like a greenhouse' and the Centre Pompidou 'a giant rattle-trap air-conditioner dropped from a sky-hook'). Paris, it seems, is the place we love to hate, and yet where we always want to go.

But even the American love-in had its limits. By the Thirties, the affair was on the rocks, and then the war saw it off. When the American writers finally returned in 1944, they wondered how anyone had ever loved the city. 'The sun never seemed to rise over Paris,' wrote Arthur Miller, in 1947, 'the winter sky like a lid of iron, graying the skin of one's hands and making faces wan.' But for Isaiah Berlin, it was more than a matter of weather. The city was finished:

> Paris seemed terrifying to me – so cold and abnormally clean and empty and more beautiful than I had ever seen a city to be . . . but empty and hollow and dead, like an exquisite corpse; the metaphor is vile and commonplace but I can think of nothing else.

And that, broadly speaking, is much how Flint remembered Paris.
'I don't think we ever understood exactly what they'd been through.'

56

Nowhere would the suffering have been more apparent than along the Rue de la Huchette.

It was now much as it was on the eve of war – a short, vaguely raffish alley that dog-legged through the Latin Quarter, along the edge of the river. It was so narrow that one could almost lean out, window to window, across the street. Then (as now) it saw few tourists, just those curious for medieval, pre-Haussmann Paris. No one knows how it got its name, or who first settled it, except that they were probably the first Parisians to venture off the islands on the Seine. It had been slow to gentrify, and several of the houses were derelict. The little theatre had been performing Ionesco's *The Bald Prima Donna* every night for the last fifty years. Meanwhile, below ground, the street seemed to disap-pear into a series of ancient cellars – like Le Caveau – all green and damp and of indeterminate intent. Set into the walls were huge ovens, pieces of iron machinery and giant brass taps, as if Quasimodo were the cook.

Now, the street was owned by Greeks, refugees from a war of their own (although which, they couldn't remember). At night the air was oily with lamb, and the waiters would smash plates across the cobbles in an effort to generate trade. It had always been a street of outsiders. Back in the Thirties, it was Balkan communists, Bretons, Jews and a beautiful Serb called Milka (whose boyfriend was killed in Spain, when a hand grenade tore off his head). Now, there were immigrants again, and a kebab shop, a fondue bar, two Swiss restaurants and a Cuban café, with a little sign in English, saying SEXY BAR FOR CRAZY NIGHT. This, I felt sure, was where the writers would gather, if ever they returned.

The residents still gossiped across the alley, and on weekends a few of them gathered up their rods and went fishing on the Seine. There was once a time, in living memory, when the poor were dependent on what they caught in the river, or on a dish of stuffed cat (*chat farci*). At this level, the destitute were known as *les imprévoyants,* literally the 'non-fore-sighted ones', and – every now and then – their clothes were taken to the *Blanchisserie des Imprévoyants,* and boiled to a colourless pulp. According to Elliot Paul, it wasn't much better for those higher up the scale. Barber's itch was an undiscriminating affliction, and money was always tight. If, between the wars, a cat died in a middle-class home, it wouldn't have been eaten but it would have been skinned, and the pelt salted and sold off for winter mittens.

It wasn't so easy to be *imprévoyant* now, although there were still people living under cardboard along the river. I often saw them in the *métro* station, like a new, subterranean sub-class. Some huddled, some sang. A few even formed little quartets, belting out gypsy songs, whilst another man made his living by balancing matchsticks on their ends. Who'd defend these people, if they ever needed help? Nobody, I suspect. In 1936, it would have been everyone. The Rue de la Huchette was in a constant state of revolt. They resisted the Fascists and the *Sûreté* and sent volunteers to Spain. When a group of Nazis appeared in the street, dressed as German tourists, it was Milka who saw them off by pouring a pisspot over their heads. The next year, the communists went on strike and were joined by all the whores and by most of the street, including the goldfish-seller at number 28, La Vie Silencieuse. (Monsieur Maurice was hardly a revolutionary, but they got him in the end. One morning in 1939 he was taken into custody and then three days later, the police turned up and dumped his fish in the Seine.)

There was once a police station at Number 14, but it was never a source of order. *Les flics* didn't see it as their place to stop people being poor, or saying what they thought. Besides, they were so hard up themselves that the chief's wife was out every Saturday picking up gentlemen on St-Germain. The only time the police were ever truly roused to action was when a burglar killed one of their own in 1926. This time, they brought him in and kicked him to death on the station floor. Now it was a souvenir shop, blissfully unaware of its bludgeoned past.

There was no one to remember any of this, except for Elliot Paul.

'What about old people?' I asked. 'Don't you have any?'

Everyone shook their heads. 'No,' they said, 'they must have moved away.'

I stayed next door to the police post, across a passage called the Rue du Chat Qui Pêche (The Street of the Fishing Cat). It was said to be the shortest street in Paris and admitted no doors and only two other windows apart from mine. In fact, all I ever heard coming up the street were the blades of icy wind that came scything off the Seine. If I leaned out as far as possible, I could just see the Île de la Cité in one direction – caught in a flash of frosty lights – and the Greek waiters in the other, stamping around on their frozen plates.

My hotel had once been a dairy called À la Vache Indolente. It was now Greek and had the more vigorous name of Les Argonautes. Every wall was painted with heart-warming scenes from Cretan life, and there were rattan hats at reception in case sunlight ever found its way into the Rue de la Huchette. My room was up in the eaves, with huge black tree-trunks over my head. This was where the milkmaid, Collette, had slept. Elliot Paul says that although she was only a teenager, she was much admired for her well-rounded rump. She spent most of the Thirties trying to defend it from the locals, and most of the occupation trying to get them to buy it.

It was the same story everywhere, of either desperation or panic. As war approached, Number 7 became an air raid shelter for ninety, and many people fled. Those who could afford to left town, and foreigners like Elliot Paul went home. Georges, the suicidal waiter, unable to face the prospect of a life behind wire, stole an army uniform, tagged on to a passing regiment and was never seen again. Meanwhile a few doors down, at Number 19, Madame Luneville had also seen trouble coming and threw herself out of the window. As she fell, her petticoats snagged on an iron brace, and – for a moment – she dangled there, contemplating the awful turn that the century had taken. Then her underwear gave way, and sent her fluttering to her death. All that remained of this tragic vignette was the iron bracket, now festooned in berets and postcards and 'I ♥ Paris' dog-leads for pooches that can read.

At the end of the street was another swingers' club called the Georges Café. In the window it advertised cocktails with names like Love Boat and TGV, as if one could choose the pace of debauchery from either 'Bobbing along' to 'Going like a train'. I never went inside, although perhaps I should have done, for the sake of the old hag who'd once run the place as a shop. Madame Absalom had put up more of a fight than most. When the Germans finally arrived in Paris in June 1940, they'd smashed down the *blanchisserie* with a tank, and then come to take her stock. For a while she fought them with a cane, but even she saw that resistance was useless. 'All right, *mes lapins!*' she howled. 'Take the fucking stuff! We're all in the soup together . . .'

Paris died as thoroughly as anywhere else in the war that followed. To begin with, the Nazis enjoyed themselves, reopened the strip clubs and started to court the city with cameras and a visit from the Führer. They even talked of a marriage between Germany and France, but it soon became a funeral. One idea had been to create the myth of common heritage, and the remains of Napoleon's son were returned from Austria to be reunited with his father. It was a gesture wasted on the Parisians. 'What we want is meat,' they said. 'Not bones!' Soon, the union began to rot. A curfew tightened itself around the city, and the *métro* began to stink.

To ignite affection, the Germans tried to blast away everything anti-Teutonic. Over 200 statues were dynamited and scores of heroes were melted down, including Edith Cavell. Even Voltaire went to the furnace. Then, when the Nazis had finished with the city's statuary, they turned on its people.

The awkward, ungovernable people of streets like mine took the full brunt of their resentment. I now realise just how much this war explains the vacancy that the Greeks have so gratefully filled. For four years death and disappearance were casually visited upon Rue de la Huchette. Nobody will ever know how many lives were lost. In July 1942, all the Jews were carted away, along with the communists and Serbs. Meanwhile, the actress who lived next to Elliot Paul killed herself after only a few months of Nazism (her suicide note reached him eight weeks later, after she'd gassed herself with a brazier). The beautiful Milka was another never destined to survive this tale; she was interned and died of dysentery in 1941. Gone too was Mary the Greek-American. She was arrested at the Hôtel du Caveau and taken off to the camps. 'I hope someone gives her Dubonnet . . .' wrote Elliot Paul, but she was never seen again. She had two sons in Detroit who, if they're alive today, would now be in their eighties.

57

I once ate at the kebab shop, a place the French found curiously exotic. Maybe Parisians are amused by eating meat that's been irradiated for a week, stuffed in a cotton-wool bun and then dished up on a salad as promising as autumn. Or maybe they just weren't as discerning as they'd have us all believe. For years, I'd been labouring under the impression that Parisians only furred up their arteries on the best of food, like lark pies or little *tartiflettes* of snails. Now, after a week on the Rue de la Huchette a different picture emerged. When Montesquieu said 'Lunch kills half of Paris, supper the other half,' he had in mind not so much heart failure as a ruthless outbreak of salmonella.

I could see why people liked it. Apart from being cheap, La Maison de Gyros was in the grip of a fantasy that made it oddly compelling. The whole place glowed turquoise, like sea-water, and was decorated with beach towels, pictures of supertankers and furniture that looked as if it had come in with the tide. Although it never felt like Mykonos exactly, it never felt like Paris either, which was good enough for most. On Saturdays, whole families came here to feed themselves on Greece.

In Elliot Paul's time, the kebab shop had been possessed by fantasies of a different kind. Back then, it was all decked out in chinoiserie, and was the place a man could enjoy a modest meal, a game of cards, or 'a little moment' with one of the girls. It was a difficult choice, deciding which to favour: there was Consuela who wore a wedding dress for 'the hard to please', a Negress called Dora, a Scandinavian girl who'd dyed all her hair green, and old Armandine, who allowed herself to be whipped for fifty francs (in the full knowledge that she wasn't going to make such money any other way). If the punter wasn't feeling up to much himself, he could always hire the peephole and watch his neighbour letting off steam. According to Paul, the wives never seemed to mind the brothel; sex, so to speak, kept their husbands out of their hair. The little shop of fantasies was called *Le Panier Fleuri*, or the Basket in Bloom.

It struck me as typical of Paris that fantasy should move so seamlessly from sex to kebabs. As with food, one minute the Parisians could be totally undiscriminating in their sexual antics, and the next, sex was an art form and a matter of age-old expertise. Often, too, lunching and wenching seemed indistinguishable. Paris's favourite listings magazine, *La Nuit Sexy*, gave equal coverage to both and was a bewildering directory of the steamiest fleshpots and the sauciest places to fill your face. All tastes were catered for, and it wasn't long ago that there was a *maison de rendez-vous* specialising in women over seventy.

There was not much left now of Le Panier Fleuri, except a heavy old door with a scalloped grille. It had continued to service the toiling artisans of Rue de la Huchette until 1940, when it was requisitioned by the Germans as a whorehouse for the lower ranks. But *la Madame* had a curious sense of honour, and – having told the girls to leave – she set the place on fire. They say she was dragged away, singing 'La Marseillaise'.

This was an uplifting thought as I sat chewing my kebab. Although I was sorry to think of all that fantasy going up in smoke, here – at last – was a sign that the people of the street had found their courage again, and had risen in revolt.

58

All along the street there are plaques to those who died. Some of the victims still had no name; some were shot by the Gestapo just before the uprising and others died on the barricades. *Honneur aux défenseurs*, say the signs, *du fortin de la Huchette*.

Beyond Huchette, the plaques thinned out and almost disappeared. Like Marseille, Paris was not always as heroic as it liked to think. Although most Parisians detested the occupiers, few were prepared to do anything other than wait. Even the artists became *attentistes* (literally, 'those waiting'), resigned to the tyranny and grateful not to be noticed. 'Les Boches left me alone,' recalled Picasso, with some relief. 'They didn't

The humiliation of Marseille. The Vieux Port looks much the same today, and there are still bitter memories of the Nazi years. At least 90 of the city's inhabitants were executed and thousands more were taken into slavery or perished in the camps.

Nancy Wake in about 1934. Shortly afterwards, the Kiwi journalist witnessed an assassination in Marseille, married a notorious Corsican and decided to stay.

Nancy at her 94th birthday, 2006. For her exploits in the resistance, she'd become one of the most highly decorated women of the war.

To begin with, *Marseillaises* like Nancy were prepared to be merely awkward towards the Vichy regime. But then, in 1942, the Germans arrived and cleared the Panier district for one of their greatest atrocities in France.

The German's choice of Mayor: a ranting one-eyed haberdasher called Simon Sabiani.

February 1943. The Nazis dynamite much of Le Panier district. The Hôtel de Ville (centre right) survives.

Le Panier district today. It was never the 'cancer' the SS claimed, and is now merely attractively down at heel.

For Marseille, liberation came in August 1944. As they left, the Nazis pelted the city with artillery, blew up the fort and sank over 176 ships in the port.

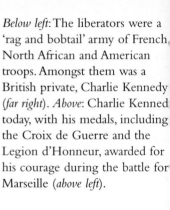

Below left: The liberators were a 'rag and bobtail' army of French, North African and American troops. Amongst them was a British private, Charlie Kennedy (*far right*). *Above*: Charlie Kennedy today, with his medals, including the Croix de Guerre and the Legion d'Honneur, awarded for his courage during the battle for Marseille (*above left*).

am Flint and his brother, Vasmer. As teenagers
drove across the US in a Buick Roadster, and
ld both distinguish themselves in war. Vasmer
a pilot, and was killed in the Korean conflict.

In 1942, Putnam Flint signed up with
the infantry. The US was hopelessly
unprepared for war, and relied heavily on
equipment made in World War I.

1943, Flint was transferred to the 824th Tank Destroyers (*Back row, 3rd from right*). Although
e battalion fought with distinction, in its original role it was obsolete before it had even
gun. But there was no doubting its esprit de corps. Heller and Warren (*bottom row, 1st and
2nd from left*) remain friends of Flint's to this day.

For three months, the 824ᵗ (the 'Panthers') and the SS slogged it across the plains Lorraine. Now all that remains of this titanic strug are the bunkers, the wire, a the occasional corpse.

Flint was surprised to find himself reunited with a US half-track. It was a 'useless thing', he declared and had performed like a bucket on wheels.

The church at Guiderkirche in happier times. It became a victim in the steeple war.

The church after Flint's bombardment. Its steeple had housed a nest of SS forward observers.

Rue de la Huchette today. The *otheke* was a hotel in the war, and owner died in the camps. Mme neville jumped from the building posite. (*Right*) Across the river, the rising began next to Notre Dame. re, the panzers take on the police.

ring the liberation, nco-American tions began like a vie but would end squabbles. Soon Americans became own as the 'new upiers'. By the e Flint arrived in cember 1944, the ers had died away, is was for sale, and was cheaper than colate.

During the long Lorraine winter of 1944, GIs often supplemented their d rations with rabbits a a little 'enemy deer'.

Finally, in March 1945, the 824th were supplied with the Hellcat. It was like an armoured sports car, the fastest tracked vehicle of the war.

Flint on the citadel at Bitche. This had been the last resort of the Nazis in Lorraine, and he'd never been up here before. It was a cathartic moment; the war he'd fought with most of his life was over. Almost 70,000 men had died along this front.

like my work, but they didn't punish me for it.' For many, resistance simply meant being rude. Students started wearing black ties, and waiters fought the war with their thumbs in the soup. Elsewhere, Parisians took to ignoring the Germans ('What Germans?' they'd say), calling them *ces messieurs*, and refusing to speak their language or understand their French. After a while, the Germans came to think of Paris as 'The City that Never Looks at You', a feeling countless foreigners have shared ever since.

If I wanted to find real resistance, I'd have to look underground. All the great acts of early defiance happened way below the surface. At the *métro* station of Barbès-Rochechouart, they were still celebrating – with photographs and plaudits – the assassination of a young German midshipman in August 1941. Although, as shootings go, it was not the most heroic (and cost thirty lives in reprisal), it marked a turning-point: for the Germans, Paris was now not merely cussed, it was dangerous.

Another day, I found myself deeper still, beneath the Place Denfert-Rochereau, in the Roman catacombs. Parisians insist that this was the nerve centre of resistance. I've always thought there was a touch of the Victor Hugos about these stories. On the other hand, the city's rebels have always ended up down here, or at least their components have. It's said there are over five miles of bone-lined tunnels, sprawling out beneath the city. Seemingly without beginning or end, such a cistern would, it's true, have been almost unassailable. ICI COMMENCE L'EMPIRE DE LA MORT, read the sign at the entrance. Seventy feet underground, however, this great cemetery seemed so much more warren than empire. Dead Parisians even smelt like rabbits, or, at the very best, beautiful shoes not worn for years.

The insurrection finally broke surface a few streets to the east, at La Santé. It's still a prison, and still enjoys the irony of its breezy name: the Health. I noticed that only the top floor of cells get any sunlight above the 30-foot walls, and that the bricks were dark with damp. From the narrow slots under the eaves, the impedimenta of bleak institutional lives spilled out on to the sills: cans of milk, buckets and sodden colourless clothes. In July 1944, there were only twelve showers for 3,000 inmates, and even revolt must have seemed better than death by mildew. But it was an unequal contest, spoons and bricks against the guns. The Milice cut down twelve prisoners and shot another thirty-five the following day out in the Bois de Boulogne.

As I stood looking up at a tablet of their names, a little stooped figure appeared at my side. 'Some place, eh?' he said.

'Er, yes,' I said, rather uncertainly. 'Probably better out than in.'

My new companion smiled. He wore red trousers and a bow tie, and said he was once a doctor at the prison. 'And we had another one exactly like it,' he said proudly, 'in Hanoi. You've probably heard of it: the Hanoi Hilton.'

We talked about the uprising, which occurred when he was seven.

'The Germans panicked. Santé in *revolt*! What would happen next?'

Soon, he said, the Paris sky was black with burning files, and non-essential staff began to leave. 'They left on horses and carts, camouflaged with grass and bits of trees!' He smiled. 'We thought that was funny and rode after them on our bicycles, also covered in twigs . . .'

Meanwhile, over on the Boulevard Saint-Michel, the survivors of Huchette assembled on the corner to watch the convoys go. They waved toilet brushes as the carts went past, but the Germans were too demoralised to care. Without even stopping, they loosed off a few desultory volleys of fire, and then rumbled off towards the country.

Behind them on the Île de la Cité, the insurrection – having recovered from its false start – was about to surface in full.

59

It was only a few minutes' walk into the old stone heart of political France. From the end of Rue de la Huchette, all I had to do was turn left, negotiate a few last bookstalls and cross the Petit Pont. The Seine was more like a moat here, or a river crushed between two forts. The furthest fort was an island, the Île de la Cité.

Here, a space opened up, the Place du Parvis Notre Dame, which was probably where France first began. Around it were the great redoubts of French political thought; there was a cathedral (Notre Dame) that celebrated not so much the indulgence of God as the ingenuity of man; next to it was a vast medieval hospital (the Hôtel Dieu), which – according to early travellers – the sick were not expected to survive but where they could at least die in the full glory of government; finally, at the other end, there was a palace of public order (the Préfecture), whose magnificent gates might at any minute have started erupting cavalry, off to chasten some restless section of the city. So, there it was: in one square, everything the French held true. It was a place to be enjoyed on an icy February day – as I had – with no sound but the frozen crack of footsteps and the fluttery panic of pigeons.

No one seemed to mind me wandering around the Préfecture. The courtyard was full of police cars instead of cavalry, and every now and then they burst from the building with a long nasal wail, a bit like a siren except with a cold. Apart from them, the place was curiously serene, and I clambered up an enormous scrolled staircase to Driving Licences, and then back down through Lost Property and Immigrant Affairs. Along the way, I came across a billiard table, several statues of elegant revolutionaries, and a man who was waiting to hand in a sword.

Across the courtyard was a monument to the uprising of August 1944, draped in laurels and flags. It's ironic that, in such an ordered city, it should be the police who began the revolt. Some say it was because they feared that the Germans would disarm them. Others think it was simply that the police – like all Frenchmen – see revolution as unfinished business and an attractive option whenever there's doubt. Either way, on 15 August, they went on strike, and then, three days later, several thousand of them locked themselves in the Préfecture, hoisted the tricolour (which hadn't been seen for four years) and challenged the Germans to fight. On the face of it, this was a foolhardy gesture: even though the Americans were closing in, the enemy still had 22,000 soldiers in town with 100 tanks, and 90 bombers at its disposal.

The Préfecture paid a high price for its cheek. The walls were still cratered with gunfire and much of the ornery had been shot away, fruit shattered and acanthus cut down to the brick. It was under siege for almost a week, with horses being cut up in the billiard room and men firing pistols from the roof. Almost 200 *agents* were killed, although it could have been worse. The German counter-attack was never enthusiastic. They had no high-explosive ordnance, and their armour-piercing shells merely punched neat holes through buildings before vanishing into the blue. Once, an armoured car drove into the *place*, ploughed the gates with cannon fire, and then rumbled angrily away. The gateway looked much the same now as it did then, gnawed and crumbly, like half-eaten cake.

The Germans, it seems, had had more pressing problems. All around them, the city was up in arms.

*

From the square, I could just see back across the Seine, and up the Rue du Chat Qui Pêche. For a while, this was a blizzard of small arms fire, but then the fighting spread out, moving from quarter to quarter. The Parisians had few weapons, except some shotguns and the guns they'd stolen from soldiers clubbed to death in the street. Occasionally, if they had champagne bottles and sulphuric acid, people made Molotov cocktails, and – at the Sorbonne – the Nobel Prize laureate, Professor Joliot-Curie, made some beautiful bombs that burst on impact. But, for most people, participation simply meant digging a barricade. Almost every street, including Rue de la Huchette, became a castle, fortified with anything from paving stones to grand pianos. The biggest was at the *carrefour*, or crossroads, of Saint-Michel and St-Germain, and so conspicuous it became known as the *Carrefour de la Mort*.

This was still how the Parisians liked to see themselves, bare-chested and atop a barricade. There was a touch of Delacroix about everyone, and this remained the most popular image of the war. *'Tous aux barricades!'* went up the cry, and almost everybody did. In the last week of occupation, membership of the *résistance* rose from 15,000 to nearly ten times that number. In the grainy images of this time, one can see bands of lawyers, doctors, *zazous* (boppers) and *naphtalines*, the ex-soldiers who'd sat out the last four years with their uniforms in mothballs. Amongst them, too, there are famous names, like Camus, Cocteau and their little bug-eyed friend, Jean-Paul Sartre. It often horrified Sartre, the sight of Paris in revolt. Once, he spotted a crowd gathered round a burning truck with a young German trapped inside. 'Let him roast like a pig!' roared the crowd. This gruelling scene was only relieved by the sight of another onlooker, who took pity on the German, braved the flames, and shot him in the head.

Paris in revolt was always richly surreal. People continued to swim and sunbathe along the Seine while tanks fought overhead. Ricochets caught people indiscriminately, splashing brains across breakfast or felling a man as he hauled in a beautiful perch. The dead were stored in the meat freezers at Les Halles, and the rubbish piled up in the streets. Vlassov's men – *les Mongols* – were seen again, hacking off jewellery and blasting everything that moved. Once, a circus was caught in the cross-fire but the housewives were soon there, cutting up the animals to eat.

Parisians always chose beautiful places to die. Some of the worst wounded were taken off to the calm, cool cloisters of the Hôtel Dieu (which now, after nearly six hundred years of medicine, is about to close). Others went to La Comédie Française. For a dying Frenchman, this is as good as it gets, with expensive marble at his back and Victor Hugo gazing down from above. 'Tragedies in France always have a touch of Vaudeville,' wrote Arthur Koestler, 'and the place where they play tragedies is called la Comédie Française'. The old theatre had come out well in the battle, although this had little to do with its defence. At one point, all that stood between *tragédie* and tyranny was Edith Piaf, a band of actors armed with stage revolvers, and her boyfriend, Yves Montand.

'We freed ourselves!' the concierge told me. 'No one came to help!'

Funny how easily people forget the giant armies, massed around the city.

60

From Notre Dame, I walked out across the beautiful, pampered battle-field of Paris. Baron Haussmann would have been proud to see how his great design had worked, opening like a sluice to flush disorder from the city. 'Architecture is nothing more than administration,' he once said, as he cleared the slums for his exquisite military scheme and his interlocking fields of fire. For him, planning cities was like sketching the outlines of a campaign, and all it needed was armies to bring it all to life. The only thing that would have surprised him about the battle of 1944 is that the forces of disorder were German, and that the Army of the Republic was barely French at all.

I began at the *hôtel de ville*. Few buildings in the world have played such a pivotal role in convincing bureaucrats that civic duty shouldn't look like work. Even in its name there was no suggestion that this was the place in charge of litter, or licences for drains. It was an outrageous spectacle of stone – towers, twiddles, drunken nymphs, poets tottering along the pediments, and philosophers in every niche. It seems that such confusion had served it well during the German siege. For five days it was pitted with cannon fire without anyone realising that between them the *fonctionnaires* had only seven firearms, most of which were harmless. Unless the city was to be pecked to bits, it was going to need some help.

At first, the town hall's pleas were ignored. Eventually, however, with the revolt on the brink of collapse, Eisenhower dispatched a huge African army of 12,000 warriors. It was commanded by a magnificent viscount, whose *nom de guerre* was 'General le Clerc'. Amongst his men were foot-soldiers from Chad, Moroccans, Senegalese, some pom-pommed marines, several hundred white officers straight from the desert, *les Chasseurs d'Afrique* and a detachment of Algerian mountaineers. They must have made an extraordinary impression as they tore through the Norman countryside, like something from the pages of Rider Haggard. At the very sight of them, Paris opened up and that evening the first of their tanks reached the *hôtel de ville*, and there the crew got out. Despite their outlandish costumes, the crowd was surprised to discover that they were Parisians. They'd been on the road for four years, had fought across two continents and now they were home.

The city dissolved in pleasure. For a while the *hôtel de ville* almost disappeared in a cacophony of bells, gunfire, squeals and flags. The Germans even added a few sound effects of their own. Sensing that the end was near, their anti-aircraft guns opened up all night, even though there was nothing in the sky. It was like 1812 all over again, except this time France had won.

Actually, there was still a battle to be fought, and so I followed the Africans up Rivoli and into the Place de la Concorde. With all its granite emptiness and crushing parallel lines, this has always struck me as the bleakest feature of the Haussmann design. It's fine for guillotines and cenotaphs but there's not much here for the living. For several days, the two sides' tanks slogged it out across this urban plain, crashing through the Tuileries and smashing up the trees. During one of these duels, a panzer took a pot-shot at a Sherman, way off under the Arc de Triomphe, but his shell missed and fizzled harmlessly overhead. This was a fatal error; every French schoolboy knows that the Champs-Elysées is exactly 1,800 metres long. The *chasseurs* turned their gun on the German, recalibrated the sights and ruptured it in one.

There was much damage in the spats that followed but Paris has worn its indignities well. The Quai d'Orsay was never a carcass for long, and the twin clocks were now back in their towers goggling over the city. Gone too were the charcoal hulls and the wreaths, and the epitaphs written in soot: *'Ici sont morts 3 soldats Francais'*. Even the Grand Palais had recovered from a spiteful fire, and had risen again like a giant soufflé of glass.

*

From Concorde, I turned into Rivoli and walked back, along the arcades. It was now mostly just tourists here, grazing their way through the souvenirs. But on 24 August 1944 it was the *Tirailleurs de Tchad*, flitting from arch to arch. They were looking for the Hôtel Meurice.

The Meurice was still surprisingly unobtrusive, considering it had been pampering the rich for almost two hundred years. I noticed that, from the outside, the only sign of its stupendous hospitality was a liveried footman and a revolving door, made, it seemed, from gold. It was here that I paused, wondering whether they'd let me in, in my well-kebabed coat and a pair of wintry boots. The Africans had held no such qualms, and had rolled a phosphorous bomb through the golden gates and then shot their way into the lobby. I can only imagine that this intrusion produced much the same reaction as my own, which was another line-up of flunkies affecting a look of pleasant surprise.

This seraphic welcome continued all the way inside. I think I'd expected that – at any moment – I'd be picked up in tongs, and dropped down a chute. But, of course, it never happened and instead I was swished through what seemed like several acres of eau-de-Nil and gilt. Almost every wall was covered in period hunting scenes, blushing shepherdesses and winsome young bucks like girls with guns. Meanwhile, entire orgies had floated up into the frescos, and a cup of tea, I noticed, cost the same as a night on Huchette. Like Hausmann's city, it was all so overwhelmingly grand that if a person wasn't welcome, he'd usually work it out for himself.

At some stage, I came across a list of those who'd stayed here. It was printed on thick cream card, and looked like a menu for people who eat kings and queens. I could see Queen Victoria, the Sultan of Zanzibar, the Maharaja of Jaipur and a handful of other imperial Zogs. The Meurice, it seemed, was also a refuge for those heaved out of their homes. Amongst the royal refugees I spotted the Duke of Windsor, the Shah of Persia and the kings of Spain and Montenegro. Perhaps that's why General von Choltitz, the old *Kommandant* of Paris, had stayed here. It was as good a place as any to enjoy one's fall from grace.

'He had Room 213,' said the receptionist, as if he'd just checked out.

People were odd like this, in the way they remembered von Choltitz. I once heard a tour guide describe him as 'The Saviour of the City', when all he'd ever wanted was to save himself. His great advantage in life was that everyone assumed he was something he wasn't. The Parisians held him in awe, assuming he'd destroyed Warsaw (which he hadn't). Hitler, on the other hand, assumed it was the sort of thing he'd *like* to do, and therefore when Paris rose in revolt, he put von Choltitz in command. 'Paris must not fall into the hands of the enemy,' Hitler told him, 'except as a field of ruins.' No monument was to be left standing, the population were to be pounded into oblivion and von Choltitz was to perish in the rubble. He even looked the type to carry out such a fatuous endeavour. He was ruddy and monocled and shaven like a walrus, and although he was middle-aged and stubby, he tended to bounce around as if he was looking for a fight.

But von Choltitz was no philistine, saw no point in the destruction of Paris, and had little truck with Hitler. For a while, he kept his master happy by sending him ludicrous reports that only the saner staff would understand: he'd put three tons of dynamite under Notre Dame; he was about to topple the Eiffel Tower in order to block the river, and he'd be blowing up the Arc de Triomphe to provide clearer fields of fire. Von Choltitz, of course, was merely buying time. All he really wanted was for the Allies to arrive so that he didn't have to surrender to the mob. He even sent them messages asking them to hurry (although he warned that Prussian honour forbade him from giving up without a fight). That night, as the Africans entered the city, he sent them directions to the Meurice, and settled down to dinner. He wished his officers well in the days to come, and – just for the record – told them to fight to the end.

But, when – eventually – the Africans found the hotel and came bursting into the lobby, there was no one firing back. Instead, their lieutenant was taken up to Room 213, where he found von Choltitz resplendent in his monocle.

The lieutenant couldn't think what to say. 'Do you speak English?' he tried.

'Yes,' said the *Kommandant*. 'Probably better than you.'

With that, he was taken away to the Préfecture. But it was not the last he saw of the Meurice. He returned in 1959, when the manager found him wandering round the lobby. 'Can I help you?' he asked.

'I lived here for a while,' said the general absently, peering into the gilt.

It was immediately obvious who he was, and a strange scene followed. It was almost as if everyone had forgotten the roles they'd played in the past. Paris fêted the general for saving the city but von Choltitz never looked comfortable in laurels. Although he was pleased to see the city restored, there was always a sense of shame. Against all his military instincts, he'd disobeyed his orders from above.

With von Choltitz gone, the last of the fighting moved back across the river.

I found it hard to imagine how the gardens here had become a last resort. There was almost no cover and the School of Mines was mostly made of glass. Nature was long ago banished from the Jardin du Luxembourg, and replaced with a cleansing vista of gravel and geometry, and lacy cordons of espaliered pear. On a crunchy winter day it looked magnificently exposed, far too formal for human incursion. The only people I ever saw here were old bearded men like prophets – dressed in greatcoats and newspaper – and the police, trying to herd them back to the city.

Over on the other side of the gardens, I came across Liberty herself, or – more formally – *La Liberté éclairant le Monde*. Although much smaller than her sister statue in New York, she had at least witnessed liberty in action. That last day, 25 August, she'd have seen the gravel sizzle, and the *Ecole des Mines* shudder and dissolve in a shower of glass. Some of the last explosions were caused by people stumbling into booby traps, or children playing in the junk. Meanwhile, the SS continued to hold the Senate, at the far end of the gardens, until the evening, when loudspeaker vans brought them news of the German surrender. Over 250 of them staggered out of the building, which still looks painfully nibbled.

From the Senate, I turned down Rue de l'Odéon on a detour I knew was futile. This street had always been quirky; Thomas Paine wrote *The Rights of Man* at Number 16, and these days it was the place to come and buy an opera costume or drink Guinness at the *bistro Irlandais*. But it was Number 12 that I was after. For much of the early twentieth century, this was the bookshop for the writers in exile: Stein, Pound, Joyce, Eliot, Virgil Thomson and Man Ray. Shakespeare & Co. had even arranged for the publication of books that no one else would take, like *Ulysses* (which was seen as filth), and during the occupation it had offered its own literary resistance. When the owner, an American called Sylvia Beach, refused to sell a German officer a copy of *Finnegans Wake*, she was interned and the shop was closed. But the stock survived this ordeal, and was hidden away in the flat upstairs, which it shared with Samuel Beckett. Sadly, all trace of this had now gone, and although

Number 12 was still a bookshop, it dealt only in yoga and Ayurvedic massage.

I suddenly felt rather spare, wondering what to do next. Perhaps Miss Beach had felt the same, on her return from prison. But liberation day was always full of surprises, and suddenly shooting started, up on the roofs above. Soon a band of wild and filthy *maquisards* appeared, to blast away a sniper. To her surprise, Miss Beach noticed that at the head of the band was her oldest and best customer. It was Ernest Hemingway, enjoying a private war.

Hemingway was delighted to be back in Paris, and at the head of his own little army. Technically, he was a journalist working for *Collier's* magazine, but he could never resist a fight (he was later court-martialled for this breach of the rules of war but – with friends everywhere – he soon had the whole thing dropped). By attaching himself to Leclerc's army, he arrived in Paris well ahead of any other Americans and then struggled to get into the action (his efforts were once described by the historian Stephen Ambrose as 'brave, foolish and sentimental'). He was almost killed in the Bois de Boulogne when a chestnut tree exploded, and then – when he got lost – he ordered his men to torture a German by applying a candle to his toes.

For Hemingway, the liberation was a disappointment. He declared it 'chickenshit as to fighting', and then, after flushing out Shakespeare & Co. and the Travellers Club, he set off to liberate the bars.

61

My own little tour of the liberation ended where it began, in front of Notre Dame.

I'd always enjoyed this extraordinary building, and so did many others. Every time I went there I saw the same man covered in pigeons, and even the touts looked businesslike and sleek. Everything seemed to thrive in its Gothic glow and after seven hundred years the stone was still alive. Despite its mountainous height, it all looked as light as a tent, and I wasn't surprised to read that the transept walls were nearly two-thirds glass. There would surely be no better place to celebrate the wonder and freedom of France, which is what de Gaulle did on 26 August 1944.

Almost a million people joined him as he marched across the city, to celebrate the Te Deum. It was their day; without them, Paris would have fallen, but not with so much ease. There was no mention of the role taken by the Allies. 'Paris liberated!' de Gaulle boomed. 'Liberated by herself!' He wasn't even deterred by the crackle of snipers, and when firing suddenly burst from the belfry and the congregation ducked, he was the only one left standing. Here, if only France had known it, was a tantalising glimpse of the next twenty years, many of which were de Gaulle's. (Some say the moment was staged, a risky strategy amidst such chaos. The Free French had already fought a costly battle with themselves, across the River Seine.)

It was also a valedictory for Leclerc, who'd led a measured and courageous campaign. Three years later, he was killed in a mysterious plane crash which left nothing but a molten medal. How differently the twentieth century might have been if he'd survived. He'd always argued that Ho Chi Minh should have Vietnam, and that the West should leave it alone.

But this was also a day of celebration. Outside, the children sang, *'Nous ne les reverrons plus/ C'est fini, ils sont foutus'* ('We won't be seeing them again/ It's over, they're completely fucked'), and the adults went wild. Some say it was the party of the century, but others weren't so sure. Simone de Beauvoir describes a *débauche de fraternité*, an entire city in a state of jubilant copulation. Even the *Sunday Telegraph* correspondent, a hard-drinking, curmudgeon called R.W. Thompson, found himself head over heels in more than he could handle:

> I remember climbing out of a tangle of limbs, on a vast divan on which my companions of the night still slept, peacefully and extraordinarily beautifully . . . Perhaps the genius of Paris is that sin is seldom sordid and often beautiful.

Well, perhaps, but the Catholic Church didn't think so. 'In the gaiety of liberation,' it urged, in some hastily printed tracts, 'do not throw away your innocence.' Never was advice more roundly ignored, especially in a city rediscovering pleasure. For a while, it looked as if life was blooming again. Yehudi Menuhin began a new season of concerts, and Ernst and Miró held exhibitions. But Picasso's pictures infuriated the Parisians. 'Explain! Explain!' they shouted, as they tore them off the wall. After four years of Nazism, they'd forgotten what it was to be surreal.

Meanwhile, with victory came the Americans (or perhaps it was the other way round). Three days after Notre Dame, two US divisions appeared, and so the new occupation began.

62

Six months after the American arrival, Flint turned up on his two-day pass.

'We arrived' he said, 'at the Gare du Nord.'

Thousands of trains later, I found myself pulling in behind him. I'd done this journey several times before, and yet it was always full of surprises. London was only two and half hours up the track (and Alsace about the same), and one moment I'd be sitting down to a Full English, and the next I'd be in the heart of Paris. The statistics of this transition were bewildering: every day, Eurostar staff washed 36,000 glasses and 80,000 pieces of cutlery. Of course, it was different for Flint. He'd spent the journey bunging himself up on K-rations, in a train that was freezing, boarded up, broken and foul. The soldiers joked that it was all deliberate, designed to deter them from taking leave, but this was hardly true. Eisenhower had set aside 10,000 beds for the use of combat troops.

The next surprise was always the station itself. From the inside, the Gare du Nord looked like an art gallery full of trains. But on the outside, it was guarded by huge stone women, voluptuously naked and armed to the hilt. This was a startling sight for new arrivals and a portent of things to come. In Paris, sex was a sure-fire seller, and everything – from railway tickets to yoghurt – came with a face full of rump. Pert breasts, knotted couples and tight buttocks were now the constant motifs of French commercial life. Sex even sold sex, and these dangerous-looking doxies would have been perfect for the American purpose. Every soldier coming down from Normandy carried an inch-by-inch guide to Parisian brothels, entitled *France Zone Handbook No. 16*. As General Patton put it, 'A soldier who won't fuck won't fight.'

A surprising arrival would then turn into a curious walk through the city. It only took about half an hour to get to the old reception centres around Opéra. Along the way, there was a little Jerusalem and a little Beirut, and it was quite common to see a whole family on roller-skates or a drunk with a bottle of VSOP. This was the Paris one either loved or loathed, with its dog-pee grating, its sexy ads and gypsy quartets. I was always surprised at how helpful people were, offering directions if ever I paused, and at how many women were scavenging through the bins. SANS RESSOURCES, said their little signs, SANS DOMICILE, which I always thought made their destitution sound almost geological and magnificently bleak.

But if Paris now wore its poverty rather ostentatiously, it was even worse in 1944. 'The Parisians were in tough shape,' warned Flint, as if he expected me to find that nothing had changed. The city, he said, had been black with grime, the fountains didn't work, and there was no coal or heating during one of the coldest winters ever. The Parisians themselves had looked raw from washing in icy water, and clacked around in wooden shoes because there was no longer any leather. Girls wore their skirts short, not because it was fashionable but because it was all they could afford. According to an official report, one in ten people were *défavorisé*, or chronically poor, and one in six buildings in a state of ruin. 'Family life is at the point of total disintegration,' wrote the official, 'and the level of promiscuity is quite beyond belief.'

Flint had said much the same. 'Sex was cheaper than chocolate.'

As in Marseille, hunger had brought people on to the streets. Parisians became connoisseurs of rubbish and would fight for the pickings in the gutter. Half-eaten K-rations were the real prize although there was also a brisk trade in cigarette ends, which were sold in bundles of ten. 'You'd even see pretty girls diving into the garbage,' said Flint. But many found it easier to barter: a pack of Luckies for a grapple in the dark.

Flint still winced at the thought of Parisians. To have witnessed their collapse of dignity was one thing, but to understand the insult they'd suffered was quite another. Even years later, Americans would find themselves unnerved by the amorality of Paris. In 1947, Arthur Miller took a room in a hotel around the corner from mine. It was an eerie time to be living in the quarter, with a concierge dressed in disintegrating coat-tails, and a 'hungry-looking prostitute' who sat in the lobby all night watching passers-by 'with a philosopher's superior curiosity'. Like Flint, the experience would never leave him. As he later wrote, 'There really was such a thing as a defeated people.'

63

Opéra had long since swept away the American suburb that settled here in 1944.

It was now back to being what it always was, a lunchtime quarter of sandwiches and cut flowers, and shutters down at five. At one end of Boulevard de la Madeleine was the Opéra itself – like a box of imperial jewels – and, at the other was the church of La Madeleine, which the rich seemed to think was grand (but which everyone else thought was merely big and ought to be a station). Few areas of Paris felt so emotionally uninhabited. At night, the entire boulevard glowed orange and the only sign of life was the vapid white aura that surrounded McDonald's. Ironically, this building was once the very heart of American life in Paris. When the Red Cross were here, a combat soldier could have had whatever he'd wanted – or at least a shower, or a shoeshine or a night between white sheets.

Perhaps Paris had never forgiven Madeleine for being so foreign. The city hadn't taken long to resent its heroes from overseas. The problem was mostly one of supply and demand; the Americans had all the supplies and yet they made all the demands. Many Parisians complained that their requirements were even greater than those of the Germans. There was much to resent: Americans had their own eggs, fish, meat and butter; they'd requisitioned 167 heated hotels; they rode in jeeps whilst the Parisians walked; they had free movies, free cigarettes, free transport and yet they kept demanding more.

The Americans had, on the other hand, supplied their own crime wave, an embellishment that Paris could have done without. By December 1944, there were over 17,000 US deserters living rough in the city (and this would double during the battles of New Year). Only one of them ever found his own way back to the States, and the rest became drifters. Many took up gangster lives, trading in stolen gas and tyres and shooting up the local hoods ('The Americans are barbarians,' declared the French military governor. 'Worse than the Russians'). Other runaways simply shacked up with a whore, and waited for it all to end.

There were still girls working the American bars along the Rue de Seze. As I walked past they'd spring out into the freezing night, wearing only their bikinis. There was something other-worldly and reptilian about these half-naked figures hissing in the cold. If I was to understand anything of Flint's Paris, I'd have to move north and settle down amongst the vice.

64

I decided to begin with a little sexual archaeology, and moved up to Montmartre.

It was a curious part of Paris, easily given to fantasy. I often felt that Montmartre was like an island, bobbing around several hundred feet above the city. Almost everybody living up there had exiled themselves from the ordinary. All the dogs were Dalmatians, and most people did something baroque like gilding, lute-making or barometer repair. I once saw an old man wearing headphones made of rags and wire, as if unable to bear any further intrusion into this world of his own.

But Montmartre was not so much dislocated as dissipated. As on previous visits, I had the feeling I'd just missed something – a spectacular drinking binge perhaps, a demonstration (*'Non à la sobriété!'*) or a spirited riot. I'm sure other tourists felt the same, and – as we waded through the placards and fruit peel – there was a collective sense of disappointment as we realised we'd arrived a day too late, or perhaps even a century. Exploring Montmartre was like climbing up through the remains of a very old hangover. Even though it was early in the morning, the locals were still shaking out tablecloths or crumpled over a brandy, trying to 'kill the worm'. A few hadn't even got out of the clothes of the night before – loud check tracksuits and sparkly shirts – and by lunchtime the only creature left standing at my local bar was another huge dog, with its tongue lolling over the taps.

But whatever had sapped Montmartre, it had been sapping it for years. My favourite eatery, the Café des Deux Moulins, was so chronically dissolute that it had turned a spectacular liverish yellow. Despite this, the food was always inspired and recklessly cheap: lemony swordfish, rocket and huge slices of *chèvre*. Most of the other customers seemed to be in the throes of either galloping alcoholism or a creative breakthrough. Some were dancers, who'd wafted up from Pigalle, and they all ate like birds and smoked like fish. Oddly enough, it was the Americans who were the first to discover the pleasures on the hill – at least in numbers. After the Great War, thousands of US soldiers, mostly black, had settled up here, and the place became a *nouveau* New Orleans. 'After the sun went down,' wrote the great diva, Blacktop, 'Paris did become the city of light, and Montmartre changed from a sleepy little village to a jumpin' hot town.' Well, maybe – although nowadays the *quartier* is more slumpin' than jumpin'.

Of course it wasn't long before people started mixing sex with their swordfish and rocket. By the Twenties, the Rue Houdon – where I'd selected a crumbly hotel – had a well-founded reputation for good value, and whores at 'rock-bottom prices'. Such claims no longer surprised me in Paris, and the only mystery was how Montmartre had managed to get more than its fair share of the action. Just what was it that had made so many gallants clamber up the hill to clamber on to an *entraîneuse*? A persistent, puerile thought kept pointing me upwards to Sacré-Coeur, whose huge, milky-white mammary domes were a constant taunt to the imagination of Parisian men. The artists had always been the first to weaken at Montmartre's charms, and both Degas and Lautrec had sprawled its girls across the canvas. The poster artist, Aristide Bruant, had called them *les Pierreuses*, the Ladies of the Stone, and Guy de Maupassant brought his friend, Flaubert, up here to demonstrate that he could ejaculate at least six times a night and probably more.

For a moment, it seemed my hotel had survived its energetic past and that my archaeology was about to be swamped in real life. ALL COMFORTS PROVIDED, said a sign outside, although this promise clearly wasn't architectural.

'The bathroom's on the fourth floor,' said the owner.

'And my room?' I asked.

'On the sixth.'

A narrow staircase led up through the building, like a coiled spine of cast iron and lino. At each floor, narrow passages dog-legged away into the darkness, all strung with wet clothes and heaped with boxes and bottles. I passed the bathroom, which – despite its vegetative colouring – I never saw unoccupied again, and continued into the roof. My room, like all the others, was tiny, and had once been rented by the hour. There were only two bits of furniture, a bed that had been ritualistically scorched with a cigarette, and a wardrobe heaped with newspapers and crusts of soap. As an afterthought, I'd been left a small, abrasive towel which, I noticed, had picked up much of the bathroom. Surprisingly, these sparse features had left no room for me, and so in order to get to the window I had to vault over the bed. It was a rewarding leap because, from here,

I was almost at a level with the Eiffel Tower and could see all the way down the Rue Houdon, which was empty by day and echoed all night. As Eiffel's spotlight began to scrape the sky, I settled down in my charred bed and began to wonder what noises would come bubbling up through the plumbing.

But instead of the groans and squeaks of commercial sex, all I ever heard were vaguely Saharan sounds, the dithyrambic gurgle of Arabic and the clatter of metal pans. It seems that a new underclass had taken over the hotel, and that I'd got the place quite wrong (the clue had been in the name, the Hôtel Surcouf, and in the pictures of camels and water-wheels pasted round the hall). I was back amongst the North Africans, and although I was happy about this, it was not Marseille. Here, the *sidis* (as they were known) were less obtrusive, and lived six to a room and stored their food on the sills. Although they made campfire noises by night, by day they were gone – out cleaning, begging, roasting chestnuts and, as far as they could, cultivating invisibility.

That night, I woke up, wondering what would happen if the Surcouf caught fire. On the back of the door was a fire notice, which simply advised, DON'T GET EXCITED. It was hard to imagine the state of non-excitement that would prevail as great balls of flame began convecting up the stairwell and licking through the tiny rooms. Or perhaps the notice was more a matter of social comment than practical advice. The North Africans were not supposed to get excited, and nor would anyone else. (When, two weeks later, an almost identical hotel on Rue de Provence caught fire, twenty-one immigrants died in the heat and crush. 'The most shocking thing,' said one witness, 'was to see children being thrown from the windows by their parents and there was no one there to catch them.' Meanwhile, the dead were carried into the cosmetics department of the Galeries Lafayette

North African Chestnut-seller
Saint Michel, Paris.

Beggar, near Madeleine.

although the store remained open as usual.) The North Africans, it seems, had become *les nouveaux misérables*.

This was not the only thought that troubled me as I lay awake in my chattering attic. What had happened to my research? And, more to the point, what had happened to the whores? Every time I thought about this question, I kept coming up with the same answer, which was 122.

At about the time France was settling down to its disastrous twentieth-century, 'The One Two Two' was emerging as the best brothel in town. It was only a few blocks from my hotel, on Rue de Provence (the same street, as it happens, as the great immigrant fire). It was a long grimy road of cheap hotels and detective agencies, but it wasn't long before I was outside Number 122. To the pimps of the 1930s, the number had sounded pleasingly brisk and perfunctory, and so the name had stuck.

It was still a rather undecided-looking building. At street level, it was a Roman fortress with enormous wooden doors, and from there it climbed up through a whole range of fantasies: neo-Egyptian, Italianate (Milanese plush), well-disciplined art deco, a hint of Baroque, and finally Babylonian, complete with hanging gardens and fence of spears. Such a smorgasbord of styles, it seems, had been good for business, and the choices had continued inside. During its heyday, the One Two Two had boasted a Tarzan suite, a hayloft, a Roman temple, a room decorated like the Orient Express (which rocked around at the flick of a switch), a torture chamber, a gondola, a medieval tent, an igloo, and a pirate's cabin (complete with mermaid lashed to the mast). Nowhere better exemplified the rise (and eventual fall) of the Parisian knocking shop, and no one tells the story better than its *madame*, Fabienne Jamet. In 1964, with the money all gone, she'd sat down to write her indignant kiss-and-tell, *One Two Two*.

Fabienne was perfect for the task, bereft of taste and happily uncluttered by morals. Her father had been an inspector in the vice squad, until he'd gone with instincts and started peddling girls. By the age of fourteen, Fabienne had lost her virginity, and at seventeen she was on the game. But in this, she was at least blessed with good looks. In the photographs that have survived, she has filmstar features, a full and sensual mouth and eyes that twinkle with cash. In 1935, at the age of twenty-five, she'd shacked up with her pimp, Marcel Jamet, and taken over the One Two Two. No couple deserved each other more. Jamet was volcanically violent and had been brought up catching rats on the ruined *fortifs* of the Paris Commune. But although he was gypsy by nature, he was aristocratic by inclination. He drove a huge Cadillac and even when he went to jail, he'd dine on pheasant and claret.

I was sorry to have missed out on the spectacle of the pre-war One Two Two. While Marcel fought and cheated and snuffled up champagne, Fabienne presided over everything as the Queen of Tack. New guests were led up a livid moss-green carpet to the 'selection salon' where they could choose a *courtisane* from a plinth ('a miraculous picnic of human flesh,' as Fabienne described it, still inured to the palpably grotesque). Sometimes, the guests ate dinner before repairing upstairs for their gondola ride or a roll in the hay. These dinners tended to be more lascivious than lavish; it was always the same beef but the serving girls (who were naked and painted so that they glowed in the dark) were always on hand, fluffing up the main business of the house. Amongst the guests there were a few names I recognised: Charlie Chaplin, Cary Grant, Marlene Dietrich and the dancer Mistinguett (the last two both bisexual), and a well-oiled Ettore Bugatti. I also spotted a few refugees from the Meurice, like the King of Belgium and a Maharaja who liked to get the girls crawling around on the floor, looking for his glass eye.

The sex was almost as extravagant as the preliminary manoeuvres. There were sixty girls working the premises, mostly ignorant Bretons. Each was expected to service at least four men a day, and by each bed was a little bottle, the label of which read, 'Gentlemen, be so kind as to disinfect yourself.' With her peculiar sense of pride, Fabienne noted the diversity of her clients' demands, and – if the money was right – the range of her ladies' abilities; at the punters' request, they'd pee on them or strangle them, or dress up in rubber, and – as she put it – '5 ou 6 acceptent de se faire sodomiser'. There was also a blind man who liked to pick his girls by hand, and a banker who came back time after time to lie in a coffin as if he was dead. The English were gentlemen, noted Fabienne, and the Americans 'less well bred'. The Russians, on the other hand, were like animals.

All of this was perfectly legal. The only rules were that the brothel had to have solid shutters (always closed), that the girls didn't stand under streetlamps, and that no two sisters worked in the same *maison*. The rules didn't even change when the Germans took over the city. Although the Jamets were always more chancers than traitors, the brothel thrived; there was an endless supply of smuggled champagne and American cigarettes; the stars still came, and Edith Piaf sang in the salon. Meanwhile, during the Battle of Britain, the place was full of *Luftwaffe* pilots, all popping amphetamines and belting out the words to 'Tipperary' and other English marching songs.

Strangely, the liberation had been less kind to the whores. At first they rushed out to greet their new clients, but all was not as it seemed. The Americans were difficult customers; they kept demanding stewed maize ('What kind of a dish is that?' shrieked Fabienne), and then they shot up the Japanese Room and tried to strangle the black girl. Almost worse were the French themselves, who'd developed an awkward case of self-righteousness. Within a year, all brothels were banned, and more than 7,000 registered prostitutes were turned out on to the streets. Marcel went back to jail, and Fabienne began a new life selling oysters, smuggling gold and running an illicit cathouse in Les Halles. She was eventually sentenced to three years' loss of civil rights, and never went back to 122. Ironically, the house itself passed to a trade association dealing in leather and skin, and now – after several changes of ownership – it's become a little bank.

'What *salon*?' said a man I caught on the steps. 'It's nothing like that now.'

As if to prove it, he asked me in, and we both stood, peering up into the void.

'See?' he said. 'Nothing.'

Six fancy floors had been scooped away and replaced with rafts of steel and glass. The banker had never heard of the Jamets, and had no idea of the great and varied loins that had wriggled around his head. When I told him about the hayloft and the mermaid, he started looking at me strangely and so I let the matter drop. There was just one last thing.

'Do you still get prostitutes on the Rue de Provence?'

'Of course,' he said. 'They've worked this street for years.'

I was reminded of this two weeks later, when I heard about the fire. It's said that the girls were the first on the scene, and the first to brave the flames.

65

France, of course, had long since recovered from its severe attack of virtue. Although the great *maisons de tolérance* would never reopen, prostitution had returned to the economy. In Paris, the authorities now estimated that there were over 20,000 people fully engaged in the sex industry, providing a range of services from domination to dressing up as sheep. The city also came up with the puzzling statistic that there were another 6,000 at it 'part-time'. I had no idea that there were degrees of harlotry, and that one could simply clock off and become something else.

'But where's the Red Light District?' I'd ask my French friends.

'Everywhere,' said the Alsatians; 'the whole city's ablaze.'

'Nowhere,' said others. 'They all do it on the web.'

Most however agreed that the fornication was probably at its most pantomimic in Pigalle. This, of course, suited me fine, because Pigalle began at the bottom of my street. It had also happened to be the first port of call for every GI looking for a specialist to scratch away his itch.

66

It would be possible to spend all day and much of the night browsing the sex souks of Pigalle. Even on a brittle Sunday morning, it was business as usual; the streets were puddled in neon, the air was slick with onions and the touts were twitchy and manic. It was remarkable the things I could have bought before the rest of Paris had even stirred. One place was like a human tack-shop, selling bridles and harnesses, and whips that would have made a carthorse weep. Another specialised in devil-wear, all finished off in squeaky red rubber, together with '*aphrodisiaques, inflatables et poppers*'. There was also a Supermarché Erotique, and a Museum of Sex, which was really just a fancy collection of priapic art (including a statue of an indignant-looking memsahib getting her comeuppance from a tiger). Even the saunas were open at this early hour, offering FREE ENTRY FOR COUPLES, and ringside seats for everyone else. Live love, it seems, never sleeps.

Along the Boulevard de Clichy were the peep-shows and the promise of no holds barred. These stalls always seemed amusingly amateur with their star-spangled curtains and feverish doggy-pleasured photos. One even bore a sign that said: MODELS WANTED. BEGINNERS ACCEPTED. But however half-hearted they may have looked from the outside, the touts were perfectly serious. Once, one of them grabbed me by the arm and hauled me into her onion-scented aura. I remember thinking what enormous nostrils she had, and had a sudden vision of toppling into the void. She meanwhile saw only euros toppling into her pockets, twenty-five to be precise.

'Private massage included,' she rasped, in English.

I tried to shrink from her grip. 'Just looking,' I croaked.

The nostrils flared. 'Listen, *copain*, you come to Paris to relax!'

She was still shouting out prices as I wriggled away, ducking down a side-street. There was more relaxing to be had down here – American bars, with stringy Asian girls pressed up against the glass. Some of them were dressed only in little patches of PVC, and were vigorous in the marketing of its removal. 'Good time, Mister?' hissed one, through a chink in the door, 'Blowjob? Two on one?' Only once was I almost tempted to further investigation. A middle-aged woman approached me, immaculately dressed in a cardigan and pearls, and at first I thought she'd lost her poodle or wanted some help with her shopping. Instead, I found myself being steered towards some ominously tinted doors. 'Come inside,' she said, with a flawless American drawl, 'I want to show you what happens next . . .' In this world of the bleakly obvious – this desert of the imagination – this was an intriguing offer but one I was happy to decline.

The soldiers of December 1944 had been faced with some similarly bewildering choices.

Hunger and liberation had brought on a sex boom. To men who'd seen nothing for the last eight weeks but mud and forest and wooden-shoed Alsatians, it was all too good to be true. According to the army newspaper, *Stars and Stripes*, 'Paris in privation had produced one of the prettiest crops of girls in living memory. For four years they had not eaten too much or loafed. And, above all, they'd had to travel by bicycle . . .'

Even better, this bumper harvest seemed to be up for sale. As always, the battalion newspaper, *Panther Tracks* was more forthcoming on the details. 'Gals, gals and all for you!' wrote one of Flint's men. 'A sharp chick walks up to you and whispers "Baby, zig zig, 200 francs" [\$4] and if you agree (and who doesn't?) you're taken to the nearest hotel for a wonderful evening.' Soon, every issue carried news of the going rates, what to expect, and comparisons with Brussels. 'An especially vivacious and well-rounded harlot,' reports one Private Finnigan, 'might demand a price of 600 francs. However, the price scales downwards for fair merchandise and mediocre stock. Some fairly delicious cold cuts can be had for 150 and 200 francs.'

Although Flint never shared his men's enthusiasm for this market in women, it was hard to avoid the girls. 'Soldiers on combat duty wore green felt flashes,' he said, 'and so the girls headed straight for them, because they were the ones most interested in sexual activity.'

These women, said Flint, would do anything to catch a soldier's eye. 'Sometimes, if you put a coin on the table, they'd pick it up in their vagina.'

But, whether for wheeled trollops, plump beauties or coin-eating genitalia, nowhere was quite like Pigalle. According to *Yank* magazine, this was the 'gaudiest, loosest, honky-tonk section of the continent'. Just as they'd done a generation before, the girls here had become adept at harvesting soldiers. One such greenhorn was the novelist, John Marquand, who seemed surprised to find that they'd done it all before:

We soldier chauvinists called it Pig Alley and GIs in filthy fatigues and muddy boots were hauled in from the front by six-by-six tracks and dumped loose on a forty-eight hour pass. The whores gathered at the truck stops to select the evening's clients, removing a man's helmet liner, running fingers through his scalp to check for lice.

Happily for me, with Flint there was no participation to copy. 'I was no goody-goody,' he told me, 'but *this* was depressing.'

The experience of Marseille had affected him, he said, and he found it all too much to bear. Besides, he was newly married, and Dorothy was eight months pregnant. No one would think any the worse of him if he saved his condom to keep his rifle clear of ice. Instead of sex he went to a show, and – as I was notionally bobbing along in his footsteps – I felt I ought to do the same. I therefore walked up the Boulevard de Clichy and bought a ticket for the Moulin Rouge.

I still despise myself for enjoying it all so much. Although the music was Cop Series *circa* 1970, and the décor ersatz sleaze, the show was outlandishly spectacular and gloriously silly. Momentarily, our cruel world was filled with girls wearing only sequins and coloured feathers ('Splendid girls,' recalled Flint, 'some of them very well structured'). This was how the rest of Pigalle would have looked, if only the punters had come by the coachful. At one point, the stage was a heaving mass of semi-naked Khmer queens, and then came Indian nymphettes, topless pirates, a troupe of well-greased contortionists, and a statuesque girl wearing only a *cache-sex*, astride six tiny, snorting ponies. This was followed by the Amazons again, like a tidal wave of feathers, and then, in the Grand Finale, one of them stripped off and dived into a tank of pythons. All around me I could hear the sound of Koreans dying of happiness.

Sure, it was overwhelming entertainment but – at €95 a pop – it was hardly soldierly. I had a feeling that I ought to experience the €10 show, three doors down, billed as the *'Spectacle Sexy'*.

67

It wasn't long before I came to realise that the show wasn't 'sexy', and that I was the only 'spectacle'.

It seems I'd misunderstood the concept from the start. Somehow, I'd imagined that I'd slip quietly into a scene by Toulouse-Lautrec, like *Au Moulin de la Galette*. It would be full of cheerfully grotesque people savouring a moment of pleasure in their gruelling lives, and I'd take a seat at the back, where I could sip an *anisette* and make my notes. Eventually, after some excitable chatter, a plump and popular woman would waft into the salon and, to roars of approval – and a tinkle from the piano – she'd peel off her corsets, and then, standing there in just her bloomers, toss her rhinestones into the crowd. If only.

The reality could hardly have been more different. Instead of a cheery salon, I was shown into a dark, mirrored room lined with banquette seats and lit with ghoulish scarlet bulbs. Despite the gloom, I could see that there was only one other figure waiting, and that was me – looking rather anxious and endlessly reflected from mirror to mirror, trailing off into infinity. As I sat down, the same Serb who'd whistled me in off the street brought me an inch of whisky – which was part of the deal – and placed it before me, on another abominable mirror. Then, out of the corner of my eye, I noticed two girls, who looked suspiciously like his daughters, flopping round the dance floor. I might have wondered what they were doing, if they hadn't been almost in the buff. They both had thin waxy bodies, and tiny grubby-looking breasts, and were convulsing to the music. It was only then that it dawned on me, the sheer poverty of my predicament. How had I ended up in a darkened room – alone – with two demented, half-naked teenagers, each entirely lost in a macabre world of her own? There wasn't even any way I could avert my gaze because the whole scene was repeated – infinitesimally – wherever I happened to look.

Miserably, I prayed for it all to end, which ten seconds later it did. This, however, only made matters worse, because the attention then turned from the dance floor back to me. Suddenly, I was covered in grimy limbs, the smell of old carpets and two weirdly thrusting waifs. I then felt hundreds of little bony hands probing through my coat, although it was hard to tell whether I was being groped or merely mugged. Neither, at that moment, was an attractive proposition and so I felt myself wriggling down the banquette, trying to extract myself from the tangle. At any other time, I might have found this funny, watching – in thousands of different dimensions – a tourist wrestling with a pair of Serbs dressed only in their knickers. Right then, however, it was more participation than I ever could have dreaded. Even now, I can still hear my slightly shrill efforts at conversation, and their grunted animal offers. It sounds like a management training video, richly spliced with horror.

'. . . I'm just doing a little research . . .'

'You want private massage?'

'. . . Suck-suck?'

'No, I, er . . . what's it like working here? Is the pay OK . . . ?'

'. . . Like my tits, you? Get some drinks, I eat you . . .'

'. . . Lickings . . .'

'. . . Buy champagne, my pants off . . .'

Eventually, even this lively exchange petered out, and the Serbs scrambled off the table and skulked off into the dark. As I sat there, alone, my whisky untouched, I realised that this was as good – or as bad – as Pigalle ever got. The girls may have been unhappy, or even miserable, but at least there were always people like me, ever willing to play the fool. Far-off, I could hear helpless whoops of laughter. Perhaps it was the Serbs. Or perhaps it was the distant howl of Panthers, echoing down the years.

68

But the ghosts of American Paris were nowhere more lively than on the Place Vendôme, at the Hôtel Ritz.

One evening, I scrubbed down my jacket and spruced up my boots and set off there for a drink. As soon as I arrived, however, I realised I needn't have bothered with such sartorial fuss. It was fashion week, and everybody else was kitted out in parachutes and baskets of ocelots, and I looked relatively inconspicuous, dressed for a walk in the woods.

It was typical of the Ritz to be so ambivalent in matters of style. With its saucy friezes, gold-plated light switches and swan-shaped taps, it occupies the operatic end of the hospitality spectrum. Upstairs, I discovered even more pinkness and swans, and ever more bell-pulls to bring maids and valets tumbling out of the panelling. The Ritz was said to provide more flunkies and more bread rolls per guest than any other hotel in the world, and – according to its musical website – it got through more than 100,000 orchids a year. It was hardly surprising that everything that's ever originated (or been filmed) here is just a little bit over the top – like Peach Melba, Grand Marnier or that great fluffy classic, *Love in the Afternoon*.

A line of sparkling glass cabinets led deep into the building. With a grocer's flair for opportunity, Mr Al-Fayed had rendered his flagship all things to all men. It was either a large hotel where one could shop, or a large shop where one could sleep. On the other hand, I wasn't entirely sure who was buying all this stuff; there were cravats, $50 socks, designer chopsticks, crystal buckets decorated with dying pheasants, pigskin co-respondent shoes, glass flowers, and some gruesome golden instruments, perhaps something to do with camels. After what seemed like half a mile of this extravagant bric-à-brac, I found what I was looking for, and that was the Hemingway Bar.

They were all here at the end, the best of America's wordsmiths. Even before Paris had finishing mopping up the Germans, the literati had assembled, and were throwing back the cocktails. There was Walter Cronkite, Ernie Pyle, Andy Rooney, a young sergeant called J.D. Salinger (enjoying what he described as 'the most rewarding minutes of the war'), Martha Gellhorn – fresh from the carnage of Normandy – and Mary Welsh, who was here with the *Life* crew, along with her boyfriend, the scriptwriter Irwin Shaw, now driving around in a jeep festooned in flowers. But chief amongst them, and buying all the drinks, was Gellhorn's husband, now in an advanced state of marination, Ernest Hemingway.

The bar still bore his name, a tribute not so much to his literary output as to his conspicuous consumption. Mr Al-Fayed had even managed to assemble a few pieces of doubtful Hemingwalia – fishing rods and sharks' jaws – as if Ernie was still here, bashing out his stories. In truth, he'd hardly done any work in Paris (two articles in as many months), and after liberating the bars he settled down to some serious drinking, beginning with the Ritz (his first order was for fifty dry martinis, one for each of his filthy guerrillas). His wife had only turned up to ask for a divorce, to which Hemingway happily agreed. As a parting shot, he gave a public rendition of a song called 'Martha Gellhorn's Vagina', and then liberated Shaw of his girlfriend, the winsome Mary Welsh. She, in due course, would suffer the unenviable fate of becoming Mrs Hemingway the Fourth.

His eponymous bar was still a convivial place to nurse a cocktail, taking it gently at a euro a sip. But, however genial and Father Christmassy he may have looked in the portraits hanging over the door, Hem of course had taken nothing gently. Most of his time at the Ritz, he'd behaved appallingly; he tried to bed Simone de Beauvoir, drank six bottles of whisky with Jean-Paul Sartre and challenged André Malraux (France's future Minister of Culture) to a fight; another time, he gave Picasso a bloodied SS tunic, telling him he'd killed the man himself. ('It was a lie,' wrote Picasso airily, and, in return, gave Hemingway a box of hand grenades.) Even Hemingway's more glittery friends found him rather tiring. For a while Marlene Dietrich hung around, singing on the edge of his bath. But it wasn't long before she tired of his language, and moved to another hotel.

It was usually Mary left mopping up, after long nights out with the troops. 'Your friends are drunks and slobs!' she once screamed. 'They threw up in my bathroom. They probably lost me my job. They drove Marlene away. They may be heroes in Germany but here they stink, stink, stink!' Typically, Hemingway punched her on the jaw, and then passed out. The pair always made it up the following day. Later, when Mary tried to curb his drinking, he ordered the bar staff to invent an odourless cocktail. It was clearly a success, and is still drunk to this day.

'Bloody Mary,' he boasted, 'didn't smell a thing.'

*

Not everyone enjoyed the Ritz. Simone de Beauvoir despised everything about it. For many Americans it was typically Parisian, and fitted neatly into the love-it-or-hate-it debate. As I wandered back through the glass flowers and dying pheasants. I heard two fashionistas purring away in New Yorkese.

'You know what this place needs?' said one.

'Yep,' said the other: 'a good smack widda baseball bat!'

Even Hemingway had been given to moments of overload. Once he took a pair of machine-pistols to his bathroom and shot it all to bits. He being Hemingway and this being the Ritz, everything was repaired the following day, and a brand new *salle de bain* was added to his bill.

69

I spent my last few days visiting the heroes of liberated Paris, or at least those interred in its clay.

Sartre and de Beauvoir were buried in a frozen graveyard in Montparnasse. Their tomb was curiously matrimonial considering that de Beauvoir was hardly domestic, and Sartre was seldom at home. They'd fought a gallant battle against received wisdom, Nazis and convention. On Sartre's grave was a huge bunch of carnations which I doubt would have pleased him greatly. Such a gesture implied that 'being' continued after 'non-existence', and that – in his long life of existentialism – he'd probably been wrong.

I found myself amongst less complicated heroes over at Père Lachaise. Leafy, ornate and compact, it was a city almost like Paris, except that everyone was dead. I padded the steep cobbled streets until gone dusk, looking for those I felt I knew. At one point, I nearly tumbled into a family residence that had been prised apart by roots, and then I had to clamber away, uphill past Balzac, Géricault and Proust. But, eventually, I found those I was after: Edith Piaf, her brutal life now just pictures in the granite; Alice Toklas, buried, it was said, in a suit by Pierre Balmain; and the great shapeless slab of Gertrude Stein. After twenty years' absence, she'd bought herself American forgiveness with a deathbed work, called *The Mother of Us All* (1946). 'It's not so much what Paris gives you,' she once said, rather obliquely, 'as what it doesn't take away.'

Over in the furthest corner, I came upon the fighters themselves in a street of angels and propellers. Pride of place went to Colonel Fabien, who'd fired the first underground shots in the Battle of Paris, and the last shots outside the Senate. Like many thousands of Frenchmen, he'd joined the regulars after liberation (within six months, the number of French divisions in the country had grown from one to seven). Like Flint, he served on the Alsace front, where the resurgent French would put up an astonishing fight. More than 30,000 of them were killed – twice as many as the Americans – including Fabien, who was caught in a volley of shells.

This wasn't quite the end of my valedictory tour. I happened to be in the church of Les Invalides the day Paris saw off one of the last heroes of its dwindling Légion d'honneur. Jacques Andrieux had escaped France in a lobster boat in 1940, only to return in a Spitfire cockpit, astride eight murderous high-speed cannons. Twelve kills later he was a national hero, earning himself a life in gold braid and a funeral in the finest of mink and drill. Even the altar was dressed in black, and the route of the hearse was lined with firemen in silver helmets and magnificent flame-proof suits. As the old *général* disappeared off to his place in the clay, a guard of aviators marched into the Grand Court and unleashed a volley of shots into the blameless, unblemished sky. At this, a vast untidy cloud of pigeons rose from the rooftops, hovered chaotically for a moment, and then crashed off over the city.

70

As the time came to leave, I found myself back on St-Germain. Although I was happy in most parts of Paris, I enjoyed the spontaneity here and the freedom from parallel lines. Perhaps that's why the artists had always liked it, out of range of Haussmann's ruler. There was once a time when the cafés here – Les Deux Magots and Brasserie Lipp – were packed with writers and painters, doing anything but work. People still crushed inside in the hope of glimpsing genius, but at €25-a-salad, the mood was hardly artistic. Now, most of the clientele were Japanese and camouflaged, or kids from Berkeley and Yale, who seemed to think no one would ever understand a love life described loudly and in English. It was easy to make mistakes like this, and to see oneself in a fantasy. 'Just remember,' warns one American guidebook, 'Paris is not Disneyland. That's still a train ride away.'

It hadn't taken the Americans long to rediscover the city after the disappointments of the Forties. Some were merely passing through – Gore Vidal, Saul Bellow and Truman Capote – and saw the cafés and sleaze as a sort of cultural rite of passage. 'Despite the waterfall hangovers and constantly cascading nausea,' wrote Capote, 'I was under the impression I was having a damn good time, the kind of educational experience necessary to an artist.'

But for those who'd stayed it was different. For them, unlike the moneyed Americans of the pre-war years, Paris was more a place of exile than excursion. Almost all of them were fleeing something peculiarly American: for Irwin Shaw, it was McCarthyism (seven years after liberating the Ritz, he was denounced, by studio boss Jack Warner, as 'a covert communist', and fled back to Paris for the next twenty-five years); for 1,500 blacks, like Chester Himes and Richard Wright, it was segregation (and Wright never went home again); for others, it was the cultural piety of the Fifties and the strictures on being homosexual, different or perhaps just mildly weird. Then there was another category – escapists of a sort – men like Lawrence Ferlinghetti and James Jones, who'd seen the full horrors of war and who'd drifted here in a state of lifelong disbelief.

It occurred to me, as I pottered along, from quarter to quarter, that – however happy I was, losing myself in Paris – I wouldn't be sorry to leave. Perhaps everyone reaches this point in the end. Paris was an alluring city, but it seldom felt accepting. With its museum streets and galleried stations, its public courting and its peep-show sex, its lofty populace and its magnificent tombs, nowhere had ever made me feel more alone, or more like a spectator. During the 1960s a report on Parisian prostitutes had noted that the girls never wanted their clients to be wholly satisfied, and they very seldom were. In this – and this alone – Paris was like its whores, averse to any redefinition of its relationships. Perhaps the greatest strength of Parisians – or their greatest weakness – was that they didn't care if they were despised. In his parting words to Paris, Hemingway wrote, 'She is like a mistress who does not grow old, and she has other lovers now.'

No one had felt this sense of dislocation – or intimacy denied – more keenly than the soldiers of 1944. According to *Yank* magazine, Paris was not all it was cracked up to be. 'After forty-eight hours,' said Flint, 'I was happy to go back to my men – despite the fact it meant returning to the front.'

Even the great American writers had found it hard to participate in Paris. Few learnt much French, and they invariably felt like outsiders. Chester Himes reported that, as an American, he was always overcharged and shunned by the girls. Paris, it seems, was a place to freshen up the soul, but stay too long and it would fester. By the mid-Sixties most of the writers had gone.

It surprised me how little of the place they'd taken away. Paris had been food for the mind, a treat for the senses, but it had seldom given them a plot. Perhaps, like all outsiders, they'd enjoyed the fragmentary surprises – the abundant nudity, the bread, the *flics*, the worship of art, the drunks covered in pigeons, and the bicycles with ladders – but they could never assemble the whole. Few ever wrote about Paris, whether in fiction or memoirs. Jones wrote his Pacific War classic, *The Thin Red Line* (1962), on the leafy Île St-Louis; James Baldwin wrote about Harlem; Ferlinghetti wrote *Her*; and Wright and Himes wrote about the predicament of the American black.

Over at the Beat Hotel, meanwhile, they'd written about little that made any sense at all.

71

The Beat Hotel occupies a curious place in my journey back to Paris. It's like an anarchic footnote that bears no relation to whatever's gone before. Whilst Flint, and those who'd sent him, had tried to restore sense and order to the confusion that they'd found, here were Americans making an art form out of chaos. Although they were of the same generation, the Beats were the very antithesis of those who'd fought the war: drugged, marginal, tangential and poetic. It wasn't even very easy to find their old hotel, which was hidden down a narrow, cobbled alley called the Gît-le-Coeur.

Time had been cruel to the Beats, by freshening up their lair. At its most inspiring, the 'no star hotel' (it never had a name) had provided accommodation of legendary depravity. It was never cleaned. There'd been forty-two rooms, each with a 40-watt bulb and a squat-hole down the hall. Most of the guests had been painters, whores and hustlers but the landlady – a grotesque old hag with pale blue hair – had always managed to keep the cops at bay. This state of Augean squalor might have continued into the Seventies but for the developers. Now, I noticed, it had a name and stars, and a glossy lick of paint.

'We get a lot of the kids coming back,' said Madame Odillard, the new owner.

'What, artists, writers, that sort of thing?'

'Oh, no,' she said, surprised, 'they're all doctors now, and seem quite rich.'

Around us, amongst all the polish and gleaming brass, were pictures of the Beats, grinning gauntly for cameras. Madame Odillard was proud of her pictures although, in her rose-watery, chintzy way, I doubt if she'd have appreciated the experiments that went on, up in Room 15. The poet, Gregory Corso, was the first to arrive in 1957, followed by William S. Burroughs and his lover, Allen Ginsberg. Burroughs had been on heroin since 1944 and was still struggling with the fact that he'd killed his wife while trying to shoot a wineglass off her head. He'd spent much of the last decade in Tangiers, hadn't had a bath in a year and could easily have spent a day looking at his toe-cap. 'I was only roused,' he later wrote, 'when it was time to stick a needle in the fibrous grey wooden flesh of terminal addiction.' Foul as it was, Room 15 was something of a sanctuary.

For two years, the Beats had lived here, staring into an old record-player which they called the Dream Machine, and horrifying the French by peeing in the sink ('So fuckin' *European*,' gasped Corso, 'even to *detect* such an action'). Most of the time they lived on dope, and on mussels they boiled in their room. But they were also cooking up the language, chopping up words and newspapers and blending them together in a pixillated soup. Somehow, despite the stink, they'd even produced a few enduring oddities (like 'flower power' and 'heavy metal'), and – most cryptic of all – *The Naked Lunch* (1959).

Then they left – Ginsberg wandered back to the USA and Burroughs was expelled – and, in time, the old hotel was sold and redeveloped. I noticed from the visitors' book Corso hadn't returned until 1997: 'Dear old Beat Hotel', he wrote. 'The sun was as bright and happy for us as for the rats . . . Now forty years later, the rats are gone and so are we.'

72

I'd had an idea I might find just one last vestige of American Paris down on the riverfront, at Rue de la Bûcherie. 'Shakespeare & Co.' had inherited the title and reputation of Sylvia Beach's old bookshop on Rue l'Odéon. The owner, George Whitman, was said to have arrived in 1946, with the idea of helping children orphaned in the war. When the orphans no longer needed him, he bought an old Arab greengrocer's shop in the Latin Quarter, and started selling books.

It was a curious place, with its fruit boxes and peeling books and persistently grocerish air. Parisians seemed to enjoy the association between literature and vegetables. Outside – and all along the river – books were sold in little sloping boxes, like winter cloches, as if they'd been growing in the sun. Perhaps they grow on trees as well? Certainly, every year Paris sells twenty times as many books as London. Shakespeare & Co. was merely the bohemian – or rather American – end of this retail phenomenon, and called itself 'The Rag and Bone Shop of the Heart'.

A keen sense of the haphazard continued inside, up a staircase made of books and a ladder to the loft. I spotted a wishing-well in Fiction, a large looking-glass covered in scrawl – called 'The Mirror of Love' – and a flyer for some experimental verse. (Burroughs gave his first readings of *The Naked Lunch* here. 'No one was quite sure what to make of it,' wrote George Whitman later, 'whether to laugh or to be sick.)' For many lonely Americans, however, the shop felt strangely like home, prompting some curiously unrestrained outbursts of regret. 'I have spent the last hour trying to decide if I should end my life' began one of the messages, glued to the Mirror of Love.

A few Americans had even moved in and made beds amongst the books. Any wandering soul can sleep here, I was told, in return for a few hours at the till. 'I'm doing Europe from the shop,' said one of the young Californians, as if an entire continent could somehow be catalogued in matter of weeks, like Children's Books and Travel. George himself, on the other hand, was harder to pin down. It was said that he still lived up in the attic, now aged ninety, singeing his hair off with a stub of burning candle. But, try as I might, I could never get hold of him, or penetrate the bank of improbable, Californian excuses.

'He never comes down, except on Sundays.'

'He's overseas, I guess, but I don't know where.'

'He hates publicity, never speaks to anyone.'

So, like a character from one of his thousands of books, George had repaired to his garret. The only publicity that he now enjoyed was his own, and strange little tracts still found their way down into the shop below (or Kilometre Zero, as he called it, 'where the Streets of the world meet the Avenues of the mind'). He didn't even stock his own biography ('It's about a time he no longer talks about,' said the Californian), which endeared me to his shop. All booksellers should be discerning and brutally selective (just as you'd expect of the man who sells you carrots) and Shakespeare & Co. must still rank as one of my best little bookshops in the world. Ferlinghetti had liked the place so much he'd even set up a version of his own in San Francisco, known, of course, as City Lights.

But what of George? Had it been a love affair, his years in Paris?

More like a Shakespearean theatre set, he once wrote. 'The Romeo and Juliets are forever young whilst I have become an octogenarian who, like King Lear, is slowly losing his wits.'

73

Soon after my return, I reported back to Flint, with the news that Paris was more magnificent than ever.

Depravity and chaos were now the exception. If anything, it had gone too far the other way; too controlled, serious and over-designed. After all, where else can one buy a contraption '*for carrying twelve shopping bags*'? Or a rucksack for a dog?

Part 6 – Mash Lorraine

Our own sausage manufacturers could learn a thing or two from these Lorraine and Alsace charcutiers if they chose to do so.

Elizabeth David, *French Provincial Cooking*

Gastronomically, Lorraine may not be as advanced as Alsace.

Bernard Newman, *The Sisters Alsace-Lorraine*, 1950

I could not avoid being struck with the appearance of poverty and wretchedness ... particularly in Lorraine, where in every town where we stopped to change horses, half the inhabitants seemed to be beggars.

Robert Arbuthnot, tourist, 1785

I hope that in the final settlement of the war, you insist that the Germans retain Lorraine because I can imagine no greater burden than to be the owner of this nasty country where it rains everyday and where the whole wealth of the people consisted in assorted manure piles.

General Patton in a letter to the US Secretary of State of War, October 1944

As each local offensive faltered, as German resistance stiffened, and, above all, as the incessant rain and movement of armies ploughed the battlefield between Switzerland and the sea into a quagmire, commanders progressively diminished their expectations and moderated their ambitions.

Max Hastings, *Armageddon*, 2004

74

With the Paris interlude over, this story returns to Flint and Jeff, and our travels in Alsace. But not for long. On 8 December 1944, Flint and his men were ordered north towards the German frontier, and so we followed. It was a drive that took us back into the forests of the Vosges, and into the tail end of the neighbouring *région*, Lorraine. Now – and for the second time in his life – Flint had the feeling he'd never see Alsace again.

None of us were happy to be back in the forest. Although gentler than the mountains to the north, the Vosges du Nord were just as ominous and dank. For hours, it seemed, the sun was swallowed up in maple and ash, and even the clearings were dark with meaty rocks and the carcasses of forts. Like the Alsatians, *les Lorrains* have always believed that anything is possible in the forest, and their mythology is rich in druids and ghosts, and cracks leading down to the underworld. Meanwhile, of all Flint's memories of this darkened world, the strongest was the persistent fluttering of terror.

We only stopped once in the forest, at Mouterhouse. It reminded me of a child's drawing, with its dark green sky, and a cluster of spiky trees and coloured houses on the edge of a silvery pond. At the centre of the village was a field of rotting trucks, like a crop of rust and glass, and in the local bar everyone went quiet when we walked in, and then carried on in *Platt*. Most of the customers were dressed in hunting camouflage, and the barmaid shrugged at the sound of French and busied a finger into her ear. We tried some German but no one knew anything about the war.

None of this made any sense to Flint. He'd once spent a fortnight here, lobbing smoke and shells into the hills behind. Since then, it had all been rebuilt, and was unrecognisable – and an eighth of its former size. Not even the battalion records brought the battle back to life, the entries merely functional and bleak: the infantry capture Hochkopf Hill; Flint's company destroys an enemy strongpoint (killing six); incoming 88s destroy the army's mobile showers; the removal of casualties is delayed by unexploded mines. Every shell is counted, sometimes 500 a day.

It was a low point for us all. Jeff wondered why everything looked so deadbeat and decrepit, whilst Flint wondered why it looked so whole. For me, it suddenly seemed that we were too late for our journey, and that the events that had happened here had now been rendered perpetually obscure. In silence we got back into the car and drove onwards into the gloom. We didn't stop until we reached the edge of the forest, where, all of a sudden, we burst into the light.

I gasped at the sight spreading out below.

'Holy *Moses* . . . !' said Flint.

It was the great ribbed plateau of Lorraine, and the panorama of his past.

75

It felt good to be soaring over the plain. The valley walls that had encased Mouterhouse had now turned into two parallel ridges, running broadly north to south. From up here, I could see that there were more ridges beyond, rippling off into the German haze. It looked like a giant, corrugated sea-bed, which – many millions of years earlier – is exactly what it would have been. Now it was just an ocean of grass riven by huge extinct rivers and deep green chasms of forest. There's never been a better place for tanks to slog it out.

Our own ridge was a huge, well-rounded lummox of land, about five miles long and shaped like a slumbering hog. It was a popular roost for little fortress-farms and villages, especially those preferring exposure to surprise. There were three or four settlements along the ridge, and its flanks were patched with large, knotty fields of cabbages and onions. Flint too was happier here, against a familiar outline. He'd last arrived here on 23 December 1944, and – although he didn't know it at the time – this plain topographical blob was about to become his home for the next four ferocious months. Strangely, it had never had a name, and so, for want of anything better, we called it the Hogsback.

Now, for the first time, Flint was no longer troubled by his profile.

'We were always a potential target, silhouetted against the sky.'

The ridge opposite was even more exposed, and had once been scraped of trees. The woods had only been replanted twenty years after the war, and until then the southern slope had risen like a wall. Along the top there was said to have been a fortress called Schiesseck, one of eleven interconnected concrete units sunk deep into the hillside and armed with battleship guns. Beyond that, in the next valley, was another, much older fortress, built by the arch-fortifier Vauban in 1680. To the Americans, even its name was impressively grim: Bitche.

'And *that*,' said Flint, 'was our objective. Never before taken by force.'

He'd only ever seen it once before, by creeping up on to the Schiesseck ridge.

'Well, then, let's go see it again,' said Jeff, and plunged us into the valley.

A few minutes later, we were up at the entrance to Schiesseck. The fortress was still there, like a great cake, crumbling under the trees. Mould and damp were now quietly finishing off the work of seventy-eight bombers. That December, they'd ploughed the German positions with high explosives, and only then did the 'doughs' move in. They were the same men Flint had been with since Alsace – the 100th Infantry Division – but they'd never fought like this. It was a wild, cramped struggle, and men brought back stories of fighting with their bayonets and even with their teeth. The breakthrough came when the Americans captured part of the workings and studied its design. They then brought another 5,000 lb. of TNT up to Schiesseck, and a howitzer to blast away the doors. Finally came the armoured bulldozers and buried the last defenders, still fighting underground. The US engineers, declared Nazi radio, were the 'underpaid Butchers of Bitche'.

By the time Flint got here, Schiesseck was nothing but a smouldering tomb.

'And that's when I crept to the edge, and took a look at Bitche.'

It was still a discouraging sight. Opposite us, rising from the valley below, was a colossal sandstone plinth mounted with some daunting purple ramparts. It looked like a giant fortified island, all that was left when the sea had drained away. For the soldiers who got this far – the Centurymen, or men of the 100th Division – there was always something mystical about this fight, and for years afterwards they held dinners and reunions and called themselves 'The Sons of Bitche'. But it wasn't theirs yet, and – for the time being – the edge of this ridge was as near as they got. On 21 December 1944 came news of disaster, and suddenly everything stopped.

Two hundred miles to the north, German Tigers had punched their way through, and the line was beginning to collapse.

76

'I'd never heard of the Battle of the Bulge,' said Flint, 'until long after the war.'

Its reverberations, on the other hand, had been felt all down the line. There were now four million men confronting each other across the dirt, each waiting for one false move. Amongst the Tank Destroyers, the talk was of massed waves of Tigers, spies, fifth columnists, and SS men dressed as peasants or disguised as American Joes. 'The Nazis are getting desperate,' warned *Panther Tracks*, 'and resorting to every means fair and foul.'

Amongst the generals, however, the talk now was of a long campaign, or even possible defeat ('We can still lose this war,' said Patton). For them, the spectacle of thousands of young replacements scattering before the tanks was almost too much to bear. The disasters in the Ardennes had revealed the fatal weakness of the American forces, which was inexperience. Had it not been for the courage of a few stalwart units and the defenders of Bastogne, the entire Western Front might have turned into this: a litter of abandoned helmets, discarded K-rations, burning doughnut trucks and undelivered mail. In desperation, the generals had sent in everyone they could to staunch the breach, even cipher clerks and convicts. Meanwhile, in Lorraine and all along the southern front, every division would have to move one space to the left, in order to close the gap. To Flint, this meant moving to the other end of the Hogsback and taking up position on a farm.

The farms here were smaller than Alsace, more like fortified cottages than castles. Up on the plateau, the soil was less generous than down on the Rhine, and so often a small stone barn was enough, with a few rooms at one end and a cellar underneath. But, however slight their dimensions, the farms were always ambitious in design. Many of them had incorporated Roman arches, heart-shaped windows, enormous sandstone gateposts and a cellar door like the entrance to the underworld.

'And the giant dunghills!' said Flint. 'Same as Alsace!'

The *Lorrains*, like the Alsatians, had always been a mystery to the Americans. Even at the height of the shelling, the farmers would appear, dressed in their finest apparel, bearing Christmas trees and ginger biscuits or little silver bells to summon the children to their presents. 'They displayed a physical fortitude of Spartan qualities,' reported *Panther Tracks*, 'which did much to offset the calamities and hardships that modern warfare has placed upon them.' In fact, so mysterious were these jingly, guttural people that they were often referred to as 'the Germans', a misnomer the farmers could have done without. The insult still irritated Flint.

'It's typical of our culture. Never knowing quite who anyone is.'

It had been a curious Christmas, spent moving from cellar to cellar. Berlin Radio played American band music, and the farmers decorated their trees with streamers of tinfoil, dropped as aircraft chaff. Some of the men went off hunting for liquor, and somehow one of Flint's sergeants came back from the forest with 15 quarts of schnapps. Others went to Mass, even though the church had lost its roof.

But whatever the vagaries of farm life, it was better than life in the open. The winter of 1944 would turn out to be the coldest for fifty years, and across the slopes the gun-pits hardened and froze and then vanished under snow. Frostbite would be as much a hazard as the occasional incoming shells, excoriating hands and – in the worst cases – clipping off fingers and ears. Winter warfare outfits, or 'spook suits', still hadn't arrived; even when they did, many fell into German hands, only adding to the sartorial confusion.

Even the slightest injury provoked disproportionate dread, not least because of the cold. Injury too often meant evacuation to the rear, separation from the unit and redeployment somewhere else. No one wanted to end up in the infantry. So when Flint developed haemorrhoids – perhaps after days spent crouched in the icy 'spoons' of his gun – he readily agreed to an operation in the field. ('It was performed,' he recalled, 'under a Coleman lamp, on a stretcher placed between a sewing machine and a bureau.') This fear of separation was felt just as keenly by the men. When Private Altmore was hit in the groin, he sent countless appeals to the Panthers, begging to return. The letters came from hospitals in Paris and England, and – every week – the battalion newspaper would set them out in full.

'Why,' I wondered, 'did it keep printing these appeals?'

Flint shook his head. 'I guess they just showed how lucky we were.'

77

We spent several days up on the ridge, in an old mining village called Rohrbach-lès-Bitche. It was the largest of the settlements on the Hogsback, and was tucked away on the southern flanks, amongst some ridges of its own. In this bowl, so little wind ever reached Rohrbach that, on a calm autumn day, the wood smoke only just seemed to wriggle away in crooked spindles of grey. The dust too was blearily inert and had settled across everything, long after the mines had gone. There was once a time when everyone here had spent his days digging plaster but now all that remained were the rows of miners' cottages and a tiny mineral line curling round the hill. To my surprise the line still ran, and – every day – two little carriages came squeaking up from Bitche and then rattled off down to the Saar.

Only two things happened on the Sunday we arrived. In the morning, the older villagers came down to Mass, and, in the evening, the younger ones took to their cars. The elderly performed their rituals in silence and in black, and the young with as little as possible of either. For a few deafening minutes the high street was a blaze of sparks and fluorescent spoilers, and a collection of battered cars assembled to blast off into the hills. We were the only people watching this launch, except a very fat girl in the bus shelter. It was hard to know if she was impressed because she had so much jewellery nailed through her face that it could no longer move at all.

By Monday, it was obvious that there was more to Rohrbach than simply prayers and scrap metal. There was also the Albert Schweitzer nursing home, a flower shop, a bar (where the old men drank their beer with little flutes of detergent-blue liqueur), and an *auberge* called La Croix d'Or. This was always a highly luminous place to eat, with all its shiny copper and tanks of tropical fish, but it was hardly ever open. Whenever it was, the news somehow got through to Germany, five miles to the north, and the Saarlanders would turn up in coaches, in the sure hope of cheap quails and cheap *Bananen Split*. Even Flint, who enjoyed good food almost as much as a bargain, was puzzled by the prices.

'How do they do it so cheaply?' he said.

'Perhaps they grow it all themselves,' suggested Jeff.

This would have sounded fanciful, but for Madame Neu. She and her husband, René, lived on a huge vegetable patch at the edge of the village, and for most of the year they disappeared under a forest of cabbages, marigolds and sofa-sized courgettes. It was, I imagined, only in autumn that our lodgings reappeared, a little house of cement and polished rock. Inside, however, the vegetation was still in charge, a sort of indoor forest of orchids, epiphytes, bamboo furniture, dried flowers and some thuggish-looking gourds. But, in spite of their jungly fittings, the Neus were faultlessly generous and forgiving. They didn't even seem to mind when

I added whisky to the flavours of the forest. (We'd been in Flint's room, commemorating the twelve bottles of Ballantine's that he'd finished near here in 1944, when our own bottle had jumped like a fish from my hands and landed in a splash of splinters on the stone. As the whisky trickled off through the foliage, I caught a glimpse of Flint, tears streaming down his cheeks, silently convulsed in heaves of helpless laughter.)

René, of course, hadn't forgotten the last time the Americans were here. Although he was only eight at the time, he'd even remembered his English. '*Shewing gurm!* he kept shouting. '*Gimme shewing gurm!*'

When he heard that the Americans were back, the old schoolmaster, Herr Kirschner, was soon pounding up the road. It wasn't so much chewing gum that interested him, as putting history in its place. Arsène Kirschner had spent much of the last seventy-eight years gathering up the stories of his beloved Bitscherland, and all he'd ever needed was an outlet. We were the lecture he'd always been waiting for, and the jam and cheeses were barely off the breakfast table before he was beating at the door. Almost everything about him was reassuringly professorial, from the little gold glasses and quick, bright eyes to the lumpy old cardigan fastened with a bull-clip. Across his shoulders, however, he was carrying a very large and heavy aeroplane, carved from gateposts and painted cheese-plant green.

'*C'est un* P-thirty-eight,' he said. '*Der Jägerbomber.*'

'Did you make it?' asked Jeff, studying it tactfully.

'*Oui! Mit mein* own hands!*'

This, I soon realised, was Herr Kirschner's Esperanto, a curious scrambling of French and *Platt* with a smattering of GI. It was a patter he could sustain for hours – as he did – and without the usual requirements of respiration and refreshment. In front of him, a thick wedge of Madame Neu's raspberry sponge cake remained untouched, although it was often dive-bombed by his hands, which, as the stories got airborne, took off after them in flight. Herr Kirschner was always a lively narrator of Rohrbach's story – combative and slightly dangerous – and, in the way he spoke, there was always the vague promise of a joke. These, I suppose, were just the tricks he'd learnt teaching boys who'd rather be out smashing up their cars.

It was also a story that began long before the beginning.

'*Ma famille* was here for *dreihundert* years. My father was a black-smith . . .'

As the twentieth century approached, I got the hang of the languages and a sorry tale emerged. Rohrbach had never recovered from the insults of the Forties, and if the village felt dislocated now, that was probably why. In 1939 the entire village was cleared and mined, in readiness for battle. The uprooted *Rohrbachois* were then dumped in Limousin, several hundred miles to the west, where they lived amongst a fiery red-faced people they neither liked nor understood. *'Maintenant, les gens ressentaient leur déracinement et le début de la vie d'un flichtling'* ('Now people resented the upheaval, and the beginning of life as a refugee'). The German occupation, a year later, brought liberation, or at least the journey home. Rohrbach was now part of Greater Germany again, and Monsieur le Maire was replaced with a *Bürgermeister*, and the gendarme with a *Schupo*.

'I remember it all very well,' said Herr Kirschner, 'because when we're young we remember extraordinary things.'

He then looked doubtfully at the cake in front of him, and was about to take a pick at it when he remembered the arrival of the Allies. 'The B-24s had been bombing us all through the summer. They even tried to bomb our little barracks, although the bombs fell short . . . And then came the P-38s,' he said, poking a finger at the great winged log, now pancaked over the table. 'And they shot up everything, or at least anything that moved.'

The Germans responded to this onslaught with a massive show of earth.

'We were all ordered out, to dig the *Vogesenlinie*.'

Large holes, it was hoped, would keep the Americans at bay. But with so many holes in his war, Flint couldn't even remember Rohrbach's contribution.

'I recall the dirt all right,' he said, 'but not particular bits of dirt.'

'It was all pointless,' said Herr Kirschner. 'But what could we do?'

He was only seventeen when he joined the *Schanzarbeiter*, or Earthworkers. 'Of course, we stopped when we heard the Americans were coming. But then they sent some armed officials up here – the *Sturmabteilung* – from the town hall. Get digging, they said, or you're on your way to the Eastern Front. Well, I was still digging a tank-trap when the first Americans appeared.'

'And were you pleased to see them?' said Jeff anxiously.

'We didn't know what to expect. Every day planes flew over, big ones and little Piper Cubs. Then they shelled us – for fourteen days non-stop! You never forget that. But, thank God, a lot of people managed to get to the mines, and the rest of us hid in our cellars. It's a miracle no one was killed. A *miracle*! You know 80 per cent of this town was destroyed? That's something, eh? I did some drawings back then, in my school book. You want to see them? Look, here we are: the bombing.'

Across the yellow powdery sheets I could see little cartoon planes trickling bombs on to stick-like homes and railway lines and bits of mangled cattle. The young Arsène had included himself in these drawings, cowering in the margin, but no sign of any Germans.

'*Où sont les Allemands?*' I asked.

'Ha! They'd already gone!' he said, waving his hand at the hills beyond the Hogsback. 'We were then all alone, and there was a terrible fear of what would happen next. Then, one morning – it was still November – the GIs suddenly appeared, with all their wonderful modern equipment.

Flint smiled. 'To your great relief, I hope?'

'*Oui*,' said the schoolmaster. '*A la joie de nous tous.*'

78

This wasn't the last I saw of Herr Kirschner. I met him again at the supermarket, which was built on an old minefield next to a concrete fort. The bunker's sullen, grey lumpiness seemed only to activate more history, and the old *professeur* towed me over to the window and waved an arm across the battlefield below. The joy at the arrival of the Americans had soon dispersed when the fight began again.

'See that? Two great armies fought over these hills for three months. *Three months!* You know, it took the Americans ten days to capture Erching, and it's only up the road! Eventually, they attacked it with P-47s. I'll never forget the sight of that. There were eight of them. That's sixty-four machine-guns! It's surprising there's anything left . . . And then three weeks later the Germans took it back again! Are you surprised we didn't take sides?

'And while they both fought over our heads, we had to bury ourselves in whatever was left of our homes. For the first month we ate nothing but potatoes! You can hardly imagine the stink, and the dirt. *Et la confusion!* Every day shelling! *La stratégie Américaine consistait à écraser l'ennemi par l'artillerie.* God knows how anything survived. All our cattle were killed and lay in the fields for weeks. Even the hills began to stink.

'I don't think we ever knew what was going on. And nor did the *Amis*, the Americans. When they found our boys hiding in the woods, they thought they were spies and would've shot them all if it hadn't been for the priest. Sometimes, they even shot each other! The P-47s often bombed their own men, and then the Americans would have to shoot them down. For three months this was a scene of carnage! *Une scène d'enfer!* I remember watching the Germans heaping up their dead *comme du bois de chauffage* – like firewood – and the Americans bringing theirs up here on strange little trailers . . .

'You say your friend, Monsieur Flint, was up here, with his men? I'm sorry we never made them more welcome. We were never sure if they were staying. Or if they'd win. Or if they were any better than the Germans. By then, we didn't really care who won, we just wanted it to finish. If anyone had ever asked us whether we wanted the Americans or the Germans, we'd have said, *"C'est la même chose."* We no longer cared. *C'était la guerre.'*

79

In all the chaos, the warring factions seldom discovered what became of their ordnance once they'd let it fly. Flint had thought a lot about this over the next sixty years. 'I remember firing on a church once,' he said, 'and I often wonder what became of it.'

The church, as it turned out, was easy to find. By working through the old battalion message log – all beautifully typed in misty blue and finished off in copperplate – I came across an order, timed at 10.30 a.m.

The view from the Hogsback.

on 30 December 1944: 'B company commanding officer ordered by Frolic 3 to fire at church steeple in Guiderkirch containing possible enemy observation post.' Intriguing though 'Frolic 3' sounded, none of us knew who this was. Guiderkirch, on the other hand, was a small village four miles to the north, and, if we moved along the Hogsback to Bettwiller – where Flint had been – we could just see it, out in the grass below. At this point, Guiderkirch had also been well within range of the company's three-inch guns.

'Both sides put artillery observers in steeples,' said Flint. 'It wasn't new.'

I remembered Herr Kirschner talking about this steeple war. 'Whenever the Germans retreated,' he'd said, 'they left men behind in the steeples, to direct incoming fire as the Americans entered town.'

'I always let George Nowicki take shots like this,' said Flint, and then added, by way of explanation, 'His brother had been killed further up the line.'

It was a hard shot: Guiderkirch was almost two miles away to the north. The log reports that twenty-two rounds were fired – twenty high explosive and two armour-piercing cap. 'All hits,' reads Flint's report, 'but damage could not be clearly ascertained.'

We spent ages peering out along the line of fire. But there were no clues in the landscape. 'If you don't mind,' I said to Flint, 'I think it's time we went down there, to find out what happened next.'

It was obvious that Guiderkirch had long since been cheaply patched and repaired. All the houses had been re-roofed and clad in asbestos

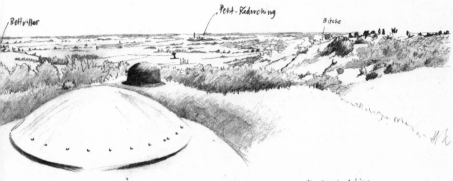

Outworks of the Maginot Line

shingles. The church meanwhile had been re-rendered and now had a tower instead of a spire. It also had new windows, new pews and a coat of primrose paint. But despite all this architectural surgery, the village still had a listless, overwrought feel. All the cars seemed to be sagging with rust, and even the village watchdogs had merely slumped on to their haunches, after a few perfunctory snarls. Opposite the church was a small asbestos house, and in front of it sat four elderly people dressed in slippers and coats. The oldest of the men had a little dog with orange pom-pom ears and ballet dancer's feet. I could see they were all puzzled by our Dijon plates and our unfamiliar hats and shoes.

'*D'où êtes-vous?*' said the older man.

I explained who I was, and that Flint had been here in the war.

'*Il est Allemand?*' said one of the others.

'*Non, Américain.*'

The very mention of the word 'American' seemed to release a distant latch, and caught us in a torrent of stories. I barely had time to flick my Dictaphone on before we were swept along in the debris of the past, immersed in broken childhoods and lives caught in the crossfire. In the recordings I have of that afternoon I can still hear their four voices, tumbling over each other in the rush to tell the tale. They said they were from the same family, called Loutz, and that they'd all been here throughout the war. Each of them had different memories of growing up, although the theme was always the same.

For Gabriel, it was the Americans arriving eight days before Christmas.

'*Et le chocolat!*' recalled Anne-Marie. It was the first she'd ever seen.

But for Yvonne it was the burning bodies, although she was only eight.

'. . . *et les tanks, et les bombes* . . .'

And the Germans who recaptured the village on Christmas Day.

'. . . *et tous les jours, la peur* . . .'

And the months spent in the cellars.

'*C'était arrosé,*' said Yvonne. The village was literally 'sprinkled'.

More than a hundred were killed.

We'll take you to the memorial, they said. A beautiful place, just up the road.

'And what about the church?' I asked. 'What happened to that?'

'*Détruite,*' they said. '*Totalement détruite.*'

Gabriel explained how it had been caught in the American bombardment just after the Germans had returned. He then went off and found some photographs. In the older pictures I could see people – women in full skirts and men in wide-brimmed hats, riding ancient horse-drawn machines – and always the church, with its little spire, smaller than the tower today. But in the later pictures there are no people, and the village has been stripped of branches and roofs, and the streets have been ploughed up and scattered with chunks of the church. I could even make out the asbestos house, stripped to the rafters, a skeleton of itself.

Keep the pictures, said Gabriel, and let people know how it was.

Flint was horrified by the destruction, but also fascinated. It was like peering behind the curtains of his past, and completing a story until now half told. He never volunteered the information that it was he who'd bombarded the village, so nor did I. Perhaps he was right. After all, what could he have said? What would have sounded adequate? Candour, it seemed, had given way to tact.

Jeff looked puzzled. 'I guess our troops did *eventually* come back?'

Of course, said Gabriel, but they didn't re-take the village for another three months. The last struggles were amongst the worst. In the end, it was left to the diehards to defend the village, SS troopers of no more than seventeen or eighteen. For days, the Americans harangued them through loudspeakers. 'DO YOU REALLY WANT TO DIE FOR THE FÜHRER?' they shouted, but the boys wouldn't surrender. Eventually, an American tank rolled up past the church, and caught them in its sights.

'*Ratatatata TATATATATAT!*' chattered Gabriel excitedly.

It got them all, said Anne-Marie. They were only children.

They died right here, said Yvonne, right where you're standing now.

80

While the great wheeled suburbs of the 100th Division sprawled over the Hogsback, another city was quietly mouldering away, deep below the surface. Flint told me that, if he'd ever known about the Maginot Line, he'd forgotten all about it. It was irrelevant; it faced the wrong way and it felt like a trap. The great armies across the plain wanted to fight a war in the open, not deep underground in a warren.

'I never even went inside,' said Flint. 'There was never any point.'

This was all the more surprising given that the line broke surface only a few hundred yards from his old positions. Along the crest of the ridge, an enormous mushroom of concrete bulged out of the hillside. It looked like the tip of some strange subterranean citadel trying to nose its way up through the turf. All around it were smaller domes, and little rusted cupolas that had once popped up out of the earth, sprayed the area with fire and then slid back underground. I'm not surprised that France saw these forts as impenetrable. This one – known as Fort Casso – was protected by armoured gun-ports, walls ten feet thick, ditches that could be swept with automatic gunfire, gas filters, bulletproof searchlights, flood zones, minefields and interlocking fields of fire. Even time had failed to digest this fortress, and – to the touch – the concrete still felt soapy and new.

From the top of the dome I could see others, on the ridges off to the east and west. Beyond those, of course, there were more, stretching away across France. The scale of construction was Pharaonic: between 1929 and 1938, the French had shifted some four million truckloads of earth and concrete (enough to bury the City of London to a depth of 20 feet). But, of course, it was all in vain. Bomb-proof, gas-proof and impregnable, the Maginot Line had simply been ignored. The only time Casso was ever fired upon was from the French side, by Germans who'd merely driven around the defensive line and who'd already captured Paris. The fort still bore the marks of this battle. All around the southern embrasures were divots ripped from the concrete, and pits in the steelwork like scoops from molten chocolate.

But a long string of follies looping off through France was only half the picture. Beneath these fungal domes a city spread out, iceberg-like, below the surface. Casso was said to disappear way inside the Hogsback, the equivalent of almost thirty storeys underground. The fortress immediately to the west – Simserhof – was said to be bigger still, and even had a little railway to carry people into the depths. One afternoon, we drove over there and bought three returns to the Centre of the Earth.

Ahead of us, vast armoured doors opened up and swallowed us into the dark.

'It's like something from a Bond movie,' gasped Jeff.

Flint shook his head in awe.

'Pure fantasy,' he said, as we rumbled into the hill.

Jeff was right to think of SMERSH and Scaramanga. Deep inside its mountain, the city of Simserhof was both uncannily futuristic and ludicrously sinister. Our little train wobbled through armouries, subterranean bakeries, industrial latrines, a network of rabbity barracks and a long damp tunnel of hospitals and morgues. Everywhere we went a cold, hard voice echoed out of the concrete, replete with the cold hard facts. '*This railway runs for five kilometres . . . You are now thirty metres underground. The temperature is always thirteen degrees . . . Up to 700 men lived down here, with an armoury of 35,000 shells . . . The fort could generate its own electricity, and could survive by itself for a month . . .*' A month? How could anyone survive a month of Simserhof, and emerge with their wits intact? Little thought, it seems, had been given to the sanity of its defenders. I noticed that the only place to eat was in the service tunnel, off little metal tables that folded down from the walls.

But Simserhof had triumphed in its way, or at least – in the words of the Voice – '*it had done what it was supposed to do*'. Like the other great *ouvrages* along the line, it had never been penetrated by the Germans, and had even been a little nation for a while. For eight days after the fall of France, Simserhof had fought on, firing 14,000 shells. Then, finally on 30 June 1940, the defenders had seen the futility of their action, and had thrown open the huge armoured doors and surrendered to the enemy. They'd gone six weeks without any natural light.

Now the ammunition elevators stood empty, and the big guns had long since gone. At some stage during the occupation, the place had been picked clean, and the guns had ended up on the Atlantic Wall. But, after that, the Germans couldn't think what to do with such an awkward underground city, and so they'd used it for storing torpedoes. They didn't even rearm it as the Allies approached, but preferred to fall back on a hole of their own, known rather grandly as *der Westwall*. But it wasn't quite the end of Simserhof's military career, or that of the Maginot Line. During the Cold War, French military strategists revived the idea of hiding underground. It was hoped that the forts would hold the Eastern hordes at bay just long enough to allow the forces of democracy to muster. By 1965 even this idea was abandoned, and Simserhof was sold.

Back at Madame Neu's, I asked Flint what he'd made of the city beneath his feet.

'A great monument,' he said thoughtfully, 'to the stupidity of man.'

81

On the outskirts of Rohrbach, we found an old half-track parked in the grass.

'Never thought I'd see one of these things again,' said Flint.

It was an unemotional reunion. Although machines had provided him with some of the happier moments of his war, Flint still seemed to regard the M3 as more of a torment than technology. It was an odd-looking object that seemed to begin as a car and end as a skip. This one had been so mercilessly roasted and spattered with hail, that – after more than half a century – it had turned a sickly, boglike green. This only made it look more prehistoric, like a reptile due for extinction. It even had armoured eyelids and a snout of thick steel scales.

'Useless,' said Flint, 'useless from beginning to end.'

But despite the contempt, he and Jeff were soon all over it. They couldn't resist machines. While Jeff disappeared under the camshaft, Flint scrambled up into the bucket and, naturally, I followed. As he ran his fingers over the familiar flanges and levers I realised that, of all his months in the field, this was probably the only place he'd ever really known as home. The feel and texture of the metal seemed to awaken an old check-list, which he'd long thought forgotten: 'Toolbox. Ammunition lockers. APC. HE. Charge windshields. Illumination shells . . . Hey, where's the ring-mount? This is where the .50cal would've been. Right here, our big machine-gun . . . And here, this is the locker where we kept our wine and spirits,' he grinned. 'People always wanted to be in my platoon. I used to think it was because I was humane, but I guess it was probably just the liquor . . .'

After several happy minutes back at the controls, Flint scrambled over the armour again, and we lowered ourselves off the treads and dropped down the side. 'Ten tons of junk,' said Flint, as he patted the armour one last time.

But the M3, it seems, hadn't taken kindly to these insults. All of us, I now noticed, were covered in thick black smears of rubber. Many months on, the satchel that carries all my notes and cameras is still richly streaked in black. Like it or not, Flint's accursed machine – or at least a smudge of it – will probably now be with me for ever.

82

The people of Bettwiller wouldn't easily forget the last day of 1944, and nor would Flint. It was the day all expectation faltered, the moment when all the hopes and strategies of the months before seemed suddenly diminished. It was also the beginning of an imponderable age, a time of intense periods of destruction followed by long interludes of nothing, and with never an end in sight. Was it weeks or was it months? No one seemed sure. In the minds of those who'd survived, the war on the plateau was now drained of definition. Until that point, it had seemed like chess played with field guns. But, from now, there would be no pattern, no set-piece moves and no restraint. It was almost as if every piece now moved to its own rules, and one moment everything would be hurtling forward, and the next it'd be tumbling back in retreat. Then, for weeks, everyone would vanish below the surface and to the outside world it would seem as if the battle was almost over.

Bettwiller had seen all this before. There are few places that have ever been so methodically destroyed. During the Thirty Years War, the Swedish – *les hordes barbares suédoises* – brought such mutilation to the land that it remained uninhabited for almost half a century. The villagers have lost count of the number of times they've had to rebuild it all since then. Occasionally, I noticed, they'd rebuilt it from the debris of the battle-field – recycled masonry and old armoured doors – but, whilst the sandstone was still pimpled with bullets, the rendering hid a multitude of sins. The villagers had even painted it the colour of make-up – peach and suntan and peacock blue – a constant reminder that beauty's skin deep and is easily wiped away.

Bettwiller was still wary of outsiders. I could feel people watching us, but there was nothing there when I caught their eye. Once, we stopped to talk to an old miner, who was sitting on a trough. He told me that he couldn't think of anyone who hadn't attacked them in the war. First, there was the French Army, then the Germans, then the British in their aeroplanes, and the Americans with artillery. When I told him that Flint had been here during the great German counter-offensive, he hardly seemed to react. 'I remember,' he said, and that was all.

It was much the same in the other villages along the northern side of the Hogsback. In Petit-Réderching, we were greeted with a curious indifference – although at least a dog tried to eat us. It was a huge mastiff, and I'd barely got a foot inside the bar when it made a lunge for my throat. Yelling out some earthy expletive, I managed to slam the door just in time, and this gruesome missile of teeth and hatred spattered harmlessly into the glass. Through the slather and dog-snot, we could just make out the barmaid. At the sound of English, she'd turned, and carried on polishing the bar.

A few miles to the north, a new enemy had gathered. They weren't like the Germans of before, and many of them weren't Germans at all, but Belgians or Russians. Thrown together the previous year, they were the 17th SS Panzer-Grenadiers, and along the Lorraine front they could muster 14,000 men. But, although this sounded impressive enough, the 17th was a mongrel division, of mongrel ideals and mongrel intentions. They relied more upon fervour than skill, and if there had ever been any hardy veterans in their ranks, they'd long since perished in Normandy. Their real strength lay in their ruthlessness, and in their acceptance that, if they failed in their purpose, they'd probably die in the process.

They were perfect for the plan that Hitler had devised. The 17th would form part of a magnificent wave of German aggression that would roll through Lorraine and into Alsace. It was a plan of unparalleled futility – Hitler's last great counter-offensive and the product of his now enfeebled logic. There was no particular objective beyond inflicting damage, although – somehow – the Führer had envisaged that his armies would disappear into the Vosges for while and then burst into Strasbourg, spreading panic amongst the Allies and bringing the war to an end. Hitler even called his madcap operation *Unternehmen Nordwind* (Operation North Wind), a name aptly unpredictable and wild. Perhaps the best thing about it was that it would begin on New Year's Eve. 'The Americans will find it an unpleasant surprise,' Hitler told his generals, 'because they don't celebrate Christmas, only New Year.'

So confident were they of taking the *Amis* by surprise that the 17th set out with only their weapons, half a loaf of bread per man, and no fuel for their return. Their orders were to forage amongst the enemy. They were to fall upon him, rearm themselves from his stores, destroy his infrastructure, and feed themselves on whatever they could find.

83

But if Hitler had thought his men would find the enemy in party hats and festive mood, he was much mistaken. Over on the American side, the atmosphere was one of anxiety and vigilance. 'Your husband,' wrote Flint to his wife that evening, 'is sober and very blue.'

The Americans had known for days that an attack was pending. They'd seen it in the coded messages they'd intercepted, and in the furrowed snow on the German side. The difficulty was in knowing what to do about it. The line was already overstretched, and, once again, Eisenhower was plundering service units and sending cooks and clerks to the front. He even went to the stockades, offering convicts a reprieve if only they'd agree to fight (an offer few of them took up). In desperation, the army then abandoned its long-standing policy of keeping blacks away from the action, but even that was too late to make much difference. Manpower remained alarmingly short, and this wasn't helped by the crippling rates of desertion. Taunted by the prospects of his army drifting away from the front, Eisenhower was forced to resurrect the death penalty for deserters, and, that December in Alsace, a hapless small-time criminal called Eddie Slovik was hauled against a post and shot. It was the first such execution since the American Civil War.

Meanwhile, the troops waited and the snow thickened. By New Year's Eve, Lorraine was covered – in the poetic words of the official report – in 'a deceptively innocent coating of white, giving little hint of the coming struggle'. I've often tried to imagine how it was in those last few seconds before *Nordwind* began, and to picture the lives of those on the Hogsback: the Panthers dug in across the slopes; Arsène Kirschner, asleep amongst his father's potatoes; Flint in his farmhouse, writing a letter to his wife; and – some miles north of Bettwiller – the cold, excited men of the *Volkswerfer* brigade, fitting their missiles into a launcher.

Then, the *Nebelwerfer* are ready, and somewhere a minute-hand falls into place, and a lanyard tightens, and the black-frosted sky is suddenly filled with the feathery trails of rockets and the awesome, concussive sound of battle.

Eleven o'clock rings out on the town clock [wrote Flint soon after-wards] . . . And before the last ringing has faded, an eerie whistling is heard. It sounds like a roaring lion – it puts fur on your back and leaves you in a cold sweat. The next thing, glass is flying, the buildings are shaking, and you are practically deaf. At first you are stunned, and then the instinctive law of self-preservation takes hold of you, and you find yourself in the cellar . . .

After the rockets, there was silence and then another sound. It was the *Panzer-Grenadiers* wading up the Hogsback – hundreds of them, dressed in 'spook suits' – all screaming in English and roaring as if they were drunk. 'Die, Yankee bastards! Come out and fight, you gangsters!' The Panthers had never been so close to enemy infantry, and had never imagined it like this. Suddenly they were all fighting for their lives – O'Moore, Kinzel, Loychik, the comic Sammy Piltch, Harrison, Nowicki, Cardona the Cuban, and the farmboys from Tennessee. 'They just used whatever they could,' said Flint. 'Hell, they even unbolted the .50cals from their ring-mounts and set them up, right here on the ground . . .'

It took all night to fight off the attack. By dawn on New Year's Day the SS troopers had withdrawn, leaving ten dead in Bettwiller and eleven prisoners. In the lull, the Panthers too pulled back, to the higher slopes near Rohrbach. No sooner had they done so, than the attacks began again. This time, when the *Rohrbachois* saw the white-clad Germans ('*les fantassins Allemands*') closing in on their town, they began to panic. Arsène Kirchner and three of his friends took to their bicycles, and – dodging the American patrols – pedalled west along the railway. ('The Americans would have shot us,' he said, 'thinking we were spies.') Meanwhile the rest of the villagers were evacuated from the southern end of Rohrbach, leaving the Joes and the grenadiers to fight over whatever remained.

As we drove north along the Hogsback, I realised just how close the armies had become. These gentle slopes of wheat and eagles had once been fought over field by field. Throughout that New Year, the adversaries had meshed together, burst apart, interlocked again, encircled one another, bled into each other's ranks, and then punched their way out before scattering backwards in horror. Occasionally, gun crews had found themselves without supporting infantry, and once they'd had to abandon their guns and crawl off through the slush. But no guns were lost. That night, Sergeant Ready (or, as he was known, 'Apple Knocker') and his men had crept back to within a stone's throw of the enemy, hitched up their guns and dragged them back to safety.

B Company had lived under an incessant squall of shells. 'For three days,' reported *Panther Tracks*, 'everything landed around our positions except the kitchen sink . . . The first day we didn't eat, not because there wasn't anything to eat but because we'd lost our appetites.' But, despite the fact that the men had never expected such an intensity of fighting, they responded with extraordinary resilience, and there were many more episodes of courage: Sergeant Mohr had driven through a lacerating barrage of fire to rescue an injured man, and Sergeant O'Connor had earned the incredulity of everyone after his refusal to withdraw in the face of frenzied frontal attack. But shells and fanatics in snow suits weren't the only hazards. Every now and then, an enemy tank clanked up to the ridge, including, on 9 January, a 'Hunting Tiger'. Although, at 79 tons, the *Jagdtiger IV* was the biggest land monster ever to fight in the war, it was no match for the determination of the men up here, and by noon that day it was nothing more than battlefield scrap metal.

Apart from a few last knots of barbed wire and the neglected blobs of the Maginot Line, there were no clues now as to the battles that raged here. Rimling, the village at the northern end – or snout – of this great slumbering hog had been rebuilt almost as if nothing had happened. This was surprising considering that it had been so bitterly contested, and had been shelled, battered, set ablaze with phosphorus and overrun three times in a week.

Flint had never been this far before. Of course, he'd listened while the battle for Rimling raged below. But only now, with copies of the records, was he able to appreciate exactly what had happened. We found the old church tower that had once been held by a lone lieutenant armed only with a carbine, and the rows of sandstone cottages that the two sides had fought for door to door. It was hard to reconcile all this with the dormitory village that Rimling had become. The catastrophic screech and boom of shells had long since given way to the sleepy whirr of mowers. For almost a month, the villagers were unable to bury their dead, and dogs and horses had lain, chunked and tattered, in the street. One of the grenadiers, we read, had found some paint and a surviving section of wall, and had daubed the words: WE WILL NEVER SURRENDER. But then neither would the Americans. At one point, they held the village with just a handful of men – a company bugler, some command post staff, and a hoary veteran called Sergeant Carey. The barn from which they'd repelled an assault by tanks was still there, and was now a builder's yard.

Opposite was a small garden of fruit trees, marigolds and marrows. This was where Sergeant Carey had died, caught at last in some whirling scimitar of metal. The last thing he ever said was, 'Damn! That was close', words that might easily have described the battle for the Hogsback.

Miraculously, by the end of the week it was still in American hands. More remarkable still, this sector – held by Flint's company and the soldiers of the 100th Division – was the only sector along the entire Seventh Army front to have withstood the attack. Had one been able to watch the front line from the moon, one would have seen the American lines everywhere shrinking away to the south, and a lone pimple of resistance. That of course was here, the Hogsback. 'Your great accomplishment,' General Devers later told its defenders, 'forced the enemy to give up offensive action on your front.' This was true; after eight days of fighting, the German High Command had realised that in this sector a breakthrough was hopeless, and had settled again for stalemate. It had suffered suicidal losses. One of the captured panzer-grenadiers told the Panthers that, of the hundred men in his unit, only nineteen remained. The attack on the Hogsback had shown that the German soldier still knew how to fight and die, but that – for the time being – the ridge was secure.

Meanwhile, all around it, the American army was in retreat.

84

From the highest point on the Hogsback, it was possible to understand the full extent of the catastrophe.

To the west, the plateau faded away in a series of pale grey folds to the Saar. It was a beautiful landscape, rinsed in haze and the delicate, lacy light of the plains. At first, it seemed empty, and then my eyes adjusted and I realised I was seeing much more than I'd imagined, an ocean of land that vanished perhaps fifty miles ahead. Now, I could make out villages stippled across the pleats, and the pewtery forests of Saarland. By Christmas 1944, the Panthers' A Company, together with the 44th Division, had already reached Germany – but a week later they were reeling back in surprise. *Panther Tracks* tried to make light of it, with light-hearted reports from the farmboys, who'd been forced to abandon their new charges: two horses, a goat, seven chickens, three pigs and a cow. But it all masked a darker story: A Company had come under withering fire from 88s, which had shredded a half-track and killed two of their finest men. Now the company was hurtling backwards, and the enemy had reached the Gros-Réderching, only a mile to the west.

For several days Flint's men had watched, as the village turned German, then American, then Free French, and then German once again. It was a vicious fight, uncomplicated by the rules of war. At one point, the SS played dead and then rose up in a blaze of murderous gunfire (which gave rise to a new rule: the SS were not to be treated as prisoners until they were unarmed and in the open). Another time, the panzer-grenadiers recaptured the village dressed in American uniforms, which prompted several months of paranoia. 'If we ever came across suspects,' said Flint, 'we'd ask them questions about Babe Ruth or the Red Sox. Or, where do you put quarterbacks? Or, what's a Juicy Fruit? What's the capital of Illinois? Who's Mickey Mouse's wife? If they didn't get it right, we'd take them in.'

But if things weren't looking good to the west, off to the east, they were even worse.

From the right flank of the Hogsback, we could look back over much of the journey we'd already done. Opposite us were the dark, coniferous ridges that surrounded Bitche, and, beyond them, the surly outline of the northern Vosges.

By the end of the first week of 1945, it was all back in German hands. The fortresses of Schiesseck and Simserhof had both been recaptured, and so had Mouterhouse with its tiny silver lake. Months of effort and bloodshed now seemed in vain. The SS saboteurs had even penetrated the gullies and woods at the south end of the Hogsback, and although – for the time being – it was a peninsula, it was in danger of becoming an island. The Tank Destroyers' guns, which were always supposed to be way back in defence, were now under attack from German front-line troops. 'They were good soldiers,' said Flint, 'you have to give them their due.'

Further east still, there was almost nothing left of the Americans in northern Alsace. Overnight, another ghost-white SS division – this one fresh from Finland – had swept in, through the forest. Although they'd had no tanks (and some of them didn't even have helmets) they caused panic amongst the thinly distributed Americans. Many of the defenders simply took to their heels, clogging up the roads ten miles to the rear. In places, the front line would be rolled back almost twenty miles, and the Lauterbourg salient – that shoulder of eastern France that buts into Germany – completely collapsed, and disappeared. But not everyone fled, although those that didn't were mauled. Amongst the hardest hit were Flint's old comrades in the 45th Division. Some of their cooks and mail clerks fought until the ammunition ran out, and in the rear echelons the radio operators could only listen in horror to the desperate cries for help ('*Send reinforcements now. My men are being cut to pieces*'). By the end of the first day of 1945, the great farmhouses of Alsace were ablaze and the SS troopers were helping themselves to American weapons, feasting on spam and stripping down the dead. They then plundered the farms for carts and horses, and set off after the Joes.

Meanwhile, the Alsatians watched in disgust as those who'd come to liberate them now fled down the road. It was what they'd always feared. '*Vous nix parti?*' they shouted. 'No, just shifting troops!' the Americans lied. In some places, they were booed and the children pelted them with snow.

'Well, I guess we deserved it,' said Flint: 'we'd been caught out again.'

It would take the Americans nearly three weeks to stem the advance, and only then at terrible cost. They'd have happily pulled off the plain altogether, if it hadn't been for Strasbourg. De Gaulle insisted it be saved. It was only the prospect of him flouncing off and fighting a war of his own that persuaded the Americans to stay. By the end of *Nordwind*, more than 16,000 of their men had died, along with more than 30,000 Frenchmen and 23,000 Germans.

Perhaps Hitler's nihilism would triumph after all. In his New Year broadcast, he told the German people, 'We're going to destroy everyone who does not take part in the common effort of the country, or who makes himself a tool of the enemy', and then – with a flourish more triumphant than desperate – he added, 'The world must know that this State will never give in.'

85

Who knows what Jeff made of it all? I had the feeling that he was frustrated by the past, by the failure of its systems, and its refusal to be more spatial. He might even have enjoyed history if only he could have explored it with a spanner. I often caught him staring hard across the ridges, trying to make sense of the battle. But he told me that all he ever saw were Grade Tens, Baby Heads and Bear Traps – the surf-like topography of mountain bikers. As to the lumpy red villages and this ancient graminiferous landscape, he couldn't relate any of it to his past, to America, to his grandfather, or to his mother come to that. Kitora Anne Flint was born on 3 January 1945, while her father was up here, fighting for his life.

'It was another two weeks before I got the news,' said Flint.

By then the German attack had stalled, and he'd been promoted to lieutenant.

'I didn't drink much – I couldn't afford to – except the night we got news of Kitty's birth . . . Blue eyes, doing well. The whole platoon was drunk! If the Germans had attacked that night . . .'

Panther Tracks (which tended to call Flint 'B Company's favourite') had reported all this discreetly. 'Congratulations, Lt Flint,' ran the editorial, 'I hear the cigars were OK.' Flint smiled when he read this again, although there was also a hint of sadness. The last time he'd stood up here, the news of Kitty had seemed providential and auspicious. Now, it was harder to bear. Kitty was ill and had cancer, and every day Flint wrestled with the imponderable idea that the life he'd been so grateful for might merely prove an interlude in the uncertain progress of his own. 'I remember how it was for Dotty before she died,' he once told me, 'but I don't think I could bear to lose a child.'

'She's fine,' said Jeff. 'A lot of people have cancer and live with it, don't they? And she's *tough*, like her dad. Yes, I'm sure she's going to be fine.'

86

During January and February 1945, life on the Hogsback acquired a rhythm of sorts. The Winter Guard had turned into a frozen solstice, in which neither army moved but shrank under the sleet. 'There are no dashing heroics,' wrote a soldier further down the line, 'but instead there is only the drudgery, weariness, exhaustion, boredom, chronic anxiety, and a desperate unceasing striving to survive.'

For much of the first month the sound of battle was incessant. Mostly, it sounded as if it was raining rail trucks, and everywhere the terrain erupted in stupendous geysers of ice and earth. But, occasionally, the softer, crackly sound of rifles could be heard. Sniper fire was a constant scourge on the Hogsback, with officers a favoured target. Saluting had long since been abandoned, and Flint now covered up his silver bars of rank. He also carried a rifle, so that, at a distance, he'd look like an enlisted man (This rifle was a detail he'd kept ever since, and he got it out a few months later, when I paid him a visit at home. It was a slim black German model, which he'd taken off a sniper).

There were few let-ups in the shellfire. Although the Americans always had more to throw, both sides were overly impressed by the spectacle of bombardment. It's said that during the campaign in Alsace-Lorraine, an average of 10,000 shells a day were loosed off across the landscape (Flint's battalion alone fired 4,624 rounds of high explosive during January, and they weren't even artillery). Little of this ordnance did anything to shorten the war, most of it simply plunging into the ridges, smashing up the trees and burning holes in the earth. At nine miles distance, a shell could miss its target by over 50 yards, enough to leave it quite unharmed. But, however empty these duels may have seemed, there was – as Flint tried to convey in his letter home – no saying when they'd start again, or if they'd ever end:

Guard, Guard, Guard. Hold! Be alert! Listen! Oh, hell, they don't have any goddamn arty left. TAKE COVER! Whoa bang whoa bang – the lousy so and sos . . .

Some soldiers even became inured to the sound, and found a curious elation in not being afraid. When this happened, they wondered if it was their nerves getting stronger, or the explosives getting weaker. This was always a dangerous moment, because the next stage was not caring what would happen, or if one lived or died.

But, for most people, there was no getting used to the shells. For them, the struggle was to avoid 'screwing up', or showing the fear that one felt. But even this was too much for many. Almost one in ten American soldiers suffered some form of 'combat fatigue'. It was a humiliating condition. In its worst form, a man might feel his personality suddenly gush away, and then he'd feel nothing at all. Such victims were like newborns – mewling, incontinent, unhearing, unseeing and mute. Nearly a quarter of all cases had to be repatriated, only to live lives taunted by guilt and the ghostly whinny of shellfire.

A few men were unable to leave their future to fate, and preferred to mutilate themselves. Self-inflicted wounds, or SIWs, were a criminal matter, but those determined on this course discovered that by shooting through a loaf of bread they could blast a foot off without the tell-tale marks of powder. In the records of B Company, there was only one officially recorded SIW. But there were others who fell under suspicion. 'One of them,' said Flint, 'was my first platoon sergeant, who'd injured his foot – theoretically, cleaning his rifle. He wasn't court-martialled because you needed to prove motive. Personally, I tended to believe him. He had guts. It was him who'd set up the machine-guns on New Year's Day.'

Gradually, the rhythm began to ease. By the end of January, there were days when there was hardly any shellfire at all, and – against the whip and snap of rifles – the men got used to new sounds, like the wind, the guttering of diesel fires, and crack of frozen blankets. In the lull, Flint's men were ordered to return to the positions they'd occupied almost a month before. It took them nearly three days to creep back along the ridge to the southern end of the Hogsback. There, they found themselves in Enchenberg again, the village of little castles, and – much to their delight – the prettiest girls in Lorraine.

Nowadays the traffic speeds through Enchenberg, and everyone's forgotten the beautiful war of 1945. But Flint hadn't.

'We were seven weeks here,' he said, 'although it never felt that.'

Enchenberg had obviously fared well in the bombardments and the sixty years that followed. We found the village pump where the men had filled their canteens; the old priest's house, with a frieze of roses round the door; and the doughty cottages where the officers had taken rooms. Most of the men would have happy memories of their time here. One opened a schnapps dealership, and another started taking bets on the Kentucky Derby from his home in Pillbox 99. Here too Cardona the Cuban had been reunited with his brother, Alfredo, who was a cook in the neighbouring division. 'Their first meeting in three years was a happy occasion,' reported *Panther Tracks*, 'and was celebrated in true Latin style with much embracing and fond caresses.'

Over on the other side of the main road, the ridge fell steeply away, disappearing into the forest below. There was still a path down to the valley. It began by ducking through the apple trees, and then descended into sycamores and firs. This was where some of the gunners had lived, in little sylvan suburbs, with names like Pine Boulevard and Spruce Lane. It's surprising how easily these ordinary Americans had adapted to their life in the leaves. Their dugouts were merely outlines now but back then they'd had log roofs and stoves, and had been decorated with old shell cases, and at night the men had sat inside, curiously proud of their work, while the snow dripped on to their heads. Further down still was where the minefield had been, and a dense weft of booby traps and trip-flares, marking the outer limits of American rule.

Every day, the Tennessee boys had collected up the animals killed by the mines and shared the meat around. Despite an order that there was to be no wildlife killed on the Seventh Army front, the boys still hunted. Sergeant Zwipf was an accomplished deer-hunter (and equally adept with the enemy), whilst others went after smaller game. Often these expeditions took them deep into the forest, and once Private Kent was gone for several hours. 'That was a goddamn *enemy* jackrabbit!' he panted, on his return. 'That jacktrooper was leading me straight to enemy lines!'

The fighting was never vigorous here. Most of the time was spent clearing snow and mines and trying to pinpoint the enemy. 'The farmboys were quite exceptional when it came to spotting camouflage,' said Flint, 'but we didn't shoot everything we spotted. Most times we let it go. Shooting would only bring something on yourself.'

Back in Enchenberg, a small wedding party was filing out of church. Amongst the ill-fitting suits and oily hair, a bride appeared. With her great rick of yellowy hair and her magnificent all-engulfing cleavage, she fitted neatly the stereotype of a country girl, and rather less so into her tiny metallic dress.

'Gee . . .' said Flint, with a mixture of admiration and alarm.

Jeff tutted. 'Big girls need lovin' too.'

It was not how Flint had remembered the girls of Lorraine. Back then, they were rather buttoned up and black, and wore big silk bows and clogs. But there was always something rather sensual and demanding about *la Lorraine*. In his book, *The Sisters Alsace-Lorraine*, written in 1950, Newman describes a society of curiously wistful women, women so needful of men that they'd even turn to magic in their search for a perfect specimen. Young *Lorraines*, according to Newman, were always throwing boys' names into streams or touring their houses naked at night, looking for lovers in the shapes of the shadows. One can only imagine the pheromonal turmoil that had ensued when several thousand Americans landed amongst them, in varying degrees of cleanliness, pulchritude and gallantry. Down the valley, in Lemberg – a town better known for its glass factory – the men of A Company were reported to have cancelled all their Paris leave because they were 'getting their full share of zig-zig from the local belles'.

I realised that things had been calmer in Enchenberg – although there was clearly more to the girls than bows and buttons. If *Panther Tracks* is anything to go by, restraint and desire were in constant struggle, here in the thick of the battle. Who would ever forget Adèle, the 'lovely blonde' who'd happily posed for photos in the snow? She was, as it turned out, already a war widow at the age of twenty, and had a baby two months old. Her unavailability was tantalising but there were plenty of others: Marie, Louise and Irene. Sergeant MacLean, the foul-mouthed cook moaned that it was all his boys ever thought about, trying to tempt girls into the barns with chocolate and bars of soap. Some even succeeded, especially those that spoke some German. At least one panther was 'going strong with a local deb' ('Affectionately known', according to Private Finnigan, the sex correspondent, 'as Horseface'), and there'd be plenty of tears when the time came for the war to move on.

It was hard to find women who remembered the Americans. The old shopkeeper said she'd been evacuated during the war, and so did several others. But I did meet one. She was a handsome woman with salt and pepper hair, who might easily have been eighty. No, she was not Adèle, she said, but more than that she wouldn't say. I suddenly felt ashamed: I'd gone too far, and my innocent exploration had become nothing more than prying. I changed tack, and told her instead about Flint. But, with such a gulf of time between them, they couldn't say they'd ever met. We said goodbye and, as I turned to leave, she caught my arm, and smiled enigmatically. '*Nous avons connu des moments terribles,*' she said, '*mais aussi de très heureux.*'

We lived through some terrible times, but also some that were happy.

That, I suppose, is much how Enchenberg would like to be remembered in this war. As we drove away, we saw the wedding party again, and the husband squeezing his great brassy bride into the back of a four-wheel-drive. His friends had let the tyres down and pulled the wipers out, so that they now flailed around like a pair of demented conductors.

Newman wrote about similar rituals sixty years ago. Marriage for *la Lorraine* was a moment of triumph, but here was a little reminder that the road ahead was bumpy.

And so it was for the Panthers. With the hiatus of February behind them, it would soon be time to face the full wrath of March.

87

Some months after my visit with Flint, I returned to Lorraine, to walk back across the plateau. I'd been curious to know what it felt like to live – however briefly – up on the plain, and to sleep a few nights in the grass. So far, I'd only ever experienced a single ridge in this great corrugated vista, and – whilst it was an important ridge – I realised that after New Year 1945 the fighting had moved down on to the fissured, open land to the north. Here, in the frozen grass and gullies, a dirty battle had yet to be fought.

I started in Rohrbach, and spent two days zigzagging back and forth across the plains to Bitche. First, I headed for the far north end of the Hogsback, and then veered west through the orchards of Rimling and down on to the grasslands below. From here, it was a beautiful, empty walk, and one that I realised thousands of young Americans had done before me, taking months instead of days.

The countryside would, of course, treat us very differently. Lorraine is famous for its mud. 'If you're off to Lorraine,' people said, 'you better take your boots.' With these dismal warnings in mind, I decided to set out in summer. The American infantrymen, on the other hand, had had no such choice. For them, Lorraine would be relentlessly soggy and unforgiving. Water would well up out of the grass, and their boots just seemed to absorb it. They soon realised that if they stood around like this for long enough, their toenails would fall out and their feet would turn first white, then purple and finally black. In the worst cases, toes had to be snipped off, or even everything up to the ankle. During December 1944, 56,000 Americans succumbed to trench foot – the equivalent of three or four divisions. Worse, it was unimaginably cold, and another metre of snow fell across the plateau. Tank engines froze and so did the wounded. General Patton became desperate, and even sent a message to Labrador, asking for six teams of Inuit sledge-dogs. (Naturally, they were sent, although by the time they arrived the snow had long since thawed.)

Whilst my Lorraine, with its crickets and its great swathes of hissing grass, would sometimes seem more like Africa than Europe, wartime Lorraine had been just as beautiful, in its own sort of way. Or that at least was how Anita Leslie, the Irish *ambulancière*, saw it:

There was something fantastic and ghostly about this winter ballet ... We could see the far-off Vosges cloaked in mist and storm, while around us the landscape remained white and black and scarlet – for wherever men had been there was blood, frozen tracks of rubies that glinted in the snow ...

This troubled me; what, if anything, was there to be learnt from tramping off after the infantry? Not much, perhaps – except that here was a landscape in which man still seemed piteously small.

Solitude – that fickle state between anxiety and pleasure – remains perhaps my strongest memory of that walk across the plains. Throughout the first day, I saw no one at all. It was like walking across my own planet, a strange turfed moonscape without a beginning or end. There were few signs of human life, and even they were hard to explain. Once, I came across an enormous tomb in the barley, carved with oak leaves and roses. Another time, it was a long straight road of grass, called the *Koenigstrasse*, or the Street of the King. When a hare jumped into my path, it was only natural that he was a giant. I think we both panicked, although he was the first to run, and for the next hour I watched him scissoring furiously into the distance, clearly mad at my intrusion.

I was happy enough to be alone, but happy to find a village in the evening. Even better, Hoelling had a little restaurant, where I sat down with a large party of locals, who happened to be Germans. In scratchy French and English, they told me they were retired miners from just across the border. Although, between them, they were missing a thumb, two fingers and an eye, they made good company. Several trays of beer arrived and then a trough of fluorescent pink paella. We all agreed that this was a funny thing to eat so far inland but then the miners reminded me that this was once the sea. I half wondered whether the suspicious-looking crustaceans now peering up at me weren't the fossilised harvest of this long-lost ocean. But there was nothing there that couldn't be washed away with Pils, and it was long after midnight before we all said our *auf Wiedersehens* and I tottered back into the grass.

Night-time on the plain was almost as surprising as the day. The sky was brilliantly black, and the uplands now glowed a spectral pearly grey. It was like looking backwards through the negatives of the day before. Darkness had also brought with it some new and disconcerting sounds: scratching, pain, rusty springs, a sneeze and a click like a safety catch, and then the whoosh of feathers followed by a thud. I carried on walking until I was well clear of the village and its barking dogs, and ended up in a vast grey space, marked on my map as *die Krammenacker*. I had an idea this meant the Crooked Land, and whilst 'crooked' wasn't quite the word I'd have used for this long-lost sea-bed, it perfectly described my sleep. All night, I was taunted by thirst and DayGlo prawns, and the sound of animals making a dinner of each other. But, at some stage, I must have drifted off, because the next thing I knew I was surrounded by church bells, my sleeping bag was drenched in dew, and there were daddy-long-legs slathered all over my face.

For a long time I lay there, thinking about the grass. Right then, there didn't seem anything else to think about – except perhaps the only other commodity the plains had in abundance which, of course, was solitude.

Few of the soldiers would forget the loneliness of their lives out on the plain.

In earlier wars, they'd have been linked together, usually by a network of trenches. During the Great War, the Western Front was – broadly speaking – defined by a single human ditch, stretching right the way across France. But by 1945 the geography of war was different. The battle-field was more sparsely inhabited for a start (the Allied Force of 1918 was almost three times as large as that of 1945). There was therefore never the manpower for a single magnificent trench, and instead the landscape was peppered with thousands of tiny, hand-made pits, known to their burrowers as foxholes. Sometimes these pits were mingled in amongst those of the enemy, or were so close that the soldiers could hear each other eat.

But the slightest noise might also bring a salvo of gunfire, and every soldier would take home his own mental snapshots from these vicious exchanges of metal; it might be a helmet, spinning through the air; or a stretcher-bearer with his hand blown off; or perhaps the body parts, gathered up in buckets.

One of those on this front was Paul Fussell, later Professor Fussell, who'd recall this tale from one of the soldiers out in the muck:

Gordon got ripped by a machine gun from roughly the left thigh through the right waist. He told me he was hit through the stomach as well . . . We were cut off . . . We were in foxholes by ourselves, so we both knew he was going to die.

We had no morphine. We couldn't ease [the pain] so I tried to knock him out. I took off his helmet, held his jaw up, and just whacked it hard as I could, because he wanted to be put out. That didn't work so I hit him by the head with a helmet and that didn't work. He slowly froze to death, he bled to death.

Soon, a new sort of silence had settled over the grasslands. From the Hogsback, Flint had said, 'it looked as if the Earth had swallowed up all human life'. But below the surface life went on, with whatever adjustments were needed. The men made stoves out of oil cans, and their own 'spook suits' from old mattress covers and sheets; they grew beards, and cut the tails off their greatcoats, which always got soaked and froze; they wore their wet socks round their neck and peed on their frozen weapons; they draped blankets around their shoulders, and never slept in sleeping bags (in case they were attacked); they hardly ever cleaned their teeth, and seldom washed (perhaps a rinse in an upturned helmet) and, if they needed to shit, there was always a sheet from *Stars and Stripes*, which was then lobbed over the edge. At least there was never any doubt where the front line ran – a foul strip of garbage looped its way across the plain, scattered with faeces, tins, paper, old shell cases, burnt-out vehicles, body parts and discarded ammunition. Happily, this grotesque frontier has long since disappeared.

By night, the men would often leave the safety of the turf and pad around across the moonscape. These patrols always held special terrors for the soldiers. Quite apart from the rich litter of booby traps and mines, the darkness distorted distance and position, and – just as it was for me – the plateau was a constant source of mysterious clicks and screams.

But whatever their fears, many young Americans carried out their duties with bewildering courage. The only thing that worried Eisenhower was that they were never more idealistic, although he needn't have worried.

For men reared on such a potent dose of democracy, this war was not an end in itself but merely a job that had to be done. Front-line newspapers, like *Panther Tracks*, were always picking away at the questions that really troubled soldiers, like 'When will this be over?' or 'How soon before the Russians arrive?' To many of the men living up here, creeping through the grass, there was no big picture, just a desire to be somewhere else. Most felt like the Joe who appears in the memoirs of Lester Atwell, a medic on this front: 'Ah'm tellin you, boy, if Ah ever gits home for a furlough, they're gonna have to burn the woods and sif' the ashes to find me again . . .'

88

At the eastern edge of the plateau, I entered the labyrinth of dark, dank valleys that lead eventually to Bitche.

For several hours, I followed an ancient sunken path through the forest. Here the sunlight was strained through beech and spruce, and in the moss my feet made deep, velvety prints which probably stayed there for months. It was a cheerless place. At one point I paused to inspect a puffball, only to discover that it was growing from a rat. I've never much liked forests, with all their gloom and their gruesome souvenirs of decay, and this was no exception. But at least I could saunter through it. Ahead of me, the infantrymen had taken every step in dread of mutilation. The forest floor had been littered in *Schuh*-mines, and sometimes worse; there were huge Teller mines to catch tanks, and a horribly animated device called an S-mine, which would burst out of the leaf mould, leap angrily into the air and explode in a lacerating squall of TNT and shrapnel. Decay or not, I had much to be grateful for in that, once again, this was just a walk in the woods.

It was always better when the path climbed up and over the ridges. Now the trees fell away and I'd find myself back amongst clover and ox-eye daisies, or jubilant clumps of cornflowers. Many of these hilltops looked like giant green eggs and the path would lollop along over several at once, before plunging back into the forest. From the top of one of these eggs – which the Americans had called Hill 429 – I could see all the way back across the plain to Germany. Soldiers, it seems, had enjoyed this spot long into the Cold War, because deep in a tuft of broom I found an old radio truck, now rusting out its retirement.

On the ridge just below Hill 429 was the village of Glasenberg. Its inhabitants had obviously spent so many centuries defending their knoll that all they could think of for their village shield was a picture of a skull. It was a bleak emblem for such a pretty place. Every miniature farm was clustered with apple trees, and on three sides the hill tumbled giddily away into the valley below. At the end of Rue de la Fontaine, I found three vast stone tubs where, once, I imagine, medieval man had rinsed his smalls. Reckless about the risk of some antique laundry disease, I was about to plunge my head into the first of these tubs when I heard a voice above me.

'*Bonjour, Monsieur. Vous êtes Américain, n'est-ce pas?*'

Down the stairs from a stone balcony came a man of about seventy. He wore green overalls and gritty boots, and had a moustache like an ill-fitting smile. Monsieur Steiner, as it turned out, had assumed I was American − not because I was about to take a bath in his trough but because Americans were the only people who'd ever come up here. The old soldiers had been back several times, he said, always the same ones: Fox Company, the 398th Infantry Regiment. They'd even brought their families.

What was it they wanted to see? I asked.

'*Un endroit dans la forêt,*' he said, '*qui s'appelle Suicide Hill.*'

I must have looked surprised.

Let me show you, he said.

We then set off across his little weedy farm, towards the edge of the forest.

This is where the Germans were, said Monsieur Steiner.

At first, there didn't seem to be anything under the trees except rubbish from the village, old pails and bathtubs, a mattress and a mangle. But then the path cleared again, and we emerged amongst an enormous network of earthworks and trenches. Below us, these great crests of soil and rotting wood rolled off into the forest, and way beyond them I could hear a river and the steady lop of an axe.

'*Voilà,*' said the farmer, '*Suicide Hill.*'

I asked him what had happened.

'*En Janvier 1945, ces bunkers ici furent attaqués par les Américains . . .*'

Monsieur Steiner described a battle of almost incomprehensible violence. As Fox Company closed in on the top of the hill, the earthworks had suddenly erupted in a firestorm of hot metallic chatter. In a matter of seconds, thousands of machine-gun rounds were ripping up air, smashing through trees and roots, kicking up vicious spouts of earth, and then scything bloodily through the men in the snow, wantonly tearing them apart, bursting faces, and nipping off arms and legs. In the years to come the survivors would tell of their astonishment at the speed and ferocity of this catastrophe, and their surprise at how easily their bodies were cropped and pruned in that invisible hail of steel. If it hadn't been for the quick-thinking of the radio operator in calling down some smoke-shells, Fox Company might have perished altogether. As it was, eleven men were killed and twenty-six injured, many of them so badly that they'd never walk or work again.

And you were here when this happened? I asked Monsieur Steiner.

Of course, he said, I was only ten but I've never lived anywhere else.

These were terrible things for a child to see.

The old farmer nodded. The dead were piled up in the laundry troughs. I remember one in particular, he said, because it didn't have a head. We walked back towards the farm.

'*Entrez*,' said Monsieur Steiner. '*J'ai quelque chose à vous montrer.*'

Inside, the debris of that day was nailed up around the walls. Every year, he said, the earth seemed to yield up more and more – cutlery, rifle bolts, shattered bayonets, helmets ragged and sieved, and the thick, greased leather of the German grenadiers. It was like a museum of gunfire, assembled from mildew and rust. But these were precious items to the Steiners, their own memorial to the people who'd died. The survivors hadn't been back for some years, said Madame Steiner. She worried that they were too old now, and that she'd never see them again. They were always welcome here, she said. ('I'd always cook them sauerkraut and sausage. This was their home in France.')

Now, all that ever came were letters, which they didn't understand. I said I'd try and help, and Monsieur Steiner went off and found the small bundle of envelopes, postmarked from Alabama to Salt Lake City. Even in my faltering French, it was poignant correspondence, replete with affection and regret. Some of the old soldiers had sent money ('Buy the children some candy'), whilst others recalled their first sight of Suicide Hill in over fifty years. 'To our surprise, we found the place where the Germans were positioned and where we were wounded,' wrote one. 'Snow and SS last time,' wrote another. But the last letter seemed to put the events of that day into the wider context of a life beyond. The writer described how three bullets had hit him: one wrecked his left arm, one his right hand, and the third crashed into his chest, burying itself harmlessly in the bible in his pocket. But, despite the paralysis and the months of surgery, the wounded man had never found defeat on Suicide Hill. Instead, he said, he'd gone on to do what he'd always wanted to do, and had qualified as a doctor.

When I stopped reading, I looked up, and saw Madame Steiner smiling, and the tears pouring down her face. Our heroes are safe, she said. We only hope they're happy.

The sacrifice of Fox Company was not in vain.

All through the forest and across the plain, hundreds of similar assaults had gradually driven the grenadiers back. As February turned to March, the grasslands were cleared and loudspeakers were wheeled out to broadcast the attractions of surrender and hot American food. Wherever they could, Germans gave themselves up, and hundreds of deserters scrambled through the slush. Guiderkirche, Simserhof and Schiesseck were all liberated, once and for all. Sometimes these assaults were led by tanks, and beneath their tracks the *Schuh*-mines crackled and snapped like popcorn.

Little by little, the Americans clawed their way back through Lorraine. Even Erching was retaken eventually – or, rather, it was engulfed in an upheaval of seismic proportions, induced by repeated waves of P-47s and some 10,000 kilos of bombs. Whilst little of the village survived this cataclysm, it was at least the end of the SS up here on the plain. Veterans say that when the artillery ceased – for the first time in three months – the birds began to sing. Shermans rolled back to their depots, and the civilians crept out of their cellars. Soon they'd be digging their gardens again and the shops would reopen, although there was nothing to buy except paper flags.

Over in Alsace, it was the same. In their sector, the Americans rallied and took almost 6,000 prisoners, while the southern end was recaptured by the French general, de Lattre. This last struggle was vicious and bloody, as *ambulancière* Leslie would remember: 'Occasionally, the Germans, themselves in frantic retreat, ran through a field and were blown to pieces by their own frantic contraptions. Legless German soldiers, abandoned by their comrades, lay calling for help while our own sappers, advancing cautiously with detonators, had terrifying casualties . . .'

But by mid-February it was over.

'The Germans,' announced de Lattre, 'have spent their last night on French soil.' Whilst this was a rousing thought, it wasn't entirely true. There'd be Germans in Lorient and Dunkerque until the end of the war, and – over here – the Americans still had one giant nut to crack: the legendary fortress of Bitche.

89

My last night in the open, I spent on the ridge, overlooking the fort. It was quieter here, on the edge of the forest, and the only other person I met was a horse-breaker called Monsieur Leininger, or Alexandre. Like me, he was sleeping in the bushes although, unlike me, he had the beginnings – or perhaps the tail end – of a wooden hut which he called 'The Ranch'. This was decorated with Marlboro packets and camouflage netting, and had a set of antlers nailed up over the door. Perhaps in his imagination Alexandre saw the whole place many thousands of miles to the west, in Montana, and he even had a little sign pointing to THE PRAIRIES. Although he wasn't overjoyed to see a stranger, he greeted me politely, as he would any wayfarer who'd just stumbled out of the Rockies.

'*Ne vous en faites pas pour le chien. Ni lui ni moi n'avons de dents.*' (Don't worry about the dog. Neither of us have teeth.)

The dog looked at me sleepily. Alexandre said they'd both been up all night delivering a foal. I wondered whether the dog also smoked, and whether it too mixed midwifery with brandy. Both of them had the same watery eyes and silvery-ginger hair. Alexandre said there'd also been a wife once, although she'd long since fled down the valley.

'*Et vous? Qu'est-ce que vous faites ici?*'

I told him about Flint, and the Americans poised above the town.

The old horse-breaker nodded. He said the forest was always turning up their things, sometimes just a box of bullets and sometimes a case of shells. It had been a dangerous place to grow up. For years, there'd been tanks lying around, and mines all over the forest. Sometimes, they'd made the bombs into fireworks, which were invariably spectacular, and every so often lethal. It was all stuff the Germans should have cleared away.

'*Les Allemands?*' I asked. Which Germans?

'*Les prisonniers!*' he said. '*Les prisonniers de guerre.*'

I don't suppose anyone will ever know how many grenadiers died, picking up their mines. Alexandre shook his head, and said he didn't know. The forest was a cruel place, and was still throwing up the bodies. Only twelve years ago he'd found an American, right up here on the ridge.

'*Avec une balle ici*,' said Alexandre, plunging a finger into his hairy cheek.

Shot right here. Just like someone asleep. Twenty-two for ever.

I'd been on this ridge before, of course, several months earlier with Flint.

Back then, we were celebrating the day he'd crept to the edge and looked down on Bitche, assuming – like everyone else – that it would soon be theirs. 'But that was before *Nordwind*,' he said, 'and the long battle to follow . . .'

It would be another hundred days before the Americans were back up here, on 16 March, looking down on the town. But this was a different army to the one before. Not only was it more experienced, it had been gradually building in strength. Along the Western Front, Eisenhower now had four and a half million men and ninety-one divisions – mostly American – at his disposal. A year earlier, he'd had not a single soldier deployed in Europe north of Rome, and now, within a fortnight, he'd have nearly a million in Germany itself. Meanwhile, along this section of front there were an extra 130,000 men, together with a mobile factory for making bridges and enough ammunition to pound the enemy under 2,000 tons of shells a day. As Flint wrote in his letter home:

> Time moved slowly in measured step right through the Ides of March, right through that period in which the armies of the past made the push-off for their campaigns. There was an electric tension in the air. All were wondering when it would be. Then, one night, came the answer. [On 15 March 1945] our artillery opened up and blasted away all night long. All night we could hear the shells whistling overhead, some high, some low, like a dragon rushing on to crush the foe . . .

Flint and his men were not part of the battle plan for Bitche, and wouldn't therefore see it again. Instead, they were ordered to head straight for Germany, and – on the day the Big Push began – they set off, crashing through the minefields and the last desperate salvoes of rockets.

90

From the ranch, I found a muddy path that led to the town. It was the same path the 397th had taken as they'd crept off the ridge. As I scrambled downhill, I wondered about the twenty-two-year-old. What had he been thinking as he clambered over the top? The battle ahead, or life beyond? A girl maybe, or even a child? Inspiring thoughts perhaps, until that bullet had smashed upwards through his face.

In the forest, the air fizzed with insects and was already sticky and warm. At the bottom of the slope, the trees opened out and Bitche looked momentarily magnificent, erupting from the corn. This was as near as any army had ever got before, but – that day at dawn – *les Bitchois* crept out to the fields to meet the Americans and guide them back through the mines. The enemy, however, was still buried deep inside the rock, and the Americans took no chances. The damage caused in the ensuing barrage of gunfire and rockets has never been fully repaired. I was surprised that the wall around the cemetery was standing at all, it was so deeply pocked and cratered. Odder still was a small farmhouse on the edge of the town, which looked like a case of structural smallpox. It even had bullet holes through the shutters, each hole repaired with a tiny patch of tin.

The owner said her father had done that, on his return from captivity. Madame Cuisse had never had the time or money to patch up the rest. She told me that the Germans had taken everything while they were away, every piece of furniture and everything from the farm. Her father had never recovered. In 1946 he'd wallpapered over the holes, fixed the shutters and then died of despair. No one had touched it since, said Madame Cuisse, and now she lived with her mother and all that remained of their farm, which included three dogs, six cats and a cage of pigeons and pullets.

'*Voyez vous-même*,' she said, and invited me inside.

She was right; time had stopped in 1946. The wallpaper was now a spectral sepia yellow, and there was no furniture except an enamel stove, two metal beds and a chair. On one of the beds sat a tiny figure, crumpled and pale as if made of tissue. Madame Cuisse knelt down and asked her mother to tell us about the war. Instead, the figure slowly uncrumpled and began to howl. Amidst the sobs and pleas, I heard the words 'stars' and 'blood', and something about a zoo for the dead.

'*C'est la maladie d'Alzheimer,*' explained Madame Cuisse. '*Elle a 93 ans.*'
The little figure was now screaming, and blocking up her ears.

This was new, Madame Cuisse told me, her mother's reaction to the war.

In dementia, it seems, she'd somehow found an unobstructed view of the past.

The trauma that had nibbled away the lives of the Cuisses still infested the town. Although the rubble had long ago been cleared away, Bitche had about it an air of lingering municipal shell-shock. Many of the houses looked cracked and chewed, and even the great fortress – which loomed, bloodshot and volcanic, from the centre of the town – was now slowly picking itself apart. Its once-mighty redans and ravelins were sagging into the weeds, and where the peppered masonry had fallen away there were jagged holes, each a disconcertingly meaty pink. This constant geological reopening of wounds can't have done anything for the fragile wits of those still living below.

The feeling of time so utterly paralysed was compelling. It sometimes seemed as if Bitche had reacted to the insults of the past by stopping the clocks and closing off the present. The town washhouse still functioned but much of the railway had failed (only one line had survived, I noticed, and the rest converged under a heap of rusting trains). Some of the older citizens still lived in the wooden huts built for them after the war, which they called 'barracks', and in which they said they'd frozen every winter for over sixty years. Meanwhile, the shops sold things I'd only ever seen in museums – demijohns, bamboo carpet-beaters, wool combs and copper bed-warmers – and there was usually thick yellow cellophane over the windows to seal out the sun. It was almost like a community of Miss Havishams, deeply rooted in a moment of cruelty almost two generations before. In the three days that I was there, I never saw anyone out at night, and even early in the morning the streets were empty except for the jackdaws waiting for something to happen.

Les Bitchois often looked dazed by the relentless inertia of their lives. In the bars men seemed to sit around for hours, just waiting, like the jackdaws. Even my own arrival aroused interest, and people would hobble over and shake my hand as if we'd all survived the same sudden and inexplicable disaster. One of these bars was down amongst the gaunt sandstone barracks which the Germans had built during their first invasion of 1872. Breakfast here meant either coffee or brandy, and the barmaid was a proper trooper's girl, with carrot-coloured hair and a wolf tattooed on her shoulder. Most of her customers were old *cuirassiers*, men who'd stayed on after their units had trotted away. What did that make them – the opposite of 'deserters'? Persisters, perhaps. Anyway, the cavalry had long since abandoned its barracks, and now they were empty, the windows flapping in the breeze. Poor Bitche, it was always either just too much war, or not quite enough.

At the top of the road that led to the fort was a heavy steel door, still punched with holes the size of teacups. This blast of gunfire was all that was needed to persuade the last of the panzer-grenadiers that further resistance was futile. It's said that they only ever fired six shots in their defence of the citadel. Their surrender would finally bring to an end the myth that Bitche was invincible (a blow from which, it seems, the town had never recovered). It would also bring to an end the Nazi occupation of Lorraine, and, across the region, more than 22,000 Germans were taken into captivity. The tragedy of *Nordwind* had finally blown itself out.

With the battle over, attention now turned to collecting up the dead.

91

From Bitche, I took a train out to the largest single gathering of Americans in Europe, a city for the slain.

St-Avold was only half an hour to the west, along a railway line that weaved in and out of the old front line. It was hard to believe that anything had ever happened here. From the train, I could see Rohrbach (which had remained without electricity until 1946) and Erching (which had once almost vanished altogether). Now it had all been restored, the villages rebuilt, the woods replanted, and the churches resurrected with spires and onion domes again.

The human damage had been harder to repair. Along this front lay the corpses of more than 70,000 soldiers. The Allies, as the new tenants of the land, at least had the luxury of being able to marshal their dead with a degree of stringency and respect. Here, in the words of ambulance driver Anita Leslie, is what happened to those killed on the German side:

The softening ground allowed graves to be dug, and the dead were gathered on carts. At one crossroads we encountered three shire horses dragging one of those wide platform wagons used for transporting tree trunks. And its load looked strangely like trees, for the hundred or more dead Germans were frozen stiff in every attitude. Their arms, held out like branches, showed how they had been killed in movement; but their faces, crystallised by the cold, were masked by the peace of the dead. The little old farmer, trying to control his plunging horses, waved to us merrily. His apple face was wreathed in smiles. 'Haven't I a funny load?' he shouted.

The Americans could afford to be more methodical with their own. Travelling with their wheeled city was a task force of battlefield undertakers, called Graves Registration. It was staffed almost entirely by blacks – victims of the army's strange ideas about who was capable of what – and, although their efforts have never been properly recognised, this was amongst the most gruelling and emotionally difficult work of the war. Their first and perhaps most difficult task was to remove the KIAs ('Killed in Action') as quickly as possible from the view of combat troops. Although, unlike the Eastern Front, there were occasional local truces for the collection of the dead, this usually meant working under fire, or, at the very least, in the volatile environment of unexploded ordnance. The dead themselves were often reluctant participants in this task, especially those crisped inside a tank. Before they could be excavated, and taken away in 'the meat wagon', they'd have to be sprayed with creosote.

The next task was to sort and identify the corpses. This was known as 'the stripping line', and here the undertakers had to work quickly with only thick rubber gloves between themselves and perhaps several weeks of putrescence. To start with, the dead man's clothes had to be cut away, and his personal possessions bagged up for sending home (less condoms and pornography and anything else that might offend his family). Then his identity discs were taken from around his neck. 'We all had two dog-tags,' Flint once told me matter-of-factly. 'You nailed one to the grave and the other stayed with the corpse.'

Any bodies – or body parts – that could not be identified were known as 'x-bodies', and were sent to the Ardennes. There, specialists got to work, injecting fingers with fluid to bulk out the prints, and making records of the teeth. If the dead man had neither a recognisable head nor hands, he was buried as 'An Unknown American Soldier'. (Nowadays, all remains found on the battlefield are sent to a similar laboratory in Hawaii, as happened to the dead soldier in the horse-breaker's tale. There are still very many to go. By the end of the war, there were almost 79,000 Americans whose bodies were never found, many of them lost at sea.)

The final task was burial. While the war continued, the KIAs were laid to rest in local divisional cemeteries. It was a Herculean task; on the Alsace-Lorraine front there were up to 16,000 American corpses, and – in the frozen soil – each grave took four hours to dig. Then, when hostilities ceased, they were all disinterred and their relatives were given a choice: the dead could be buried here with their comrades, or the US government would deliver the body to any place of the family's choosing, anywhere in the world. It might be a mountain village in Colorado or the slums of Manila, or alternatively a man killed in Italy might be transported to France to be reunited with a brother killed in Lorraine. There was only one restriction: no one – at least officially – was to be buried in German soil.

Soon the dead were on the move. Between 1947 and 1954, over 172,000 corpses made their final journey around the globe. In Europe, almost two-thirds of the dead sailed home to the United States, and in Lorraine those that were to remain were taken to St-Avold.

My train arrived at exactly the same time as a consignment of brand new tanks. St-Avold needed something new. My taxi driver told me that the mines had just been closed, throwing everyone out of work. He said he'd spent all his life working down there, 900 metres underground, and now all he had to show for it was this old car and cancer of the throat.

'*C'est drôle, n'est-ce pas? Mais ainsi va le monde.*' (Funny, isn't it? But that's the way it goes.)

He laughed, a tricky manoeuvre through a tracheotomy tube. In order to produce any sound at all, he had to clasp a hand around the ruins of his larynx. The crackle that this produced sounded like a radio, buried deep inside his chest. When I asked him about the American cemetery, there was a distant rustling and then, from the tube, the strange paper-dry, unglottal voice. There are, he told me, as many Americans buried under St-Avold as there are people living on the surface.

For a second, I had a vision of St-Avold in cross-section: the quick, the dead and the miners. Then the driver's mobile phone rang, which he answered, one hand to the throat and one to his ear. This left us flying through the town centre steered only by his knees. Now, I had another sudden vision, of mangled cars and people and me somewhere in amongst them. Perhaps my premonition system wasn't working, or perhaps it was just the thought of 10,489 young Americans curled up in the soil. Whatever it was, I was grateful for the cemetery, and a long calm avenue of linden and Scots pine. Whilst the old miner sat, coughing and rattling by the gate, I got out, and set off through the rows.

It was an astonishing feat of geometry and mowing. From wherever I stood, perfect parabolas of crosses arched away in every direction as far as the eye could see. The effect, presumably intentional, was bewildering: all perspective had been redefined and overwrought by the repetition of a single, innumerable shape – that of the soldier's grave. This was hard to enjoy, but then the cemetery was always intended to be admired rather than enjoyed. Amongst the tombs there were giant altars and a vast and spartan chapel. It occurred to me that these structures would have been better understood by the generation that built them, a generation more readily inclined to see death in battle as a feature of public duty rather than as an act of personal sacrifice. The mowing was part of this. I could see at least ten groundsmen at work, their presence living proof of the state's commitment to honour those who'd died in its service

Even in amongst the tombs it was hard to get a sense of the men beneath, rather than the army in which they'd fought. Each grave – startlingly white and uniform – was inscribed with the sparsest of information: name, rank, unit, place of birth and date of death. There was no indication of age, residence or family. In such a drought of detail, all I could tell was that sometimes I was amongst Texans and New Yorkers, sometimes Puerto Ricans, and sometimes men without heads or hands. But I did find at least four of the Panthers – including Eugene Whitener, who'd died on the Hogsback when, all of a sudden, a beautiful January day was torn apart by shells.

In the middle of the cemetery was another public building, smaller than the others but made with all their solemnity and stone. Inside, oddly enough, it contained an all-American living room (with buttonback chairs, floor rugs and a log-effect fire), some solace perhaps to those who'd made the trying journey through France. But, if this wasn't enough to make visitors feel at home (a delicate task in a cemetery), there was also the homely, well-polished figure of Mr Horace Thompson, himself a veteran of several conflicts and now the Superintendent of St-Avold.

I immediately took to Mr Thompson, and soon we were deep in the statistics.

'We got 151 unknowns here,' he told me. 'And 28 brothers laid side by side.'

I asked him how much the US government spent each year on cemeteries.

'About $50 million. That's less than the cost of a bomber.'

Mr Thompson obviously loved his garden of soldiers, and he even had a computer which could track the dead after their travels around the world. I tried to think of a name I knew. What about Sergeant Carey, who'd kept the Panzers out of Rimling?

Click. Click. 'Impressive . . . Medal of Honour. That's the highest award . . .'

'And do you have him here?' I asked. The question sounded odd.

Click. 'Nope. He's in the Ardennes. Probably an issue with ID . . .'

Poor Carey, the wounds he'd suffered that day must have taken much more than his life. I was sorry not to have found his grave. It's possible that, but for his courage, the Panzers would've got on to the Hogsback, and then this would have been a very different story (or perhaps there'd have been no story at all).

It was time to find the old miner again, and begin the journey back to Bitche.

Time too to rejoin Flint, and our journey of the summer before.

92

We had one final task before leaving France: an ascent of the citadel of Bitche.

It took Flint almost an hour on the cobbles and broken rock. At times, the road disappeared altogether, vanishing into the cliffs, where it curled upwards through giant subterranean casemates and through a complex of stables, smithies and ancient gunpowder stores. Often it was hard to see anything in the dark, although Flint was determined to go on, as if he'd promised himself this moment some six decades before. Clambering upwards through the sandstone, it was as much a feat of imagination as exertion. To me, the citadel felt more like the epicentre of a Victorian battle than the hub of mechanised warfare. But for Flint this was the end of the battle, a sight he'd yet to see.

Eventually, we emerged through a hole on to a plateau at the summit. The rock here was so dimpled with warfare that only a single building survived. Now the lizards had it all to themselves, although when they saw us they panicked and rippled back into the ground. Flint crossed to the parapet and peered out across the dark forests that had been the worst three months of his life. He could never have envisaged tranquillity like this, and I suddenly noticed how happy he was, happier than I'd ever known him before. Although – unlike me – he could never feel any great affection for France, its restoration was now a source of unimagined pleasure. I had no idea how much this meant to him until the following Christmas, when he sent a photograph of himself – happy on the citadel – to all his friends. It's over, the picture seemed to say: the war I've fought with most of my life has finally ended.

Town Hall, Brêche.

This, of course, was not how it felt at the time.

Even after France, the war was far from over, and some of the most vicious moments were yet to come. But at least, after this, there was the feeling that some-thing had given way within the Nazi structure, and that – from now on – things were rushing to an end. 'Much more to be told,' wrote Flint in his last letter from Lorraine, 'but time is now in his measured stride.'

93

Soon, our little French car would be free of national speed limits and soaring off through Germany. Jeff, who claimed that in the States he always slithered along at fifty, was thrilled by the prospect of the autobahn.

'It'll be like *flying!*' he said.

Unfortunately, he was right; flying is more or less exactly how it felt as we entered the Pfälzerwald at 180 km/h., except that, instead of several miles above, we were actually swooping *through* the trees. But even at this brain-jangling speed, we were still being overtaken by the locals. Wasn't German society supposed to be constrained? How could they be so unrestrained on the road?

The only other thought that occurred to me as I lay there, crushed flat by the G-forces, was that – at this speed – we might miss Germany altogether. We'd only just crossed the border, and already we'd sliced through most of the Rhineland Palatinate and were heading straight for the Rhine.

Flint, on the other hand, loved it.

It reminded him of the last time he did this journey. Indeed, speed was probably the most memorable feature of that wartime dash. The 824th had even been given a smart new machine for racing through the Reich. In mid-March 1945, the half-tracks and artillery pieces were finally dumped, and replaced with a sort of open-topped armoured sports car. It had a sleek, low profile, an aircraft engine and a high-performance thirst of just over a mile to the gallon. Although at 19 tons it was hardly nimble, it turned out to be the fastest armoured vehicle of the Second World War, and – in the right conditions – could manage a heart-stopping 50 m.p.h. All it needed was a fancy name. Officially, it was called the 'Gun motor carriage 76mm M18 ', and those who drove it called it the 'M18 TD'. Unofficially, however, it became known as the Hellcat.

'A beautiful machine,' said Flint, 'something that could really move . . .'

Everyone, it seemed, loved the M18. For the Treasury, it was a cheap alternative to tanks (at $55,000 a piece, instead of $70,000 for a Sherman). For the military planners, it would reshape the chessboard, like a castle that was everywhere at once. But for the men the attraction was simpler: the Hellcat would be the drive of their lives.

The problem was, it was just too clever by half. The speed was ingenious but it had only been achieved at the cost of durability and punch. With its 12mm of armour and its open top, sending the Hellcat into battle was like unleashing the family saloon. The only advantage of such thin plate was that shells tended to go straight through the bodywork and out the other side. Whilst this may have killed the crew, it did at least mean that the machine could be reused.

More troubling still was the fact that, although the M18 called itself a 'tank destroyer', it struggled with tank destruction. Its gun was just too light. In order to be of any real danger to Panzers, it had to sneak up on them, and then hit them right beneath the mantlet. Small wonder that, in the two months that the 824th had Hellcats, they'd only destroy a single Panzer (although, in fairness, German tanks were becoming scarce). This meant that the Panthers had to rapidly reinvent themselves; instead of hanging back in defence, from now on they'd be flying around with infantry. This was a costly use of armour, and never part of the plan. In fact, Hellcats had been declared redundant long before arriving in Lorraine. Production had stopped five months earlier, and of the 5,000 ordered, only 2,507 were ever made. Washington couldn't even persuade its lend-lease customers, Britain and the USSR, to take the Hellcat on. No thanks, they said. They wanted battle tanks and not a little roadster.

Meanwhile, Flint's men surged into action. Having not advanced an inch for more than three months, they now covered ninety-two miles in two days. Like us, they tore through the Pfälzerwald, and on 24 March 1945 – like us – they found themselves peering into the Rhine. Before them lay Swabia, and the single certainty that the journey ahead would be different to anything before.

Part 7 – Sauerkraut und Blitzen

The customs of the Germans are entirely different . . . They spend all their lives in hunting and warlike pursuits, and inure themselves from childhood to toil and hardship.

Julius Caesar, *The Conquest of Gaul*

Germany is nothing, but every individual German is much, and yet the Germans imagine the reverse to be true.

Goethe

There is a sense of richness over this land. It is in the Rhineland too; that feeling that this Reich, with its dreadful ambitions, has such an abundance of wealth in and under its soil.

R.W. Thompson, *The Devil at My Heels*, 1947

In this twilight of the Gods, the defenders of the Reich displayed the recklessness of fanaticism and the courage of despair.

Col. Stacey, Canadian military historian

94

As we crossed the Rhine, Jeff slowed just enough to allow us a glimpse of the waters below.

It was an arresting sight, a vast conveyor belt of barges and whirlpools sliding over the plain. Huge muscles of water – the colour of liquid pewter – would flex and ripple together, and then sprawl apart before plunging out of sight. Europe's greatest waterway was, it seemed, still in vigorous form after gushing out of the Alps. In the hundred-odd miles between here and the Swiss border, it had dropped an astonishing 420 feet. It was hardly surprising that navigation looked like an exercise in white-water shipping: the Rhine was literally hurling ships downstream, and would fight them all the way back up again. They couldn't even be sure they were making the same journey up as down, because the river was always changing its course and wandering off across the plain. Three hundred years ago, the village of Alt-Breisach was in Alsace but then the river had a change of mood, spilled round the other side and captured it for Germany.

Not everyone's impressed. Although the Rhine looks like a molten glacier, many Germans say it's more a torrent of chemicals than snowmelt (and that if you toss a bit of paper in, it'll come out as a photograph). Ruskin, on the other hand, thought it was just plain dull, or at least not half so grand as 'the Thames at Chelsea'. Perhaps this was just another silly Ruskinism (he also declared that Cologne Cathedral was 'an enormous failure' and that all German Gothic was 'abominable') or perhaps his protest-too-much views masked the underlying anxiety that so many Europeans have felt at this stage in their journey. After all, until now, he'd only dipped a toe in Germany, and soon he'd be fully immersed.

95

Few countries have ever managed to inspire in their neighbours such a subtle blend of fear and wonder. From the very earliest, it seems, awe has been the recurring theme of visitors' accounts. Julius Caesar described the *Germani* – or 'The Shouters' – as a hard-working and warlike people, probably best avoided. Tacitus thought much the same: 'Germans have no taste for peace; renown is more easily won amongst perils.' But he also described a people who were honest and hospitable, and who were devoted to their children and proud of the incorruptible chastity of their

South-west Germany

0   25   50   75   100 km

0   25   50 mls

S W A B I A

Mannheim
Eberbach
Heidelberg
Neckargerach
Speyer
Neckargemünd
Bad Wimpfen
Neckarsülm
Heilbronn
Mainhardt
Karlsruhe
Murrhardt
Althütte
Pforzheim
Winnenden
Waiblingen
Stuttgart Fellbach

Rhine

F R A N C E

Strasbourg

Neckar

G E R M A N Y

Ulm
Donau

Lech

Munic

Mindelheim

Kaufbeuren

B A V A R I A

Marktoberdorf

Lechbruck

Trauchgau

BODENSEE

Grainau
Garmisch-
Partenkirchen
Mittenw
Leutasc
Seefeld

Innsbruck

A U S T R I A

Heilbronn

Unter-
eisesheim

Audi
Factory

N E C K A R S U L M

Ober-
eisesheim

Neckar

Power
Station
Factories

ASSAULT
BOATS

US ARTILLERY

Kanalhafen

Neckar

Wartburg

HEILBRONN

0   1   2   3   4 km

0   1   2 mls

wives (an adulterous woman was shorn, and then flogged from the village). These same women, he noted, had an important role in this culture of warfare, and would urge their men into action by the simple expedient of showing them their breasts.

This military striptease may not have lasted but Germany remained a daunting prospect. In the twelfth-century Byzantine poem *Digenis Acritas*, (Διγενής Ακρίτας), the stereotypical German is open, invincible in war, gout-ridden and ends his life in wine (the typical Frenchman, by contrast, is childish, perfidious in war, and passes his time in fraud). Even in the age of the Grand Tour, visitors to Germany would find plenty to surprise them. It was Europe's dystopia, an unruly confederacy of over 1,800 separate political and cultural units. There was no single ruler, no fiscal system, no national army, no road network and therefore only the most primitive system of inns (English tourists in the eighteenth century were advised to show their guns to the landlord and tell him they weren't afraid of superior numbers). Boswell had to sleep on a table in Vellinghausen, and in a cowshed in Hanover. But despite its somewhat bosky amenities, visitors still found much to admire. 'The Germans in general are a good natured people,' wrote one tourist, William Lee, in 1753, 'lovers of pomp and magnificence.'

Writing two centuries later, Winston Churchill was rather less generous. 'The Hun,' he said, 'is always at your throat or at your feet.'

The Panthers had experienced their own moment of Caesarean awe during the crossing of 1 April 1945.

It began with a spasm of Ruskin-like reproof. Many of the soldiers were disappointed to find themselves not amongst fairytale Rhineland castles, but in a huge American traffic jam. 'It seemed the whole US army was pouring into Germany,' wrote one of the soldiers in Flint's division. There was further dismay when they found that the river was cluttered with sunken boats, and that the only bridge was a flimsy pontoon which, under the weight of the Hellcats, bobbed beneath the surface. Worse, on the other side, there was no welcome: no flags and no happy villagers. The Panthers were, of course, in hostile – or 'bandit' – territory. 'SEE GERMANY AND DIE,' read the graffiti: ONWARD SLAVES OF MOSCOW! Somehow, this was not what the young Americans had expected.

But disillusion soon turned to horror. The battle for Germany (known rather modestly as Operation Undertone) was now a week old. On its very first day, the Americans had brought 2,000 pieces of artillery to bear on Germany, and had attacked it with 1,500 bombers and an airborne invasion comparable to that of D-Day. By 1 April, Germany was already looking ragged and medieval. Ahead of Flint's men, the leading units ran into a *Wehrmacht* column consisting entirely of horses and carts. 'The tanks brought all available guns to bear on the column,' runs the official history. 'The Germans and their horses panicked, and wagons and their horses were strewn all over the road. A tankdozer was brought in to clear up the mess, and the advance continued.' For a while, the Joes tried to capture the surviving animals so that they could ride instead of walking, 'but the horses were still too skittish for that'.

Meanwhile, the magnificence and pomp of Mannheim (a feat celebrated these days in concrete) had all but disappeared. The old baroque city was nothing but a field of caves. Swallows returning from Africa found their old roosts gone, and had to make new nests out of plaster picked from the ruins, feathered with matted horsehair and strands of anti-radar tinsel. Strangely, the only structures to have survived intact were the factory chimneys, which had somehow withstood the bombs. This made the Rhineland cities look like petrified forests, and amongst the first to wander through them was the British novelist, Mervyn Peake:

They are no more [he wrote]. They are relics. Terrible as the bombing of London was, it is as absolutely nothing – nothing – compared with this unutterable desolation. Imagine Chelsea in fragments with not a single house with any more than a few weird-shaped walls where it once stood, and you will get an idea in miniature of what Mannheim and Wiesbaden are like.

That afternoon, Flint's Hellcats, now in support of 'Combat Team 398', drove west through the turnips and apple orchards, coming to a halt in what's now the well-scrubbed village of Plankstadt. At some stage, news came through that – two hundred miles to the north – Hitler's army in the Ruhr had surrendered and over 400,000 men had handed in their arms. Along the line, the Americans held church services under the blossom – not services of thanksgiving (for that would have been premature) but services to commemorate the fact that, improbable as it seemed in this Armageddon, it was actually Easter Sunday.

96

Soon we were soaring again, through a landscape throbbing with work.

It was exactly as Caesar had described it, with only the hardware updated. Everywhere, the *Germani* were contorted with effort, although nowadays their world was latticed in ring roads, canals, gas pipes, *Autobahnen*, and high-tension cables snapping out the volts to industry. Even the little dormitory towns looked determined and chaste, their houses the colour of overalls and fitted with shutters as if they were shops or roll-top desks. Most of these places had name plates too, so that every street read like a roster, a community ready for duty. The Swabians, a friend from Mannheim once told me, are famous for their thrift and industry.

'They live to a simple code,' she said: '*Schaffe, schaffe, Häusle baue.*' (Toil, toil, and build a little house.)

But were they really thrifty, or just saving for a 7-series? Swabians can't resist a sporty pair of wheels. Often, their houses were completely dwarfed by the car they kept in the drive. Perhaps the *Häusle* was just the rather dull thing one kept by the street whilst real life was lived in the car, tearing round like Batman? Already, I had the feeling that there were two sides to the Swabian character: in public, the steadfast, po-faced worker; in the privacy of his little metal box, a comic-strip eccentric never more comfortable than when speeding along in his tracksuit.

On reflection, perhaps this love of cars wasn't as odd as it seemed. After all, cars had started here; Mannheim was the cradle of motorisation. Had we been driving along here on a fine spring day in 1888, we'd have seen one of the earliest specimens, the work of Mr Benz. At the controls was his wife, Bertha, who'd taken the contraption without her husband's consent. She and her sons were on their way to Pforzheim, sixty miles to the south. Not only was this the world's first case of joyriding, but Bertha was the first ever woman to take the wheel. Along the way, she'd used her hatpin and suspenders to repair the ailing engine, and had stopped at a shoe shop to replace the brakes.

Later, on another trip to Swabia, I caught up with the Benz machine in the state capital, Stuttgart (which, of course, has several museums of cars). It looked like a little leather sofa mounted on a threshing machine. I often think that if cars had never progressed beyond this stage I might have understood the Swabian affection.

*

Swabian prosperity might also have been measured in food.

Entering this *Musterländle* – this model state – was like driving into a salad. Wherever it wasn't sprouting industry, the land was sprouting radishes and lettuce. We passed through forests of cabbage, and an area that looked like the Serengeti for pigs, the horizon heaving with pork. Germans, it seems, just can't get enough of the stuff and – every year – they get through an eye-watering 110 lb. a head (usually stuffed into one or other of the 1,500 different varieties of sausage). With consumption like this, it's not surprising they need such solid cars, to convey them from pork fest to pork fest.

Remarkably, this abundance had continued throughout the battle. Only the cities starved ('*Wir hungern*,' the citizens complained as the Americans took over). But in the country it was breakfast as usual. The Swabians could even afford to be generous to their conquerors, and the *Amis* were offered omelettes, bowls of milk and sandwiches, which were nibbled to show that they weren't poisoned. Elsewhere, the Moroccans helped themselves to the livestock. *Ambulancière* Leslie watched as they caught a ewe, cut its throat and let the blood drain away ('I felt glad,' she wrote, 'that death could be so simple and comparatively painless'). The North Africans then settled down to a *schwäbisch* feast of roasted mutton and chicken, cooked with grapes and apples, potatoes, onions and steaming hummocks of spicy cabbage.

'This,' said Leslie, 'was their kind of war.'

97

Aboard *Le Missile*, we all felt slightly differently about being in Germany.

My own feelings were probably the least developed. This was largely a matter of upbringing. Like most Britons of my generation, I was always taught to believe that Germans were, by turns, both hilarious and sinister. It was a theme repeated everywhere. Schoolmasters couldn't resist *ze funni akzint* (and even the occasional goose-step). On television, there were good French cops, nice Dutch detectives and amusing Spaniards, but the Germans were always incorrigibly wicked. In the cinema, too, they invariably looked either mutilated or monocled, and were usually dressed in coal scuttles. Even intellectuals took up the theme, encouraging the idea that anything dark and nasty (like *Realpolitik*, *Weltschmerz*, *Schadenfreude* and *Angst*) was always better expressed in *Deutsch*. Worst of all was the popular press, which was delighted to have found a victim in perpetuity. There was never any distinction between Nazis and Germans, and the joke was set to run and run. If anyone ever commented on this, as the German Culture Minister, Michael Naumann, once did, the tabloids would respond by simply running off some pictures of Dachau 'just to jog the memory' (particularly inappropriate in Naumann's case because his family were Jewish, and had joined the battle on the American side).

Aside from all this, I also had some earlier travels to contend with. During the late Eighties, I'd been to Germany many times to represent British soldiers at their courts-martial. Usually, I'd stayed in old *Wehrmacht* barracks and had seen no one but Britons. Germany without Germans was an unsettling experience which seemed only to feed my preconceptions. I noticed that every German car was equipped (by law, apparently) with a pair of surgical gloves, and that all lavatory bowls had a little shelf in order for one to inspect the departing stool. Equally disconcerting were the TV listings, where dead actors were identified with a crucifix and the date on which they'd died. To make matters worse, I then had to appear – dressed in a gown and horsehair wig – at a military courthouse still adorned with concrete swastikas. None of this did anything to dispel the impression that either the British had got rather stuck in the past, or the Germans were as weird as we thought.

Jeff had a slightly more telescopic view, but at least one uncluttered by the past. Americans have never suffered the triumphalism of the British. Most simply think of Germany as somewhere foreign, clean and far away. When I asked Jeff what it meant to him, he said 'Volkswagens'. At least he could think of something German. I suspect that many others have no idea that the German things in their life (the Löwenbräu lager, the Braun toothbrush and the Adidas shoes) aren't actually American at all. This is an easy mistake in a country which is itself so inherently German. Flint's German-speaking platoon was by no means unusual in the mid-twentieth century. You only have to look at a Louisiana phone book to realise that you're back in Swabia, except with French towns and English streets. The old story that the US Senate only passed by one vote a resolution to adopt English rather than German may be a myth, but the immigration was real. Between 1820 and 2006, some seven million Germans migrated to the USA, more than from any other European country. Even now, Germans are heading for the States at the rate of around 40,000 a year.

All this gives the two societies much in common. For a start, they're both Protestant, federal, republican, beer-drinking and highly carnivorous. They're also both ardent plutocracies, and yet insist that their citizens are equals (all Germans, according to a recent study, are upper-lower-middle Middle Class). In work too they share a similarly rigorous attitude, and can be censorious of leisure. Much of this is lost on the British. More than once I've felt that, if only the Americans spoke German, we Britons would probably understand them better.

Naturally, there are also huge differences between the two republics. Perhaps the greatest is that Americans feel they've found their destiny, whereas Germans believe that theirs has been denied – a factor that may explain why the human traffic is all one way.

Flint was thrilled to be back. For days, I'd been aware of his mounting excitement, as if – once again – Germany was the destination and France just a stage to be endured. 'The Germans were cleaner,' he told me, 'more progressive, and more ambitious. People like us. They're far more *sensible* people.'

It didn't seem to matter that they'd been the enemy before. Soon Flint was singing along in German, and calling out the place-names. From now on, whenever we got to a hotel, he booked himself in as '*Oberleutnant Flint*', which always made the Germans smile. He liked everything: the beds, dinner at seven ('instead of the middle of the night, goddammit'), and sausage-meat for breakfast. He also thought the ladies more prepossessing on this side of the Rhine, a view shared by the soldiers sixty years before:

> For months, [wrote one] the only thing female that we had seen were the klutzy, husky rural French farm women clomping around in their wooden shoes and slinging manure with pitchforks. [German women, by contrast] were nicely shaped, dressed, and coiffured, and obviously knew that there were strict rules against fraternisation with the enemy. However, they flaunted their femininity, committing a little hormonal sabotage . . .

Flint's pleasure, however, was always more ancestral than hormonal. He told me his family had been coming to Germany for over a hundred and twenty years, beginning with his grandmother. 'My father was sent to

The Neckar Valley. Flint's men were almost relieved to have reached Germany. A third of them spoke fluent German, and, to them, the natives were cleaner and more honourable than their allies, the French.

The city of Heilbronn lay ahead. It would become a mini Stalingrad.

Although badly damaged by air raids, its population would put up a vicious resistance. It still bears the scars.

Flint was astonished the city's restoration (although these days the interior of the Rathaus is finished i polystyrene).

memorials in Garmisch-
[G]enkirchen. Germany would
[pay] a heavy price for the war
[it ha]d begun. Seven million of
[its c]itizens were killed and, of
[thos]e, 1.3 million corpses were
[neve]r found. Of them, all that
[rem]ains is a plaque.

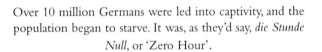

Over 10 million Germans were led into captivity, and the
population began to starve. It was, as they'd say, *die Stunde
Null*, or 'Zero Hour'.

(*Left*) Amongst the PWs, Josef Ratzinger, now
Pope Benedict XVI. (*Below left*) Another prisoner was Field
Marshal Rommel's son, Manfred, who was serving as
a flak gunner, aged 15. (*Below*) Between 1976 and 1990
he was the mayor of Stuttgart, and is now retired, living
amongst the trophies of his great democratic career.

Hitler's Olympic Stadium, Garmisch-Partenkir
To the Nazis, the Alps was a mystical place,
a repository of the Teutonic spirit.

The Americans made a dash for the Alps,
expecting to find one last massive army,
and a Nazi Shangri-La.

The Leutasch Valley. A labyrinth of passes, forests, corridors and choices, Flint would remen
Austria as wilder than anything he'd seen before. Back then, there were dead bodies along
road, German soldiers killed by the SS for their shirts.

A long tradition of Alpine travel. In 1910, Flint's father set off through Germany in a 1906 Oldsmobile, with his wife, two small children and four spare tyres.

Flint and his grandson, Jeff Bartley. Jeff was only a few years older than Flint had been in 1945, and found Europe equally curious.

Not every visit was so happy. The last time Flint was in the Alps, an assassin tried to kill him - although it cost the marksman not only his *drillinger* (which Flint still has, right) but also his life.

The main street
Innsbruck. Back
in March 1938,
it provided the
Nazis with a
rousing receptio

The Tirolean Austrians provided Hitler
with some of his most dogged support.

(*Above right*) In a remarkable city like
Innsbruck, it was unsurprising to come
across a man like Bruno.

(*Right*) In 1945, as a young GI, he'd met a
starving woman here and had married her
and stayed ever since.

...e 'beach' at Oberhofen, with Hohe Munde behind. Every morning a beautiful naked girl ...ad appeared and bathed in the Inn River. (*Inset*) Flint on the same beach 60 years earlier.

...e Oberhofen *Schützenfest*. A huge army of feathered rebels assembled on the Americans' old camp ...The *Schützenkameraden* still march with the WW2 rifles they'd hidden from the Americans in 1945. ...*et*) Alfred Kirchmair and his niece. He still recalled the last American visit sixty years before.

The summit of Hohe Munde (2,662m), and the Inn Valley (Telfs in the foreground, and Oberhofen just beyond). Having survived eight months of fighting, in June 1945, Flint and his gunner decided to try their luck on the mountain.

(*Left*) Almost exactly sixty years later, the author set off after them.

(*Above*) Flint in Oberhofen at the end of the war, as portrayed by a concentration camp survivor.

Dresden for seven years of his education. Matter of fact, he was there with the owner of Zeiss, and with Hjalmar Schacht, who became Hitler's Minister of Economics . . .' Later, just before he joined the FBI, Lawrence Flint returned to Germany to teach the science of fingerprinting to the German police. 'He always loved it here, and in 1907 he brought my mother over, on holiday.'

Three years later, the Flints returned again – with two small babies – for their greatest adventure of all. 'Father decided to bring his automobile, an open-topped 1906 Oldsmobile Runabout, called Merrywheels. He had it shipped to Hamburg, and from there my parents drove it down to the Alps, with my brother and sister in the back – aged one and three! I guess they must've made a curious sight. Father knew he'd never find spare tyres and so he brought four of his own, and – as there were no gas stations – he had to buy his benzene at the drugstore. And the automobile itself was considered so valuable that at night they brought it into their hotel, and kept it in the ballroom. But they made it, and my mother became the first American woman ever to climb the Jungfrau . . .'

'And then it was time to head back?' I gasped, 'and do it all over again?'

'Sure, although by the time they got home Merrywheels had to be scrapped.'

All this made our autobahn adventures seem rather modest. Whatever else can be said about touring, it's not what it was.

98

The natural American affinity with Germans alarmed the generals of 1945.

'We have to get tough with Germany,' declared Eisenhower. 'And I mean the German people, not just the Nazis.'

He himself had no difficulty working up a little hatred. Eisenhower was appalled by *Nordwind*, the Germans' pointless resistance and what he saw as their 'conqueror complex'. He told his wife that they were 'beasts', and – despite his own Teutonic ancestry – he had no compunction about killing them. 'People of the strength and warlike tendencies of the Germans do not give in. They must be beaten to the ground.'

Down the line, he ordered a new era of hostility. Regimental newspapers were used to announce strict rules (mostly ignored, according to Flint) against speaking German, fraternisation, gifts and playing with the children. *Panther Tracks* also carried hair-raising tales of saboteurs, ten-year-old gunmen, and Americans lined up and shot. In such an atmosphere, Eisenhower himself couldn't help sounding rather Roman (which is probably much how he felt): 'You're entering Germany not as a liberator but as a victor! The only way to get along with the Germans is to make them *respect* you, to make them feel the hand of The Master!'

As always, it was left to General Patton to put it in more soldierly terms:

> We're not going to shoot the sons of bitches, we're gonna rip out their fuckin' goddam guts and use them to grease the treads of our tanks! We're gonna murder those lousy Nazi cocksuckers by the bushel-fucking-basket! Rip them up the belly! Shoot them in the guts! We're gonna go through them like crap through a goose . . .

Powerful words for a man who wrote poetry and believed in reincarnation. But Patton was always a GI's general, and fought his war with three mistresses, a pair of nickel-plated revolvers and a Cadillac. His effect on the enemy was devastating, and who knows what impact he might have had in the post-war years (he'd wanted to push the Russians out of Germany). But it wasn't to be. On 9 December 1945, his Cadillac was making its way through this countryside when it was hit by a two and a half-ton truck. Patton broke his neck, and was carried to Heidelberg, where he died a fortnight later. When his funeral was announced, more than 20,000 soldiers volunteered to carry his coffin.

99

If ever there was a German city that could be described as having been at the heart of American affection it was Heidelberg.

Even now, its citizens are puzzled by their survival. Whilst all around them, great Swabian cities had tumbled into dust, Heidelberg had remained virtually untouched. Some people told me that this was because Patton and friends had already earmarked it as the capital of their American army in Europe. Others said it was saved by Mark Twain, who'd spent the summer of 1878 pottering round the city, and who'd described it as 'the last possibility of the beautiful'. But was that really the sort of sentiment that made strategists go weak at the knees? It seemed to me that only a

Broadway hit could work magic like that – and then I discovered that there *was* one. For several seasons, from 1924 onwards, Sigmund Romberg's *The Student Prince* (a tale of ordinary royalty, set in Heidelberg) had played to packed houses. It was obvious that amongst the little boys in the audience was the future membership of Tactical Air Command. To them, bombing Heidelberg would have been outrageous, like bombing Toytown or the long-lost kingdom of Narnia.

Heidelberg's war even had a Broadway ending. By Easter 1945, the Nazis had destroyed all its bridges, and it was surrounded by Americans. But on that Good Friday a young schoolgirl, called Ami Tham, had rowed out across the Neckar to meet the foe and ask that her home be spared. A few hours later, and without a shot being fired, the great green and friendly giant was settling down in the city.

And that, I later discovered, is where it's been ever since. There were still some 10,000 troops in town, making up one in twelve of the populace. During the course of several visits over the next few months, I'd meet a number of these soldiers. Some had come from Saudi Arabia ('Shit all there but sand') and some were going to Iraq ('It's just a phone call away!'). Like soldiers everywhere, they were accomplished grumblers: the coffee was too strong, the showers too weak, the beer too bitter (they had to drink it with lemon), the bells drove them nuts, and they didn't know 'what the fuck was going on in the soccer'. One of them even had a T-shirt describing himself as an 'Official Member of the Piss and Moan about Everything Society'. But, actually, they loved Heidelberg, and, every night, I'd see their shaven heads bobbing through the crowds, bringing a new accent to this fairyland, which was mostly that of jive.

Flint's only complaint about Heidelberg's tale is that he wasn't part of it. Hellcats weren't needed in Narnia (and, besides, further up the Neckar, there was another battle – small but extraordinarily vicious – which had yet to be fought). We decided to make up for this historical injustice by diverting *le Missile,* aiming it at the city, and dropping it – in contravention of some truly Narnian traffic laws – right down the high street. Heidelberg wasn't built for cars, of course, but only for hobgoblins and elves.

100

It was reassuring to find that the city was still nine-tenths fantastic and the rest improbable. Tucked into its own little gorge, Heidelberg has its own weather system (five degrees warmer than the rest of Swabia), its own caveman (the oldest European ever found) and its own bright-red version of Jericho. Every now and then either the French or the weather had done battle with this castle, blasting away the ramparts with gunpowder or 20-gigawatt bolts of lightning. Most agreed that this had improved its appearance, making the fortress more improbable than ever. Mark Twain thought it was the King Lear of castles – 'deserted, discrowned, beaten by storms, but royal still and beautiful'. Well, little difference there, I'm pleased to say.

Meanwhile, the town below looked as if it had been designed by cake-makers, using gingerbread and icing. Most of the buildings seemed edible, especially the gatehouse over the bridge, and the Hotel zum Ritter which was decorated with delicious sixteenth-century fruits and a flock of biscuit-coloured sheep. It's sad to think this is how much of Germany must've looked before the Allies bombed it into crumbs, and – if Heidelberg's anything to go by – a lot more was lost besides. Here, right in the centre, it was still possible to buy a fox's tail, an armful of LPs, a bottle of absinthe and a battle-axe. Even McDonald's was a delicate rococo, raspberry pink.

'Oh, darn it,' said Jeff, 'and now here come the cops.'

As far as I was concerned, their intervention was heaven-sent. That first morning, our car found itself caught up in a surge of students, and was being carried backwards down the *Hauptstrasse*. Being the longest high street in Germany, it could have taken hours, if not days, to extract ourselves, and even then there was no guarantee we wouldn't be swept back in again on a small tsunami of Koreans. A gauntlet rapped on the window, which Jeff opened. Towering above him was a beautiful sylph-like girl, dressed in leather, white, gold and bullets. 'Gee, I'm awful pleased to see you, officer,' said Jeff, in his broadest West Virginian, and then with just a hint of adultery, 'I thought we'd had it there.' To her credit, the policewoman blushed prettily, and showed us where to go. Her directions were magnificently gruesome, and involved a square where the gibbet used to hang, the old imperial prison and a street called 'The Devil with a Chopper'. It all sounded like a warning, a sort of parking ticket in baroque.

I was sorry to have got off on such a bad note amongst the modern-day *Homo heidelbergensis*. It always seemed they had enough to worry about. Perhaps all Germans were worriers? Or perhaps it was the burst castle above them (or their own brush with pulverisation)? Whatever it was, I soon discovered that everyone seemed edgy. Waitresses worried about acid rain and nuclear power, and a physicist once told me that the nation was getting lazy. Meanwhile, taxi drivers were always fretfully grooming their cars, as if they were horses, and would turn their engines off at the lights. Being stressed, or *strapaziert*, was merely an expression of normality, which was odd in a city so patently improbable. During that first visit, with Flint and Jeff, our hotelier was so stressed by our appearance that he would tut and cluck whenever we went near reception. I couldn't face this again, and so when I returned on later visits I stayed at a place in the centre, where at least the old *Gastwirt* had managed to calm her nerves with vodka.

But, despite this anxiety around the edges, there was always a seam of pleasure running through the city. The statues, I noticed, often wore lipstick, and one of the most prominent shops on the *Hauptstrasse* was a place selling large recreational breasts. Every morning began with a parade of giant dogs around the Heiliggeistkirche, and a procession of men in Monty Python moustaches. This, of course, was not quite what I'd expected of the Germans.

Naturally, 30,000 students made their own contribution to this levity, and until 1914 the university had even been obliged to keep a prison. Imprisonable offences had included smoking in public, kicking street lanterns, taking dogs into class, bearing weapons, disguising oneself on a sledge, 'misinterpreted gallantry', and attending a theatre in the presence of an actor. Surprisingly, this *Studentenkarzer* had survived, preserved with all its bars, iron beds and lamp-black graffiti. There were four cells – Sans Souci, Solitude, Villa Trall and the Palais Royale – in an attic above the university administration. But, although it had a certain dramatic gravity about it, life for *captivus academicus* was never particularly hard. In all the photographs of that time, the prisoners look louche and dressy, in their fancy jackets and pillbox hats, and are either singing or smoking or walloping back the wine. Life in the *Karzer* was, it seems, merely a continuation of life on the outside, except slightly more compact.

Meanwhile, in the drinking dens the fun had continued unabated. These places weren't like the fussy little outlets we think of as bars. Many of the *Studentenlokale* have been swabbing out the beer and spew for the best part of six hundred years. With all their soot-black panelling, antlers and tree-trunk tables, it was like going for a drink in the middle of a forest, or in the Hall of the Mountain King. Some even had elfish names – 'Zum Sepp'l', 'Schnitzelbank' and 'Schnookeloch' – and 'Zum roten Ochsen' (The Red Bull) was decorated with a huge portrait of a dead hare, and another of Kaiser Wilhelm II. Flint loved it here, and – if he'd had an axe – he'd have added his initials to those already hacked into the woodwork. It was also the place to get his tongue round German again, and to sink his face into a mound of pork and noodles, or, as they called it, *Schwäbische Schweinerückensteak mit Speck und Zwiebeln*. Not something one wants to say after a couple of buckets of Wonder Brew.

Here, in matters of beer, the locals were truly legendary. It wasn't just that the stuff was good, but the way they put it away. Pots arrived, were drained, refreshed, and drained all over again. Sometimes this was done to music, perhaps a baritone singing 'Morning has Broken,' or – in Zum Sepp'l – a maniac thrashing it out of a piano. But most of the time these evenings had no rhythm or shape at all – or at least as far as I was concerned. Not so, the Swabians. Whilst, by midnight, I'd be singing along with the baritone, they'd still be looking intelligent and thirsty. Countless tourists before me (including Caesar, Tacitus, the Byzantines and Coryate in 1608) have made the mistake of trying to keep up with the Germans. It's impossible, forget it. Here, inflating oneself with lager is a hereditary feat, or at the very least an act of devotion. In fact, the only thing Heidelbergers can remember of Luther's stay in town is his unguarded utterance that 'who loves not woman, wine and song, remains a fool his whole life long'.

I soon discovered that the only real cure for Heidelberg was to keep running up into the hills. Sometimes, these excursions took me up the *Eselpfad*, the old donkey path, to the castle. But, even here, it was impossible to completely escape the sights and textures of the night before. After all, the *Schloss* was built by the King of Boozers, Francis IV, whose only surviving diary entry (9 July 1598) reads *'Gestern voll gewest'* ('Yesterday a skinful'). Close up, his fallen, pot-bellied towers even looked like drunks, making it all seem more Humpty Dumpty than King Lear. Worse still, at the heart of the castle was the biggest barrel in the world, made from 130 tree trunks, and with a dance floor on the top. Although the chatelains had long since drained off the 50,000 gallons of grog (they could happily drink a thousand pints a day), even empty it was enough to tempt some dangerously nauseous thoughts. Obviously, the American soldier who appeared at my shoulder didn't think the same.

'Huh,' he grunted, 'I could kill this keg in two days.'

Twain, too, had given much thought to the barrel, in the summer of 1878. Like me, he was on the run from the town (although trying to escape the heat rather than the hooch). He was also on the run from Connecticut, which – despite the success of *The Adventures of Tom Sawyer* – he'd begun to find rather pricey. So, in April of that year, he'd put together a large retinue of family, friends and servants, and set out for the financially gentler climes of Europe. (Of course, he wasn't the only American out, sniffing around for a bargain. On later voyages, he met the banker, J.P. Morgan, and Flint's mother who, at the age of ten, was on a family trip in search of jute. As a parting gift, he gave her a copy of his book, which Flint still has to this day.) Meanwhile, in Heidelberg, Twain settled down in the Schloss Hotel, a bold idea that's long since rotted away.

His penny-pinching adventure turned out to be richly creative. Somehow, the plunging views of the Neckar seemed to send him into a flurry of work. Not only did he write parts of *The Prince and the Pauper* and *Huckleberry Finn*, he also learnt German, explored every inch of Heidelberg, and gathered the material for one of the most enjoyable (and least reliable) travelogues ever written. *A Tramp Abroad* is everything good travel writing should be: opinionated ('All Rhine wines are disguised vinegar'), original ('The Germans are the very children of impulse. We are cold and self-contained compared to them') and frank ('Drat this stupid yodelling'). His treatise on the language ('In German, a young lady has no sex whilst a turnip has') must be the most comical ever written although, in fairness, there's not much competition. Meanwhile, as to the barrel, he wrote: 'An empty cask the size of a cathedral could excite but little emotion in me. I do not see any wisdom in building a monster cask to hoard up emptiness in, when you can get a better quality, outside, any day, free of expense.'

How lucky for him, to think only of its emptiness.

Another feature of my convalescent walks was a hillside of mansions, owned by the student *Korps*. At first, it wasn't very clear who the

Korporationen were except that, at night, other students crept up from the town and pelted their villas with rocks and paint. Every morning, these little palaces – some of the most lavish and expensive properties in Swabia – were covered in new splats, or a rash of angry posters: KAPI-TALISME ABSCHAFFEN! said some, or YOU MIGHT NOT COUNT IN THE NEW ORDER. What, I wondered, had the *Korps* done wrong?

There were few clues up on the Schlossberg itself, and so I asked around amongst my German friends. I had two who lived in, or near, Heidelberg. One was a doctor, who'd been at school in England (which was how I knew her). She said the *Korps* were merely the relics of the private armies that had sprung up during the chaos of the nineteenth century. Most of them had patriotic names like Suevia, Allemania, Normannia and Vandalia – although they were later joined by armies of mathematicians (Markomannia), Catholics (Unitas), God-squadders (Wartburg) and swots (VDSt). These *Korps* were everywhere once, and had even given the Germans their national flag. But nowadays, she said, they were more inter-ested in drinking than guerrilla warfare. Joining one merely satisfied a German need to form together in clubs. *Hier sind wir unter uns*, people liked to say (Here we are amongst ourselves).

'A bit like American fraternities,' said the doctor, 'or English public schools.'

'And what about women? Are you allowed in?'

'Of course!' she said. 'Although we're not allowed upstairs.'

My other friend, a young economist called Markus, thought the *Korps* were anything but harmless and hearty. They were secretive and ritual-istic, he said, and their membership was invariably white, privileged, rich and well-connected. They insisted on the 1937 borders, maintained an insidious influence throughout the German establishment and adopted ludicrous clunky slogans, like *Ehre! Freiheit! Vaterland!* (Honour! Freedom! Fatherland!). If you want to see a boy systematically and expensively brutalised, enrol him in the *Korps*.

'It's no wonder,' said Markus, 'that people attack these places with rocks.'

But the truth, I began to suspect, probably lay somewhere in between. After all, I discovered, the *Korps* had never been Nazi. Hitler distrusted their self-sufficiency, their aristocratic loyalties and their tolerance of Jews. When the head of the student SS, Hanns-Martin Schleyer, suggested, in 1935, that Suevia expel all Jews, he himself was expelled from the *Korps*.

Fascism was probably not therefore a charge that would stick, but what about brutality?

'They like chopping each other up with swords,' said Markus.

'What, *still*?' I exclaimed. I'd read about this in Twain.

Markus smiled knowingly.

'Go to the Hirschgasse,' he said, 'and you'll get a feeling for what goes on.'

The Hirschgasse was a short walk down the Schlossberg and across the river. I almost missed it at first, hidden as it was under an enormous quiff of creepers. It was equally over-foliated inside, a jungle of tree trunks and chintz. These days, it described itself as 'one of the Leading Small Hotels of the World', which usually means that – in place of anything interesting – there's probably now a trouser press. In the Hirschgasse's case, this wasn't strictly true, and – despite several fires and changes of law – it still looked like the sort of place to bring your opponent and hack him into pieces. In days gone by, this was a *Mensurstube*, or a pub in which to duel.

All around the breakfast room were grim mementoes of the hotel's earlier facilities. There were iron nose-guards, goggles, padded armour, spattered sashes, coloured pillbox hats, and long *Schlagers* – or cutlasses – that were once ground sharp enough to shave. In their photographs, the duellists, dressed in this lot, look like beehives, with just their heads available for slicing. These, of course, were just the photographs suitable for breakfast guests (I later saw a picture of a *Korps* taken on Duelling Day, or *Mensurtag*, 1911. It looked like a team of freshly chopped Frankensteins, everyone crudely hacked and stitched together). 'In those days, they were allowed to cut deep,' said the manager. 'Now they just slash each other around the head.'

No one knows where the fights happen now, but after Twain's accounts of 1878 I was rather glad I never found them. He'd missed nothing of the detail of *Korporation* duelling. All contact between the *Korps* was forbidden, to encourage a culture of bloodshed, and each new recruit – or 'Fox' – was trained for a year in the art of mutilation. It was like topiary for human beings: the fighters had to stand stock-still, slashing away at each other's heads. (To flinch or duck meant instant dishonour.) Then, on *Mensurtag*, the opposing sides assembled here, along with their seconds, some bent physicians (by then, it was all illegal), Twain and seventy-five spectators. Soon the first duel got under way, and the hall was sparkling with blades. 'In the midst of the sword flashes,' wrote Twain, 'I saw a handful of hair skip into the air as if it had lain loose on the victim's head and a breath of wind had puffed it suddenly away.' Between bouts the swords were cleaned with surgical spirit, although the fighters were proud of their scars (a good *Schmiss* could be manfully accentuated with horse-hair or salt). That day's wounds included a peeled scalp, a ripped lip, and both men drenched in crimson. 'The injuries were a dreadful spectacle but better left undescribed.'

'And this really *still* goes on?' I asked my doctor friend.

'Sure. I see it all the time in the Mannheim police reports.'

'It's true,' said Markus. 'Some kid lost a piece of his scalp last week.'

'And no one does anything to stop it?'

'How can they? This is Heidelberg. That's what happens here.'

101

'And if you think that's weird,' said Markus, 'what about a Nazi *Thing*?'

As I wasn't sure what he meant, he said he'd show me. It would involve crossing the river, and climbing up through the forest to the top of Holy Mountain. Up there, said Markus, was an old hill-fort. It was a place so outlandishly *völkisch* that Goebbels had decided it must be Nazi, a sort of direct line to the German soul. On 22 June 1935, he led the people of Heidelberg up to the summit, bearing torches, and – almost exactly seventy years later – we set off after them, in search of the Nazi *Thing*.

As we climbed through the maple and beech, Markus talked about the trees.

'You know, here we are, one of the most densely populated countries in the world, and yet a *third* of it is forest! We don't just live next to the forest, many of us actually live in it, both mentally and physically. It's almost a mystical relationship. You British always think about the sea and what's beyond. We always think about the forest. That's why we worry about acid rain, in case there's no more forest. We came from the forest, didn't we? Two thousand years ago, it was from the forest that we emerged to defeat the Romans, and now it's to the forest that we retire. It's a prim-itive thing, a bit of us that's never grown up . . .'

'You make yourselves sound like the Flintstones,' I said.

Markus laughed. 'Well, maybe. But the Nazis knew all about our affinity

with forests. They even cultivated a crazy ideology called *Blut und Boden*
– Blood and Soil – which was like a religion of the forest. The idea was
that we were a proud warrior race, born of the earth and trees. Can you
imagine anything so absurd? That's what this was all about: an "assembly
of Germanic people" (which is what a *Thing* is) to speak directly to the
spirits.'

Ahead of us was the summit. There, the forest cleared and the ground
fell away into a vast, subterranean stadium. Enormous arcs of stone
descended stepwise to the west, enough seats for 20,000 people. At the
bottom was a large stone podium, where Goebbels had stood with his
sorcerers, goblinising politics and shouting at the trees. 'This,' he shrilled,
'is a veritable church of the Reich!' But the German people weren't so
sure, and within a year the *Thing* movement was all but over. Plans for
another 1,200 stadia were shelved, and – up here – the *Thingstätte* was
abandoned. Now it was almost empty, except for a woman practising the
tom-tom drums, and a party of US Marines having a *Thing* of their own
with some Budweiser and a smouldering tree trunk.

Marcus turned to go.

'It's all so ridiculous,' he said, 'that even now I could cry with shame.'

102

Goethe once wrote: 'Just thinking about Heidelberg gets one into a very
peculiar state.' Peculiar states and peculiar thinking have continued to
trouble the city for much of the twentieth century. In the Faculty of
Psychiatry, the brilliance of madness and the madness of Nazism have
been constantly recurring themes.

I went up there once, to see an exhibition of pictures by the mentally
ill. It was housed in a large red-brick clinic, where the only sound was
the ticking of a clock. The artwork, which I had all to myself, had been
collected together by Dr Hans Prinzhorn, between 1919 and 1921. It
portrayed a curious world: the sky raining apples; a field of angry heads;
coiled lovers, drawn on scrap with nurses' purple pencils. There were
also photographs of the artists, each of them with the eyes of genius and
the aura of Neanderthal Man. Prinzhorn believed that, in their primi-
tivism, they were uniquely capable of depicting the human condition.
His book on the subject, *The Artistry of the Mentally Ill* (1922) had a
profound effect on the artists of the time, particularly Ernst, Klee,

Schlemmer and Dubuffet. Brilliance, it seemed, was merely a variant of disorder.

The Nazis hated this idea, and – under them – the collection was suppressed. As far as they were concerned, there was no role for the sick and the weak in German culture. At least ten of the artists were killed: shot or gassed in the Nazis' camps. Meanwhile, in the faculty, a new professor was installed, the notorious Carl Schneider. Under him, psychiatry lost its reason, and patients were sterilised, poisoned and slaughtered. In Heidelberg, a total of 211 inmates died, many in the name of 'work therapy' and eugenics. Schneider's speciality was children. Having examined them with admirable thoroughness, he then had them killed and their brains removed, so he could compare his clinical observations with the patho-anatomical findings. But even Schneider realised that science would never excuse him, and so – shortly after his capture by the Americans in 1946 – he strangled himself in his cell. In his search for the 'causes of idiocy', he'd found nothing but barbarity.

Nazism returned to haunt the faculty in February 1970. This time it was the belief that capitalism – of which Nazism was a mutated form – had created a society of mental patients, and that the only cure was Marxist revolution. Sickness, the theory went, would become a weapon, and the group tasked to change the world was the *Sozialistisches Patientenkollektiv* (SPK), or Socialist Patients' Collective. 'The system has made us sick,' they proclaimed. 'Let us strike a death blow to the system.' 'Iatrocracy', or Rule by Doctors, would be violently overthrown and replaced by the Rule of the Mad. *Kraft aus der Krankheit*, ran the slogan (Strength through Sickness). The man behind this loopy ideology was one of the faculty's psychiatrists, Dr Wolfgang Huber. The university would have sacked him sooner if his patients hadn't threatened to commit suicide *en masse*. Instead, he stayed on, and his group therapy sessions became classes in explosives and karate. Eventually, even the government tired of this, and in June 1971 Huber and his wife were carted away to begin four and a half years in jail.

It was the end of the SPK as a force for change (although it still exists as a website and a one-man war of words. 'Amazing!' said Markus, when I told him. 'I thought all the German weirdos had wandered off to Paraguay'). But, although the SPK was spent, some of its patient-revolutionaries drifted away to join other movements and continue their lunatic war. Embassies and aeroplanes were blown up, and there were shoot-outs with the police. The campaign even returned to Heidelberg from time to time, with rockets fired from the *Schloss* and a bomb at the American barracks. This last attack was a heartless operation, and provided Heidelberg with the unforgettable spectacle of a man's legs, left hanging from a tree.

That, however, was the final chapter in this madness. Now the faculty was quiet again, with just its purple lovers and its thunderstorm of apples.

103

From Heidelberg, Flint and the Hellcats had raced across the hills to Bad Wimpfen, arriving on 4 April 1945. Sixty years later, he, Jeff and I had taken the same route. The following summer, I decided to re-do this journey, this time walking the fifty-odd miles along the banks of the Neckar.

I had hoped that Twain would be my companion on this walk, in the literary sense at least. *A Tramp Abroad* was the only guidebook I had, and I could almost picture us all setting off together, me in my jeans and boots, and Twain and friends dressed in turbans and blue army shirts, and equipped with opera glasses, parasols and alpenstocks. But Twain was a useless walker. No sooner was he out of the main square than he spotted a train, and he and his friends jumped aboard for Bad Wimpfen. They didn't even walk the last part of our journey – twelve miles to Heilbronn – but, instead, caught a lift on a cabbage cart drawn by a cow. As for the return journey, they drifted back downstream on a woodcutter's raft, making a spectacular reappearance in Heidelberg. According to Twain, the raft hit the central pier of the bridge and 'went all to smash and scatteration like a box of matches hit by lightning'. All this, meanwhile, meant that I had to read *Tramp* backwards, a century out of date, and with a large pinch of salt.

I had a sudden German moment as I began to climb, a wave of pure, endorphinous pleasure brought on by the presence of trees. This was uncharacteristic of me, but then this forest was uncharacteristically enchanting. Everywhere I looked there were little animals – red squirrels, jays, cuckoos, tangerine-coloured slugs and newts the colour of flames. There was no one else up here in the beech woods but I often came across grottoes and tiny gardens where, I suppose, people liked to come and imagine themselves once again the creatures of their sylvan past. I can't blame them. Away from the *angst* and the rumble of the river, life in the walls of the valley was alluringly serene. 'Germany in summer,' wrote Twain, 'is the perfection of the beautiful.'

At the rim of the valley, I paused before descending again to the river. The painter, J.M.W. Turner, had spent hours here, perfecting perfection (and in 1836 he'd return to England with over 440 Rhineland scenes). The Neckar was different now to the river it had been then. Whilst it still flowed like a snake through this pretty green crack in the planet, it had been a crazy grass-snake then; these days it was a fat and silvery python. In 1933, the river had been calmed by a series of dams and weirs, and so now it was deep enough for barges. In Twain's time, he said, it was so narrow you could throw a dog across. Nowadays, the Neckar is two and a half dog-throws wide, and even then, he'd probably get his paws wet.

Twain would, however, have liked the barges. They were like huge floating gypsy camps, loaded with old cars, coal and scrap metal. Some were Dutch and some were Swiss, part of a strange community of water-tinkers endlessly plying the rivers of central Europe. A few even had little gardens, and swings for the children, or a Mercedes for the shopping. The bargemen always waved back. One that I spotted was black, a Twainesque figure, who'd somehow mislaid the Mississippi. To Twain, the bargemen would have been irresistible characters, and Huckleberry Finn might even have ended up German. But in 1878 the only barges were inglorious wrecks, being hauled upriver using 'sails, mule power, and profanity'.

On the other hand, the days of rafts, were – sadly – over. In Twain's day, these disposable, powerless craft made up most of the downstream traffic. Somewhere upriver a long crocodile of logs would be lashed together and then dropped into the currents, where it would be hurled through Germany on a one-way trip to the Rhine. Facilities aboard were sparse (a booth) but, for Twain and friends, it was a pleasant place to sit, dangling their toes and twiddling their umbrellas. The only problem was that, once under way, the raft couldn't be stopped. This was almost fatal for the Twain party. As they passed by the Eberach quarry (which is still blasting out bathrooms today), the Italian masons detonated their charges, sending up a barrage of rocks. Happily, only one boulder fell amongst Twain's group, wrecking an umbrella. 'It did no other harm,' he wrote, 'but we took to the water just the same.'

While Twain was bobbing around on the water, I carried on, plodding along the bank. Sometimes I was on little roads, sometimes tracks and occasionally four feet deep in the grass. It was never hard going (the Germans had teased Twain mercilessly for his Alpine outfits), and no one was in the least surprised to find me walking from city to city. Germans, I realised, were always pounding round the countryside, setting themselves appalling feats of endurance involving either bicycles or boots (I remember a Frenchman once telling me that just watching the Germans at leisure made him feel exhausted). My own excursion was merely a jaunt, without even the prospect of starvation. There was spring water everywhere, and – in the villages – there was always something unusual to eat like black sausage or giant croissants filled with rhubarb and cream.

Most of these villages were fortified. The Neckar valley was like a corridor of castles. It wasn't just a question of a few walls and a big door. Each of these bastions was a stupendous, almost Disneyesque creation of posterns, machicolations and half-timbered barbicans. Neckarsteinach had three of these fortresses, all built by thugs with names like 'Bligger of Steinach', or '*die Landschaden*' (The Grand Wrecker of the Country). Hirschhorn had only one, but it was a particularly virulent orange and dangled off the top of a hill. By the time I'd climbed to the top, it was all in cloud and there was just a pair of F-16s jousting round the summit. I half wondered if the pilots were Twain fans, and had come to deliver an epilogue (*Tramp* describes Hirschhorn as a dirty village 'stocked with deformed, leering, unkempt and uncombed idiots'). Fortunately, however, at the last minute they must have spotted the tea-shops and geraniums, and merely waggled their wing-tips and shot off down the valley.

But, when it came to rarity, there was nothing quite like Dilsberg. Built astride a huge topographical egg, the entire village had been squashed inside the castle wall. It was all so tightly packed that there was no room for cars, pavements or anything else of post-medieval design. Everybody seemed to be either breeding rabbits or growing herbs, and although the signs said WARNUNG VOR DEM HUND, all I ever saw were witches' grimalkins and the occasional Chihuahua. Twain of course loved it, and realised that in Dilsberg he'd found a rich source of vertiginous tall stories; there were land-pirates, giants and a bottomless well. He even reported that the Dilbergers had been interbreeding for 1,500 years, that the village was a 'thriving and diligent idiot factory', and that there was a vigorous government campaign either to get everyone into an asylum or to get them to marry beyond the walls. This, I suspected, was pure Twain. I'd probably have thought nothing more of it had I not dropped a euro down the castle well and heard nothing in reply. In German folklore, it seems, even Twain had met his match.

At night we went our separate ways. Twain and friends would book into an inn, usually somewhere with ghosts or a collection of stuffed animals. I, on the other hand, still had walking to do and would carry on until it got dark, and then sleep in the forest. Surprisingly, this had appalled people in Heidelberg. 'Beware of the ants!' said one man, but, for everyone else, the worry was wild boar. To me, this just sounded like green *angst*, or perhaps a touch of Twain. But that first night it sounded altogether different. All around me, I could hear the *Wildschweine* snorting through the grass, ripping out roots and ploughing up the turf. For hours, I lay there wondering what the pigs would do if they suddenly took against me. Would I be trotted to death, or merely guzzled up like swill? Eventually, at dawn, they simply snuffled away, leaving the hillside looking bombed and muddy, as if I'd spent the night under enemy fire.

But the Neckar at sunrise was a rich reward for the snuffles of the night before. Long feathery wisps of vapour lifted off the water, and the forest looked opulent and dark. My only encounters that morning were with an owl, a dozen squirrels, a farmer digging his way out of a barn (by pitching the dung through the windows) and a small snake, made from parquetry and killed by the postman's van. Only once did I have to leave the valley, when the path turned into cliffs. Then, I climbed out and for the next five miles wandered across a plateau, feeling rather lost and sunburnt. It was odd to be back in the light again, amongst ancient farms like Tudor galleys, and villages of haylofts and dung. But eventually the roads wriggled back to the gorge again, and down to the river at Neckarelz.

There, I found myself on a little beach of gritty sand and nettles. It may not have looked like a D-Day bridgehead, but this was where the first American armour had landed on the eastern banks of the Neckar. Upstream, tanks had been mangled and sunk, but, here in Neckarelz, they were soon clambering clear, and racing off across the flood plains beyond.

I spent my last night in the ruins of Hornberg Castle. Not only was it pig-free but the *Burg* also enjoyed a bandit's view of the valley below.

This was obviously the perfect place from which to rob one's neighbours, and everything about it was splendidly raffish and debauched. It had bee-striped shutters, statues of robber barons (all well-coiffed and curly), vine-yards up to the door, and little rat-runs that zigzagged off through the forest. The barons' family shield, I noticed, depicted a wolf devouring a sheep.

I also discovered that not all the castle was ruined. Somehow the eastern ramparts had survived five centuries of neighbours and revenge. It was now a hotel, as it had been when Twain called by, and so that night I sat down to a baronial dinner in a hall with a floor that sloped like a cave's. With some difficulty, the waitress managed to clamber up to my table – laden with venison, dumplings, cranberries and half a bottle of castle wine – before slithering back to the kitchen. But, however Twainesque the evening may have seemed, I didn't feel that my literary fieldwork justi-fied a night in a boutique room. So, while I went off to hunker down in the graveyard, Twain repaired to his baronial suite, which he'd share with the greatest ghost of all, the redoubtable Götz von Berlichingen.

Götz occupies a curious place in the German imagination, somewhere between Captain Hook and Conan the Destroyer. Born in 1480, he was said to have found 'deep joy in battle', and hardly noticed when, at the age of twenty-four, his hand was blasted away. He simply had it replaced with an iron one, which served him brutally well over the next fifty years of warfare, and which, in Twain's words, 'was nearly as clever a member as the fleshy one had been'. Meanwhile, in 1517, Götz moved into Hornberg where he dabbled in robbery for a while, swooping down on the barges and then thanking God for remembering him in his needs (Twain said the bedroom still smelt of Götz, and still had a hook for hanging up his fist). But Götz's real love was splitting French heads and cutting up the Turks, both of which he could still manage in his sixties. In the popular imagination, he's still out there, chopping his way through the enemy. His most famous words are probably the only ones that anyone ever remembers; when the French once demanded his surrender, he replied simply 'KISS MY ARSE'.

Naturally, the Nazis loved Götz. His iron fist became part of their mili-tary jargon, and, in its search for something thuggish and Gothic, one of the SS Divisions had even adopted his name. Coincidentally, this was the same division (the 17th SS Panzer-Grenadiers), that had clashed with Flint's men in Lorraine. I don't suppose either side ever thought they'd see each other again. But they were wrong. By 4 April 1945, *die Götz von Berlichingen Division* was waiting – like its namesake, mutilated, brutal and defiant – for its last and most bloody clash of arms, in the hills just beyond Bad Wimpfen.

104

From the escarpment on which Bad Wimpfen sits, it was possible to look out over the entire battlefield of April 1945. The escarpment itself was a last ripple of contour after the gorge, and – beyond the town – it ran parallel to the river for a while before gradually sloping away and merging with the banks.

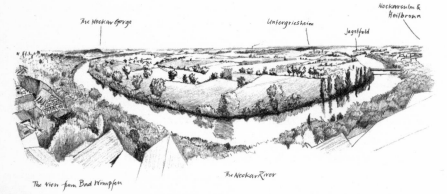

The View from Bad Wimpfen

The Neckar Gorge · Untergriesheim · Jagstfeld · Neckarsulm & Heilbronn · The Neckar River

During my travels with Flint and Jeff – to which I now return – we'd spent ages up here, picking out the features in the landscape below. To our left, or north, was the entrance to the gorge, and directly in front of us, across the river, was a vast expanse of water meadows and foothills. Then, to our right, also on the other side of the river, were the pink roofs of Jagstfeld, and beyond that the chimneys of Neckarsulm and then the biggest prize of all, the city of Heilbronn. 'That was the objective,' said Flint, 'and the idea was we'd cross the river here, and attack it from this direction.'

But the plan soon changed. Jagstfeld and Neckarsulm were viciously defended, and it proved impossible to throw a bridge across the river. Whenever troops did get across they found themselves fighting in glass-works, or lost in a labyrinth of factories. Fearing that they'd be cut off, it was decided to move the bulk of the 100th Division upstream, and throw it into the heart of the city. Only a fraction of the force would be left on the escarpment, to slog it out with Jagstfeld. It was a vicious duel. Across the river, the Götz Division had had weeks to sight their guns and dig them into the suburbs. But they hadn't reckoned with the speed and cheek of the Hellcats. That day, 4 April, one of the B Company sergeants, called Haglund, won a Silver Star after careering into the open, and – in a mighty fit of shells – destroying three machine-gun nests and a self-propelled gun.

It was hard to imagine how anyone had survived in the villages on the escarpment side, Ober- and Unter-eisesheim. But they had. Everything had been rebuilt of course, and all that remained of the pre-war villages were the root cellars built into the banks of the road. But up on the top, we found the turnip fields from which the Hellcats had launched their unequivocal response. Now, it was quiet again, nothing there except a kestrel, and a farmer paring onions with his knife. Flint told him that he'd been here before.

'I was only six!' said the farmer, 'but I remember it well.'

He described how the first American tank appeared.

'It was hit. Boof! I think seven Americans died, all burnt alive. And then everything was destroyed. Shit everywhere! We spent the rest of the week in the cellar.'

'Horrible,' said Flint. 'Just fortunate we never had time to think.'

105

Two days later, Flint's men had covered the retreat of a reconnaissance platoon, as it pulled out of Jagstfeld and rowed back across the river.

The German resistance was bewildering. Hadn't the *Wehrmacht* already been defeated? Aerial pictures before the battle had shown almost no activity in Heilbronn, and now here was the army making one of the most desperate stands of the war. And where was it getting the men from? Even since its annihilation in Normandy and Russia, the *Wehrmacht* had formed another twenty-five divisions of 'People's Grenadiers', albeit a ragtag of policemen, pioneers and demonstration units. It was like fighting the Hydra, snapping off one head only to find six squeaky-new minia-tures sprouting in its place. The OKW, or High Command, had even trawled schools and hospitals for anyone fit to bear arms (resulting in the pitiful spectacle of amputee battalions, or units of the partially deaf). Perhaps the most tragic of all was Germany's very own 'Tank Destroyer

Battalion', a unit of grenadiers who were expected to ride into battle on bicycles.

But military resistance was one thing, civilian another. In Heilbronn, civilians were feeding the soldiers, directing the artillery and keeping the battle going. The children were the worst, having never known anything but Hitler. '*Ein deutscher Junge*,' they'd chime, '*is zäh wie Leder, hart wie Kruppstahl, schlau wie ein Fuchs*' (A German boy is as tough as leather, as hard as steel, and as cunning as a fox). But even the adults could put on an unsightly show of force. For the last six months every male in Heilbronn between the ages of sixteen and sixty had been obliged to serve in the *Volkssturm*, the German equivalent of the British Home Guard. Although their training was mostly in slogans, they could also muster a fearsome collection of arms. There were 'burp guns', *Schuh*-mines, potato-masher grenades, contraptions captured from the Russians, and rifles seized from the Dutch (sometimes with Greek bullets re-machined to make them fit).

But, from Flint's perspective, the worst of their weapons was probably the *Panzerfaust*. 'It was an ingenious device, a bit like our bazooka.'

So it was, except that even a child could fire it. Over a third of all American tank casualties in Germany were caused by the *Panzerfaust*. Unlike the American model, it was light and disposable, and could be operated by one man alone – as long as he was mad enough to creep right up to a tank. (Its only weakness was that it was assembled by slave labourers who soon discovered that, if they mixed sand with the charge, this rendered it inert.) But, once the missile was on its way, the warhead did the rest, blasting through up to 140 mm of steel plate with a jet of hyper-heated gas and high explosive. 'It was an extraordinary sight seeing one coming towards you,' said Flint. 'I remember the man who fired it, but fortunately he missed, and the rocket hit the ground and exploded. Even the shock was enough to throw me back against the ring-mount, and – although I didn't know it at the time – it seems I fractured a vertebra. I still get a bit of pain from this, just a little reminder of the *Panzerfaust*, I guess.'

But if the question of *who* was resisting the Americans was puzzling, even more puzzling was the question of *why*? Few Germans had responded to Eisenhower's rather rural invitation to surrender (he'd suggested they go back home and plant their seeds). But, I realised, the reasons for this obstinacy tended to vary, almost from person to person. Officially, the explanation was resentment, and in Heilbronn the civic authorities still made much of the great RAF raid of 4 December 1944, in which over 6,000 people died. As Hitler himself had said, 'Bombing actually works in our favour, because it's creating a body of people with nothing to lose ...'

Anger, however, was only part of the story, and there were other emotions at work. A few Heilbronners still felt a childlike tug of loyalty towards Hitler and the Nazis. They believed either in some mythical 'wonder weapons', or – perversely – in the idea that defeat was somehow worse than death. But for others, it was more fear than fidelity. In the first five months of 1945, nearly 6,000 political dissenters were officially executed. Countless others were summarily shot, or hanged under a placard that read '*Ich bin ein Feigling*' (I'm a coward). It hadn't taken many placards like that to stiffen the civic resolve.

Coercion, on the other hand, didn't explain the general mood of defiance. Here, something more Germanic was involved: that strong instinct for authority. '*Alles in Ordnung*,' people would say, as if life wasn't life until 'All is in order'. For Germans, society was far too foresty and riven with misunderstanding to function without rules, and in April 1945 they were in no mood to slide back into the chaos from which they'd long since emerged. Rules would therefore be rules. Even bad rules would be rules until they were replaced with something else. What wouldn't be tolerated was anarchy, or even transition, and so – until the American *Ordnung* was installed – the old *Ordnung* would prevail.

Bad Wimpfen was an endearing example of the German weakness for order. It had all been built plumb in the middle of the German chaos, and yet had emerged relatively unscathed. There was a thick town wall – which had somehow engulfed our hotel – several towers all nibbled by lightning, a house for a giant, dated 1532, and another only four feet wide. In fact, the entire centre looked as if it had been designed by the brothers Grimm, and built from wattle, daub, tree trunks and crystal lights. Twain described it as 'tumbledown, dirty and interesting', and although the place had obviously had a good scrubbing since then, the overall impression was strangely much the same.

But just because Bad Wimpfen was higgledy-piggledy, this didn't mean it was wildly spawning disorder. Far from it; it was the very model of nicety, citizenship and hair-splitting social conventions. All its dogs had to have nameplates, and all its windows net curtains. There was a general duty to clear snow, and a personal responsibility for leaves. Even better, I discovered, everybody had their own title in this antiquated bumbledom; there was Dr Engineer, Mr Senior Baker, and – my favourite of all – Mr Master Roofer (*Herr Dachdeckermeister*). What's more, not only were they all expected to keep their place but so, in a sense, were we. No sooner had Jeff parked the car than we had an old lady rattling on the windows, railing at some breach of parking conventions. What upset her was not that we were causing an obstruction but, rather, that we'd found a rule and broken it. '*Ordnung muss sein*,' as people kept saying, 'Order must be'.

Few places in the world enjoy such a mood of mutual admonition. Before Bad Wimpfen, I'd never seen so many people telling each other off. Children were especially vulnerable, because they could always be trusted to drop litter or play with a ball. But adults too were ripe for reprimand, and a vast jurisprudence had developed tackling such social evils as the inappropriate hanging out of washing or the leaving of toys on the lawn. Naturally, noise was the richest source of rebuke, and there were reams of rules about radios, music, mowing, children and dogs. Of course, all rural communities everywhere have a touch of this, but nowhere made it sound so lofty. RUHE IST DES BÜRGERS ERSTE PFLICHT, said a little notice in Bad Wimpfen: 'Silence is a citizen's first duty'.

There were mixed reactions to all this from my American friends. Flint, as always, found it pleasingly German and as satisfying as ever. Although lopsided and archaic, Bad Wimpfen, it seemed, had always done the right thing. (In 1945, the 100th Division had pounced on it so quickly that the citizens had hardly noticed the change of regime, and were seamlessly compliant.) But, for Jeff, the town had rather less appeal. Never one for quaintness or rules, he kept calling it *Bad Woomfler*.

106

There were no niceties about Flint's final clash with the Götz Division.

From Bad Wimpfen, we could look down on to the low hills where the SS had made their stand. It was a magnificent landscape, lavishly embellished with orchards and vineyards, and limpid washes of purple and green. From our escarpment to the downs around Untergriesheim, it was only a fifteen-minute drive – a journey that sixty years ago had taken almost a day. Back then, with the frontal attack on Heilbronn now locked in stalemate, a fresh assault was ordered, this time curling round the north of the city and attacking from behind. On 7 April 1945, Flint and his men were ordered to join this assault, and to do so they'd have to drive back downstream to Neckarelz, wobble over the river on a sunken pontoon, fight off an air attack, slosh through the water meadows, ford the frothy white Jagst, and then scramble up on to the downs.

Up there, it was still a wide, open space, perfect for this one last duel. At the crest of the hill we stopped and got out. All around us were bright orange pumpkins, like Dr Prinzhorn's heads leering out of the landscape. Beyond them were luxuriant flanks of sugar beet, cabbages and turnips, and then finally Heilbronn tucked into a horseshoe of thickly wooded hills. Goethe had loved it up here, and in 1797 he wrote: 'Everything you survey is productive. Firstly, the vineyards, and then the city itself, lying in a swathe of gardens. It conveys a feeling of calm, expansive, satisfying pleasure.'

But Flint now felt none of this pleasure, just the vague rekindling of pre-battle nerves. In his mind, he was peeling back the harvest, and trying to recall the wintry scenes beneath – the frost-burnt straw, the soggy earthworks of soldiers and the slopes of military trash. Only the sticky soil was the same, and the soft wet curves of the down. 'The M18s could go over this,' he said absently, 'just like taking a walk.' He recalled how they'd churned over the crest of this hill and then ploughed down on to the slopes below. Then, suddenly, there it was – just as he remembered – a line of stunted trees and ditches. 'This was the outer limit of the enemy defence,' said Flint. 'Machine-gun pits and men armed with *Panzerfausts*.'

I asked if he'd been frightened.

'No, fatalistic,' he said. 'In combat, you hear guns, and it's like a musical score. The story unrolls from there.'

In Flint's case, it was a complex score, and no two recitals were ever quite the same. Over the years, the seconds had elasticated and the hours had crumbled away. But the basic plot was unchanged, and Flint was never more vivid in its retelling than the morning we stood on Untergriesheim hill. In the cold language of the battalion records, four enemy gun emplacements were 'put out of action' that day. But in Flint's version, there was the hiss and spit of bullets, the sight of Norwicki pumping off rounds, a blurred charge of armour through the mud, a man with a *Panzerfaust*, the sky the colour of flesh, and then – in the finale – the distant sensation of impact, as the Hellcats rode up over the foxholes and crushed the men beneath.

Flint would never talk about the people who'd died. It was almost as if some soldierly pact existed between him and those he'd killed. He wouldn't humiliate them with description, and they wouldn't torment him with his guilt. In this way, killing had become an intensely personal matter, known only to those who'd had no other choice. This could often make the fighting seem rather abstract, and, with Flint, it sometimes felt like an unearthly clash of machines. 'It was either *ours* or *theirs*,' he'd say, as if humankind had stood back from time to time, and let the big cats fight it out.

On the south side of the downs, a great plain of sugar beet curled away, ending in a distant lip. 'It was over there,' said Flint, 'that the enemy put their 88s, probably the worst thing I ever faced in the war.'

There were several miles of beet between us and the lip, marked on the map as Oedheim. For three days, from 8 to 11 April, the great machines had blasted away at each other across the plain. From the air it must have looked like pinball, Hellcats hurtling up the field only to be battered about by light and sound. The 88 was a formidable obstruction. Although, as a gun, it didn't look much – grey pipes and long splayed legs – it had an astonishing capacity for killing. One moment it might be spattering its way through a tank, and the next it could raise its barrel and blast an aeroplane out of the sky. Its shells, meanwhile, travelled far faster than the speed of sound, and so, as Flint put it, 'they were already bursting all around before you'd even heard them coming'.

But the Hellcats had speed on their side.

'We drove so fast that their shells kept falling behind . . .'

Eventually, the Götz Division began to dissolve. On the first day of the skirmish, Flint's platoon had fired 21 rounds of high explosive, and then 57 on the second. Then, on the last day, Flint delivered the *coup de grâce* by calling in an air strike. 'Until then, I had no respect for the air force. They were sissies who slept between sheets! But it was a joy, a great relief, to watch the 88s getting the shit knocked out of them . . .' By the end of the sortie, the defenders were in tatters, and the 88s no more. According to the official record of this battle, the Americans who fought on this plain 'decimated a regiment of SS troopers entrenched in almost impregnable positions, and aided materially in the ultimate capture of Heilbronn'.

The Panthers had come a long way in the six months since the Vosges. 'The SS was still the SS,' I suggested, 'but you'd been transformed?'

'Yes,' said Flint softly. 'We were ready for them, and blasted them to hell.'

107

Heilbronn had done well to cultivate a little tourism on its scanty raw materials.

It was clearly no longer the garden city of Goethe's day. Since then, it had been a garden of rubble and now it was a garden of factories. We seemed to spend hours driving through these great allotments of industry and ground-up stone. When I returned the following summer to walk this route, the hours had seemed like days. Every factory was the same, a giant sprawl of cladding built on the shingle of its past. There were pickle factories, breweries, sugar refineries and Audi plants, all dressed in the same ephemeral, envelope grey. Not even the Neckar seemed to vary any more, but had now been straightened and calmed. This enormous industrial channel – the *Kanalhafen* – seemed to loom over me for much of my walk, like some vast insurmountable spire.

Heilbronn was relentless, which made its tourist office all the more surprising.

I asked what was left of the city that Twain had known.

'Lots of things,' said the *Herr Direktor* bravely.

In the end, we whittled it down to four or, more strictly, three and a half. The Hafenmarkt Tower had only partly survived the great *Luftangriff*, or air raid, of December 1944, and now threw long shadows down the high street like some half-eaten carcass. The cathedral and the *Götzenturm* (where Götz was confined between his bouts of robbery) had fared better, and had now been reassembled from their constituent shards. But the most remarkable recovery of all was the *Rathaus*. Twain had declared this town hall to be 'of the quaintest and most picturesque Middle-Age architecture', and had described a portico of life-sized rusty knights, and clockwork angels that blew trumpets through the night. It was then almost completely destroyed in the war, and, in pictures, it looked like a broken picket fence leaking sunlight and ash. Now, somehow, it had been restored to its clockwork glory, and the trumpets were tootling again, and the façade was wriggling with knights. Its vaulted cellar had even become a restaurant, which was where I ate with Flint and Jeff. Although in Twain's time the wild boars were nailed up round the walls, now they came on a plate, with a *jus* of raspberry and port.

'Some restoration,' said Flint, looking round appreciatively.

The waiter laughed. 'It's all fake!' he said. 'Just clever polystyrene!'

Back out amongst the factories, I saw the word HEILBRONX daubed on a wall.

It was odd to think of despair as American (Heilbronnograd would have been better, or maybe even Hell-bronn). During the first fortnight of April 1945 the Americans had liberated this city, although not without a bloody and pointless struggle. It was like Warsaw in miniature except that – here – the ferocity was harder to explain. As *Stars and Stripes* put it, 'For nine deadly days, the Centurymen suffered all horrors in a knock down, drag-out, slug fest . . .' Remarkably, they suffered only 400 casualties, including sixty killed. It's not known how many Germans died, especially as many were irregulars – cadets, stragglers, old men with Greek rifles and children with bazookas. Not even their fortitude would save them as the awesome technology of the New World bore down upon them.

The fighting was at its worst out here in the factories. Back then, they were made of stone, and each was its own little fortress to be battered into gravel. One by one, the Centurymen cleared them out, often fighting room to room. But then, just as one plant was cleared, the enemy would tunnel back beneath them, make a new fortress from rubble, and begin the fight all over again. There was a bitter fight for the Knorr factory, and a slaughter at the glassworks. Men would never forget the claustrophobia of these struggles, and the sound of enemy voices seeping through the walls. For some, the abiding memory was of child-guerrillas, or their first sight of slaves – wild, half-starved Russians freed by the confusion. Others, like one Private Logan, would remember only the appalling injuries they suffered amongst all that machinery and glass. Years later, Logan recounted how he'd lost an eye in the power plant, and how he'd recovered to find some SS grenadiers about to sever his head with a shovel. (He was spared because of his cigarettes, and spent the rest of the war being frog-marched into the Alps on a diet of snails and raw potato.)

Eventually, Heilbronn gave way. By 8 April, it was surrounded on three sides, and its defences began to implode. The inner city fell the next day, and from there a sense of defeat started to ripple outwards into the suburbs. The rag-tag defenders either gave themselves up or fled across the horse-shoe hills. 'The enemy, who had turned at Heilbronn like a tiger,' reads the American official report, 'was leaving like a jackal.' Hundreds got away but more than 1,800 surrendered, and marched off into the American 'cage'. Amongst the last to flee the city were Flint's old adversaries, the remnants of the Götz Division. They thought they'd never surrender, but they did. Three weeks later, and the day before the end of the war, they gave themselves up in the Alps.

Meanwhile, Heilbronn lay in ruins. Over three-quarters of the build-ings had been destroyed. The decision to make a stand here had been entirely that of the Nazis (perhaps the only thing they'd ever learnt in Russia was to thread their main defensive line straight through the heart of a city). If their purpose was to delay the Centurymen by a week, then the battle of Heilbronn was theirs. In every other sense, however, it was a futile waste of human life and endeavour. Heilbronn had never fully recovered and was still a fractured city with a polystyrene heart. But, at least by 13 April, the killing had stopped, and the ruins fell silent at last.

That morning a new sound was heard in the city. It was Chopin's 'Polonaise', played by a young soldier called Donald Waxman on a Steinway he'd found in the wreckage. Somehow this ennobling, mellifluous music seemed to soothe the raw and ruptured air. When they heard it, people wept – wept for what they'd lost, for those who'd died, and for the myste-rious course that German life had taken. No one would forget that moment. Waxman would return home and become a concert pianist, and the composer of more than fifty pieces of music. But for those who'd heard his war-torn recital, it would be like a fulcrum in their lives, the point at which Nazism had died and their long and painful restoration had begun.

108

Before leaving Heilbronn, we drove up into the horseshoe hills. They were now all forested with vines again, and Jeff stopped to pick some grapes for Flint. Twain had compared the local wine to vinegar but it can't have been from this fruit. Each grape burst in the mouth like a cold, wet bomblet of spices, apple and dew.

'But it's theft!' protested Flint, as the juices dripped off his chin.

'Think of it as booty,' I said.

'Or payment,' said Jeff, 'for services to the city.'

At the top of the horseshoe ridge was a tiny fortress, like a stack of little stone burrows. In military terms it was no more than a tube, with a heavy wooden door at the bottom, and a view of Heilbronn from the top. But this, it seems, was all it had ever needed: Wart Castle had stood here for over a thousand years, and during the battle of 1945 it was the last place to fall. With the city quiet, the 399th had fought their way up the hill, only to find the tower abandoned and a note attached to the door. In it, the Americans were asked to spare the life of the caretaker, and to help themselves to the wine.

'Heilbronner Trollinger!' said Flint, smacking his lips at the memory.

Strangely, 1945 turned out to be one of the best years ever for wine. The vines had done badly during the war. But, just as they'd failed at the beginning, so they'd flourished again at the end.

109

After Heilbronn, a dam burst, and the great wheeled city poured into the German countryside and spread out across the land.

Originally, I'd had an idea that we'd follow the old campaign trail, and go touring in the wake of the troops. But the speed and complexity of the advance was breathtaking. In the twelve days after Heilbronn, Flint's men had cleared some 250 kilometres of 'bandit country,' logged thirty-five towns and villages, and skirted hundreds more. It wasn't even as if they were sticking to main roads. Often, they were belting off through the forests, or fanning out into the back of beyond.

Just trying to follow them on the map was exhausting. Erlenbach. Löwenstein. Hösslinsülz. Breitenauerhof. Sometimes, I'd lose them for a moment, and then they'd resurface in another tangle of Swabian names. Willsbach. Affaltrach. Weiler. Hohenacker. Occasionally, the Panthers would disappear altogether, and I'd have to rush off to Stamfords the booksellers to buy another slab of maps, of ever-increasing scale. Then, after some frantic searching, I'd find them again, somewhere deep in the foliage like Unter Heimbach, Neuhütten or Finsterrot. Some of these places were towns, I noticed, and others merely dots – just one man and his schnauzer, perhaps.

Then we were on our way again. Amertsweiler. Lauxenhof. Hals. Bohringsweiler. Grab. Marbächle. What, I wondered, did all these names mean? What about Fischbach, perched on top of a mountain? With only limited German, my imagination began to reel. During the course of my cartographical travels I fancied I'd found Worm's Head, Little Nutcracker and the Lake of Brains. At least, as the trail led south, the names began to have more of a toponymic feel. Steinberg. Wolfenbrück. Althütte. Leutenbach, Fellbach and Grunbach. Then there was a long jump of several inches to Pfuhl, which sounded like a little piece of punctuation before the final descent to Ulm.

Even on paper it was a breathless journey. How anyone had managed it in three dimensions – astride a Hellcat and in less than a fortnight – was hard to comprehend. Even the Panthers had been taxed to the limits. 'The pace was devouring our energy and strength,' wrote Flint to his wife, 'but the desire to win burned ever stronger. All the fiendish obstacles of the enemy were atomised by a united effort.'

Of course, the fighting. I'd almost forgotten that. As I thumbed my way back through the records, I was able to reconstruct a bewildering programme of combat. Not only had the Panthers been trying to get from A to B, they'd also been beating off ambushes, clearing woods, carrying troops, and smashing through large roadblocks of logs and mines, known locally as *Abatis*. According to the battalion orders, they came under fire at least once a day, sometimes only a squall of machine-gun fire, other times a barrage of rockets. These clashes had a special poignancy in what were clearly the last few weeks of the war; injury and death now seemed even more futile than ever. For the generals, the answer was always the same: overwhelming firepower (northern Swabia was already heaped with the mounds of obstinate villages known as 'Patton's Memorials'). Even Flint's men responded to the challenge without any of their former reticence. In Weiler, they fired a total of fifty-one high explosive shells, enough – I presumed – to transform a smallish town.

All this left me wondering: what was to be gained by earnest pursuit? Even if we could negotiate the off-road terrain of 1945, what was there to see? The trees will have grown back, and the villages recovered. And how would Flint recognise places he'd only ever known for ten blazing minutes, sixty years before? There wasn't even anything left of the Germans' huge – and useless –*Westwall* (between 1946 and 1949, the French army had blown up more than 17,000 bunkers, a precaution elegantly described as *dynamitage systématique*). We'd be better off, I thought, heading straight for Ulm, and I raised this with my friends.

'Absolutely,' said Flint. 'Let's get on, to the Alps.'

'Yep,' said Jeff. 'Hit the autobahn, and we can do it in a couple of hours.'

Curiously, the idea of a dash for the Alps had dominated the American thinking of 1945. For months, the Panthers had been encouraged to believe that their ride would ultimately end in Berlin. Now, suddenly, the Seventh Army peeled off to the south. This was partly because it was felt that Berlin was better left to the Russians, and partly because Eisenhower now worried about the safety of the 90,000 US servicemen held prisoner in the south. But there was also something else haunting military intelligence, and that was the concept of *Alpenfestung*.

'Ah, yes,' said Flint, 'the Alpine Redoubt!'

'And what did you think it was?' I asked. 'A sort of castle in the sky?'

'Yes, that sort of thing. Superguns. Underground cities . . .'

Like all castles in Germanic lore, it had its foundations in fact. Undoubtedly, Hitler had a hideout in the Alps (although he didn't like talk of a 'last stand') and he'd always said he'd fight on until America and Russia turned on each other. Goering had been more specific, placing the last battles in the Alps (where he'd promised to die a Nazi death). But, although OKW had ordered plans for an Alpine fortress, it had taken American imagination to build it. US secret agents had even reported having seen it develop, from across the border in Switzerland. Soon the rumours, like Jack's beans, found fertile soil and were sprouting skywards. By April 1945, the Germans were supposed to have 100,000 crack troops in place, 300 square miles of tunnelling and the wherewithal for a two-year siege. It would be a beacon of Nazi resistance, perhaps for a decade. One report, in the *New York Times*, even suggested that Himmler controlled the Alpenfestung from his desk, and that he could blow the whole thing up with the simple flick of a switch.

If the Panthers had had any doubt about the lie of the land from here, they were then seconded to a mountain division. For nearly five months they'd fought within the 100th Division, and, during that time, the division had suffered over 85 per cent casualties and had taken 13,000 prisoners. Now, with the Alps in view, the Panthers were redeployed amongst the 103rd, a body raised in Colorado, Arizona and New Mexico and originally known as the Rocky Mountain Division. The Alps, it was felt, was just the job for them.

Ulm only featured momentarily in the advance of the Hellcats and the Rocky Mountaineers. They paused for the night above the Danube and the wide blue plains beyond. Then, on 27 April 1945, they surged forward, off to war with Shangri-La.

110

That night, on the same ridge above the plains, we met a man who considered himself to be the happy product of defeat.

It was a chance encounter. We happened to be staying in the same inn, admiring the same sunset. Ahead, the full spectrum of blues undulated away towards the horizon where it ended abruptly in some tiny, delicate dogteeth each glowing luminously pink. Flint made some remark about how – whatever else had changed – the Alps hadn't, and, at the sound of American voices, the man came over and introduced himself. 'I was a prisoner of the US Army,' he said. 'It was the best thing that ever happened to me.'

I searched his face for mockery but there was none. Instead, the old man seemed unduly formal, and although he was tall and regally good-looking, he spoke with incongruous humility. In this, he reminded me of Flint, and, that evening, we all agreed to eat together. He did tell us his name but – as he'd never wanted to be in this war, nor probably this story – I shall call him Axel.

'It's strange to be talking about that period of my life,' he said. 'I've never mentioned it before.'

Flint nodded understandingly, affirming a code between them.

It was an odd evening. Axel told the story he'd never told before, and as he spoke, his hands shook and his eyes filled. But filled with what? Were they tears of joy or shame? The experience he described could have been characterised as either. There was joy in defeat, and misery in triumph. Whilst the rest of Germany had sensed redemption in Hitler, he'd sensed only doom. At the age of twenty-two, he ought to have felt pride at being in an elite intelligence unit, but all he felt was disgust. There was satisfaction at the news of Nazi atrocities, if only because it confirmed the immorality he'd always suspected. Then there was admiration for the defection of his *Hauptmann* to the Allies, and a sense of elation at his own capture some weeks later. But it was only when he was transferred to the captivity of the Americans that he saw the future ahead, suddenly without bounds. 'The Americans saved us,' said Axel. 'Saved us from ourselves.'

Flint smiled appreciatively. 'You're a great idealist.'

'Maybe,' said Axel. 'But the enemy wasn't the Americans. It was right here, amongst us: the *browns* (I can't bear to call them any other name) . . .'

Flint nodded. 'I only wish others had had the wisdom to realise that sooner.'

'We were very slow,' said Axel angrily. 'I'm sure you remember.'

'Yes,' said Flint, 'I do. Back then, these roads were packed with people for whom realisation had come just too late.'

Flint and I had often talked about the great exodus along the roads to Ulm.

'It sometimes seemed the whole world was on the move,' he said.

Not every nation was represented in these great rivers of human beings, but a good few were. Flint would remember the inmates of the camps best of all, in their stinking zebra suits: Belgians, Latvians, gypsies, pretty Polish girls, Greeks (with 'Gk' stamped on their back), and a Russian in a cassock and felt hat. Then there were the slave workers – corralled from around Europe – the dregs of Vichy France and the pitiful remnants of several other desperate foreign adventures – the long-lost Koreans, the Indian nationalists, and even a few of Vlassov's men. (These were the same *Mongols* who'd fought Nancy Wake, plundered Paris and hunted the Alsatians. They'd wander around Europe for weeks trying to surrender. Eventually, the last few thousand were gathered up and sent to the Soviet Union, where they were gradually killed off with bullets and ice. Vlassov himself was hanged in Moscow in 1946.) Also amongst them was a sizeable chunk of the German population, fleeing the fighting both ahead and behind, and running helter-skelter they knew not where. 'The Germans,' wrote Australian war correspondent, Alan Moorhead, 'expected to be ill-treated. They had an enormous sense, not of grief, but of defeat.'

But nowhere did this sense of defeat seem more enormous than in the columns of vanquished troops. Flint would remember them not so much in terms of numbers but miles. In places, the lines of *Landsers* and *Grenadiere* were so long, strung out across the countryside, that there weren't the Americans available to round them up or disarm them. 'We just pointed them back up the road,' said Flint, 'and carried on with the advance.'

Many German soldiers therefore arrived at their place of captivity still with all their arms. A few had even donned ceremonial uniforms for the occasion, or had turned up with their girlfriends in tow. But, for most, captivity was a vile experience. US Army rules required that all prisoners be searched, silenced and segregated, and deprived of all their documents. If they'd lost their clothes in flight, there were no more to be had, and the rations were barely a tenth of those for fighting men (it was even worse in France, where POWs were carted around in open rail trucks, only to be pounded with bricks dropped from the bridges). Unsurprisingly, the rabbles that reassembled themselves in the prison camps were a dispiriting sight, and often included children, villains and Nazis, all thrown in together. Had Flint paused at the cage outside Ulm, he might have caught sight of a pope-to-be, Josef Ratzinger, aged sixteen, and Germany's greatest living novelist, Günther Grass, who was then an SS trooper (and who was about to spend the next sixty-one years pretending that he hadn't been). For some, the ordeal would last a year or more, although the youngsters were allowed out sooner (the future Benedict XVI left on a milk truck three months later).

I asked Flint whether his men ever simply killed their prisoners outright.

'It was war,' he said carefully, 'but POWs were usually treated pretty fairly.'

All soldiers have something to hold back from history, but this, I thought, was probably true. Of course, there were stories of GI atrocities; Germans who let off all their ammunition, shot the emissaries and then jeered at their captors could expect little quarter; nor could the concentration camp guards. (At Dachau, four GIs machine-gunned a long line of them, against the wall. 'The Germans were quite brave,' wrote an eyewitness who filmed it. 'They sensed what was happening and they just stood there.') But these stories were always the exception; unlike his brutalised adversary, the average young American was still constrained by the fundamental decencies of his upbringing. In the years since My Lai and Abu Ghraib, it's become easier to envisage the collapse of conscience, but in the Germany of April 1945 the evidence of atrocity is largely anecdotal. Certainly, the theory – advanced by a Canadian journalist, James Bacque – that over a million German soldiers died in captivity has never caught the breeze. Without bodies, mass graves or even the missing million, it's merely an idea becalmed in the statistics.

'It never happened,' said Axel emphatically.

He, on the other hand, wasn't here at the time, and was never held in the cages at Ulm. Captured in 1942, Axel, along with 400,000 other POWs, was shipped off to the States, in empty troop transports. They arrived in New York in November 1943, and stayed in the barracks of those who'd gone to fight. 'I was then sent to Tennessee,' said Axel. 'A two-day rail ride through the mountains. And there I stayed until 1946. These were some of the happiest days of my life. The farmers all spoke German, and gave us chicken pie and ice-cream. No one tried to escape. Why bother? None of us were browns, or even professional soldiers! Many were academics, and, during my time, I learnt French and English, and then studied Latin and Greek . . .'

Flint smiled, and said he remembered the POWs in Texas.

'Having a good time,' he said ruefully, 'while we were off to war . . .'

'An *extraordinary* time!' said Axel. 'A regeneration after the Hitler years.'

'And did you ever return to the States?' I asked.

'Of course. To me, it was the Promised Land. I'm only back to retire.'

He gazed out across the darkening plains and the purple dogteeth beyond.

'And you know why I like it here? Because it's just like Tennessee.'

III

Before moving on, we stopped in Ulm just long enough to get a parking ticket.

Sadly, this clash with the municipal *Ordnung* tends to dominate my parting impressions of Swabia. It seemed to take hours to find the *Rathaus* and Mr Senior Traffic Officer, to fill out the forms and buy a paper absolution. But, somewhere amongst this bureaucratic flurry, Flint and I did at least manage to visit the *Münster*, which had the tallest spire in the world. From the bottom, this great isosceles of rock looked like a Saturn V rocket, except covered in gargoyles and griffins. Just like a rocket, it was, I suppose an early device for reaching heaven. Only the Swabians – the most technically astute people on the planet – had possessed the skill, ambition and hubris for such an unearthly endeavour. Surprisingly, when the first cracks appeared in 1530 (causing the mason to flee), they'd lost their nerve and had left the spire unfinished for more than three hundred years.

My only other memory of the day is of a beautiful painting of a cardinal who was having his guts winched out with a windlass. This, it struck me, was a perfectly Swabian notion, the idea that purgatory was somehow synonymous with the loss of one's digestive system.

I was sorry to be hurrying on. In 1934, the young Patrick Leigh Fermor had climbed to the top of the Münster's spire, and had peered down on Ulm below. Forty years later, in his masterly travelogue, *A Time of Gifts*, he spoke of his despair at the idea that the Swabia he'd loved had all but disappeared in the firestorm that followed. Well, he needn't have worried. As we zigzagged back through the half-timbered streets, I came across ANDY'S MAGIC HAIR SHOP and a horse wearing a petticoat. Swabia, for all its trials and innovations, could still be cheekily medieval.

Jeff saw none of this, and his memories of Ulm will be even more distorted than mine. By some macabre twist of history, he'd developed a savage case of trench foot. After a morning at the doctor's, he was then confined to the car, with his hot, pink foot dangling out of the window. As if the sepsis wasn't bad enough, he had another problem to contend with: the only way we were ever going to get to Bavaria was by putting me behind the wheel.

Part 8 – Bavarian Waffles

Deeper into Southern Bavaria the feel of legend, and some erotic symbolism grows.

R.W. Thompson, *The Devil at My Heels*, 1947

The nature of the mountains was not, of course, unknown to his men by rumour and report – and rumour commonly exaggerates the truth; yet in this case all tales were eclipsed by the reality. The dreadful vision was now before their eyes; the towering peaks, the snow-clad pinnacles soaring to the sky, the rude huts clinging to the rocks, beasts and cattle shrivelled and parched with cold, the people with their wild and ragged hair, all nature, animate and inanimate, stiff with frost; all this, and other sights the horror of which words cannot express, gave a fresh edge to their apprehension.

Livy, *Hannibal's Crossing of the Alps* (218 BC)

The earth will shake as we leave the scene.

Goebbels's suicide note

112

Of course, I was fine on the straight bits. To begin with, the road south was so straight and Roman that I even permitted myself a glance at the Bavarian countryside now streaking past. Although it was disconcerting to realise that the speed and harmlessness of these streaks now depended on me, a pleasing picture emerged. Amongst the blur, I could see copper cupolas and apple orchards, ancient plum trees, Draculesque castles, log-mountains, and cuckoo-clock houses with frilly bargeboards and a set of horns above the door. It was only later, in the Allgäu – the baby Alps – that the road began to undulate and swim before my eyes. Suddenly, sightseeing became a function too many, and I had to muster all the skills I clearly didn't have, like swerving and braking. How did other people manage these things with so much less noise and smoke? Although he was far too polite to say so, I had the feeling Flint had enjoyed this journey rather more on the last occasion, even though he'd been in a Hellcat and under constant threat from snipers. At least he could fire back at what-ever was out to kill him.

Jeff, meanwhile, sat in the front, with the battalion records across his knee. Now it was his turn to shout out the place-names. They'd already been mangled once, by the military clerks, but Jeff still managed to mangle them again. That afternoon, apparently, we passed Wizened Horn, Mumma Gun, Cough-Baron and Market Dorf. Flint recognised none of these places although he did enjoy the footnotes; at one point, the arrival of the Americans was announced by a town crier with a bell; elsewhere, the clerk had recorded that Flint's men were attacked with 'odds and ends'; in other places, however, the war became even vaguer still ('Contact made. No front line exists'). Bells, chaos and a bumpy ride were as much as Flint remembered.

Our own bumpy ride ended by a wild green river called the Lech. It looked like liquid malachite frothing through the rocks. Just as in 1945, it wasn't immediately obvious how to cross this torrent, and so I slewed us into the grass and turned off the engine. For several minutes we sat there, saying nothing, just enjoying the watery, cow-belled clank of the Alps.

113

It's an odd one, Bavaria. The largest of the sixteen German states, it's also the most rural, the most Catholic and the most unpredictable. During its time, it's been a fantasy kingdom, a Soviet republic and the cradle of Nazism, and – even now – it calls itself the *Freistaat Bayern*. No one's quite sure what it'll get up to next. All that can be said is that, whatever else is happening in Germany, the Bavarians will be doing something different – and it won't be growing potatoes. The *Freistaat* is also home to BMW and Siemens, and every year it produces an impressive crop of millionaires, making it the richest *Land* in the land.

Other Germans regard it all as a source of both wonder and amusement. They love the BMWs but titter at all those funny costumes, the *Tracht*. In the popular imagination, the Bavarians are over-nourished, loud-mouthed and fabulously hick. What's more, their manners, in matters of business, are boorish, and their music sounds like birdsong. Bismarck once defined 'a Bavarian' as someone 'halfway between being an Austrian and a human being'.

For their part, Bavarians take all this in their stride. To them, all sober, strait-laced northerners are *Saupreussen*, or 'swinish Prussians', and are either killjoys or party-poopers (*Karnevalsmuffel*). As for the jibes, it's water off a Bavarian's back. '*Mir san mir*', they say: We are what we are.

This sense of detachment is at least partly explained by the great wall now looming up ahead. For almost 250 million years, the Alps have been bulging out of Bavaria. It's said that they're still rising at the rate of a millimetre a year, an outrage caused by Africa sliding northwards and ruckling the European carpet. According to the Austrians, if the whole thing was straightened out again they'd end up somewhere in Libya. Meanwhile, until recently, no one was able to get over, under or even through the Alps.

They're a forbidding sight, not so much a wall as a vertical landscape. From the Lech, it looked like a vast upended island, which is what it is, in a way: a stupendous work of orogenesis, half the size of Japan, or like two little Icelands flipped over on to their sides. I could hardly believe that people and cities had ever attached themselves to *that*, but they had. Now, the Alps were home to 14 million people, spread through eight countries, all yodelling away in three different languages, and all specialists in clinging on. Who can blame American intelligence for taking one look at it and deciding it had become an *Alpenfestung*, or a fortress for the trolls?

114

Like all good troll stories, this one was beautifully untrue.

There was no redoubt, no underground castle, no *Reich*-in-waiting and not a single secret weapon. Almost nothing had been built, and the great concrete complexes still lay around in sacks. The architect had fled, and even Himmler, from whose murky mind the *Alpenfestung* had emerged, was now a babbling nervous wreck. Gone too was SS General Skorzeny, the mythical warrior sent to rally the troops (being mythical he at least knew when to disappear). That left only a quarter of a million soldiers in Bavaria, but with food for only a week. In the Alps itself, there were still eleven divisions of soldiers, although 90 per cent of them weren't fighters, and only 500 were on their feet.

Not even *die Werwolfe* could keep the story going. The werewolves were another of Himmler's ideas, conceived in one of his murkier moments. He'd had a fantasy about soldiers in sheep's clothing, all completely contrary to German military tradition. The idea was a flop. In Esslingen, they tried to blow up a Hellcat and were shot by the Panther's sentries, while in Winnenden they were given away by a German army chaplain. Most Germans despised them, and wanted to co-operate with the New American *Ordnung*. Once Hitler was dead, the werewolves were called off and told to vanish into the myth.

All this is not to say that resistance came to an end. Far from it: the fight became more desperate than ever. Every diehard, bigot and zealot in Bavaria was now funnelled into the Alps. The battalion records report more SS activity than ever. It was mostly a matter of personal initiative, or what one US army clerk called 'a fantasy of violence and speed, and extravagant incident'. Occasionally, jets appeared, and then whistled off harmlessly into the blue. Once, a huge radio turned up, on a train, prompting everyone to think that Hitler himself was about to make an appearance. But the real fighting was never as grand as it promised to be, and usually began with a roadblock. Here's one that Flint described in a letter to his wife:

One day we were carrying infantry, and the advance went well until a bend in the road, and here there was half-a-mile of large pine trees felled across the road. No way to pass. On one side was a sheer drop, on the other a forest too thick to lead a cow through. It didn't take any orders. The men swarmed off the vehicles like ants and – just like ants – they hacked and sawed and lifted and sent the great logs tumbling down into the valley below. How long to clear? Perhaps half an hour and the column was on its way to close with the enemy.

Often these roadblocks were coupled with an ambush. These were pitiful endeavours, like throwing feathers into a storm. All that the attackers had, said Flint, was the initial advantage of surprise. 'We'd have to respond with a lot of MI rifle fire, just to keep them busy.'

'And then you brought the big guns to bear?'

Flint winced. 'That's right. The .50 cal took care of individuals, and splintered all the trees. And then we'd fire some shells, and blast everything away . . .'

Still the attacks went on, each more pointless than the last. On 30 April 1945 – the same day that Munich fell – the SS made a determined stand in the Alps, and suffered obliterating casualties. Meanwhile, in Berlin, their ungrateful leader sat down to one last dinner, with Eva Braun and his bunker staff. It's said that, during the meal, Hitler gave a talk about dog-breeding, and came up with the theory that lipstick was merely fat, scraped from the walls of Parisian sewers. Shortly afterwards, he poisoned his bride of one day, and then shot himself in the head.

Even this news, however, wasn't enough to convince Flint's seniors that there weren't giants and castles ahead.

115

On the day Hitler ruined a good sofa, the Panthers camped in Trochgau, which was where we headed next.

It was a pretty village, like something conjured from a children's book. All the cows wore collars and bells, and the farms were decorated with wooden love-hearts and trimmed with lace and barley. Each of these barn-houses also had a vast earthen ramp up the back as if, at night, everything could be herded upstairs to bed. Even the potatoes had their own homes, with huge doorways in the turf. Our hotel was a little way back from the village, and four feet deep in clover. It was run by two very precise men, who were described by one villager as being 'on the other bank'. All the lamps wore French knickers, and the artwork was of the School of Puppies and Kittens. It wasn't quite what we'd expected but, after a day of bouncing around in the baby Alps, I suppose a nursery was only natural.

The waitress had no place in this strangely kindergarten setting.

'I'm from the north,' she told us.

You're gorgeous, gleamed Flint (although he had the dignity not to say it).

Poor Flint. Clearly, the effort of a second all-male tour of Bavaria was getting to him. He was missing women. Flint loved all variants of the female kind, whether they were just clever or funny, or – like Lisl – unnervingly curvy and lavishly chestnut-haired.

'You must love it here?' he purred.

'Love it? God, no!' she said. 'Everyone seems to think I'm a hooker!'

We must have looked puzzled.

'This,' she said, 'is no place to be long-haired, Protestant and single.'

Sex in Germany is – to outsiders – a matter of some complexity. We can never work out whether the Germans are prurient or prudish, whether there's too much sex or hardly any at all. Both Julius Caesar and Tacitus wrote about this curious contradiction in German culture: the barbarians' womenfolk were famously prim, and yet there was all that battlefield strip-tease, and the promise of sensual reward. Since then, the travel literature has reeled with confusion. Of all the bewildered accounts, my favourite is that of the Earl of Dartmouth in 1752. Finding himself in genteel company, he was horrified to discover that he had to kiss all the ladies present, from the matronly to the outright grotesque. 'It was,' he wrote, 'sad, clammy work.'

The signals coming from Germany are still confusing. We read that there are over 400,000 prostitutes registered in the country, and that brothels are such a prominent feature of society that they now feature in architectural reviews. Lust is even an electoral issue, and there's always some sort of campaign for more action in the bedroom (*Fair beim Verkehr!* Fairness in Sex!). Most town halls seem only to indulge this national concupiscence. In Cologne, during the World Cup of 2006, the authorities set up 'performance booths' so that the fans could better enjoy the locals, albeit briefly and in a cabin by the side of the road.

But, whilst Germany sometimes seems like the very fount of carnal knowledge, it can still be a powerful source of chastity. There are great leagues who march against impurity, and many women still live to the traditional creed of *Kinder, Küche, Kirche* (Children, Kitchen, Church). Even German men are sometimes puzzled by their partners' self-restraint. In the 1960s, Oswalt Kolle brought out a guidebook to womankind, and it became an instant bestseller under the title *Deine Frau, das unbekannte Wesen* (Your Wife, the Unknown Being). But, more often than not, it's been foreigners who fall foul of German sexual mores. When a British tabloid, the *Sun,* published a picture of the Chancellor, Angela Merkel, wearing only her bikini (with the caption, 'I'm big in the Bumdestag'), Germany reacted with fury. To the British – more used to seeing Germans with their clothes off than on – this was hard to understand.

If there's any pattern to this, it's probably to be found in latitude. The further south one goes, the less frisky the Germans seem. Bavaria has no Reeperbahn, and no concept of industrial debauchery (at the very moment Cologne was encouraging a little sexual athletics, Munich was expelling all its whores). In the Allgäu, meanwhile, we discovered that life was even more buttoned-up still. 'They call this area the *Pfaffenwinkel,*' said Lisl. 'The Priest's Corner! You're in the heart of Ratzinger country. *Das Land des Panzerkardinals* . . .'

This was all discouraging news to those young Panthers now in search of some recreational love. But it wasn't just God they found between themselves and the fairer sex: there was also some ugly army chicken. 'Fraternisation' was illegal. It was against regulations to talk to girls, and still less to take them to one's heart or bed. One officer even ordered that all cigarette butts be pulled apart, to discourage any friendship. 'Don't get chummy with Jerry,' advised an editorial in *Stars and Stripes.* 'In heart, body and spirit, every German is a Hitler.' For any Joe wishing to test the army's anti-sex laws, there was a $65 fine, a sum large enough, it was felt, to shrivel all but the most ardent of adventurers.

But separation was impossible, like keeping the tide off the beach. Even Bavarian girls discovered that there was a limit to their godliness. For some, the attraction was physical, but for most it was spam. Hunger made whores of the most ordinary women, especially in the towns. Countless young GIs lost their virginity to these unconvincing amateurs, known as

Veronica Dankeschöns. Food, meanwhile, had become an expression of conquest. 'In this economic set up,' ran a US Army report, 'sex relations, which function like any other commodity, assume a very low value . . . the average young man is afforded an unparalleled opportunity for sexual exposure . . .'

Sometimes, however, the little Lotharios got more than they bargained for – a dose of 'siff' or 'clap', or perhaps even both (a predicament known as 'full house'). By the end of 1945, the US Army was treating 600 new cases of VD every day, and announced that any woman knowingly transmitting an infection was liable to be shot. But the women, too, often got more than they'd bargained for. By 1946, there were another 20–30,000 new little mouths to be fed, all half-American and born of the quest for spam. This was a curious legacy of the Battle of Germany – the equivalent of three new divisions of life – and it would take some explaining to the husbands when, eventually, they marched back home from the camps.

'What about B Co.?' I asked Flint, 'Was it a company of lovers?'

'Not so much the farmboys, but the Brooklyn lot were experts.'

Not all these encounters are easily forgotten. One of Flint's men took some satisfaction in bedding young Bavarian women and then revealing, with a flourish like a circus magician, that he was Jewish and that this was an act of revenge. Elsewhere, a few GIs took what wasn't even theirs, smashing their way into German lives. In March 1945, the US Army had logged more than 500 complaints of rape, and by the end of the war it had executed some forty-nine Joes for crimes of violence and sexual assault. Of course, plenty got away with it, especially those higher up the chain. The army simply wasn't ready for the spectacle of a major or a colonel hauled against a post and shot. One of those who ought to have been punished was a senior officer that Flint had known.

'There was some issue with a girl . . .' said Flint.

I remembered the name, a heavy drinker.

'He was always half-crocked. Really, a grade-A schmuck.'

'And what about the girl?'

There was nothing about this in the records. The officer had been expunged. One moment he was there, and the next he'd gone and there was a new name in his place. The old drunk had simply vanished into the paperwork – no questions, no investigation and no fuss. There was little more that Flint, or anyone else, could add. 'We never knew much about the girl,' he said. 'Except the poor kid was only just fourteen.'

116

Up the road was a fortress even madder than the *Alpenfestung*.

Neuschwanstein was commissioned by the King of Nonsense in 1868, designed by a set-builder and built from Bavarian debt. We could see it long before we got there, a pod of turrets and towers soaring over the flanks of the Alps. It looked more like a mountain cathedral than the castle it was supposed to be – the home of an ancient German knightly class (who'd probably never existed). As we got nearer, however, the place seemed to erupt in detail; there were fantasy barbicans, blind arcades, sculpted modillions, bartizans (big and frilly enough to drag the whole thing over), and a wealth of pseudo-fortifications, all machicolated, banded, rusticated, slotted and trimmed. Here was architecture at its most operatic, or kitsch gone super-Gothic. I had the feeling I'd seen it all before, which of course I had: Neuschwanstein is a motif of the Disney Corporation, an enduring symbol of whimsy, Kooky ideas and profligate expense.

Most visitors don't know whether to laugh or cry at this point. Neuschwanstein is not only fabulously silly, it's also confirmation of everything we admire about the Germans, and everything we fear: that they're technically brilliant and yet comically serious and dangerously vain. In the cold light of day, this thought may seem excessive – but then Neuschwanstein had an aura about it which encouraged surfeit. The Australians, I noticed, had overdone it on Pils, and one group was attempting an anaesthetic assault on the mound, tumbling backwards whenever gradient got the better of balance. The Japanese, meanwhile, filmed everything – even the litter bins – as if no one back home would ever believe that Europe was like a trailer for *The Lord of the Rings*. My American friends, on the other hand, loathed it. Jeff took one look at all the kiosks and key-rings and had another attack of trench foot, and never got out of the car. Flint did at least agree to clamber up to the castle, even though he was suspicious of history, especially history with pompoms and tinsel. 'I have a psychiatric reaction to this sort of place,' he grinned.

The Bavarians didn't. As we clambered upwards through felled trees and falling Australians, I became aware of that peculiarly German variant of happiness. It was partly the trees and the huge rococo hunting lodges, but also the fantastical landscape, like one of those miniature Chinese rock gardens except with its dimensions exploding skywards. All around us – happily plodding up into the dark – were citizens of Augsburg and Munich, all dressed in fancy, bone-buttoned green coats, and hats with hackles of badger hair and feathers. No one but the Germans make such a ceremony of taking a walk in the woods. But then nowhere are forests and fantasy so inextricably interwoven. German mythology is rife with mountain kings, secret kingdoms and powerful wood spirits. According to two German writers, Barkow and Zeidenitz, their compatriots are the products of this foresty fantasy, and in every German there's a wild-haired genius pounding through the mountains, weeping over sunsets and trying – against impossible odds – to express the inexpressible.

Bavarians, it seemed, were no exception, and Neuschwanstein was perhaps one of those rare places where the disparate threads of Bavarian personality briefly came together. Weaving all these threads as one was the King of Nonsense himself, or at least his ghost, the ill-fated Ludwig II.

Ludwig was a strange figure to find at the heart of Bavarian content-ment. He'd been almost everything Bavarians aren't: decadent, fey and irrational. In his portraits, he was girly and slender, and even military regalia only made him look like a souvenir doll. But, for Bavarians, I now realised, he was still endlessly heroic; his life had inspired hundreds of books, six films, several plays, numerous Ludwig II Societies and an annual bonfire. A whole industry had grown up around his wimpy image, and there was hardly a tea-towel anywhere that hadn't been thoroughly Ludwigged (not to mention postcards, aprons, kitchen clocks and hotel art. There was even a Ludwig dog bowl). What, I wondered, had he done, to deserve a life preserved in knick-knacks?

Little in Ludwig's life makes any sense today. His grandfather was the godson of Louis XVI from whom he'd inherited nothing but a case of *folie de grandeur* (not that he made much of his regal status: Grandfather spent much of his life shacked up with an Irish trollop who passed herself off as an 'Andalusian dancer' called Lola Montez). By the time Ludwig was born in 1845, his mother was so grand that she deigned to see him for only an hour a day. This left Ludwig with just a statue of the Virgin Mary, for which he developed an unhealthy regard, and his brother Otto, whom he often tried to strangle. Otto, however, was already extravagantly mad, and in later life he refused to take his boots off and barked like a dog (at which point he was retired from the Bavarian Army with the rank of major-general).

It was only at the age of nineteen, when he ascended to the throne, that Ludwig's fantasies grew wings and set off for a world of their own. It began with an infatuation with Wagner ('Oh, he is Godlike!' declared Ludwig. 'My mission is to live for him, to *suffer* for him!'). But soon, Ludwig's entire life was an opera. He saw himself as 'The Swan King', and often liked to float around in a giant papier mâché cockleshell dressed as Lohengrin or some other well-feathered hero. He hated ruling, and seldom visited his capital, Munich. The military, as far as he was concerned were all 'Hedgehog Heads' (*geschorne Igelköpf*), and Ludwig would far rather watch a fireworks display than visit his army (who were being chopped to bits by the Austrians). Eventually he wearied of ruling altogether, and in 1870 he sold his kingdom to the Prussians for 30 million florins.

Neuschwanstein had a leading role in Ludwig's state of delusion. With Bavaria now part of Germany, he found himself with nothing but an empire of the mind. His mountain fortress would be fit for a Sun King and the defender of the Grail. Fantasy was heaped on fantasy, and storeys were added to storeys. Neuschwanstein simply wouldn't stop growing, and it became one of the first castles of the German legends to have central heating and a river that ran down the stairs. Naturally, Bavaria went broke paying for it all, and soon this great stage-set began to unravel its creator. Initially, Ludwig tried begging – from the Duke of Westminster and the Turkish Sultan – but, later, he ordered his servants to raid the Rothschild bank in Frankfurt (an operation which they tactfully bungled). Eventually, the Swan King decided to seek a new Bavaria altogether, and sent emissaries to Scandinavia, Africa and Afghanistan to look for El Dorado or at least the Kingdom of Prester John. In the end his agents failed, although they did conclude that Norway was the nearest thing to Shangri-La.

Deeper into the Alps was another of Ludwig's follies, not a castle full of heroes but a palace made for one. We could see Linderhof on the map, tucked in amongst the vesicles of forest and rock, straddling the road that Flint had taken in 1945. We could also see a thin dotted line across the mountains which we thought might be a short cut. After ten minutes of yawing and clattering through the scree, a huge sunburnt face appeared at the window.

'Is this good for Linderhof?' said Flint in faltering GI German.

The face knotted itself into whiskers and wrinkles, and replied in faltering grunts and waves. If you carry on along here, the big hands seemed to say, you will be battered by unspecific forces, before falling over an edge, and then fluttering for a while before being smashed to bits on something hard.

We turned back, and took the Hellcats' road.

Linderhof felt uncannily serene after our morning spent swinging around in the deep green fissures of the Alps. It looked like Versailles pared down to the essentials: one ornamental garden, one façade of porticoes and columns, one Moorish pavilion, one peacock throne, one grotto, one front door, one Hall of Mirrors and one bedroom. Ludwig never shared his life with anyone other than the occasional equerry or fop, and was terrified of company. He thought marriage was repulsive ('I'd rather jump in the Alpsee,' he said), and would kick his servants if they ever dared look at him, or even cough or sneeze. Whenever plays were performed at Linderhof, Ludwig would be the only person watching.

Along corridors-for-one led a trail of violet silk and silver crocodiles. One salon had almost disappeared under gold leaf, and another had become a utopian landscape, rendered in Gobelin tapestry. There were pieces of Sèvres big enough to hide in, and a half-size equestrian bronze depicting *Ludovicus Rex* in the manner of a Roman knight. He'd spared the Bavarian taxpayer nothing in the worship of himself. It was unusual to find him only as a knight; most of the time he was the Sun King himself, and all around him were the first – and fallen – ladies of the Royal French court. Amongst the statues, I spotted Mesdames Pompadour and Dubarry, and Marie Antoinette, all looking rather fondled and worn.

A stunted banquet table was still laid for a solitary dinner. It was a golden toad of a table, and could be winched downwards through the floor so that Ludwig would never have to defile his solitude with servants. The only guests that ever ate with him were imaginary, and were addressed in courtly French. Once, however, he did invite his favourite grey mare to come and eat at his table. It was a splendid horsy feast and she ate off all the best crockery, which afterwards she smashed.

We can all escape reality for a while but we can't escape the gas bill. In the end, it was the cost of heating this gilded lunatic asylum that brought Munich out in protest. In June 1886, a commission was sent to Neuschwanstein to detain the demented king. For several days, the Castle of the Grail was truly an Alpine fortress, defended against the gasman. Ludwig ordered that all the gates be barred and the commissioners be arrested and have their eyes burnt out with a poker. Bavarians never like to forget this, the moment the philistines were defied. But it didn't last; Ludwig gave up, and two days later he drowned himself in the Starnberg See, taking his doctor with him.

So ended Neverland, the Swan Kingdom, the gas bills, and Bavaria's best ever hope of a credible *Alpenfestung*.

117

In the last pass before Garmisch-Partenkirchen, Flint felt a tremor of the past.

'It was cold, bitterly cold. The Hellcats had open tops, of course, and so we were completely exposed, and yet surrounded by freezing metal. I can't think of these passes without thinking of that cold . . .'

I looked up the date: 2 May 1945. 'Still a week of war to go.'

'Doenitz was on the radio. Said the fight went on, to repel the Bolsheviks!'

'So Garmisch was still very much at war?'

'Yes, in parts,' said Flint. 'Mostly up in the forest.'

'Not great for the sightseeing.'

Flint smiled. 'A pity. My parents had enjoyed it here on their tour of 1910.'

'I don't suppose you even found their old hotel?'

'No, we weren't sleeping much. We just refuelled and carried on.'

Most Americans would remember Garmisch like this, snatches glimpsed in the closing days. For some of the Rocky Mountaineers, the picture would be even more fragmentary still. They'd remember nothing but the fur coats, stolen from the rich and chopped up into jackets.

*

Garmisch-Partenkirchen has always been a place ripe for extortion. Straddling a long, deep crack that eventually turns into Italy, it's the perfect spot for preying on the north–south road. The mountains have made a chamber of its lush green plain, with an entrance at one end and an outlet at the other. There's no other escape; the sky has been replaced with rock and ice, and unleashes fierce white rivers down anything that looks like an exit.

Naturally, the local hillbillies, the *Werdenfelsers*, became a tribe of toll-men. Their village, at Germareskauve, was already jingling with cash long before the Romans set up a rival camp at Partanum. The two camps have never got on, and were only forced into marriage by Hitler for the 1936 Olympics (although, even now, there are two ski clubs, two fire brigades, and two clubs for dressing up in *Tracht*). Only once did they enjoy a moment of divorce, and that was during Flint's last visit, when all the bridges were blown. But the *Werdenfelsers* have never been ones to put pride before production. Even when they were engulfed by Bavaria, in 1802, it wasn't long before they were back at their tills. I once found a gallery of portraits from this time, and was surprised to see the *Werdenfelsers* strutting around again, in fur top hats and jackets made of coins.

Now, it seemed, the town was in a permanent state of Christmas. Even though the summer was still sprawling into September and the slopes were hazy with gentian, I had the feeling that Advent had somehow crept up behind us. Everything was made of pine or chocolate, or inhabited by furry animals and puppets. On all the walls were huge airy murals – or *Luftmalerei* – which were like the world according to Christmas cards (amongst them, I could see the disciples kitted out in lederhosen, and Jesus dressed in *Tracht*). Meanwhile the smell of hot wine, pine trees and spicy little biscuits had left my natural body calendar reeling in confusion. Embarrassingly, I also found it all rather pleasing – or at least pleasingly familiar – and I suddenly realised how much of my life I must have spent in a state of pseudo-Bavarian *Gemütlichkeit*. Bavaria, I now know, doesn't look like Christmas; Christmas looks like Bavaria.

This yuletide illusion felt even stronger in the main street of Garmisch. It was like walking into a Nativity scene, except one set to a Landler waltz. Nothing seemed to belong to the age we live in – neither the whiskers, the full skirts, the packs of giant dogs, the donkeys whittled out of spruce, the puppeteers, the lace-makers, nor the men now cracking

Garmisch, Bavaria

Mittenwald, Bavaria

their whips. I started scribbling notes in my diary in case this truly was a messianic moment.

At my side, I sensed Jeff, panting with disbelief.

'What kind of dog's that?' I asked.

'Search me,' he said. 'It's probably from Outer Space.'

118

Like the mountains, Garmisch-Partenkirchen has long since closed in around those last, mad days of its war.

I once climbed up into the forest, unsure what to expect. It was a beautiful walk, livid with violet and blues. At the top of Kramer Hill, I came across a little chapel with breathless views back across the chasm below. It was equally breathless inside, amongst the faces of the dead. Each wall was covered in the photographs of those who'd perished in the war. It felt odd, being caught in the cold, grey gaze of men who looked so immediate and yet who'd vanished almost three generations before: grenadiers, *Landsers*, men in forage caps and swastikas, farmers, fathers, submariners, skiers, a man with an ice-axe, and three brothers who'd all died within a month. Every frame was carved and trimmed in the same Christmassy baroque, with a sprig of edelweiss or holly. There were still plenty who came up here to tend them, and to stare back into the past. It's said that almost one in seven German war widows is still alive today.

In the inscriptions was the tale of a great, grey empire that began with its neighbours and then collapsed in the East. *Gefallen Paris . . . Russland . . . Stalingrad . . . Russland . . . Russland.* Here was a timely reminder that however great the struggle had been on the Western Front, in Russia it was almost thirty times as intense. I suspect that, of the local boys killed out there, few got a tomb of their own. Of them, all that remained was a picture on Kramer Hill.

Further down the valley, the mansions of the rich sprawled off into the trees. I enjoyed the thought of the Rocky Mountaineers up here, creeping through the rococo in their search for billets and fur. One of the houses in particular caught my attention. It was set back amongst the beech and had white walls and green shutters, and elliptical windows in the roof that looked like huge sleepy eyes. The man who'd lived there was so famous that not even the Nazis had dared come in and arrest his daughter-in-law, who happened to be Jewish. By the time the Americans arrived, he was eighty-one although 'still rosy-cheeked and vigorous'. When the GIs came bashing at the door, he answered it himself, and told them what he told all soldiers who ought to have known better. 'I am Richard Strauss, composer of *Der Rosenkavalier*.'

Further up still, the mansions turned into palaces of logs. Grainau was still a place to come and flounce around in fur. It had a high street of chalets, an onion-domed church and a shop selling designer *Tracht*. For the good burghers of Munich, this was the place to keep a mistress, or – if they had a million euros to spare – perhaps even an Alpine love-nest. Trees hear nothing and see nothing – although they do have a tendency to gossip. It was said that the Sultan of Oman kept five houses up here (but that the only reason he came here was because he liked to watch the rain). For a while, it was also rumoured that Hitler was up here, with Eva Braun, and her sister's husband, a weasely drunk called General Fegelein. This news soon had Professor Trevor-Roper plodding up the valley, although – by September 1945 – he'd concluded that it was 'pure fantasy' and that 'the whole story dissolved at the merest touch of criticism'.

It was however true that Eva's sister, Gretl, had hidden out up here.

Gretl was famously described as 'slightly sluttish', and I once met an ancient American officer who'd interrogated her (and whom I promised not to name). A strange story emerged, a bit like a nursery rhyme for Nazis. He said that Gretl had been living deep in the woods and had just given birth to a child of the ogre, Fegelein. The ogre himself, meanwhile, was long since dead in far-away Berlin. The Führer had found him with a suitcase full of jewellery (and an unfamiliar wench in his bed), and had signed his death warrant on the grounds of desertion. Fegelein was shot the following day in a garden full of craters. Eva didn't mention his death in her last letter to her sister, and – in the Braun family – the name of Fegelein was never raised again. The following day, Eva herself was put out with Chancellery refuse, and that left only Gretl with the secret of the treasure.

'*Treasure?*' I said. 'What treasure?'

'Gold teeth,' said the old interrogator, 'and thousands of pounds in cash.'

'And did she tell you where it was?'

'Yup, it was in a lake. We got a farmer to drag it out with his cows.'

'And why was it in pounds?'

The story-teller laughed. 'It was all fake! I sent one of the £50 notes to my old pa back home, and he was damn near busted for forgery! The whole thing was a crock – except the teeth . . . They reckon it came from the concentration camp at Oranienburg, where the Nazis had been getting the inmates to run up bundles of fakes. Seems they had some schmuck idea of flushing the Western world with forgeries, and sending us into freefall. Jeez! Can you imagine anything as cuckoo as that?'

'And what about Gretl? What happened to her?'

'Who cares? Far as I know, she fucked off back to the forest . . .'

Beyond Grainau, the trees closed in again, sealing out the day. Later, I went up there with Flint and Jeff, and we walked around under a chattering canopy of jays. Ahead of us there was nothing but the Zugspitze, a wall of rock that tapered off thousands of feet above. The summit was the highest point in Germany, and, for the SS, this was the end of the road. Here, according to the battalion records, they'd make their last stand in Bavaria, in this beautiful green dead-end. The idea, it seems, had been to swoop down from their fortress of twigs and leaves and kill the American-appointed mayor. Perhaps, like Ludwig, they really did think they'd found their Shangri-La? Well, so they had – until the Hellcats levelled the trees.

As we walked back, through the new growth, a strange thing happened. A fox stepped out of the shadows, and came and sat down beside us. No one said anything and yet, somehow, it felt as if a door had closed on a painful past.

119

There was still an American army in Garmisch-Partenkirchen. We often saw their military policemen, growling around in outsized vehicles more like juggernauts than jeeps. Occasionally, we saw soldiers too, always looking conspicuously foreign amongst all that badger hair and bone. They were the last stragglers of the vast Army of Occupation that had been in Germany since the war (over the years, there's seldom been less than a quarter of a million Americans in the country. In all, some 12 million servicemen have passed through, including Elvis Presley, who now has his own mock-Gracelands somewhere up near Frankfurt). Not all these soldiers were attuned to the country all around them. One I met was still trying to sleep off the effects of Iraq.

'. . . my wife goes nuts when I hear de RPGs . . .'

'RPGs?'

'Yeah, every night! Wham! *WHAM!* All round ma fuckin' tent . . .'

Even the tents belonged to a world apart. In Garmisch, the Americans lived in what the locals still called the *Hitler Kaserne*. They must have been the only pink barracks in the world – a bastion of bowling halls, movie-theatres, Pizza Huts and malls. It had a GI hotel, GI shops and a GI ski run. Even the waiters were GI, it was said, because they were cheaper than the Germans. To the locals, the *Kaserne* was a mysterious place, like a little chunk of America that had somehow landed in their midst. They couldn't see it at all behind its wall, but they could hear it, chirruping over the airwaves (*'This is Radiofreeeeurope! The VICE of Democracy!'*). It was popularly believed that the place was used as a sort of fortified university, teaching the New Europeans of the East the civilised values of the New World to the west. Hardly anyone inside spoke German, and I once met a man who sold *Antiquitäten*, who said he'd learnt his English as a schoolboy, caddying for the US Army golf club. Herr Beerman said he still found it odd, such a stronghold of isolation, tucked up here in the Alps.

'*Kleines Amerika!*' he said. 'It's like an island within an island.'

120

It intrigued me, the thought of a place so chronically Christmassy. What was it like in the winter? A few months later, I returned to Garmisch-Partenkirchen to take a second look – not with Flint this time, but with my wife, Jayne, and our daughter, Lucy, aged four months. Although this journey necessarily means jumping out of the narrative for a page or two, at least now I feel I understand a little better the Alpine war that Flint fought, literally packed with cold. I also realised, as we set out, that Lucy was exactly the same age as Flint's daughter when he was here, although he, of course, had never actually seen her.

Nowadays, the hardest part of the journey was leaving home. We seemed to spend days packing. I thought of the Flint family in 1910, with their open-topped car, two tiny children and four spare tyres. We, by contrast, moved off like the Mothercare wagon train with prams, sheepskins, four cases, sterilisers, a car seat, nappy bags, flasks, cameras, a pram hood and an armful of fleecy pink extras. Eventually, after what seemed like aeons, we managed to haul this great mound of plastic and fluff into the Alps. Disappointingly, Lucy hardly had noticed the transition from Heathrow to fairy tale.

The Bavarians had. From the moment we landed, people gave us kind but weary looks, as if we were making them tired. Germans like children, friends had told us, but only if they're inconspicuous. This was a discouraging thought as we pressed ourselves upon the locals, trailing leads and leaks and pink fluffy ears. 'Don't expect the Bavarians to get too excited about babies,' people said: 'you're not in Italy yet.' At least we only had to find our hotel. One friend, who'd been coming to the German Alps for years, said we'd never have got an apartment with a baby.

'You'd have more chance,' he said, 'with a pack of hunting dogs.'

Garmisch, meanwhile, had been transformed since the summer. The overwhelming sensations of Christmas had been almost smothered under a metre of snow. The trees had turned to lace and the lakes to sugar. A sparkling halo of fog lay across the meadows of the summer before. When I first saw people in the haze I thought they were swooping about on wires, instead of gliding around on skis.

Every day more snow piled up, packed to the height of the street signs. Cars were buried in drifts, and trucks had to be abandoned in the forest. There were icicles the size of swords, and the *Hauptstrasse* developed drifts so huge that they were like its own little Alps. The pram was useless in this, and simply sank out of sight. Meanwhile, on Frühlingstrasse, the small wooden farms had almost vanished under the snow, along with their portraits of the Virgin and their pigeon cages under the eaves. The modern-day *Werdenfelsers* did what they could to keep the town going. Each morning, Unimogs appeared to cart away the drifts, but still the silence remained. It was like the black and white film that my travels with Flint ought to have been.

We stayed next to the lusty River Loisach, now just a gurgle, trickling through ice. Our hotel, the Aschenbrenner, was built by the Duke of Ruess in 1906, and we were given his gargantuan study with views over the Zugspitze. This being a fairy tale, the Duke had married the milk-maid who'd lived at the end of his orchard. They'd enjoyed a short, sweet life in their lumpy chalet but, happily, their affection had survived – at least in turrets and green-tiled stoves. Every morning we ate a Duke's breakfast under the watchful eyes of a dozen wooden apostles.

Being new to the controls of a baby, it took us hours to get going each day. No sooner was output under control, than more input was needed. But, once going, there was no stopping us. We'd poke our heads into every tavern and every chapel. We even found a gift shop for cats (*Katzenboutique*) and an outlet for second-hand chamois-leather shorts. Then we toured the ancient barns, and padded four miles around the fabulously frozen Lake Eibsee, where the men of the *Wasserwacht* were practising the extraction of corpses from under the ice.

Then, to top it all, we scrambled up into the Partnachklamm gorge. It was a deep crevasse of ice-forts, tunnels, waterfalls frozen in mid-splash, curtains of ice, translucent organ pipes, niches, windows, alcoves, and frosted daggers and spears. All morning the path nibbled upwards through the rock, and the sky looked like a streak of crooked lightning several hundred feet above. Later, we met an old woodcutter who'd worked in the gorge until 1963, flushing timber out of the hills. 'If the logs jammed, we were lowered down to unblock them.'

'And it's a dangerous place?'

'*Ja, ja,*' said the woodcutter, 'when the snow melts!'

He told us that, each spring, the gorge spewed out great clots of roots and rock, often the size of a village. '*Die Alpen sind junge . . .*' he said. 'The Alps are young, and can still get very angry.'

121

The great thing about these adventures – whether with Flint or Lucy – was that at the first twinge of hunger an eatery appeared. The Bavarians seemed able to put restaurants in the most awkward of places. During my various visits to Garmisch-Partenkirchen I've eaten in a chasm, up a mountain, under an Olympic ski jump and in the royal stables of a lunatic king. But wherever these hostelries were, they were always cosy places, decorated with little woodland animals around the walls, and tables hewn out of logs. Often I sat under cowhide lanterns and ate off wooden plates. The waitresses always wore *Tracht* – usually laced-up blouses and milk-maid's skirts – and the *Lokal* itself would have some endearingly woody name like Zum Wildschütz or Goldener Engel. This was just how I imag-ined the pubs of the pixies.

But it was always the food that surpassed all the myths. The Bavarians seemed to take their food almost as seriously as warfare. Each meal was like a campaign, fought against overwhelming odds. Huge flanks of bullock and ram would be wrestled under control with daggers and forks, and then thrown down the hatch, followed by noodles, potatoes, ravioli, strudel, *Weisswurst*, pretzels and the occasional *Kalbskopf*, or calf's head. Once I ordered a whole leg of something called a *Schweinshaxen durchwachsen*, which came with a dumpling the size of a baby's head, and which took an afternoon to eat and a week to digest. The waitress said that this was nothing, and that during the *Oktoberfest* the feats of eating were more prodigious than ever. For thousands of hoofed animals it's like a terminal migration, as they're carried away on great rivers of gravy and beer.

Only the Bavarians can eat like this. If ever a little space appears in the digestive process, some delicacy or other is levered into the gap, and washed into place with more hot chocolate and beer. By this stage, even the puddings begin to sound dyspeptic; there are *Nonnenfürzle* (Nun's farts) and *versoffene Jungfern* (Drunken Virgins). Then, for anyone still left upright after this onslaught, there's *Obstler*, or wild fruit schnapps. Even Lucy put on a pound that week, just by being there.

But for Flint, the taste of Bavaria had a different effect, and seemed to awaken old songs. Mostly, these were tunes he'd learnt from the prisoners – a bit of belting from 'Horst Wessel', or snatches of 'Lili Marleen:'

Vor der Kaserne
Vor dem grossen Tor
Stand eine Laterne
Und steht sie noch davor . . .

Up in Garmisch, there was always some old boy willing to sing along with him. One night, we found ourselves packed into a cavernous bar with a party of locals who looked as if they'd been out hunting since the turn of the eighteenth century. They all wore thick green tunics and felt hats decorated with bits of silver and fox. The accordionist wore lederhosen, and had thick, hairless arms and could warble upwards through the octaves like a frog. It was only after my third *Mass* of beer that I realised he was a woman, at which point Flint and his new friends coiled their arms together and declared – rather incongruously – a state of brotherhood, or *Brüderschaft*.

'More beer, *Oberleutnant*?' roared the accordionist.

Flint slid his glass down the table. '*Scheissen Bären in der Wald?*'

When they'd worked their way through the prisoners' songs, the singers started on some *Gstanzlen*. These were raunchy, improvised, told-you-so verses – sung, ululated, howled and sneezed, antiphonically from table to table around the vault. The Frog danced, and the beer flowed. Flint said that Bavarian music was proper drinking music, but to me it always felt like peristalsis, booming and rumbling steadily through the stomach. It was music to digest to. Then, as we sat there, happily groaning and bellowing, a boy came in and started to dance a jig. He was wearing a white blouse, black leather shorts and pumps, braces and feathery hat. As he danced, he kicked his knees in the air, and slapped his buttocks and clapped his shoes. Jeff was struck mute with disbelief. If this wild, wriggly dance had had lyrics they too would have been plucked from the air. *Hey, diddle, shaky! Cheers! Clap, slappity, feathery, HEY!*

'*Die Schuhplattler!*' yelled the accordionist. 'The Dance of the Shoes!'

To some, like her, this was obviously the very essence of *Werdenfelser* culture. To others, it was merely a fond reminder of the days when they still had movement in the waist.

122

There was only one more town before the Austrian frontier, probably the strangest of all. If Garmisch had seemed a little fanciful, Mittenwald was having a full-scale attack of the amateur dramatics.

It was Sunday, and almost everyone was dressed for a period play. Even the shopkeepers had taken a role, in their best *Blusen* and waist-coats, with huge fur hats or pantaloons and lace. No one seemed to think it at all odd that their lives had turned into a musical. One man was wearing a frock coat made from curtains, and another – who looked like the Rat Catcher – was being towed along by a team of matching dachshunds. Then there were two very fat ladies who'd somehow managed to truss themselves up like humpback settees, and were a vision of tassels and piping and straining damask. And that was just the morning's work. In the afternoon there was a *passeggiata* of Heidis, followed by a parade of old Cinderellas. I even saw a cyclist pedalling past in a flurry of feathers, and with a very small dog peering out of his pocket.

The *Luftmalers* too had been at work, painting the town with their scriptural scenes. Goethe had described Mittenwald as 'a living picture book', which of course it is; here, Jesus goes around in a big felt hat, and the Apostles drink Bavarian beer. At our hotel, however, biblical charac-ters were rather more rigorously treated. We had St Anthony pinned up in the eaves, and another saint being skewered in the lobby. The only other picture was a photograph of some guests, all refreshingly under-clothed and frolicking around in the sauna. That night, Jeff and I tiptoed out, past the expiring saint, off in search of a drink. All we found was a gay bar, decorated with fairy lights and a picture of a *Schuh*-dancer wearing nothing but his smile.

Flint said it was hard to believe that this was the place he'd known.

'They gave us a bit of a headache,' he said.

I looked in the orders, and found 2 May 1945. The cast of Mittenwald had fought all day, and then let the Americans in.

'I guess they're entitled to be a little crazy,' said Jeff.

This was true, except that Mittenwald had always been strange. For centuries they've celebrated Nonsense Day, driving their old maids through the hag mill, in the hope that they'll come out as maidens. They once made the best violins in the world but now they make nothing but mutants – weird, stuffed foxes with eagles' wings and horns. Some blame the *Föhn*, the maddening wind that comes singing through the cracks (the accordionist told us it was still a defence in court, to blame one's crime on the *Föhn*). All this was possible but I prefer to think of Mittenwald as just a case of frontier nerves. After all, here the certainty of northern Europe ends, and from now on, there's nothing left but the south.

123

At the end of the town was a split in the mountain. I had to pay a local farmer fifty cents to look inside this cleft. It was only narrow – probably the width of a car – but a river came down it the colour of swimming pools and at the rate of two pools per second. The river, I discovered, was the Leutasch, and I looked it up on the map. Upstream, it opened out into a valley of its own and was joined by a road. This, I realised, was the same road the Hellcats had taken as they wriggled through the rock, taking a back route into the Tyrol. The Commander of VI Corps had told the invading force that they'd been specially selected for the occupation of Austria. 'All the chips,' he said, 'are now on you.'

I read this out again to Flint. 'It sounds like poker,' I said.

He shrugged. 'Well, it was, I suppose.'

Still no one knew what lay beyond. An *Alpenfestung*, or a mountain arcadia? Would the Panthers be fêted by obliging natives? Or mauled by the last few heads of the Hydra?

Part 9 – Sweet Tyrol

I loved my first sight of Austria. There was none of the mystic gloom of Germany about these rambling ancient villages within their great gateways.

R.W. Thompson, *The Devil at My Heels*, 1947

There is no better company to be found in all the wide world than that to be met with in the Inns of the Tyrol.

Ian F.D. Morrow, *The Austrian Tyrol*, 1931

Should I draw Innsbruck? . . . I must suggest the hustle and bustle, with Tyrolean women in their traditional costumes, slim Austrian officers and travellers holding a book. That would create a picture of the city. But the surrounding set is more splendid; it gives the picture depth – the city framed by the high mountains like threatening storm clouds passing overhead.

Hans Christian Andersen, 1840

GIs stationed in Austria admit that the scenery is good and that the girls are pretty, but they don't like much else. There isn't much else. The Austrians are living largely on the hope that somehow things will get better, and the GIs in Austria are living largely on the hope that somehow they can get home.

Yank magazine, 1945

124

One of the first things Flint heard in Austria was a bullet, sizzling past his neck.

'I wasn't particularly surprised. The country was pretty wild then.'

It looked pretty wild now. Although there was a wide, brilliant green band of meadows along the floor of the valley, beyond it, the rock rose up and swooped off into the sky. Down here, there were little chapels scattered through the grass, barns made of tree trunks, and huge wooden farms painted up like palaces. But up there, there was nothing but velvety greens and gunmetal blues, and a powdering of ice.

I once read that all of Austria was like this: a massif the size of Idaho or Scotland – one-third inhabited, one-third forest, and the rest a vertical, silvery void. No doubt Goethe would have called it 'a living maze', an infinite mountain labyrinth of corridors, chambers and choices. As for the Tyrol, it's like a little Austria inside a big one. Even its history sounds more like the story of a lost world than *das Land in Gebirge*, the Mountain State. Amongst the Tyrolean rulers we find Margaret the Ugly, *Maultasch* (or Gobsmack), Sigismund the Wealthy, Frederick Empty Pockets, and the Elephant League. It's also said that, whenever there's a catastrophe, the Gnomes of the Tyrol can be seen escaping over the hills (although they did return when Margaret the Ugly fled). This must be the only place in the world where the patter of tiny feet means it's time to run for cover.

We stopped only once in the Leutasch valley, at Gasse. It had changed little since the Hellcats had paused here, on their pot-shot tour. There was still a small pink shrine full of bones, a dozen houses, and a *Gasthof* with a stuffed fox on the bar. The waitress, who had a laced corset and ketchup-coloured hair, shrugged when I told her that Flint had been here before. The Tyrolese had never been much impressed by the American invasion. They'd been told that Negroes were cannibals, that radar tinsel was poisonous, and that Colorado beetles had been sent over to eat all their potatoes.

Soon we were on our way again, breezing along through the grass. Flint told me that they'd often found bodies in the meadows, a black tunic at their side. It seems that a rumour had got out that the Americans were shooting the SS on sight. When they heard this, the SS starting shooting *Wehrmacht* troops and then swapping their clothes with the dead. The irony of this wasn't lost on the Hellcat crews. A great regime, which had once vowed to rule the world, was now slaying its subjects, just to steal their shirts.

'And what about the man who tried to shoot you?' I asked Flint.

'A fanatic,' he said. 'Some crazy Austrian fanatic, making his last mistake.'

125

Austria is famous for its enthusiasm, and occasionally fanatics.

I've always been intrigued by this little country which behaves like an empire. To the outside world, the Austrians seem tirelessly ambitious. It's hard to believe there are only eight million of them. Hardly a competition goes by – from golf to cheese-making – without Austrians picking up prizes. They've produced world champions in skating and Formula 1, and now there's an Austrian – Arnold Schwarzenegger – in charge of the world's fifth economy, the State of California. It's been the same in the arts. Three of the most popular painters of the last century – Schiele, Kokoschka and Klimt – were Austrian. But it's in the world of classical music that Austria's in a class of its own. It seems to have produced almost everyone: Bruckner, the Haydn brothers, Mahler, the Strauss family, Schubert, Schoenberg and Mozart. (Webern, too, would probably have joined this list, if he hadn't been accidentally shot by an American soldier in Salzburg.) Meanwhile, Brahms and Beethoven were Austrian by adoption, having jumped the border in the hope of soaking up the talent.

Even now, the determination of Austrians is astonishing. Wherever I've been in the world, I've always found Austrians already there – with castles in Majorca, hotels in Africa and tracts of Paraguay the size of Wales. It's almost as if they've grown out of their own country, and had to start an annexe. But they're always famously charming and energetically generous. Pleasure, after all, is a serious matter, at which they also excel. The map of Austria seems to bubble over with improbable resorts: Wörgl, Gurgltal and Obergurgl. Every year, for over a century, foreigners have flocked up here to chase the locals over the moguls. They never catch them, of course, because – when it comes to skiing – the Austrians are probably the best in the world.

But, it seems, there's a darker side to this dedication. Just as in Orson Welles's masterpiece, *The Third Man*, long shadows still fall across the set. My guidebook warned of policemen 'not renowned for their friendliness towards other races', and it wasn't long before I came across the glossy,

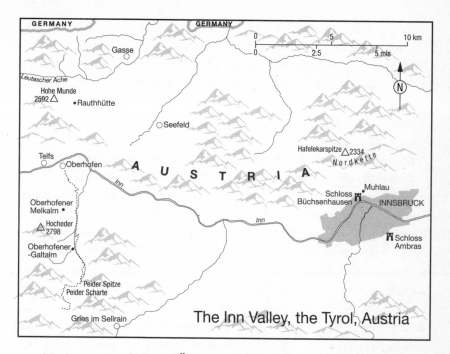

The Inn Valley, the Tyrol, Austria

neo-Nazi posters of the FPÖ. Unsurprisingly, no such enthusiasm has ever been shown for Hollywood's breezy, Alpine classic, *The Sound of Music*. With its frivolous depiction of Austrian fervour, the film was refused airtime for over thirty-five years, until January 2001.

Even now the outside world watches and waits, to see who'll emerge next whipping up a sense of destiny. Many Austrians, it appears, still can't resist the clickety-click of boots. In the last two decades, they've voted in President Kurt Waldheim – despite more than a whiff of atrocity – and Jörg Haider, who can always find much that was good in the Nazis. Almost a third of Austrians apparently agree. A few would like to go further still, and expel the Turks and reclaim the Italian Tyrol (or at least blow up the pylons and block the roads). But for most, it's simply a question of living with the utter conviction that Austrians deserve much more than they get.

The Austria that Flint had known had easily fallen for the Nazis' charms.

Once the electorate had been pruned of Jews and other outcasts, 99 per cent of Austrians voted for *Anschluss* with Germany. Support was particularly strong in the Tyrol. The city of Innsbruck had given Hitler's troops a wild welcome on 12 March 1938, and two weeks later the Führer himself was bathing in petals and praise. After that, the Tyroleans had thrown their lives away in every quarter of the Nazi adventure – from Finland to Tunisia – and had staged their own *Kristallnacht*, their own pogroms and their own little Final Solution. Overall, almost a third of Austrian Jewry perished, and more would have died if the mood of Austria in 1938 hadn't removed any doubt of what the future held, prompting most to flee.

Even Berlin was shocked by the determination of the Austrians. Although they made up only 8 per cent of the Reich's population, they provided 14 per cent of SS manpower, and 40 per cent of those involved in genocide. There were also Austrians at the very highest level of the Nazi machine. Apart from Hitler himself, there was Adolf Eichmann (architect of the Holocaust), Kaltenbrunner (Head of the Gestapo), Seyss-Inquart (enslaver of the Netherlands) and the repulsive Globocnik, who'd overseen the smooth pace of killing at both Sobibor and Treblinka. With handmaidens like that, Hitler must almost have wondered whether he needed the Germans at all.

Now, it's often the Austrians themselves who find it hard to believe, the part they played in the war. For over forty years, they've enjoyed the idea that they were merely the first victims of the Nazis. There was little compensation for those who'd been persecuted, few memorials to those who'd died, and no public statement of contrition until 1988. I remember once sharing a cable-car with two elderly American Jews in Innsbruck, and passing high over the old concentration camp at Reichenau. It had long since become a prosperous suburb, without a single word of its past. 'The Austrians,' said my fellow travellers, 'are the worst liars in the world.' As with so much about Austria, this was only half true. These days, Austrian democrats work hard on their *Vergangenheitsbewältigung*, or their 'coming to terms with the past'. Now, historians like David Irving are likely to get longer sentences for denying the atrocities than many of the Nazis got for actually committing them. This doesn't bother the diehards; they don't deny the atrocities happened. They just say that it was nothing to do with them.

But – whatever's happened to the Nazis since – by 3 May 1945, they were almost out of action. The very day that the Hellcats came rumbling down the Leutasch, the German forces in the north were preparing to surrender. If, however, the Panthers had thought that they'd take the Tyrol without one last spasm of zeal, they were very much mistaken.

126

'I think,' said Flint, 'that this is where he tried to shoot me.'

We'd left the Leutasch and were slithering down into the Inn Valley at Telfs.

'I remember these steep streets, and our tracks slipping on the cobbles.'

Ahead of us, the traffic had almost come to a halt. Very slowly, we descended through a featureless town centre. It was so nondescript that all I can remember about it was that everything was rendered in cream and pink, and that there was a very old-fashioned coat enjoying a window all of its own. According to the records, Telfs had fallen during a snow-storm, two days before Flint had arrived.

'And that's when I heard the round. But not a *usual* round . . .'

'Do different bullets sound different in the air?'

'Sure. I'd know an army round anywhere, at 2,900 feet per second.'

'And you actually thought this at the time?' I asked.

'Yes, it's the sort of thing you do think about. Until I saw *him* . . .'

'What, up here? In one of these windows?'

'That's it, second floor. So I swung the .50 cal round and let him have it.'

'Was that the first time you'd ever got an individual in your sights?'

Flint nodded. 'That was the end of the incident.'

'It must have made a mess of the house.'

'Well, the wall had gone. I sent one of the fellers in to get the gun . . .'

'And was it anything special?'

'Yes, very special. It would've been almost an honour to be killed by something like that. It was a *Drilling* – a three-barrelled gun – made by Robert Triebel of Bavaria. It had two Krupp side-by-side 16-gauge barrels, and a very high velocity 7/57 underneath –' Flint was now sketching the gun in the air – 'and it had a Carl Zeiss telescopic sight – to be used when shooting a breed of deer at a great distance . . . And the breech was all heavily engraved, with a stag and an *Alpenschneehuhn*.'

'That's extraordinary,' I said. 'How do you remember all that detail?'

'I still have the gun.'

127

After Telfs, Jeff turned east along a sort of geological motorway. The Inn River has been carving out this racetrack for millions of years, and now it comes boiling down from Switzerland with hardly a corner left. The spoil from this tireless excavation – sand, minerals and powdered mountain – has made for a luxurious valley. Cabbages here look like little fat stegosaurs, and the grass glows as green as a planet. I noticed that some of this fecundity had even seeped upwards, into rock above. Up there, we could make out tiny, plump monasteries and footholds of apple and pear.

But the Inn had also carved a natural alley for traffic. Now over half a million trucks a year came grinding through the Inntal. Sometimes the jams were over seventy miles long, like a new river made of grumbling engines and gears. Down here, the sound was muffled in cabbage and hay, but 1,500 metres above it was said to sound like a runway. Austrians hated this invasion of wheels, and were always planning an outrage. I once met a man who used to be a ski instructor in the winter and a guerrilla in the summer.

'We used to blow things up,' he said. 'Just to have a day without traffic.'

Eventually, Innsbruck emerged from the hay, a city of castles and ski-jumps. From a distance, it looked curiously vulnerable, which of course it was. The mountains were always moving around and shaking it up, or pouring rocks into the suburbs. The last great avalanche, in 1951, brought with it seven hectares of forest, including trunks as broad as trucks. As the local newspaper put it, the city is haunted by seven dragons, which hide up in the rocks planning their next disaster. Most of the trouble came from Nordkette, a great black hood that seemed to peer into the city. Lifeless, waterless and bald, it wasn't even climbed until 1870. It's been furious ever since, and now – like Gulliver – it has to be pinned down under thousands of hawsers and stakes of steel. Such fury wasn't lost on the Nazis. Even while they were still outlaws in Austria, in 1933, they were daubing the hood with their spidery mark. It took weeks to clean it off but, when they came to power, the Nazis got their revenge. In a magnificent spectacle of terror, the city was blacked out so that all that could be seen, burning, high up in the cliffs, were the gruesome words EIN VOLK EIN REICH EIN FÜHRER.

The Allies too had added to the fury, with a few violent raids of their own. I was often told that the bomber pilots panicked when they found themselves in a sky full of rock, and dropped their loads too early. 'You can see the craters from the plane,' they said, 'on the wrong side of Nordkette.' I tried looking once, but you need to be Austrian to see damage like this. All I could see was a wilderness that had been under almost constant bombardment for over 250 million years.

Just before Innsbruck we turned right, up into the southern walls of the valley. This was where the 103rd Division had halted, to keep a watchful eye on the city.

Almost everyone up here seemed to be living in defiance of gravity. We found houses dangling off the slopes and impossible stilted roads that seemed to soar off into Italy. The farmers meanwhile were always swooping around at Mach 3, even in their tractors. Every day, the *Tageszeitung* carried pictures of atomised vans, uprooted cranes and tractors shrivelled by their flight. The Tyrolese are famous for spattering themselves across their mountains. Roadside memorials – or *Martelen* – have even become an art form, usually with a crude painting of the victim's car at the moment it took to the air (one, perhaps the most famous, depicts two friends toppling over a waterfall. The inscription says that it was the beginning of a long journey, and that 'They hoped to find that the Gates of Heaven were open').

We stayed at an old farm belonging to a mountaineer. Herr Falschlunger was small, strong, nut-brown and almost unintelligible. When he spoke, it sounded as though his words had been seized by a gale, and even his writing looked like a coil of rope. Around his walls were the instruments with which he dissected his way – pitons, hammers, a *Krötel*, a *Pickel* and an *Eisbeil*. I half wondered if he hadn't used the same instruments to hack out the furniture. It was like living in the house of the Seven Dwarfs, except that there was only Mr Wiry. Even he wasn't around very much. Each morning, Herr Falschlunger gave us our eggs and blood sausage, and then disappeared over the mountains, off – no doubt – on one of his *Wanderungen*.

'Nice country,' said Jeff.

'Yes,' said Flint, 'if a little odd.'

128

Down the road, the history of Nowhere in Particular was told in oddities. Ambras Castle looked like a gay version of Colditz, daunting and yet splendidly twiddly. It hadn't always been a museum of nonsense. In 1562, it became the palace of the governor of Bohemia, a rollicking warrior called Ferdinand II. To begin with, he'd filled his *Schloss* with the arms and armour he'd acquired while cracking Turkish heads in Hungary. This in itself would have made an impressive collection for there were 17 tons of hardware, including a Turkish bow that could fire almost half a mile, a suit of armour 15 feet high, and a gun that looked like a tree. Now this great array of burgonets, glaives, lames, morions and rondaches was spread out over several floors, along with portraits of old heroes like Vlad the Impaler (the inspiration for *Dracula*) and Gregor Baci (who was painted with a broken lance embedded in his eye). Ferdinand had even clad his infants in armour, so that they looked like knights of the nursery. It was all a conspicuous reminder that warfare then was a more theatrical encounter, and that the object was not to fall over.

But there was more to Ferdinand than a fancy breastplate and a feather in his bosnet. He'd had a vision of a beautiful world full of art and machines, and defied his father and married for love. Although Philippine Welser looks a little chilly in her portrait, she was a commoner and a woman of the world. She's left behind one of the first ever celebrity cookbooks, dated 1543, and also her book of cures (thistle for fever, horsetail for bleeding, and cornflower for the eyes). She and Ferdinand had also commissioned an ingenious mechanical chair. It looks normal enough (for an armchair made out of steel) but, I was told, whenever one of their guests sat in it, secret arms would spring from the chassis and pin the victim in place. Philippine would then ply her prisoner with drink and get him to sign her *Trinkbuch*. I noticed that the first entry was that of the Baroness herself, and was typically over the top; '*Ich hoff zu Gott*' (My hope is in God).

After that, their *theatrum mundi* knew no bounds. It became a celebration of the craft and ingenuity, not of God, but of man. The Renaissance had clearly gone to their heads. Amongst the exhibits I found a pack of giant playing cards (with monkeys for royalty); a model of the Holy Sepulchre made from millions of microscopic wood shavings; eight carved ivory balls, one inside the other; a set of Javan *durga* fighting knives that blurred before the eyes; a clockwork barge full of toiling Turks and a monkey eating an apple; an antidote made from bezoar (a stone found only in the gut of an Asian goat); and a pair of beautiful *Mundbirnen*, or mouth-pears, which could be used to stop a man screaming, or expanded to prise apart his face.

I don't think I've ever come across a museum that's entertained me so much, and left me so lightly informed. Philippine and her husband had enjoyed the world for no better reason than that much of it was weird. The pride of their picture collection had consisted, not of kings and queens, but freaks, dwarfs and the chronically hirsute. One of the portraits was of a man with limbs like an insect, wearing nothing but his ruff. It was a view of life that Philippine had continued to enjoy until 1580, when, at the age of fifty-three, her liver finally gave in.

One of the first places I visited in Innsbruck happened to be Philippine's tomb in the Hofkirche. She looked icily calm again, in the chapel that she shared with her lover. The same could not be said of the other heroes of the Tyrol. The tomb of Ferdinand's great-grandfather, the Emperor Maximilian, was still empty after Innsbruck had refused his pallbearers admission to the city in 1519 (for fear that they wouldn't pay their bills). This was a shame because his tomb was surrounded by twenty-eight life-sized bronzes known as 'The Black Fellows'. With so few home-grown dignitaries, the Fellows were mostly imports (amongst them, I spotted King Alfred of England, Joanna the Mad, and King Rudolf, whose codpiece shone like a comet after centuries of fondling hands).

But there was one other hero sharing Philippine's silence. He was probably the most irrepressible of all, the man every *Tiroller* wants to be: Andreas Hofer. Three times their guerrillas had sent Napoleon and his Bavarian allies whimpering back over the Alps. On the last occasion, the French cavalry had to sneak away with their hoofs muffled in sacking. I noticed that, somewhat incongruously, Hofer's tomb was white and stately whereas, in life, he'd looked like our landlord, Herr Falschlunger, except with a beard like a hedge. In fact, his grim, hairy features could still be seen all over the city, a sort of Alpine Che Guevara. But, like all good bandits, he was betrayed in the end. In 1810, the French took him to Mantua, where they propped him up on the walls and then blasted him to bits. After that, he only took part in one more raid. It was the secret mission, thirteen years later, to steal his body and bring it back to Innsbruck, where it was placed in the Hofkirche.

Coincidentally, he'd enjoyed one of his greatest moments up here, in the woods, next to Philippine's castle. I once saw some of the weapons his men had used in this almost vertical battle. They looked like garden tools, sharpened up for the kill. Philippine would have enjoyed such oddities, as do the Tyrolese now. Two hundred years on, people were always trying to summon the Hofer inside themselves, to scare off the lorries and drive out the Turks. The man who shot Flint was probably a Hofer, as was the skier who'd blown up the roads.

129

There was even a Hofer – a real Hofer – in charge of Innsbruck on 4 May 1945, the day the city surrendered.

The surrender had looked promisingly dignified, until Gauleiter Hofer stepped in. Three days earlier, an American major in the 103rd had made a telephone call to the German adjutant, and had made him a soldierly offer: *Surrender the city within four hours, or it gets destroyed.* The major had even been on his way to a parley, when the fanatics rose in revolt. This was clearly the work of Hofer, who only three weeks before had been given the fanciful title, Head of the *Alpenfestung.* Although he was only ever a salesman, Hofer had always dreamed of a starring role – even as the curtain began to fall. The day after the revolt, he called a meeting. Although he gave his 'word of honour' that he had no guns, the Americans spotted three high-velocity rifles and had the *Gauleiter* hauled away, still squeaking 'Heil Hitlers' at those who'd gathered around. At the same moment, he was sacked by Berlin, which left Innsbruck without any direction at all.

Overnight, there was a farce of armbands and hats. The fanatics melted away, and the 'Free Austrians' appeared. They looked equally piratical. It was almost as if one lot of Hofers had vanished, and another had taken their place. 'The whole set-up looked like a Class C Hollywood movie,' wrote one of the GIs later. 'Some were in German uniform, some in civilian clothing, all wearing the red-and-white armband of the resistance movement. They all seemed very excited and keyed up, and were loaded with two or three weapons each, and had hand-grenades stuck in their belts . . .' Their worst fear was that the last of the SS, some forty miles to the east, would swoop back into the city, and so, on 3 May, they let the Americans in.

It took the band of the Rocky Mountaineers to turn this burlesque into a musical. Some of the bandsmen had played with Jan Garber and Tommy Dorsey, and so the city was taken to the sound of Boogie-woogie and Swing. Few will ever forget the spectacle of Innsbruck as it began to change its tune. It was hard to believe that, only the day before, it had been the Nazis' last resort. Now the girls sang, and there were gifts of cognac and flowers. Even the *Wehrmacht* turned out along the route, slinging their weapons in salute and shouting, '*Heil Amerika!*' The following day, 4 May, Innsbruck officially surrendered.

By the time Flint arrived late that afternoon, the party was almost over and the city was beginning to starve.

130

There was little rhythm to Innsbruck, and the tune was always changing. To begin with, I thought this was something to do with the earthquakes, and the constant shifts in the rock. The old city still looked braced for trouble, with all its stonework pinned and clamped and its cloisters buttressed in granite. But I soon realised that it was the weather creating this multiplicity of moods. One minute Innsbruck could look sumptuously rococo – all gold tiles and violin curves – and then the light would change, and it would look merely turreted and dark.

Nothing was quite as it seemed, or not for very long. Magnificent trams would come clanking through the city, and yet on board there was no sound but the slightly dental hiss of the chairs. Everywhere, there were shops selling guns, throwing-stars and crossbows – and yet newspapers were sold from lamp-posts, with an honesty box for your money. Sometimes it all felt like Germany, 28 miles away in one direction, and at other times like Italy, 25 miles in the other. Sometimes, it didn't feel like either, and we'd come across a street full of dancing Cubans, or an Australian bar with a large inflatable kangaroo. Mostly, however, it felt prim and lacy, and even the burger bars were required to have cast-iron signs and gold lettering over the door. But then, just when things couldn't get any primmer, a *Nacht Bar* would appear, lavishly advertising the local talent sliding down poles, nine-tenths naked and upside-down.

One of my favourite places was the Weisses Kreuz, the hotel where I later stayed. Unlike so much of the city, it had survived over five hundred years of earthquakes, and was made of tree trunks and granite. The staircase was like a spiral drawbridge, big enough to carry carts up – four storeys – into the roof. The rooms were no more than pigeon-holes, but the corridors were as wide as streets, and lolloped away like gullies. As I lay there at night, I always enjoyed the thought that I could hear the same sounds Mozart had heard, during his stay of 1769: the coughs and farts and the same give-away creak of the floor.

Like the city, its people were hard to call. I once saw an old lady in the Altstadt (or 'old city') reading *Vogue*, and then I realised this was all she owned – this and a trolley full of books. Another time, I saw a woman who looked like a duchess, selling sausages outside the opera. The human landscape was always changing. At times, it seemed that the only people around were Goths and punks, and girls in combat boots and barbed wire. Then a tractor would pull up with a trailer full of singers dressed in long white socks and dirndls, and – once again – everyone would be tapping along to the sound of 'Ein kleines Edelweiss'. Many people weren't even the people they said they were. Apart from the nefarious skiing instructor, we also met an Albanian yodeller, and a waiter who'd discovered the secret of pyramid selling.

But probably the most complex of all was Roland, who seemed to live around the centre. He wore a Norfolk jacket and carried a vanity case, and although he was elderly, his hair was dyed bright orange. The first time we met him, he was also carrying a capful of coffee creamers which he'd stolen from a restaurant. It was hard to say whether he was the salesman he said he was, or simply another tramp. But there was one thing that probably was true: he was here the day the Americans rode into town. 'I remember you!' he said, grinning in Flint's face.

Flint frowned. 'I'm not sure I remember you . . .'

'. . . Lounging in your jeeps, and your cops wearing space-boots . . .'

Then Roland began to sing. It was Glenn Miller, after sixty years away. '"Way down south in Biiiirmin-ham, I mean south in Aaaalabam . . ."'

When this elicited nothing but embarrassment, Roland turned to the booty.

'Grade A coffee! Pineapple chunks! The whitest bread you ever saw . . .'

Flint grimaced, as uneasy with Innsbruck's praise today as he had been then.

'Weren't you supposed to be fighting?' I asked Roland.

'*Ja*, we were meant to go out with *Panzerfausten*!'

'And didn't you?'

'My friends did! One lost his arm, another his leg, and the third was killed!'

'And what happened to you?' I asked, 'after the Americans left?

'The French came, and stayed ten years! And occasionally a Russian . . .'

'And were the pickings as good under the French?'

'*Non, seulement les Américains emportent leurs confiseurs à la guerre.*' (No, only the Americans take their confectioners to war.)

Roland, it seemed, had spent his whole life hanging around armies, picking up the carrion. These days, all he had to show for it were languages. It's a mark of the troubled times in which he'd lived that he was now completely fluent in six.

131

I knew no one in Innsbruck but I did have some contacts through friends in Madagascar. Although this sounded exotic, the Schlögl family were impressively down to earth. They even had their own voluntary fire brigade, or at least it felt like theirs. The entire family were volunteers of the *freiwillige Feuerwehr* in Mühlau: fathers, uncles, brothers, sisters and nieces. For the Schlögls, dressing up in khaki and eagles and rushing around in tenders was a matter of dynastic pride, and they'd been at it since 1874. Chief amongst them was Ulrich, who was stout and fair and looked like a mountain king. On our second night in Innsbruck, Ulrich suggested a tour of the city aboard one of his monstrous engines.

Flint had never thought he'd see this day again, an Alpine tour astride several hundred horsepower. But although our tender weighed 16 tons, including 2,000 litres of water, it was still three tons shy of a Hellcat. It made up for it with thrust, and was more a jet than a tank. We even had aircraft seats and took to the streets like a bomber, cruising along at 13 feet. 'Drives like a baby!' roared Ulrich, as we skirted the Musikschule on our starboard wheels, and blasted past the Altstadt. 'How does it compare to your M18?'

'Better!' said Flint, ecstatically. 'No need for the .50 cal.'

Innsbruck, meanwhile, seemed even more intriguing by night, and at altitude and speed. I kept catching glimpses of some distant time: men with carriages and knobbly horses; cats on a cobbled street; a tiny figure running home with a violin under his arm. Our tour finished in a street of red lanterns and girls in long white coats which they let fall open to reveal their long white legs. As we passed, they looked up, their faces blank and moonlike in the glare.

'Seems like business is booming,' I said.

'Doubt it,' said Ulrich. 'These days everyone gets their sex on the net.'

And, with that, he turned his great, red box of horses round and galloped back through the Altstadt.

132

At the fire station a group of old prisoners had assembled, to meet the returning American. They'd laid out a little welcome in the canteen, with beer and slices of sausage. As we went in, they blinked and stood up and shook hands, and soon their stories were bounding along, sometimes four at once.

All of them had spent time in the American cage. Herr Pfeifhofer, who was gingery and slight, said he'd been captured further west, and Ulrich's father, Helmut, said he'd been found under a tarpaulin near the Czech frontier (having, at the age of seventeen, fled the slaughter of Romania). But Uncle Richard and his friend, Rudolf Wille, had both been captured in Innsbruck. There was no resentment about this turn of events, just a candid assessment of Tyrolese life under American rule.

'The first wave were rough . . .'

'. . . went to bed in their boots . . .'

'. . . cleaned their guns on the curtains . . .'

'. . . ate all our eggs . . .'

'. . . some were blacks, and we'd never seen blacks before . . .'

'. . . burnt our table with the iron . . .'

'. . . the next lot were better . . .'

'. . . stayed in our house, and you'd never have known they were there . . .'

As we talked, more firemen stamped in, pulled off their helmets and sat down to enormous plates of potatoes and ham. The prisoners ordered more beer and turned their attention on Flint.

'How long were you here?'

'Did you have a girlfriend?'

Flint said they'd only been here two days.

'And we parked the M18s someplace called Mutterhaus.'

'*Mutterhaus?*' squealed the prisoners. 'That's just here!'

'Look!' said Uncle Richard, throwing open the window.

At first, I could make out nothing beyond the roar of the river. Then I spotted a line of poplars, and the silhouette of a dome. 'That's Mutterhaus,' said Helmut. 'It's still a convent. I expect you remember the nuns.'

*

By day, it became obvious that beyond the nunnery there stretched a vast medieval allotment. I often came here during my visits to the city, just to enjoy the roar and the greens, and to reaffirm the flatness of the earth. Sometimes I saw nuns at work amongst the vegetables, levering up the beets and fighting back the cabbage. One of them told me she had enough pasture here for sixty cows, and that, in the sand and snow-melt, the carrots grew as sweet as sugar.

I often wondered what else one might find in the sand. Here, on 4 May 1945, Flint's men had come to a halt, amongst the roots and salad. Soon afterwards, the great, wheeled, green suburbs of the American army had caught up with them, along with all its bakeries, workshops, chaplains and historians. Eisenhower now called it 'a mighty engine of righteous destruction'. Even the army's regulations had caught up with the combat troops. One day a spiffy lieutenant arrived from headquarters with news of Flint's Bronze Star. 'They expected me to report to the CO – in blouse and pinks! After *eight months* on the road! This was chicken at its most absurd . . .'

As for the Austrians, they hadn't seen such abundance for years. The end of the war in Innsbruck was like a second Stone Age. There were no light bulbs, no bicycle tyres, no shoes, no alarm clocks to wake the workers, and no trams to get them to work (even four years later, only 3 per cent of Austrians enjoyed a modern kitchen). Roland the Tramp told me it was the fault of the Germans, who'd requisitioned everything. 'They took all our horses,' he said, 'and all our skis, which they then sent to Norway.'

Worse still was the hunger. Eight out of ten Austrian children were malnourished. Many, like Roland, became adept at foraging and collecting up the scraps. American coffee grounds were salvaged, rinsed and reused. GIs were even asked not to put ash in their swill, because at some stage it would all be boiled up in a vat of municipal soup. For a while, children also came begging at the great allotment of Mutterhaus, until they saw it vanishing under the treads. After that, said Roland, they set off for the country, where things were hardly better.

He shrugged. 'We got used to it. Potato peel for breakfast.'

133

My only other contact in Innsbruck was still clearing up after the war.

I knew very little about Frau Schenk, other than the name of her street and the number of her house. It was only when we got close that I realised that her 'house' took up most of the street, and that she was the chatelaine of Büchsenhausen. This was one of Innsbruck's two castles, the other being Ambras, which it faced across the city. Büchsenhausen was probably prettier. It had plump, dark green cupolas like some exotic Turkish haberdashery, and the ramparts were an edible caramel orange, with chocolate windows. I later discovered that it was built by a foundryman called Gregor Löffler, who'd grown rich on fancy guns (not only was he gunmaker to the Emperor Maximilian I, he'd also cast some of the cannon with which Drake had seen off the Spanish Armada).

Frau Schenk was a worthy successor to the exuberant Löffler. She was eighty and had mischievous ice-blue eyes, and produced a bottle of whisky for tea. These days, she explained, she lived mostly on the upper watchpath, which was carpeted in Astroturf and haunted by an enormous, full-length shot of Humphrey Bogart. There was also a large, black broadsword up here, hanging on the wall. Frau Schenk said it had been used to decapitate her forebear, William Biener, Chancellor of the Tyrol, in 1651. Flint peered at the sword suspiciously, as if his whole afternoon was beginning to turn into one of those inexplicable tricks of old age.

'What had your ancestor done wrong?' said Jeff.

Frau Schenk's eyes twinkled. 'Got too close to the mistress of Ambras.' She was a Medici – Claudia de Medici – always an ominous sign. 'People say they even had a tunnel between the castles . . .'

We all gazed out across the blue haze that had settled over the city.

'Chancellor Biener was either helping himself to the treasury,' said Frau Schenk, 'or helping himself to Claudia . . .'

Teatime was rich in subterfuge. Frau Schenk would begin a scurrilous story – usually about the Nazis – and would then catch herself, and trail off in giggles. 'We were always taught never to mention them again,' she'd say, and then she'd pour more cups of Scotch and start on someone else. I was never quite sure whether what I was enjoying was an Austrian tea, or an Austrian version of an American tea. Either way, the whisky soon saw Flint restored to reality.

He didn't even flinch during our tour of the state rooms, about which nothing was entirely normal. At one point we found ourselves in a tiny chapel before the dried-up corpses of Saints Faustus and Iucundus, dangling either side of an altar. Their flesh was woolly and fibrous, like biltong except that it was trimmed in lace and seeded with minute pearls. Saint

Schloss Büchsenhausen.

Citment was laid out in the vestry, next to a pair of unused slippers which had been a gift from the Pope. Beyond lay the main apartments, and Frau Schenk led the way, unlocking doors as she went and whisking off the dust sheets. The ceilings were so busy with cherubs that they seemed to flutter, but otherwise the rooms were almost empty. There were only a few occasional pieces of gilt, and the family portraits around the walls, all now ragged with gunfire.

'Sorry about the mess,' said Frau Schenk. 'It was Section G2, after the war.'

'G2?' said Flint, 'I don't remember them.'

'The French Gestapo. They requisitioned us in 1945.'

'What, and shot up all the pictures?'

'Worse than that. The furniture you see is just the stuff we kept in the attic. Everything that was here at the time they heaped in the middle of the room and set on fire. We've never had the money to replace it. G2 did terrible things to Büchsenhausen. I sometimes feel I've been tidying up ever since.'

It was inevitable that at a tea like this, in a city like Innsbruck, someone like Bruno Grossman would turn up sooner or later.

Bruno was disconcertingly ambiguous. Although he said he was ninety-two, he was craggy and nimble with long colourless hair, and wore a black shirt and a bright blue baseball cap from Cancun. He also had with him a beagle puppy, which squealed and then flopped off into the castle, presumably in search of Saint Citment. Bruno cackled slyly, and helped himself to some whisky. I couldn't fathom him at all. Was he Catholic (as he said) or Jewish (as he seemed)? I couldn't even work out whether he was American or Austrian although – as if turned out – he was both. 'I was born in the old Austro-Hungarian empire,' he said, 'and raised on a chicken farm in New Jersey.'

Flint smiled. 'And how did you end up back here?'

Bruno didn't seem to understand him, or any English except his own.

'I was one of the first into the city! We were hunting for prominent Nazis . . .'

'*Schweigen!*' tittered Frau Schenk, 'We shouldn't talk about these things.'

Bruno ignored her, and carried on. He told fragments of stories, most without beginning or end. He remembered a German brothel in Strasbourg, and the girls lying dead on the stairs. In Innsbruck, the Mayor had given him the keys to the city, and he met a woman who was starving, and married her. 'They were exciting times,' admitted Bruno, 'and I often felt like a hero.'

At first, I didn't know what to believe of Bruno. But then, just as doubt was settling in, he'd produce some photographs. Here was the hungry girl, and Bruno looking taut and shorn in the uniform of an American officer. He also had some snapshots he'd taken off a German: Hitler laughing; the staff at Berchtesgaden; Mussolini, dressed, as always, for some pantomime war of his own. Then, after that, Bruno's life blanked out. All he ever said was that he'd stayed in Austria, pursuing American interests.

'And did you find what you were looking for, Bruno?' I asked. 'The Nazis?'

He looked at me blankly for a moment. '*Ja, Ja.* Including Kaltenbrunner.'

'Really, Bruno,' said Frau Schenk, sweetly. 'You should be more discreet . . .'

Our curious whisky tea was coming to an end.

'We took them all to the old Grey Bear,' said Bruno. 'You'd never seen them so frightened in all your life.'

134

The Grauer Bär was not as growly as it sounded but was an old, cramped coaching inn just off the Altstadt. It was the sort of place that was always recasting itself, throwing out its fittings and starting all over again. In the Bear's case, the end of one look hadn't always coincided with its replacement by another. After several hundred years of this, it had become a large unruly nest of different styles; there was a palm court, Perspex furniture, some Renaissance plasterwork, the latest up-lighters, and a lingering air of the Thirties. It felt like the sort of place to come and wait for an airship.

The Nazis must have made a curious addition to the décor. Amongst them was the leader of Vichy France, Pierre Laval – soon to be shot – and a man from the death camps called Schwammberger, who used to rip people up with his dog. But the biggest prize of all was Dr Kaltenbrunner, Head of the Gestapo. He was an apelike man, with a hectic eye and a nicked and thoughtless face. When he was first arrested, he had in his possession a huge quantity of candy and guns. Without his moustache no one knew who he was until his mistress, Countess Gisela von Westrop, appeared, and slathered him with kisses. By the time he got to the Bear, he was no longer in a kissable state but was a dampening figure of fear. No one knew more about interrogation than Kaltenbrunner. Bruno said he confessed to everything, especially when it was hinted that, if he didn't, he'd be fed to the Russians.

'He was pretty dumb,' said Bruno, 'and cried like a baby.'

Plenty of others had fled to the Alps, although not always to Innsbruck. In Berlin, Goebbels had watched in disgust as – one by one – the leaders of the Reich had taken to the hills. Nor was it an edifying spectacle for the Americans who'd had to round them up. Von Rundstedt was arrested in his bath, and Goering was found – perfumed, bloated and doped – in Berchtesgaden. The Alpine haul also included Robert Ley, the drunken, foul-mouthed Minister of Labour; three more field marshals, Kesselring, von Leeb and List; and the slimy Julius Streicher, Jew-baiter, pornographer and editor of *Der Stürmer*. Rather harder to catch was Axmann, Head of the Hitler Youth. For six months he wandered the mountains like a minstrel, singing laments for his master. But even he gave up in the end, and was given three years in the jug. After his release, he ran a little shop in the Canary Islands, where he died in 1996.

'And what about Kaltenbrunner?' I asked Bruno.

'He was hanged, at Nürnberg, along with some of the others.'

Their bodies were then sewn into mattress covers, and cremated.

'And I heard their ashes were dumped in a Bavarian ditch,' said Bruno, and smiled. 'I tell you there was nothing smart about any of them. Hell, they were as surprised as anyone at how they'd got so far.'

But not all were caught. There were a few who'd slipped the net at Innsbruck. One of them felt familiar. It was Sabiani, the miniature *Führer* of Marseille. Once again, as the noose tightened, he'd slithered away – first to Milan and then to Buenos Aires. For the next seven years he could be found in La Boca, selling watches on the quay and ranting like a seer. Eventually, he returned to Europe, where he died unknown in 1956. He's buried in the forgettable village of Casamaccioli, on his native island of Corsica.

'Goddammit,' said Bruno. 'How did these people ever find power?'

Juvenal knew. It was Fortune's little joke, wrote the Roman jurist. 'Village pierrots yesterday, arbiters of life and death today, and tomorrow keepers of the public latrine.'

135

Amidst all the distractions of the Tyrol, the end of the war had been almost overlooked.

Eisenhower's announcement was typically flat and formal. All offensive action would cease that day, 7 May, and the war would end in two days' time, at one o'clock in the morning. *Der Krieg ist beendet*, the Austrians were told, and they shrugged as if they already knew. B Company, meanwhile, had already left Innsbruck, and was camped next to a thunderous volley of snow-melt, twenty miles upstream. There was no fanfare and no church bells, just a deadening sense of relief. '*Alles kaputt* at last,' wrote Flint in his letter home that day. 'The future, who knows, for the individual it may not be secure, but for the world – Kitty-Ann's world and posterity – it has a better foundation . . .'

Few celebrated. *Stars and Stripes* printed a victory edition, and a band tootled off through Innsbruck. Some of the men got drunk, and a few let off their guns. But for most, they simply couldn't think of a gesture that properly reflected the enormity of the occasion, and so they let it pass. For 337 days there'd been American soldiers in northern Europe, just waiting for this moment, and now they didn't know what to say. Even Eisenhower had struggled to find his euphoria. 'The route you have travelled,' began his *Victory Message to the Troops*, 'is marked by the graves of former comrades . . .'

Probably the strangest sight that evening was distant Innsbruck ablaze with lights. Millions of young Americans had only ever known Europe looking blacked-out and dead. 'You can't imagine the feeling,' said Flint, and I don't suppose I can.

But not everyone was so sure Europe illuminated was any better than Europe in the dark. It was a day riven with uncertainty. Far to the south, in Cannes, another veteran of Alsace seemed to express the curious ambivalence felt by all. It was Audie Murphy, America's most highly decorated soldier, and now a movie star in waiting: 'I feel only a vague irritation. I want company and I want to be alone. I want to talk and I want to be silent. I want to sit and I want to walk. This is VE day without but no peace within . . .'

Part of the problem was that the war hadn't ended at all. The very same day the Panthers were given news of victory in Europe, they received their orders to proceed to the Pacific. For a few weeks, the Tyrol would be a beautiful tank-park, and then they'd start all over again.

136

Apart from the arrival of an army bound for Japan, only two things have ever happened in Oberhofen. Neither involved Luther; the village has remained sumptuously Catholic. Christ dies in every gable, and the Virgin is pinned down in the church with seven bright swords through her chest. Even the cobs are hung out to dry in the pattern of the Sacred Heart. Life is lived piously, to a rhythm like the swish of a scythe. Occasionally, much older rituals resurface, to show that times may change but Oberhofen doesn't. There are ghost dances – or *Schemenlaufen* – winter festivals, harvest rites and communal exorcisms, when the evil spirits are driven off in a purge of cowbells and birch twigs. At these times, the villagers – Wegscheiders, Hollrigls, Fögers and Eckers – will dress up in huge shaggy costumes made from clumps of lichen and string. The elephant-headed *Luzifer* might even appear, armed with a pitchfork and attended by his little winged toads.

No, the first great event in the village's history was the arrival of nails. This wouldn't alter the way farms worked, but it would make them bigger. A few pre-nail snuggeries had survived, with their ingenious pegs and joints, but pinning had changed all that. Nails had opened up whole new realms of carpentry, and by about 1650 the village had begun to loom up out of the grass. Now it looks like a fleet of hulks anchored in the bottom of the valley, all smelling vaguely of fodder and tar. No one, it seems, has ever seen any need for further innovation. Old cart tracks still bump around amongst the barns; there are marigolds in the butter-tubs and goats in the orchard; the corn dries in ladder-racks up to the roof, and – as always – the dung is piled up, rich and sour. Even the flies haven't changed much, except that they're several thousand generations on.

The second great event in Oberhofen's history was the First World War, which had completely wiped out its militia. It would take over eighty years to reassemble the *Schützenkompanie*, and to find enough feathers and guns. Many villagers still regard the annihilation of the original *Kompanie* as a cruel and inexplicable outrage. They'd prefer to carry on as if nothing had happened. In one sense, therefore, it wasn't an event at all.

If so, that leaves only the arrival of nails.

*

We parked in the meadow between the village and the river.

The grass was long now and mumbled with crickets and bees. I could see Flint mentally stripping out the shoots and tearing up the turf. 'Yes, this is it,' he said, and suddenly he seemed to see their big green tents again, and the Hellcats under the trees. 'We were here *five* weeks . . .'

'Doing what?' I asked.

'The first two, occupational duties – guarding prisoners and so forth.'

'And the rest?'

'Well, training for Japan.'

We walked over to the place where the big guns had blasted away at some imaginary Okinawa. It was now the village tip. I was intrigued by the things still thrown away; we found a wooden *Pflug*, or plough, an ancient television with doors like a garage, and a child's homework dated '1952'. Flint was less surprised by this. He remembered the old villagers swollen with goitre, and an ancient laundress who'd repaired his shorts with thousands of tiny stitches. 'And down here, they grew radishes. Nothing but radishes. It was all they seemed to eat.'

Along the river bank was a fringe of hazel, and a beach of fine white silt.

Flint stopped, as if he'd seen something move in the bubbling shallows.

'Every day, a maiden appeared, flaxen-haired and magnificently structured . . .'

Every day, she'd peeled off her aprons and waded into the melt-water.

'Without the aid of a bathing suit . . .' whistled Flint.

'I hope you didn't abuse government binoculars,' I said.

'Didn't need to, she was that close . . .'

We asked about the maiden in the village. I was surprised that Flint had the vocabulary for an enquiry like this. But all the old ladies shook their heads. If they'd ever paraded before a company of enemy troops 'flaxen haired and magnificently structured', they weren't about to admit it now. One of them said the Americans had stolen her radio. Another said they'd made her sleep in the cellar, with her brother only four months old. Oberhofen, it seems, hadn't appreciated the invasion of its time-line. There was no sign anywhere of the American intrusion, except perhaps a cheap, varnished cabin which some wag had renamed Beverle-Hill.

But I did at least meet a man who was curious to meet his first American in sixty years. 'I was six when you were last here,' he told Flint, and pottered off and brought him a handful of grapes. 'You had big green boxes of chocolates and biscuits. And chewing gum! Children have the best experience of war. All soldiers treat them well, even Russians. And you arrived in jeeps and wonderful crawlers, which my grandfather pelted with stones. Yes, it was a great time (although I didn't know what was going on). A few years later, I found an American hand grenade. *What a thing!* A shame it didn't have a fuse . . .'

It was Alfred Kirchmair: goatherd, ski-lift operator, story-teller, militiaman, and keeper of the village peacock.

I still get Christmas cards from Alfred, written with muddy hands and sealed up with dirt. We met several times over the months to come, and developed a strange friendship, which lacked for nothing except comprehension. In order to understand what he said, I had to record him and get his words translated. Even then, the translator wasn't sure it was German. 'Who was *that*?' she'd say. 'It sounded like Oetzi the Iceman.'

Alfred didn't seem to mind this lapse between his words and their reception. He was kind and phlegmatic, and his eyes glittered at the very thought that – one day – I'd probably know what he meant. Perhaps he was just glad to have me as part of his collection. Alfred collected all sorts of things on the basis that they might one day be needed. Apart from all his jobs ('One's not enough for a farmer here'), he also gathered old chairs, wood from the river, building scraps, greeting cards, rifle targets and the little animals that died on the road. This entire collection he'd reassembled down by the river as a shack called Animal Heaven, or *Paradies der Tiere*. I suspect, however, it was more paradisaical for Alfred than for the animals, who'd spend eternity stuffed with sawdust, locked for ever in their last, failed leap. *Paradies*, said Alfred, was where he came to get away from it all, and he'd never been anywhere else.

Once, he invited me down to *Paradies*, to talk Oetzi-babble and drink beer from a vase. It was a beautiful evening and we sat on his driftwood terrace, peering up into the mountains. 'Hohe Munde,' announced Alfred, and then he turned round to a malevolent spike of black on the opposite wall of the valley, '*und* Hocheder.'

My heart sank. I felt I already knew them. Flint had revealed that when he wasn't fighting off waves of imaginary Japanese, he was up, scrabbling around in the clouds. He and his gunner, Norwicki, had climbed both Hohe Munde and Hocheder. The great thing about old age was that he was neither tempted nor able to repeat this youthful folly. That he could leave to me. After all, it was part of our travels, and I felt an unwelcome compunction to go wherever he'd been back then. This was a journey we'd begun at sea level, and I couldn't possibly let it peter out at 600 metres, when there were still over 2,000 to go.

It would mean returning – without Flint and Jeff – the following summer.

'I have to go up there,' I told Alfred, unhappily.

He needed no translation for this one, and lay on the ground and laughed.

137

I returned to Oberhofen on Midsummer's Day, to find it preparing for war. People were rushing around, looking for guns and swords, sponging tunics and polishing belts. As darkness fell, the summit of Melk-Alm was set ablaze with burning tyres and wool. It was *Bergfeuer*, or mountain fire, I was told, and had been offered up to the Sacred Heart every year since the Bavarian invasion of 1796. That night, from deep inside a hulk, came the sound of a band, thumping out the 'Schneewalzer'.

'What's going on?' I asked.

'*Morgen ist das Bataillonsschützenfest*,' people said.

The militias, I gathered, were on the way.

Dawn the next day was ruptured by reveille and the boom of cannons. I hurried down to the church square, only to find the village *Schützen-kompanie* on parade. Having somehow recovered from the Great War, the little battalion was now gearing up for manoeuvres. It looked like a squad of mountain cavaliers, short only of horses. Each of the militiamen, or *Schützenkameraden*, wore a wine-coloured tunic, a green silk wide-brimmed hat (decorated with egret plumes), charcoal suede breeches, a cravat with a horn toggle, long white socks and silver-buckled shoes. In addition, the officers wore sabres, and the *Bürgermeister* sported a full white beard, like Captain Birdseye, and a belt of solid silver Marie-Theresa thalers. The lower ranks, I noticed, were armed with axes and old, charred rifles, dating from the war.

As the battalion came to a halt, I spotted Alfred.

'*Guten Verlauf*,' I said, as if he were off to the front.

He grinned and doffed his hat. Across his chest was a long row of medals for godliness and shooting. He said his rifle was German, a

Karabiner 98K. I asked how the village had managed to get hold of them, and Alfred's eyes twinkled thievishly.

'They were just lying around,' he said, 'so we hid them from the Yanks.'

Soon, more militias arrived, from the surrounding villages. The Americans had missed a lot of guns. A huge army of feathered rebels assembled on the field of the Hellcats. Some companies wore purple and bottle-green felt, some carried giant set-squares and others bore battle honours captured from Napoleon. The cannon were fired again, and then Oberhofen – as hosts – unleashed a crackle of shots up the valley. Next, the *Schützenkurat* blessed the troops and pinned medals on their banners, and then the Commander of the Tyrol gave an address about *Vereine* (union) and *Bruderliebe* (brotherly love). It all seemed harmless enough. The last time the companies strayed into politics – just before *Anschluss* in 1938 – they were mistaken for Nazis and banned. Now, according to Alfred, all talk of politics was forbidden.

The sky turned a brilliant steel-blue, and the rocks began to shimmer. In the heat, the great padded warriors began to fall. Now, women dressed in bottle-green dirndls and lace floated in amongst the silken heaps, dispensing iced water and schnapps. Eventually, once the *Landeshauptmann* had said all there was to be said about brotherly love, the cannon fired and a trumpeter called the retreat. With that, the companies gathered up the fallen, and marched back up to the village.

A great skirmish soon turned into a feast. The swords were collected together and the rifles stooked, and a seventeenth-century catering corps appeared with carts of beer and roast chicken. The troopers seemed to steam as the beer went down. After a while, one of them got up and yodelled like a cuckoo, which no one seemed to think strange. I, meanwhile, had never seen such an extravagant display of facial hair. Apart from the beards, there were handlebars, walruses, mutton-chops, carpet brushes, cake-sieves and cacti. One man I met – a delightful violin-maker called Wolfgang – had two beautifully waxed curls that looked like a pair of whippet tails bobbing around in front of his face. As it turned out, he was something of an expert in hair. Every one of his violins, he told me, was strung with American mustang, because home-grown tails were too brittle.

The beer flowed, and the *Kuckucksjodler* sang. At some stage I sat next to an old man with a horribly mutilated arm, which turned purple in the sun. I also remember a well-feathered railway guard, who wanted to travel the world. He told me he'd go anywhere, as long as it didn't have Indians

or blacks ('South Afrika shoundsh OK,' he sloshed). To my disappointment, he picked up first prize in the raffle, which was a drum of universal
tractor oil. Second prize, as I recall, was a mint-condition cowbell.

138

The day after the *Schützenfest*, I set off, up Hohe Munde.

Deep down, I'd hoped that people would tell me the whole idea was
crazy and that it was far too dangerous to venture up out of the valley.
In this respect, my best hope had been the tourist office in Innsbruck.
To my immense gratitude, they told me that the snow was still far too
deep, and that I'd probably vanish for good. The Alpine Club had disagreed.
There, I spoke to a man with a wild, untidy beard like an eagle's nest.
He'd produced a large map of the crumples I wanted to climb, and – for
what seemed like hours – he'd stared into a whorl of contours, as if he
could sniff out the snow. Then he'd nodded slowly and wisely, and told
me it was all right. As for the Hohe Munde, it was merely a 'steep hiking
trail', or – as he'd put it – a *Wanderpfad*.

Discouraged by this optimism, I'd asked around in the hope of something more grim. Being Austrians, however, everyone had said I should
go, although, when it came to mountain advice, they were all obligingly
Gothic. I was warned about bottomless crevasses, bloodcurdling ticks,
poisonous snakes, and awesome storms that could suddenly blow up from
nowhere and blast everything away. One man had even inspected my
boots. 'One slip,' he'd said, 'and you're dead.'

At the mountaineering shop there'd been worse news still, at least in
financial terms. I was told I'd need dried food, an axe, a shovel, flares, a
compass, alpenstocks and an emergency blanket. I'd hesitated. Did I *really*
need all this? Flint, who'd also climbed in June, said he'd gone up in just
his combat gear ('I don't think we even had the brains to take water'). In
the end I'd settled for a pair of sticks. I never mastered them, but, as it
turned out, they had their uses: they kept my hands busy, and – in
moments of sheer terror – prevented me from fastening myself to the
mountain (to which otherwise I'd probably still be attached).

There'd been more discouragement in Oberhofen. From the bottom,
Hohe Munde looked like a pillar that had been hit with a hammer and
then polished up in the wind and ice. I couldn't see anything to hang
on to. The summit, which was almost two kilometres directly above,

sometimes disappeared altogether in streaks of icy vapour. No one knew quite what it was like up there. Some of the farmers had never been to the top, and even Alfred hadn't climbed it for forty years. 'What's the point?' he said. 'There's no grass, nothing up there for cows.'

So it was that I set off, wondering whether a great adventure was about to unfold or a little one unravel. I got a lift as far as the road would go, and then took a path through the woods. It led gently upwards through scabious and beech. This is easy, I thought, as I poled along with my brand new purple sticks. After about an hour, I came to a clearing, where a stag slowly raised his huge, sleepy head from the clover. For a moment he winked at me lubriciously, before suddenly remembering his place in the food chain and crashing off into the forest. It was flattering to have been so undeservedly loved and feared in an instant.

I quickened the pace, and was just about to congratulate myself at the ease with which I'd adapted to the Alpine wilds when I came upon Frau Rautte's coffee shop. After sixty-five minutes without human company, I felt bizarrely impelled to reconnect with the world. Frau Rautte, standing five feet tall in her slippers and housecoat, clearly felt rather differently about humankind. She had a Welcome Scowl, and a huge yellow dog with industrial claws. After a chilly exchange of euros and coffee, the air outside felt suddenly warmer, even at 1,600 metres. Good, I thought, only one kilometre to go.

Seldom have I worked so hard to cover a single kilometre. At first, there was only the mild inconvenience of alder. This ingenious shrub has learnt – in its alpine form – to snag hikers in its claws and then lash them with long barbed whips until they promise never to come back again. Ugly and uncompetitive, you can't blame it for defending its corner. It's also the only shrub that can survive the thousands of tons of rock and ice that, every year, come rumbling down from above: it simply flexes flat against the ground, and then springs back up in the thaw. To those that know it, it's therefore a timely reminder of the glacial chaos to come.

After a good thrashing, I found myself being kicked upwards through a steep band of scree and broken boulders. The poles were now useless and skittered around on the rock. In places, I slipped and took a hard granite boot to the backside. I was surprised that, every time I sought a handhold, ants came swarming out and licking over my fingers. What powerful evolutionary pressure had forced them to take their chances up here, on this upended surface of Mars? The pace slowed. I worked out that I was now travelling at about the speed of tortoise, a lumbering 300 metres an hour.

Then I found myself in the snow. There were only dollops of it at first, like scoops of cold, wet bread. But further up it had gathered in drifts amongst the boulders, and – if I stood on it – it would hold me for a second before snatching me into the crack. Soon, I could feel my shin bones stinging as the mountain began, little by little, to grate away the skin. It was small comfort to know that it had been worse for others. I came across at least three tablets commemorating those who'd lost their way, toppled over the edge and ended up in Telfs, several thousand feet below.

For almost two hours I continued like this, levering myself upwards from boulder to boulder. 'The last bit was wicked,' wrote Flint in his letter home. Now I knew what he meant. The only sounds were that of my breath, sawing through my chest, and a bird that sang like a gearbox. By the time I reached the clouds, my fingers were a gruesome shade of ham. I cursed the internet geek who'd described this as a 'no hands climb'. Did he think we were all Austrians, with sticky feet like a fly? I cursed the internet, the ants and the metallic bird, and – when the mist thickened, and the snow came over my knees – I even had a pop at Flint. What did he think he was doing, coming up here? He'd just fought through three countries: why did he need another encounter with death?

I felt only slightly better after staggering through a crust of snow to the summit. At least, I *assumed* it was the summit: visibility was negligible. There was however a large crucifix and nothing very obvious left to climb. I also signed a book, and wrote something about the sixtieth anniversary of the 824th Tank Destroyers. It must have sounded as if I'd driven up there in a Hellcat. Then I sat, wondering what to do next. Opposite me was a swirling black chasm, up which came the sound of church bells and the river, almost a mile below. I was still troubled by the pointlessness of my endeavour. Was all mountaineering like this? Mountaineers, I decided, must be people of peculiar piety, able to overcome even the most intrusive feelings of futility.

Such surly thoughts remained with me until about halfway down. Then, suddenly, the clouds parted and Austria appeared all around me – green, cool and jewelled. It was, I realised, just a little mountain trick, to get me to climb the other peak, Hocheder. But I'd already decided that one 'up and down' was enough. If I was going to die in the Alps, I'd rather die on a journey than on some hearty sporting workout. Then I spotted a nick in the horizon, just to the left of Hocheder's summit. According to the map, it was a high pass, at 2,650 metres. Just the job, I decided.

I'd potter over that and see what they got up to in the valley beyond.

139

Between these excursions, I stayed on a farm called Reasnhof. The owners, the Fögers, had once employed Alfred as a cowman. They'd had thirteen cows, five acres of hay and five acres of roots. By Oberhofen standards, they were therefore considered to be people of quality and wealth. Even now, few farmers could whistle up more than half a dozen animals. The Tyrol is one of the last places in Western Europe where the cows are still known by their names.

For over two hundred years, Reasnhof had been the envy of the village. Built in the year of the French Revolution, it was something of a revolution in itself; it had thick stone walls, ramps to carry *Laderwagen* into the loft, and a trapdoor system for distributing hay into the stalls below. It was all still there, a little cow factory fitted out in wood – butter moulds, milking stools, creaming spatulas, threshing poles and rakes. Best of all, the house was separate from the barn. 'Everything still stank of cows,' said Martha Föger, 'but at least we didn't have them belching under the bed.'

She found me a room in the eaves, decorated with rag rugs and sheaves of corn. After Reasnhof's minor industrial revolution, further refinements had been slower to come. Martha said most of the changes had happened in her husband's lifetime, and he was only sixty-three. Hermann remembered how they'd made cheese by a fire in the middle of the room; how they'd cured pork where the smoke gathered in the eaves; how they'd got their first chimney in 1945 (just after the Americans left); and how all the work had been done by oxen until the first tractor appeared in 1961. All summer, his father had lived with the cattle up on the *Alm*, the richer grass at 1,600 metres. Hermann meanwhile had stayed behind, making hay in the valley.

'*Schwere Arbeit*,' he'd say: 'hard work, and not much reward.'

The last refinement was, in every sense, the most dramatic of all. It was said that one of the new machines had snatched Hermann by the hand, coshed him, dragged him to the ground and ripped out his fingers. Surprised and disfigured, he'd never felt quite the same enthusiasm for the land after that. When his father died, he'd sold the cows and turned the barn into a theatre.

I got to like Hermann. He had a funny way of pointing and wagging his stump, as if he had a fantasy finger. Although the barn didn't see many actors, he'd adapted well to the role of Alpine impresario. He wore orange sunglasses and a CND badge, and at weekends he lay on the lawn dreaming of plays. It didn't worry him that tourists had yet to discover his theatre, and he was busy learning English for the day when all that changed.

'And what about the cows?' I asked. 'Do they still go up to the *Alm*?' The Fögers looked puzzled. 'Of course, that's how we survive.'

Hermann described a perpetual cycle of grass and herding cattle.

'They're taken up in spring, and brought back in September . . .'

'You'll see for yourself,' said Martha, 'as you walk up the pass.'

'Why not stay with the herders?' said Hermann, 'It's not four-star but . . .'

Martha shuddered as memories of the past loomed into view.

'It's a hard, dirty life,' she said: 'only for simple people.'

140

If the road to the Oberhofen *Alm* had been any steeper, it would've been a ladder of gravel. Only the most ancient and unloved cars ever came up here. I could hear them for miles, squealing uphill behind me, and then they'd pant into view, trailing pipes and vapours. One of the *Bergbauern*, or mountain farmers, had a prehistoric black Mercedes with no hubcaps and a case of terminal rust. It looked as if, at any moment, it was going to lose its grip on the gravel, roll over the edge, and somersault into the gorge. The traffic coming the other way – or to be more precise, the tractor – was more alarming still. It descended like an avalanche, and on the front was a mechanical bucket in which sat three small children packed with cushions. As we passed each other they grinned demonically, and then whirled off into the dust.

Apart from these occasional machines – and the finches – I had the forest all to myself. It was a bewitching place. All the trees had beards, and the darkness was alive with water, as thousands of tiny, icy capillaries wriggled off into the void. The track seemed to sizzle with heat, and yet there was snow in the pass above. At one point, the way ahead was blocked by a cast of enormous ants, heaving slabs of leaf. I also came across an old felt hat, a dead weasel, and a saint's grotto which could only be reached by a rope. Hermann had said that it was a dangerous life up here, and that cows were often killed. If they all survived the summer, the village would hold an *Almabtrieb*. This, he explained, was a sort of bovine victory parade, and all the cows would be marched back down, dressed in ribbons and silk.

After two hours, the forest began to thin, and I came to a one-man chapel and a field of ponies with long blond hair. They looked as if they'd been shampooed, and were soon wafting over the meadow to lick me clean of salt. It was like being pelted with rancid marrows. I wondered if Hermann had run this blond gauntlet as a child. Every few days he'd done this half-day climb, to bring food for his father. 'My mother visited him once a week,' he said. 'It was a lonely existence, a different world.'

Meanwhile Alfred's father had been up here the day the Americans arrived. Alfred thought this funny. 'He was still at war, long after everyone else had surrendered!'

Eventually, towards the end of the afternoon, I arrived at the *Alm*. It was like a giant lawn on the shoulder of the mountain. All the turf at this altitude was owned by the community and administered by the village *Gemeinde*, or council. It was an impressive feat of collectivisation: there was a carved trough, a communal shrine, and a knobbly house for the council's herders, made from shingles and rock. Even the cattle looked strangely communistic as they clanked out of the furze, surrounded me with strings of drool, and then queued for a lick. I hurried on, to the herders' house.

The chief herder was out when I called, but his girlfriend said I could stay. Heike looked young and tired, and wore big leather boots and an apron. Her job was to cook, to turn all the milk into cheese, and to look after any visitors that called. She led me up to a communal room in the roof, which had seven mattresses side by side on the floor. 'It's all yours,' she said. 'It's hardly ever used. Some days we don't see anyone at all.' In the shadows I could just make out walls of rough-sawn wood, nails for clothes, and a cat with luminous teeth and murderous hiss. Downstairs, it was more beckoning but equally spartan. There was a wood stove and pine benches, and walls of whitewashed stone. The only decorations were some antlers and a crucifix. From the front door, a sprawl of tricycles and plastic dumper-trucks trailed off down the *Alm*.

'What'll happen,' I asked, 'when the children need to go to school?'

Heike sighed. 'They'll have to live with their uncles, down in the valley.'

Suddenly, with an almost perceptible click, the sun switched off the *Alm* and the air began to freeze. Two small muddy boys came scrambling up from the river, and the herders returned and threw themselves down at the table. To my surprise, they all wore thick black lederhosen, steel-tipped boots and alpine hats. When the meat arrived, they ate as a pack – hungry, wordless and hunched. Their day had been hard. At this gradient, the herders had little use for machines, and only in the last five years had they had electricity. It occurred to me that, like old American cowboys, they lived their lives on the very fringes of agricultural possibility. Certainly, Hermann had thought so.

'Up there,' he'd said, 'even the chickens wear crampons.'

When Rudi, Heike's boyfriend, had finished, he rolled cigarettes for each of his men. Although only in his late twenties, Rudi was already eight years into his ancient way of life. The hardship seemed to suit him. He had a ponytail, and a sunken whiskery face, and eyes that narrowed at strangers. I sometimes wondered if he didn't sometimes wish that life was harder still, as it had been in the past. The day Flint and Norwicki drove up here must have felt like the end of the Middle Ages. The *Bergbauern* were still making their own felt clothes from boiled wool, and growing barley at 4,000 feet. Every year the soil was washed to the bottom of the field, and every year men like Rudi would haul it back up again in baskets. It was said that, during his life, every mountain farmer carried an entire field on his back.

Heike appeared with bad news.

'There's no food left – just a little *Speckknödel mit Zuppe.*'

Although aromatic and spicy, it was ghostly soup that did nothing for my hunger. That night, I climbed onto my enormous seven-man bed and ate all my emergency chocolate. In the darkness, the teeth glowed and hissed, and up through the floorboards came the sound of the herders, snapping and growling over a game of cards.

141

The next day turned out to be the most frightening of my life. That's not saying much. For most of us, modern life is happily devoid of terror and my life is no exception. There have been accidents, of course – usually involving roads – but by the time I've realised I ought to be frightened, events have usually moved on. Either that, or there have been others around – fellow passengers, Brazilian riot police, soldiers on a volatile frontier – and I've never felt entitled to take more than my share of the communal fear. But this day was different; I was alone, and the feeling of extinction was protracted, like the frames of a bad dream clunking along in slow motion. It was also a day that stands as a useful marker in my life, the point when I realised something I'd always suspected: that, faced with adversity, I'm not very brave.

It all began well enough, with a dollop of cheese. The new batch was ready, and Heike scooped off a bowlful and parcelled it up with a slab of fresh black bread. She also gave me a pint of yellowish milk, still warm from the cow, and showed me the path through the *Alm*. Here, my outing and that of Flint, sixty years earlier, went separate ways. He and Norwicki turned west and climbed for five and a half hours to the summit of Hocheder; I turned south for a twelve-hour climb through the Peiderscharte, or Peider Gap. During this time, I'd see no one – another rarity in my waking life.

It was strange to be setting off so unsure of what I was doing. Part of me felt cautious and disapproving, and had hoped that the herders would hold me back (but they didn't. They merely grunted and got on with their cards). Another part of me felt curiously elated, thrilled at the prospect of doing something I shouldn't. I'd also managed to convince myself that it was not a day that could possibly be flawed; the sky was as blue as sparks, and the air so cold and sharp it had thrown everything – crags, peaks and ice – into startling high definition. It almost felt as if, until then, I'd been looking at the world through gauze.

All morning, I clambered upwards through the inverse hierarchy of the mountains: cows, then goats, crows, ants and finally nothing. It surprised me, the tiny gardens that grew, once everything else had fled. I came across lawns of wiry campanulas, rusty pink roses, and of course gentian, like wisps of purple mist. Several times I had to take my boots off and wade through a torrent of ice-melt that came clattering down from the pass. Surprisingly, I always found the path again, even though it was no more than a disturbance in the stones. I fondly imagined that it was an old trade route, scuffed from the slopes by *Kraxenträger*, or mountain pedlars. According to Hermann, they'd been a familiar sight up here for many years after the war. 'They carried huge backpacks, or *Kraxen*,' he said, 'full of wonderful things – like silk ribbons, tin toys, alarm clocks and sea-salt.'

After the ants, I found myself mostly amongst crusts of old winter snow. There were no footprints in it, leading to or from the pass, which was both troubling and momentarily exhilarating. More troubling still, I was now in a huge white bowl, perhaps half a mile across. I suddenly felt a mad wave of panic at the thought of being so alone. There was no sound any more, no creak or caw, or friendly snap of grass. Even the river had gone quiet and was now nothing but a small, dark hollow of emerald ice. I could feel my ears straining to hear something, anything but the sound of my breath. Wasn't the worst torture supposed to be like this, to be deprived of everything but a sense of yourself? I could always turn back, I thought, but that would mean climbing back down to the *Alm*, and a night of the herders' contempt. The panic subsided, and I turned back towards the bowl.

It wasn't immediately obvious how to get up and out. The path had simply vanished amongst the boulders and slobs of snow in the bottom of the bowl. I took out my compass and aligned it with the map. I suddenly realised that I'd never used a compass before, at least not in earnest. With some satisfaction, I noticed that, on the dial, everything was where it should have been: Hohe Munde like a tooth, and Oberhofen a speck in the valley below. I swore at myself for feeling so scared, and then, in a feat of magnetic faith, set off up to the rim. In some places, the boulders were as big as cars and I had to jump from roof to roof. In other places I was paddling upwards though the snow, which occasionally gave way, filling my boots with slush. I don't suppose the *Kraxenträger* hauled their gee-gaws up this way, but I did make progress of sorts. After half an hour, I was out of the bowl.

After that, however, there was another bowl, and then another after that. Each time I hauled myself on to the rim, my heart sank, as I saw that I'd have to do it all over again. The only consolation was that the bowls were marked on the map. I was at least following the trail. But knowing where I was on the map only prompted fresh anxieties. The contours here were widely spaced, and yet I was climbing hand over hand. Further up, over the other side of the pass, I could see that the contours bunched together even more tightly, and in parts they nearly touched. For the best part of a kilometre, I'd be traversing a drop that was almost sheer.

Fuck it, I thought. Fuck it. Now it's too late to go back.

I scrambled up the last of the contours, trying to pretend they were easy. I remember feeling oddly reassured by the sound of water deep inside the snowdrifts, just because it was noise. But I still panicked, and began to scuttle like a beetle on my hands and knees. At some stage a new thought occurred to me, that I might somehow tumble through the glassy crust and only be found thousands of years later like Oetzi the Iceman, shrivelled up like a glove.

Then suddenly it was over and I was in the Peiderscharte, a notch in the skyline I'd first seen from the other side of the Inntal. For a moment I lay there, counting my blessings. I'd stopped climbing; the slope faced south, and so now the snow had gone; I was lying, sprawled out, on a tiny patch of grass. Way over on the southern horizon I could see the Lüsens glacier, a magnificent swelling of fluorescent white. This sight would, I realised, have been even more impressive still to Flint; since he was here, the Alps have lost almost half their ice, 20 per cent in the last two decades. I also realised that – for both of us – we'd reached the highest point in our travels, journeys that had begun with the sea. From now on, it was downhill all the way home.

Downhill. The very thought of it unleashed fresh waves of terror. So far, I hadn't seen any way down. The Peiderscharte just seemed to end like a balcony over the valley beyond. Where there had been grass, there was suddenly nothing, or at least nothing but pale blue fields and houses almost 2,000 metres below. I slithered to the edge on my stomach, and looked over. It was only then that I saw that the drop wasn't sheer but a perfect parabola of grass and scree, ending in a scallop of snow almost half a mile to the south. I could also see a shallow six-inch groove in the turf, which led down a gully and then cut off west out of sight. This I realised was the traverse, marked on the map as a path.

It seemed to take for ever to lower myself feet-first down the gully. I tried to focus on my hands as they tightened around the tufts of grass. I could hear little stones skipping off into the afternoon. What struck me as odd was how similar terror smelt to cheese. I was also fascinated by the new pulses I'd developed in my temples, like great fat fish that had come flapping to the surface. Then my toes felt the groove levelling out and turning west. Slowly, I stood up, not upright but parallel with the slope, and not dignified but crablike and damp.

It took me two and a half hours to complete the traverse. There was no space within the groove to put one foot in front of the other, so I had to shuffle along, clutching at rocks and grass. Sometimes the groove disappeared altogether, swept away in deep runnels of snow and mud. Then I'd have to uncrab, slither down, shin up, and re-crab. I hardly ever looked to my left, although I decided I'd probably survive the fall. It would have been like dropping a dolly down a very long garden slide, except with hard obstructions to vary the trajectory and pace. At the time, this wasn't an image that was easy to displace: myself, airborne and bouncing from boulder to boulder.

By the end of the traverse, my thoughts were so surreal I wondered if I'd really survived. Perhaps, without noticing, I'd fallen into an abyss? But I also felt stupidly happy, as if my whole life had suddenly been transfused with vigorous colour and meaning. Looking back, I suppose this was merely the high that recruits mountaineers. From then on, the rest of the descent seemed easy: a boulder field, the scallop of old snow and finally a long grassy zigzag into the valley below. By the time I got to the bottom of this gorge, which was called Sellraintal, it was early evening and the light was beginning to fail.

Despite the orangey glow, there were still people out, making hay. In Gries, the entire village had taken to the hillside with rakes. It made a strange noise, a sort of communal swish and scrape. Amongst the haymakers I spotted a fireman, several toddlers and a girl, magnificently taut and glossy, wearing only a black bikini. I'd always had an idea that the afterlife would be like this, full of attractive people happily making hay. In my present state, this was hardly a comforting thought.

142

I spent my last few days in the valley of the haymakers. It was as good a place as any to enjoy the sensation of time struggling forwards.

At the farm where I stayed, the past and the future were in a continual state of conflict. Hoisnhof was a colossal Alpine structure, as much a garden as a house. The outside was a pageant of billowing pansies and forget-me-nots, whilst the inside had a rather less urgent feel. The panelling in my room had never been painted, and at least one of the bridal cabinets hadn't budged an inch since some happy day in 1798. But the house was divided in two. In my half lived Georg Haider and his wife, Veronika. Although, at 30 acres, his farm was only the size of a large parking lot, Georg had the ambitions of a rancher. He and Veronika were always dreaming of tractors, tourists and European grants. All along the hall were the cowbells they'd won, a testimony – if nothing else – to the beauty of their herd.

In the other side of the house lived Uncle Josef. No one ever went in there because Uncle Josef was known to resent intrusion. It seems that all forms of intrusion offended him, especially that of the twentieth century. Machines, as far as he was concerned, were disgusting, and so were electric fences, concrete, bottled milk and tourists. He particularly hated the way Georg made hay, which he said was 'dirty'. Grass should be cut 'clean' with a scythe.

'It was a problem,' Veronika told me, 'because we have to share this farm.'

In the end, the two men had reached a curious compromise: they'd farm alternately, one day modern and then one day traditional. Each would have his own barn – Georg's with pipes and wires, and Uncle Josef's with his racks of wooden tools.

Naturally, I thought Veronika was joking, especially that first night with hay trucks crashing up and down the drive. But then the next day began somewhere deep in the eighteenth century. At dawn, Georg and Uncle Josef started hauling their stakes and ancient tools up the slope on their backs. There, the grass had already been scythed some days earlier, and so the men started making their stooks. First, they used a *Stipfler*, or planting stick, to drill hundreds of holes in the turf. Into each hole they rammed a stake, or *Stange*, which had short arms like a stunted tree. The grass was then raked up and draped over the 'trees', and left to dry in the sun. By the evening, the tiny meadow looked like a parade of bright green yetis. After two days, said Veronika, it would all be carried down to the old barn and pitched inside. The job of ten minutes had somehow been preserved as the toil of several days.

Uncle Josef, of course, hated me. He never acknowledged my *Grüss Gott*, and never looked up from his work. It wasn't personal: I just happened to be a tourist, sleeping in what had been his bed. I think he also resented the sound of English. The last time he'd had to put up with so much foreign chatter, aged thirteen, was during the American invasion.

'This was their command post,' said Veronika, as she showed me into the breakfast room. The only sign now of a troubled past was an old photograph of a bearded Haider dressed in *Wehrmacht* uniform. The family had fared badly in the war; one of the boys was killed in Alsace and another five on the Eastern Front.

'What does Uncle Josef remember of the Americans?' I asked Veronika

She thought for a moment, trying to remember what he'd said. 'They *never* walked. Drove everywhere. Almost drove into the house.'

143

When the time came to leave Austria, Flint and Jeff had not been sorry. This wasn't because they didn't like it; for all its obliquity, Austria is compulsively charming. It was just that after several weeks on the road, they'd reached the point which – as tourists – we all reach eventually: their capacity for surprise had simply been exhausted. Jeff had even started visiting bike shops in Innsbruck, not to take an interest in them but merely to rest his eye on something familiar.

I suspect that Flint had felt much the same at the end of the war. Some months after our visit, he showed me a portrait of himself, drawn just before leaving, in May 1945. The artist had been an inmate of a concentration camp, and was making his way home through the European chaos. 'I think I paid him a pack of cigarettes,' said Flint, as he showed me the picture, sketched on old brown paper. It was a strangely impenetrable portrait; the mouth smiles and yet the eyes are full of disbelief; the young man looks wiser and yet also detached; there's curiosity there, but it's only a matter of habit. Europe had left Flint chronically weary; the fatigue no doubt would be slept off in weeks but the sense of disbelief would be harder to dispel.

After six weeks in Austria, the Panthers were given their orders to leave. The Tyrol was soon to be handed over to the French, and their army of turbaned North Africans. As for the remainder of the American Army, they'd move to a sector further to the east, where they'd create hundreds of little Americas, and thousands of little Americans. According to *Time* magazine in July 1946, 'The first crop of Austrian babies fathered by helpful GIs is sizable.' This was no exaggeration: during the next ten years of American rule in Austria, over 2,000 children would be born to American soldiers in the Salzburg sector alone. It was the same in Vienna; there, within a year of the end of the war, GIs and their local girlfriends were getting through 60,000 scoops of ice-cream a day. Many of them would even get married locally. On the first day that such marriages became legal, there were over 300 applications, including one from the US commander. These, it's always struck me, are rather touching statistics. Here, after a surfeit of hatred, was an abundance of what really can only be love.

Meanwhile, on 18 June 1945, the men of the 824th Tank Destroyers were ordered back to Innsbruck and loaded on to trucks. It was the end of an unforgettable journey. During their 232 days on European soil, they'd crossed three countries, and travelled and fought over more than 800 miles of roads. Now, it was time for the trucks to turn round, and head back for the German border.

144

It was the end of the road too for the Hellcats. Although loved by those who'd driven them, it was obvious they were doomed before they'd even begun. Few of those brought over to Europe ever made it back to the States. Of the 2,507 made, about a fifth were cannibalised, de-turreted, and used in Korea as flame-throwers and odd-job vehicles. Then, in 1957, they were finally pulled from US army service.

As for the rest, most were sold off where they lay. Many of them had long journeys ahead, as they spread out around the world. Italy took 107, Japan 10, Greece 127, Iran 55, and Venezuela 40. One of the largest contingents went to the Chinese Nationalists and played a noisy if inconclusive role in the Taiwan Straits Crisis of 1958. After that, the Taiwanese Hellcats kept reappearing in various shapes and colours until they were eventually retired in 1985.

Easily the most persistent of the Hellcats, however, were the Yugoslavian contingent. They were still slogging it out in civil wars as late as 1995. In Bosnia-Herzegovina, each of the different factions dragged Hellcats out of retirement. The Sijad Ali Brigade had them painted up in alarming green and pumpkin splodges; the Bosnian Serbs refitted them with truck engines so that they ground into battle at a fraction of their former speed. Cruellest of all was the treatment of the Serbian Army, who used them as decoys during the NATO air strikes. In this final tableau, we get one last glimpse of the Hellcats – abandoned not far from the battlefield they were designed for, and being dashed to bits by those who'd made them.

Part 10 – Schlachtteller, or Death on a Plate

So ends the bloody business of the day.

Homer, *The Odyssey*

One saw few tears. For the Germans the catastrophe had gone far beyond that point. Tears were a useless protest in front of the enormity of the shelling and the bombing.

Alan Moorehead, *Eclipse*, 2000

This Germany is a Samson, shorn now of hair, but again the hair will grow, and the strength will flow once more to pull down all Europe in ruins.

R.W. Thompson, *The Devil at My Heels*, 1947

History judges you by your success or failure. That's what counts. Nobody asks the victor whether he was right or wrong.

Adolf Hitler, 1940

The success of this occupation can only be judged fifty years from now. If the Germans at that time have a stable, prosperous democracy, then we shall have succeeded.

Eisenhower, 1945

145

Nowadays, it's hard to imagine that the German railways had once almost ceased to exist. Several months after flying out of Innsbruck, I found myself back – alone – floating along through the Swabian hills. Train travel in Germany is always like this, a mildly anaesthetic experience. There's no noise but the comforting hum of machines, and the temperature's sleepily perfect. Someone, it seems, has thought of everything – from Wi-fi to footrests – and there's a strange feeling that if you just sit there, in a state of happy catatonia, everything will be all right; the cups and paper will recycle themselves and the toilets will self-clean. If the unthinkable should happen and the train should be late, you'll even be provided with a note called a *Bescheinigung über Zugverspätung*, which can be tendered, at work, as an official excuse. In such a bumpless, soundless environment, the Deutsche Bahn has created the supremely forgettable journey.

Then, from amongst my befuddled synapses, a station appears. It's Stuttgart, looking, for all the world, like the castle at the end of *Sleeping Beauty*.

146

For Flint too this had been a forgettable journey. We'd agreed that there was no point in recreating it. Europe from a train would have been almost unrecognisable. Besides, this was a journey that many soldiers had long since put out of mind. For many, it was their first chance to reflect on the frailty of life, and was the beginning of their nightmares. Beyond the windows, almost their entire campaign was played over – backwards and at funereal pace. Garmisch. Stuttgart. Pforzheim. Strasbourg. Dijon. Paris . . . A train journey that should've taken no more than a day was grotesquely protracted into five.

That the trains functioned at all was remarkable. Germany now lay under 14 billion cubic feet of rubble. The dust released by hundreds of thousands of explosions covered everything: grass, children, clothes, food and wreckage. Unexploded bombs were still being pulled from the ruins at the rate of 1,500 tons a day, and many people thought it would take another thirty years just to clear up the debris. As for the countryside, was littered with tank-traps, barbed wire, gun boxes, wadding, hum faeces, chaff from passing bombers, burnt-out vehicles, and bodies now turning black in the hot June sun. To those on the train, it would come as no surprise to discover that 1945 was the most destructive year in human history, with more people killed and more homes destroyed than in any year before or since. 'It was macabre,' wrote one visitor, of Pforzheim. 'Not a soul moved in the ruins. Occasional houses had the names of whole families beneath the ruins chalked up. Life had ceased here in one afternoon.'

As the train slowed over the broken points, it had often been possible to catch a whiff of this destruction. The stink of putrefaction would linger for months, and was a smell no one would ever forget. Over 650,000 people had died in the ruins. The task of recovering their bodies was unimaginable and often seemed without end. Even eighteen months later, cadavers were still being pulled from the wreckage. Nor were the dead confined to their bunkers and homes. Human remains turned up in canals, rivers and reservoirs, or lodged in sewers, and deep in the woods. Many corpses weren't recovered at all. Of the 7 million Germans killed in the war, 1.3 million bodies have never been found. Many of these, of course, were lost at sea or abroad, but there were plenty too who vanished in the German dust.

Almost more disconcerting than the dead were those who'd survived. Germans, when faced with catastrophe, have an extraordinary ability to behave as if nothing is wrong. Even as the Third Reich folded up around them, they'd adopt this posture of normality, delivering post to the battlefield and repairing trains and phones (the Berlin Philharmonic, it's said, had carried on performing even as the Russians closed in on the city). But, by the end, this great effort had begun to stall. The middle classes were now out trading their clocks for potatoes, and a new artisan had emerged called the *Kippensammler*, or the Collector of Butts. As the writer Alan Moorehead put it: 'The victors observed that a physical pallor of defeat possessed the faces of the Germans, a compound of hunger, exhaus- ion and fear for the future.'

They made a curious sight, the survivors, beside the track. People now scraps of uniform or things they'd found in the wreckage, and chil- old postcards of places that no longer existed. Almost two out of ve remaining Germans were now on the move – fleeing, returning ating. Moorehead watched, fascinated: 'There was a frantic ant- ty about their activities. Life was sordid, aimless, leading nowhere.'

Every day, a further 20,000 refugees arrived from the east, and, to confuse matters more, there were another seven million former slaves and prisoners still pouring out in all directions. Some formed bands and set off into the country, searching for revenge and booty. Eventually, they too were rounded up by the Allies, categorised as 'DPs', or Displaced Persons, and dispersed through a network of huge, wire cities.

But with so many dead, and over ten million men in captivity, Germany wasn't just a nation of itinerants, it was also a land of women. In some places, like Berlin, they outnumbered men by three to one. It was a hard new world that they faced. In Swabia, many French colonial troops still regarded women merely as human plunder. Rape had not been seen on this scale since the Thirty Years War, and yet – this being Germany – people reacted with extraordinary phlegm. 'I've been raped twice,' one Stuttgart woman was heard to say, 'but at least I've kept my chickens.'

It was obvious that cities like Stuttgart had borne the brunt of the destruction. Flint's men had watched with bleary fascination as the city they'd bypassed on the way down now uncrumpled itself from the plain. It was a Neolithic apparition, a settlement of rocks and dust. Everything stank of burnt timber and liberated sewage. That month, dysentery began its work, snuffing out the old and the weak. The survivors had made paths through the ruins, just wide enough to wheel their barrows. Some of them lived in weirdly mutilated high-rise structures linked by gantries and walkways. Others had fashioned grottoes from the rubble. A new Stone Age was upon the city, exactly as Hitler had – almost wishfully – predicted. 'If this war is lost,' he'd told his architect, Speer, 'the nation will also perish. There will be no need to consider even the most primitive existence.'

Ordinary Stuttgarters, however, had another name for this time. It was a typically German expression, combining both tragedy and a sense of the need to get on. This was an end, but also a beginning. It was 'Zero Hour', or *die Stunde Null.*

147

Famine, over the last sixty years, had been lavishly replaced with excess.

Although Stuttgart didn't seem to be a large city, and fitted neatly into a bowl of vineyards and forest, everything about it was vast. It was almost as though it had been rebuilt in the wrong dimensions. There were enormous streets, enormous theatres, enormous fountains for enormous feet, and enormous parks (where people drank enormous beers and played enormous chess). Even the policemen seemed outsized, and carried huge clubs as if – at a moment's irritation – they could simply pick you up and slog you into the hills.

Probably the only place that hadn't been magnified was the station, which was already astronomically huge. It was a triumph of industrial quarrying and *Jugendstil*, and felt like a home for the Cyclops. Huge vaults of rock just seemed to fade off into the void. I tried to imagine the Panthers' troop train here, feeling tiny, like me. The Stuttgarters had never managed to fill their *Bahnhof*, despite their successes elsewhere. For a while they'd tried doubling everything; there were double-decker trains, double-sized loos and coffee-stands, and even a double layer of shops extending deep beneath the concourse. Few places in this gargantuan town made its citizens seem so small and precise. One of the waitresses told me – in flawless English – that she'd like to improve her English (although her first choice was Latin). Meanwhile, the newsagents sold four different magazines about clocks, and twenty-eight about fitness. I also discovered that this was one of the few stations in the world where it was possible to buy a full set of scalpels and forceps.

'What are *those* for?' I asked. 'Recreational surgery?'

The vendor merely shrugged, which left a curious impression. I had a sudden vision of the Stuttgarters, having transformed their city, setting to work on themselves. Until now, only food had effected such transformations. Stuttgart, after all, was famous for filling bellies both utterly and fast; meat-loaves snatched on the way to work, ravioli on the hoof, and trotters on the run. For workers still with space to spare, there was then Königstrasse, which was a whole street of pies, pumpernickel, *Schwarzbrot*, cakes, *City Brötchen* and pretzels. Stuttgarters could be found here at any time, night or day, grazing like a migration of ruminants. If they weren't the sort of people who then went pounding off to the factory, or hiking into the hills, they'd long ago have eaten themselves to extinction.

It's possible, I suppose, that, if I'd looked, I might have found a few oddballs fretting over calories and salads. But not amongst the Zero Generation. For them and their children, the sensation of hunger was still a cause for deep-rooted panic. At least one in five Germans was old enough to remember when the meat ration fell to 3.5 oz a week. That's barely more than a sausage. By midsummer 1945, the nation was starving;

the average daily intake was around 800 calories per person; and in Berlin 4,000 people were dying of malnutrition every day. Who then can forget the time when potatoes were hoarded like nuggets, and when a box of spam cost the same as a Persian carpet? Heinrich Böll describes how a whole generation became like addicts, craving the taste of bread. To them, the ghostly pangs of hunger would only ever be soothed by overwhelming feats of ingestion. The Germans now even have a word for this: the *Fresswelle*, or the Tidal Wave of Eating.

Having seen so much already, many returning Allied soldiers seemed almost oblivious to the enormous hunger around them. As the *ambulancière*, Anita Leslie, put it: 'We the conquerors seemed to be thinking of intoxication, and the Germans only of food.'

148

But, although smashed and starving, for Germans there was yet more humiliation in the months ahead. Their country, together with Austria, would be carved up like Africa, and fed to the three great military powers: Britain, America and the USSR. The chunks had been identified some years earlier in a back-of-an-envelope plan called 'Rankin C', and were agreed at Yalta in February 1945. At that stage, no one had foreseen that the Western Allies would make the gains they did, and so 40 per cent of the cake was ceded to the Russians. As for the French, they were never part of the original plan, although – later – a fourth sector was scrabbled together from the British and American shares. Berlin, meanwhile, which sat deep within Russian territory, was to be regarded as a separate prize, and was cut up like a pie into four ungainly slices.

It was a haphazard division, which would give the future Germany an accidental feel. A new, 865-mile east–west divide appeared – on paper at first, but later in wire and concrete. It sliced through thirty-two railway lines, three *Autobahnen*, thousands of minor roads and of course 78 million people. To comply with the treaty, US forces had to give up huge tracts of central Germany, giving the locals four days in which to decide between Soviet domination or taking to the road. Meanwhile, the British and American sectors simply reflected the way their troops had been quartered in England (Britons in the east, Americans in the west), and the way they'd crossed to the continent and wheeled east in the same formation. This quartering decision, which was probably made by a humble official several years earlier, would affect millions of lives for the rest of the century.

Then there was the question of how to run these sectors. Here – just for a moment – the Western Allies would suffer a total lapse of imagination.

While Flint and his men were rattling back through Germany, the official US policy towards the country was still one shaped by revenge. It was almost as if Eisenhower's anger had somehow leaked back home. He was still bitter about the Germans' futile resistance, and promised to 'treat them rough'. One of his suggestions was that upper levels of the Nazi hierarchy – including 3,500 members of the leadership, Gestapo and general staff – should simply be 'exterminated'. Another was to allow the Russians into the western sectors, and 'let nature run its course'.

But the most morbid plan of all came from Washington itself. There, the Secretary of the US Treasury, Morgenthau, came up with a truly Carthaginian scheme: Germany was to be 'pastoralised'. It would be stripped of all military capacity; its industry would be ploughed back into the soil; the Germans themselves would become a chastised race, living in 'homespun wool'. Surprisingly, President Roosevelt had liked the idea, and so too had the Nazis (it had made the last few months of the war a fight against certain slavery).

To others, the 'Morgenthau Plan' (as it was called) was pure folly. Churchill described it as 'unnatural, unchristian and unnecessary'. Even General Patton, who'd done his fair share of pastoralising German cities, thought the whole scheme rotten. Although – to the surprise of many – he declared that Germany was the 'only semi-modern state in Europe', he did point out that, if it shrank any further, it would be swallowed by the Russians.

In the end, it was this idea – of a Red Army, hungry, jaws ajar and poised – that prevailed. In July 1945, Morgenthau was dropped and Germany became a military protectorate, ruled by committees and chicken. As a former Stuttgart politician later told me, 'For several years, the German state ceased to exist.' Then in 1948, the first grain ships set out from Galveston, Texas, followed by $1.4 billion of American money. The Marshall Aid Plan was like Morgenthau in reverse, a massive transfusion of strength.

The politician told me Stuttgart had done well in the years that followed.

'We became the headquarters of the US Forces in Europe,' he said. The only surprise was how big 'Europe' had become in American eyes. 'We not only ran the North Pole, but also the entire continent of Africa.'

149

To get some idea of Stuttgart's *Wirtschaftswunder*, or economic miracle, I took the S-Bahn out to Bad Cannstatt.

Although Daimler and his successors had been producing cars here for well over a century, it felt like a journey into the Seventies. I passed through whole suburbs of funky bus stops and fruit-salad-coloured homes. Everything was glossily functional and modern and yet also faintly nostalgic. It was like the world according to Fisher-Price. The crowning glory, I suppose, was the Neue Staatsgalerie, finished in 1983. For the deconstructivists, it was all the best jokes rolled into one: grass-green floors, buckling superstructures, and windows Popeye-punched through the walls. The oddest thing about it all was that it was British (or at least its architect, James Stirling, was). It was not how I remember the Seventies. As a child of Heath and Wilson's Britain, I can only recall cities as rather grimy places, where we often reverted to candles.

Clearly, that wasn't the case here. By then, West Germany had miraculously bloomed into the world's fourth economy. Having built over five million new houses since the war, it then set about lavishing on them geometry and colour. It was hardly surprising that many ordinary Germans still regarded the Seventies as a groovy, Golden Age. I noticed that a few of them still dressed as if in denial of the years ever since. Even in Stuttgart, one of the wealthiest cities in Europe, people were still conducting experiments in velour and avocado. But it was in matters of knitwear that the Stuttgarters could be at their most obstinate. One woman I spotted on the S-Bahn was wearing a pink jumpsuit with a matching tank-top, finished in sequins and frogs.

But, whilst the evolution of Germany will never be told in its knitwear, it might be told in its cars. The *Motorenwerk* in Bad Cannstatt has always been a reliable barometer of German fortunes. Whatever pours out of its back doors is a fair indication of what's going on elsewhere. During the war, it was Panther tanks, thousands of them. Then, in the early Fifties, its skinny workforce had produced over 50,000 Mercedes Pontons. Now, the factory looked merely sleek and inter-galactic, like a terminus for the the *Starship Enterprise*. At the gate, I was sealed into a tinted pod with some other visitors and whooshed across the base. A man in a Spanish sombrero told me that this was where they made the SL500, which cost as much as a house. Mercedes, I noticed, had rewarded the Stuttgarters well for their hospitality and efforts. Quite apart from the factory museum, they'd been given athletics tracks, football fields, a giant stadium, and a vast indoor arena called the Hanns-Martin Schleyer Halle.

Hanns-Martin Schleyer? The name rang a bell.

Of course. Heidelberg. The head of the student SS in 1935.

Germany hadn't heard the last of Schleyer, and nor, I realised, had I.

150

I know now how this story will end: with Schleyer – bloody and mutilated, his mouth full of pine needles and the back of his head shot away – bundled up in the boot of an Audi and dumped in Alsace.

It's the years in between that are harder to grasp. Sometimes they feel like a long and desperate adolescence, or a revolt against the past. Germans, especially the young, seemed suddenly angry to discover who they were.

Even the Zero Generation had sometimes reacted with horror. They were swift to wipe out the apparatus of the *Reich*; every facet of Nazism was criminalised, from toys with swastikas to the Hitler salute; the once-powerful state was broken up into its constituent *Länder*; thousands of tons of Nazi flummery were burnt, ripped down or cut up; many towns too – already damaged in the bombing – were pulled apart in the frantic search for something new. To outsiders, this anxiety often seemed like denial. 'Obviously,' wrote Martha Gellhorn sarcastically, in 1945, 'not a single man, woman or child in Germany ever approved of the war.' Even now, experienced commentators, like Max Hastings, see Germany as being in a state of denial, and – it's true – a place like the Mercedes Museum can still tell the story of a motoring century without a single mention of the Nazi years.

But amongst the younger generation I've always found more anger than denial. There was a recurring sense of frustration, a suspicion that the sheer evil of the old regime had never been truly confronted. 'We've always referred to the Nazi killers as the *Hitlerschergen*,' said my friend Markus, the economist, 'as if they were robots without a soul or conscience of their own. But it wasn't *just* Hitler! It was us too. We should never forget that . . .'

It was, I realised, a frustration partly born of unfinished business. The moral fabric of German society had proved far harder to repair than its homes and factories. Having hastily concluded its trials at Nuremberg, the Allied administration then began on the rank and file. The first task was to establish who was a participant and who was merely complicit. In the US sector, twelve million questionnaires were sent out, and throughout the West over 170,000 people were put on trial.

But even before the first verdict, it was realised that guilt and innocence could not be so easily defined. In almost two decades of influence, the Nazis had permeated every level of society from the Reichstag down to the gangs that cleared the sewers. It was also obvious that former Nazis would be essential to the recovery of the country, and therefore, ironically, to the whole process of de-nazification. Men like Alfred Krupp and Hanns-Martin Schleyer would not therefore be away for long; Krupp, who'd been sentenced to twelve years for using slave labour, was out after three, and back in charge of his works; Schleyer, meanwhile, did four years for his role in the SS, and then, within a decade, was on the board of Daimler-Benz.

For the young, such forgetfulness was unforgivable, and they drifted into revolt. As it was the late Sixties, Germany was always bound to have its fair share of *Alternativen* – hippies, squatters, sexual liberationists, visionaries, and over 60,000 conscientious objectors. But many young Germans were far more than merely *antiauthoritär*; they still saw Nazis everywhere – amongst their parents, in government, on company boards and in the press. Even the American occupiers were cryptofascists. By 1971, a poll of Germans under thirty revealed that almost one in five favoured violent insurrection. The campuses erupted, professors were taunted, and buildings were daubed and burnt. 'Our children have declared war on us!' proclaimed the papers, and it was partly true. Tiny secret cells of urban guerrillas sprang up across the country, including the 'June 2 Movement', the *Sozialistisches Patientenkollektiv*, 'The Revolutionary Cells', the 'Tupamaros' of West Berlin, and – most famous of all – the RAF or *Rote Armee Fraktion* (Red Army Faction).

The killing was soon under way. To begin with the terrorists had merely tested their nerves, robbing banks and setting fire to department stores.

Then they started door-stepping judges and generals, blowing off faces, and firing rockets at cars. During the next two decades, until the late Eighties, the guerrillas – most of them intellectuals and graduates – would destroy a newspaper press and an embassy, hijack two airliners, kill the President of the Supreme Court, and kidnap countless others. They even executed their own traitors, and developed fancy logos as if it were cool to kill. Schleyer knew he was a marked man. The *New York Times* had once described him as 'the caricature of an ugly capitalist', and at home he was the focus of guerrilla contempt. By the mid-Seventies he was also President of the Employers' Association, and never went anywhere without his posse of gunmen.

Germany was aghast at this appalling renewal of brutality. How could this happen here, in one of the most prosperous and orderly societies in the world? To begin with, the weak, decentralised police force had no answer, and often panicked. There were some energetic shoot-outs, and some nights felt like the Wild West (except with more polyester and flares). I remember all this in my childhood, and the perplexity of the adults around me. The terrorists always seemed to be beautiful willowy girls, or girlish young men dressed in leather. What was happening to Germany? Perhaps all its Barbies and Kens had risen in open revolt? The German media, it seems, were thinking on similar lines. 'Whilst the rest of the world has rock stars,' remarked one journalist laconically, 'we have urban guerrillas.'

Who, I wondered, would be my guide through this war after the War? For weeks I thought it over, and then I realised I had the answer already, hanging over my head. As a teenager, in 1978, I'd painted a large portrait, which now hung in the kitchen at home. It was based on a photograph I'd torn from *Paris-Match*, and depicted a solid, middle-aged man in an overcoat, sitting smoking a cigar, with his hands folded in his lap. Although the subject made for a pleasing image – patient and self-assured – it was only years later that I'd discovered his name: it was Manfred Rommel, one of Germany's best-selling poets, the former Mayor of Stuttgart, a champion of European democracy, and the only son of Hitler's greatest general.

I immediately wrote to all my German friends. Did anyone know him? For months I heard nothing. Then I received a fax, forwarded from Stuttgart, with a minute signature: M. Rommel. In it, he explained his back pain and Parkinson's, but said that, yes, he'd be happy to speak to *'Herr Gimlette'* whenever he was next in the city. All I had to do was call him at home.

151

The Rommels lived out in the suburbs, on a lane of potholes and privet. Their house was detached and plain, with a high red roof and small dark garden of lawns and yew. I think I'd expected more of such an eminent German, but then the Rommels were famously Swabian and careful. The old Field Marshal had survived the war on bread and cold snacks, and was well known for his aversion to excess.

I dreaded the prospect that Manfred would be like his father. In preparation for my visit, I'd read three biographies of Erwin's life. It was not an endearing picture. Even those who admired his brilliance in battle described a man who was prickly and terse. He didn't smoke or drink, and had few friends. He could be ascetic and yet also vain, secretly relishing the adoration of German womankind and the favour of the Nazis. Whilst canny enough never to join them, he was also ambitious enough never to thwart them. When it came to the unpalatable suffering of others, he could all too easily shut it out where it suited his career. His letters home – almost a thousand of them – were authoritarian and lifeless. He was always giving his family advice on how to be the person that he was, or how to mourn him when he'd gone.

I now feel mean, having even suspected Manfred of such attributes. Both he and his wife, Lilo, met me at the door, she busy and alert like a small reddish bird. Dr Rommel was slower, and I noticed that he wore several fleeces and several sweaters, and that his disease had robbed him of expression. But in every other sense, he was the man in my picture, and I felt I'd known him most of my life. 'I'm sorry I'm so slow,' he said, 'I'm now taking twenty pills a day.'

I was shown into the sitting room, with apologies tumbling after me. The Rommels both spoke good English, and were adept in the small talk of a stranger in their home. I was warned of rugs that tripped and chairs that squeaked, and ushered to the sofa. Dr Rommel sat opposite me in a harder, more upright chair. To my surprise, I noticed that we were surrounded by his father: maps, biographies, metal figurines, battle plans (France rendered in coloured pencils), family snapshots, some sticky brown paintings of castles ('The only artwork allowed during the National Socialist years'), and a cluster of silver-framed portraits. In one of them, the older Rommel looked like a movie star, taut, leathery and distracted.

'That was taken by Leni Riefenstahl,' said Dr Rommel, 'during the battle for Poland. She was known as "Leni the Pistolwoman", and I'm told she took this picture at Hitler's headquarters. I think Hitler liked having my father around because he was handsome and had been decorated for bravery. Also he wasn't tall. Hitler didn't like people to be too tall . . .'

'Do you feel you have to defend your father?' I asked.

'No, I think history will speak for itself. He wasn't a Nazi.'

'But I suppose he was part of the Nazi aristocracy?'

'Not really,' said Dr Rommel, 'it was more a *military* aristocracy.'

'Then do you think he knew about the atrocities?'

'Yes, towards the end, he probably did. But not in Africa. The war there was of a different quality to Russia.'

'So what did he *want* to happen? He was never part of the bomb plot?'

Dr Rommel shook his head. 'No, he thought Hitler was better alive than dead.'

'Will we ever truly know what he wanted?'

Manfred shrugged. He said that, sometimes, his father had told him he wished Germany was like Canada, a dominion of Britain. At other times, he'd said he wished he'd been a Swabian shepherd, and had never got involved. But his most dangerous idea, that he'd deliberately collapse the Western Front (and so bring the war to an end), probably cost him his life. Hitler was acutely sensitive to disloyalty, and dispatched two generals to the Rommels' house in Ulm. They offered the Field Marshal a choice: he could either face the humiliation of a public trial or he could take poison that would kill him in seconds.

'I was fifteen at the time,' said Manfred, 'and was on leave from my battery.'

He pointed at a picture in one of the silver frames: it showed a callow, surprised-looking boy in a flak-gunner's tunic. It struck me how awkwardly Manfred had worn his uniform, when his father had worn one so well.

'And how did he respond to the generals' offer?' I asked.

'He went very pale, and told me he had fifteen minutes to live. Then he went upstairs to tell my mother. I remember he told me to lock the dog in his study, and then he gave me his wallet. I suggested that we try and shoot our way out of the house, but he wouldn't. He said the Gestapo already had it surrounded. So then we said goodbye and he left. He put on his leather coat and got in the car with the generals. They'd already bought a wreath before they came out, and had begun arrangements for my father's state funeral. There was nothing that could be done; they drove up the road, and my father took the poison.'

Dr Rommel paused, and looked across at his handsome, distracted father.

'That was the first time,' he said, 'that I understood the Third Reich.'

There was another pause, and Lilo came in with some coffee. In the tape that I made of that morning, I can hear her quick movements, teaspoons rattling in saucers and the creak of leather chairs. Then she's gone and Dr Rommel takes up the story again; there are the months in French captivity, and then release at the age of sixteen ('After twenty-one months of military service!'). After that, there were no more guns. The young Rommel trained as a civil servant and became a politician.

'So you succeeded where your father failed, and made a triumph of defeat?'

Rommel shifted modestly.

'Well,' he said, 'I always felt it was better to lose Hitler's war than to win it.'

He'd had an impressive career. By 1974, Rommel was Mayor of the city. Even his opponents would concede that his rule was marked by his own particular brand of fairness and compassion. 'We learnt a lot,' he told me, 'and the police learnt a lot – in what could've been a very difficult time. As a civil servant, I always opposed the use of force. If the students wanted to occupy the trains, I said, "Let them! It won't last for ever." But I suppose my greatest achievement was the promotion of tolerance in this racially diverse city. We've never had violence against strangers, or so-called strangers.'

Around the shelves were honours from all over the world: peace medals, American awards, an OBE, the Légion d'honneur, and the German Distinguished Service Cross. There were even plaudits from Marshal Zhukov, the conqueror of Berlin, and a group photo from General Patton's family (which now includes a nun). By the time he retired in 1996, Dr Rommel was the *éminence grise* of post-war Europe.

'Did it help that you were the son of Field Marshal Rommel?' I asked.

'Yes, without a doubt. I was an anti-hero, but my father was still a respected military figure. So, yes, an advantage. But I'm very proud that I've received these honours without suffering gunfire.'

'Would your father be proud? Or did you defy him?'

Dr Rommel looked puzzled. 'He was a much better man than me . . .'

'But you always had the courage of your convictions?'

'Yes . . .'

'He didn't. He always did what he had to do, and never what he ought . . .'

'That's not really fair,' said Dr Rommel. 'It was a dictatorship. I've always worked in a democracy, which I knew would never harm me.'

I mentioned the Zero Generation, and their angry children.

'Were you ever angry with your parents?'

'No. I belong to the Anti-aircraft Generation. We were young enough not to have been responsible for the Third Reich, and yet old enough to have played our part. We knew from experience how far people could go from reality, especially as we'd believed all that stuff of National Socialism. We'd seen what ideology could do.'

'Can you see how the next generation became so angry?'

'Yes, I can. They'd found a means of escape, an explanation. They'd read their school-books, and decided that no Germans had opposed Hitler except the Jews. An entire generation was guilty. It was very simple. And so they said that, if their parents had been wrong in accepting the authority of Hitler, they should accept no authority at all. What they didn't recognise is that a strong democracy is the only protection against a dictatorship like Hitler's.'

'And so the fighting began all over again?'

'Yes,' said Dr Rommel, 'it did, although – by the time I took over – the RAF's leaders were already in jail. We called them the Baader-Meinhof Gang . . .'

'They were locked up here, weren't they? In Stammheim?'

'That's it. Have you been there? You should go.'

I told him I was planning on going that afternoon.

Rommel nodded wearily. The prison was all that was left of this peculiar war.

'It was a madhouse,' he said. 'Full of people who somehow believed they were the only sane people in the world, and that everyone else was crazy.'

152

From the Rommels, I took a tram across the city and up into the vine-yards. It was hotter up here, and the people looked poorer, and cross. Eventually, the tram stopped in Stammheim, a small village of weedy cement houses with love-hearts cut in the shutters. I got out and walked through the village until I came to the edge of an open plain. There, bulging from the barley was a vast, bone-white behemoth of concrete, which I recognised as the prison.

It was like a fortress of slits and wire. I tried to walk round it for a while until I realised it was the same from every angle: shapeless and blind. Way up, along the roof-line was a light fuzz of razor wire, arc lights and cameras, and pylons to deter visits from the air. Occasionally, guards came and went, and sometimes I heard voices from some court-yard deep inside. But otherwise, all the windows faced inwards, rendering Stammheim inert to the outside world, and inert to those within. Although, nowadays, the metalwork weeps rust, and the concrete is blistered with damp, this was once regarded as the most perfect prison in the world, the beautiful geometry of the Seventies harnessed to the fight against disorder.

But, in reality, Stammheim, just like the Seventies, was deeply flawed. It became a metaphor for federal authority, by turns overweening and inept. The guerrillas managed to smuggle in guns, and devised a secret telephone system using the old wiring in their cells. Strangest of all was the way they were gathered on the seventh floor, like a college of revolt. 'I always thought it would be better to put them in separate jails,' Dr Rommel said. 'But no one listened, and so, every day, they were together, saying they were right and we were wrong.'

But the terrorists soon got their chance to speak to the world.

At the far end of the ramparts there was an armoured courtroom. It had been custom-built to try the leaders of the Baader-Meinhof gang, following their capture in 1972. Here was architecture at its most starkly functional: a rhomboid of concrete mounted with blast nets, mortar shields and tiny coffin windows. Despite all this, judges were still attacked and the prosecutor killed. The trial, when it finally started in 1976, would prove to be the longest and most expensive in German history, at a cost of $15 million. It also provoked a whole new wave of terrorists, known as the Second Generation RAF, committed to the release of the first.

Germany missed a beat, horrified at the prospect that here was a battle that might rumble on for ever.

It's hard now to imagine how this gang had earned such fuss. Andreas Baader was a motorcycle thief, who was only twenty when he began setting fire to shops. His co-founder and girlfriend, Gudrun Ensslin, was as thin as a knife and acid-quick. She'd been leader of the Socialist Students' Union, and believed that the police were the progeny of Hitler, that debate was pointless and that the only logic was terror. Slightly more complex was Ulrike Meinhof, who'd been a television presenter and the editor of a fringe magazine called *Konkret*. At thirty-eight, she was older than the others, and became involved almost accidentally, after helping Baader to escape. But, after that, she never lacked what it took. She wrote urban guerrilla handbooks, and even gave up her precious twin daughters, whom she called 'The Mice', in order to live underground. To ordinary Germans, such commitment was horrifying, and they readily assumed that she was a leader of the gang.

Between 1970 and 1972 half the country watched in horror, and the other half in wonder. The gang were like the characters in a film that had merged with people's lives. They dressed well and killed because it mattered, and always stole the fastest cars (for a while, BMWs even became known as *Baader-Meinhof Wagen*). Even some of the most influential thinkers of the time – like Heinrich Böll and Jean-Paul Sartre – were seduced, and came out in admiration. But many did more than think. In the years to come, some twenty-seven home-grown revolutionaries were killed.

I asked Dr Rommel whether he understood such commitment.

'Yes, I've seen it before,' he'd said. 'As a young person, you're very impressed by devotion, conviction and courage.'

But for the gang, the end was far from impressive. Ensslin was arrested in a boutique while shopping for fancy clothes. Meinhof, meanwhile, was found hiding in a flat in Hanover, and Baader was picked up sporting a quiff of bright yellow hair. When their trial began at Stammheim's concrete court, they contested everything – four counts of murder and fifty-four attempts – and then set about a war of words. Some days they attacked the judge, others American policy in Vietnam. Many days they didn't appear at all but starved themselves in their cells, and then accused the State of torture. Surprisingly, it was Meinhof who cracked first; six months into the trial, she unthreaded her towel, made a rope, and hanged herself in her cell.

Meanwhile the 'Second Generation' got to work. The bombs and the killing were more florid than ever. It didn't even stop when the court delivered its bomb-proof verdict on 28 April 1977 (guilty on the four counts of murder and thirty attempts). Five months later, the guerrillas kidnapped Schleyer, as he always knew they would. During the snatch, his driver and all his gunmen were killed. Schleyer was then trussed up and lived the life of a parcel, in Holland, Brussels and Alsace. It was the beginning of a bleak ordeal that's still known as *der Deutsche Herbst*, or the German Autumn. When the federal government hesitated in negotiations, the guerrillas hijacked an airliner in Majorca and had it flown to the Horn of Africa. Along the way, they executed the pilot in Aden, and dumped his body on the tarmac.

Here, in Stammheim, the prisoners waited in their blind white cells. Then, on 18 October 1977, they heard that West German commandos had stormed the plane at Mogadishu. All that night, the secret telephone system crackled and fizzed, but the guerrillas knew that their cause was lost. Ensslin ripped out the wires and hanged herself. Meanwhile, Baader and his sidekick, Jan-Carl Raspe, each dug up their secret guns and sprayed their brains across the tiles. Another terrorist, Irmgard Möller, stabbed herself four times with a sharpened breadknife, and was the only one to survive.

That night also saw the last of Hanns-Martin Schleyer. When his kidnappers heard of the Stammheim slaughter, they took him into the Vosges, knelt him on the forest floor, and shot him through the head.

153

So, the war about the War ended – or did it?

Before leaving Stuttgart, I decided to visit the guerrillas in their graves. This was harder than I'd expected. Most people thought the bodies had been buried secretly or removed from the city. But Dr Rommel told me that I'd find them up in Dornhaldenfriedhof, where he'd ordered them to be buried. Until his intervention the Swabians had refused to give them a grave. No cemetery would touch such troublesome spirits. With the appalling prospect of the corpses being shunted off to Bavaria, the Mayor had stepped in. 'I will not accept that there should be first and second class cemeteries,' he'd told the cameras. 'All enmity should cease after death.'

The Dornhaldenfriedhof was on a wooded ridge high above the city. Although my taxi driver was just the right age to have been a fan of the urban guerrillas, he was faintly appalled by my visit. He was a strange, bristly, nocturnal man, who spoke English as if the words were nailed up in front of him. 'They were freaks,' he said. 'Worse than the National Socialists.' Did I know that Ensslin's father was a pastor? He snorted with disbelief, and put his foot down, as if he couldn't wait to get me out of his car.

At the ridge, I paid him off and set out through the graves. All around me was a little army of sextons – snipping, digging, brushing, gathering and wheeling. They wore the same green uniforms as the jail guards (which I suppose they were, in a way: wardens of the imprisoning soil). I asked one of them for the Baader-Meinhof grave, and there was the same flicker of disgust. 'Over there,' he said, and waved me off, into some distant conifers. I was surprised by this reaction: a week after the suicides, over 2,000 mourners had assembled here, across the ridge, along with a thousand policemen, armed with machine-guns and dogs. It was the high point of the movement's endeavours, and also its conclusion. After Stammheim and Mogadishu, support began to fall away.

But, like the Nazis, someone still loved them. Around their slab, I noticed, there were fresh red flowers and candles. Apart from their names – Baader, Raspe and Ensslin – the inscription read only STUTTGART STAMMHEIM 18 OKTOBER 1977. Many on the extreme Left still believed that they were murdered by the state (although it's a criminal offence to say so). Many others felt that, although they were wrong, they were also half right: German society had never been fully purged of its past. The only trouble was that, in attempting this themselves, they'd become as foul as the Fascism they'd sought to scourge. They only ended their war in 1998. After detonating a massive explosion at a women's prison, they then issued a final message, which now seems eerily flippant: 'Today, we end this project. The urban guerrilla in the shape of the RAF is now history.'

Meanwhile, the Nazis continue to thrive, and every now and then resurface, as starkly unlovely as ever. These days, their party, the NPD, gets a sullen 5 per cent of the vote. A few of its members are old veterans – perhaps even men who fought battles with Flint – but they're usually only there to remember their dead. Apart from them, not much has changed. There are still the black shirts and shaved heads. On the anniversary of the bombing of Dresden, the NPD descend on the city with banners. The Left often meet them there, with their own banners, saying DON'T WEEP FOR THE KRAUTS. In the skirmishes that follow, Left and Right seem to merge in a furious mass of sticks and stones. Sometimes, they even swap sides – as the NPD's lawyer had done; Horst Mahler was a convicted terrorist and had been a founder member of the Baader-Meinhof gang.

One of the green sextons joined me by the grave.

'They get a lot of visitors,' he said.

'Has anyone ever tried to dig them up?'

'Are you crazy? We put over two tonnes of lead on top of these guys.'

It sometimes feels as if a small part of Germany died all over again during the Baader-Meinhof years. Just at the moment it ought to have been recovering, there was a catastrophic collapse of pride. The values of this, one of the most systematic societies in the world, had been challenged, often with bewildering violence. I wondered whether it had ever recovered, or whether Germany had been somehow permanently diminished. Even today, a fifth of all its citizens say they aren't proud to be German. Typically, a Stuttgarter will introduce himself as a Swabian first, then a European, and only finally as a German. Once, this ambivalence of feeling was so strong that the federal government felt impelled to put a notice in the back of its passports: *'If you are of the foolish opinion that everything outside Germany is worse, stay at home. If you think that outside Germany all things are better, don't come back.'*

To someone of Dr Rommel's age, everything felt smaller. Since 1972, he told me, the death rate had consistently exceeded the birth rate. 'The country's shrinking. In fact, we have the fastest shrinking population in the world. Last year, 150,000 people left. We're slowly fading away! And don't bother learning German, because we don't. Everyone wants to speak English.'

Most people already can. Children, I noticed, often spoke a sort of Teutonic Americanese, like *'Hab zie got a handi?'* (Do you have a mobile phone?) or *'Zis ist Cool'*. Advertisers too command an exotic vocabulary, with puffs like 'New fragrance for men' or 'Sense and sensibility', which they expect the public to understand. Even forecourt attendants can make a passable stab at English. Linguists say that this is how languages disappear: first in public and then around the hearth. Here, the virtual hearth is already under conversion. With programmes like *Big Brother* and *The Magic Bullet,* German television now sounds incongruously English.

Even that spark of revolt seems somehow reduced. Of course, Stuttgart had its punks, hanging around in the station, but they always looked as if they had homes to go to and mothers to cook their tea. Rebellion is still not something the Germans do well. One of the last people I saw before boarding my train was an anarchist wearing a tartan skirt and combat boots. She had cheese-white limbs and brittle, scarlet hair in which there nested two tiny, live white mice. As a statement of difference, I thought this was magnificent – but no one else did. The other commuters barely gave her a glance, as if they'd seen it all before. 'If you want to threaten us with revolution,' they seemed to say, 'you'll have to do better than a pair of fancy mice.'

154

Soon, my train was panting through the allotments and soaring off to the Rhine. One last time, I watched Germany flashing past, like the clips off the editor's floor all spliced into one: black soil, vines, crow-steps, nurserymen, a garden of wooden *Wildschweine*, turnips, car plants, Karlsruhe, and a Mercedes scattered over a road. Then it all ended where it began, with the river, and a great sheet of metallic water heaving off to the north. Over on the other side, the vast *bassins* of Strasbourg appeared, filmy and grey like blocks of captured ocean. Although buried deep inside a continent, this was once one of France's greatest ports. Now all that broke the silky surface was a small boy, drifting along on an airbed.

Ships may no longer converge on Strasbourg, but everything else does. From the train, it's exactly as the Romans described it: Strateburgum, the 'town of routes'. Roads were piled on roads, and streets on rivers and canals. Amidst this great medieval tangle, I could just make out the European Court of Human Rights, which seemed surprisingly small for the task in hand. Strasbourg had been an obvious choice as the capital of rebuilt Europe. Having for centuries been Europe's most contested city, it would now be its most conciliatory. Here, it was hoped, France and Germany would be thrown together in an embrace so tight that neither would be able to draw back far enough to hit the other. The *Strasbourgeois* had adapted well to the new regime of tolerance. After all, it wasn't long ago that they drowned criminals, and dunked dishonest merchants in the river.

Eventually the station appeared, like a cathedral for trains. A journey that had taken me two hours had taken Flint and his men almost ten times as long. But, for them, their travels were far from over. From here, their troop train would take three days to pick its way through the wreckage of France, a few hundred miles to Rouen. All that people would remember of this time was the heat and the buckets and the sight of threadbare France. Then, after a week in a city of dusty tents called Lucky Strike, the Panthers rode by truck to Le Havre, where a liberty ship was waiting. There, finally, on 1 July 1945, they set sail, many of them hoping they'd never see Europe again.

Part II – Finishing with Chicken

Only the dead have seen the end of war.

Plato, 4th century

Upon arriving in America you will be amazed at the large number of beautiful girls you will see. Remember, boys, New York is no Marseilles. Many of these girls have occupations, such as stenographers, sales girls, or beauty operators; therefore you do not approach them with 'HOW MUCH?' A proper approach is; 'Isn't this a beautiful day?' or 'Were you ever in Scranton?' Then say 'HOW MUCH?'

Panther Tracks, 1945

With the defeat of the Reich, there will remain in the world only two great powers capable of confronting each other – the United States and Soviet Russia. The laws of both history and geography will compel these two powers to a trial of strength . . .

Adolf Hitler, 2 April 1945

155

Several months later, I found myself standing on South Station, Boston.

People often say that Boston's not a particularly American city, and yet – to me – it was as superlative as any. Everything about it felt gloriously over-stimulated; dimensions higher, colours brighter, dogs the size of ponies, meat thicker, music more intense, and even the drunks in a state of happy hyperbole. I now realise that I always feel like this in America. It's almost as if an entire nation has taken too many of Alice's EAT ME pills, and is still holding out for more. No wonder Britons love it, and flock here on holiday and then flop back, exhausted. For most of us the feeling's the same: that up until now, our lives have been quaintly under-stated.

Take South Station. If Britons were ever to embark on train journeys of several thousand miles at a temperature of minus five, we'd call it an 'expedition', or at least an 'adventure'. Here it's merely a commute. Much, I know, has already been written about the sheer amplitude of the American landscape but for me even the detail is enormous. There are minute variations of everything, presenting a world of infinite options. The most obvious example is television, whose thousands of channels seem to satisfy every possible variant of human personality (at the station bar at least three were showing, all at once). Even a simple desire for yoghurt prompts a bewildering spectrum of choices from 'sports lite with cranberry' to 'low fat with lime'. It's hardly surprising that, during Flint's war, there was never a single moment when Europe felt like home.

For many millions, this is a state of perfection, a destination they've sought all their lives. Nowhere else in the world feels quite like this. Uniformed Latvians patrol the concourse, Kenyans clean the trains, and Colombians sell the tickets. For many of those actually born here, it's all too perfect to leave. I remember once an American friend saying to me, 'I'd love to travel like you. I wanted to go to Ethiopia once, but then I saw a TV show and all that dirt and cow poop, and I decided it wasn't for me'. I don't think he meant to sound so disgusted. It was merely his native instincts, speaking up for themselves.

Most of the time, my mood hovered between a sense of awe and over-load. I imagine Flint had experienced similar feelings as he'd stepped off his train in July 1945. Suddenly, colour and clamour were rushing back into his life. But a lot had changed since he'd been away. He was no longer the glass-worker he'd been but a veteran and commander, and soon he'd be happily home amongst those who were almost strangers, including his Texan wife, and a child he'd never seen.

156

Now it was Flint behind the wheel, shouting out bits of his past.

I enjoyed these impromptu tours. Although his sight was failing, and we sometimes rode bronco over the kerbs, Flint still had a keen sense of how his city had been. I sometimes wondered if he didn't steer his way around by memory, swerving to avoid horses and trolley-buses and things the rest of us no longer see. Along Stuart Street, he pointed out the old speakeasies of Prohibition, now almost all an illusory shade of concrete. 'We always got to know the fire exits,' he said, 'in case we were raided.'

Naturally, it was a landscape rich in Flints. We passed old Flint farmsteads, old Flint factories and old Flint clubs. Even when the city's freeways disappeared down a large hole, called the Big Dig, we found that we were still hurtling along through Flintian history. 'They unearthed a pewter tankard down here,' said Flint, 'belonging to one of my ancestors.' The old Welsh family, it seems, had become part of the Boston subsoil.

At one point, we found ourselves near North Bridge, Concord, and got out and walked down to the frozen river. The paths were as hard as glass, and beneath the ice the water was peacock-black. It was here, in April 1775, that great-great-great-great grandfather Samuel had led a company of militia against the British. For a while, Flint and I stood at the Redcoats' grave, staring into the snow as if we could somehow see them, curled up below. They were probably the first ever casualties of American military action.

True to family tradition, Flint hadn't stayed in the army for a moment more than he had to.

It was, however, another four months before he got his discharge. For a while, the generals had dithered as to what to do with so many Panthers, and, while they'd dithered, Japan surrendered. After that, chickenshit had taken over. Soldiers were required to wear full uniform at all times, even at home on leave. Then Flint was sent back to the Deep South and given the task of teaching 'military courtesy and sanitation' to battle-weary veterans. It was an absurd order, and one he'd no intention of obeying. 'Every day, we marched out to a beautiful grassy knoll, and there we sat and smoked and talked until it was time to march back home.'

By November, even the chicken war was over, and Flint was free to go. Veterans were now allowed to wear their uniforms for another sixty days, while they looked around for work. The only restriction was that, across the pocket, they had to sew a patch depicting some sort of bird in a state of heraldic distress. 'It was just one last bit of army nonsense,' said Flint, 'and we called it the ruptured duck.'

157

The ruptured ducks had done well in the years that followed. Many, like Flint, felt empowered by the experience of structure and command. He wouldn't be returning to the factory floor – or, at least, not until years later, when he'd acquired one of his own. For him, the Fifties and Sixties were marked by ever-bolder inventions and machines. Even now they sound like cybernauts, marching out the future: cryolators, batter mixers and viscosity controllers. In time, the family were restored to a latter-day version of Flintian splendour.

America too had been transformed by the war. For a start, it was richer, and its GNP had flared by an extraordinary two-thirds (compared to Britain, whose debt had increased by a factor of five). By 1949, the United States owned 70 per cent of the world's telephones, 80 per cent of its refrigerators, and almost all its televisions. But not only this; the experience of war had also given it a new corporate confidence. The very task of mobilising over 16 million people worldwide (and then supplying them, tending them, and priming them to defeat a determined enemy), meant that management would never be the same again. Concepts that today we take for granted – sizability, budgeting and psychometric testing – were all products of the war. Individuals too had developed their corporate side and were perfect for the tasks ahead – devising modern suburbs, creating multinationals and arranging forays into outer space. Stephen Ambrose called them 'The IBM Generation', and said their creativity was the perfect counterpoint to the desolation of their youth.

But not everyone was happy. Amongst their literary peers, the veterans were considered bland and materialistic. It was felt that the home-grown tradition of American radicalism – forged out of need – had somewhere got left behind. In works like *The Lonely Crowd* and *The Organisation Man*, post-war society was portrayed as ultra-conformist and dangerously in awe of authority. Such fears might have sounded fanciful, had it not been for Senator McCarthy. There were dangers too, in over-indulging the multinationals, leaving future generations vulnerable to vast, ungovernable corporate states, like Enron.

But perhaps the greatest danger lay in the new-found confidence in military solutions. No one can sanely dispute that the Second World War was a triumph of both might and right. But since then things have been less straightforward. The United States has bombed twenty-five different countries, and has sought the overthrow of more than fifty governments, some of them democratically elected. Ordinary Americans have never felt quite the same unanimity about these ventures, some of which – Cuba, Indo-China, Iran, Somalia and Iraq – have proved to be punishing brawls. Even now, however, US governments compare their strange schemes (like 'The War on Terror') to the fight against the Nazis. To veterans like Flint, this is a source of endless wonder.

158

When we finally got to Flint's house, I felt sure that the rest of his life would slot into place. So it did, in a way, and yet there was always the feeling that the young Flint was far better known to me than the man he'd become. This, of course, was merely an illusion generated by our travels – and couldn't possibly be true – and yet it worried me. I think what troubled me most was the thought that Flint might've felt something similar, that too much of his past felt like a time he'd rather forget.

The house played a curious role in this. It was an old, white clapboard farmstead with ox-blood shutters and a deep stone cellar. Flint had bought it with his GI grant in 1945, and had never lived anywhere else. With its huge fireplace, its maple floors, fly-screens and furnaces, it was, in some ways, still very much the house he'd bought over sixty years before. The two most conspicuous additions were the swimming pool – dug out by an old comrade from the 824th – and a barn, erected by a curate who later became the Bishop of Ohio. Otherwise few things had changed. With so little intervention, the house seemed to offer a commanding view of an earlier age.

Surprisingly, Flint's wife, Dottie, featured only fleetingly in this perspective. In death, she'd shown a remarkable lightness of touch. It was now three years since she'd died, and the house – with its Persian rugs, portraits, busts and gun-cabinets – felt comfortably masculine, as if it'd never been anything else. The sheer totality of her disappearance horrified Flint. Neither in his surroundings nor in his memory was there ever enough of Dorothy, and her death still felt like a chasm, instead of a space where her life had been.

Around the house, there was slightly more of the children. Perhaps it was merely that their accoutrements were more conspicuous. Out in the barn there were snow-shoes and lacrosse sticks, and along the mantelpiece four tiny hooks for Christmas stockings. The children reinforced their participation by actually appearing from time to time. My history had somehow never caught up with them, and it took me a moment to adjust to the fact that they were now all middle-aged. In the intervening years, they'd had plenty of time to work up some Flintian character: Margie was a herbalist, Rebecca had converted to Judaism, and Leverett now ran the factory, and made his own cars. But probably the one I got to know best of all was the oldest, Kitty, born during the German counter-offensive. She always loved the idea of journeying back into the past, and now lived in a state of uncertain euphoria. 'I've had six rounds of chemo,' she'd say, 'but – look! – here I am, still here.'

More complicated, perhaps, was the lingering presence of the war. I'd always imagined that Flint's memory was strewn with pieces of that time but was surprised to find that so was his house. Up the stairs there were snapshots of old comrades, and elsewhere we stumbled on medals, belts, the concentration camp survivor's portrait, a little black German pistol, shirts decorated with tank-munching Panthers, a beautiful tailored tunic or *blouse* – effulgent in patches and brass – and a crumbling officer's over-coat. 'I think I've got almost all my uniform,' said Flint, 'except my boots and pinks.' Out in the barn, it was like a little repository of battlefield litter – army bags and blankets, bits of a three-inch projectile, and an old ammunition box stencilled PATRONENKAST 88 (Shellcases 88). 'I think I must have picked it up when we overran their guns,' said Flint. 'You keep it. You probably know the battles better than me.'

To Flint's children, these things had always been a mystery.

'Father never told us about the war . . .' said Margie.

'. . . never let us talk about it,' said Rebecca. 'Never watched war movies . . .'

'. . . and wouldn't even let me have toy guns,' said Leverett.

This made it all the harder to see why Flint had kept his loot. He himself didn't seem to know. Perhaps he didn't hate the war quite as much as he hoped? He once told me it had created a sort of dependence in him, and that – ever since – he'd found the constant company hard to live without. Another survivor, also a veteran of the 103rd, wrote of the sheer exhilaration of having survived. 'Death has been right in front of you, reaching for you and you beat him,' he wrote. 'The knowledge that you came that close and survived is a high like no other.'

Or perhaps it was simply that the war was too much of himself to throw away? Just as millions of young Americans had reshaped Western Europe, so it had reshaped them. It was not a past that could be amputated, however broken and brutal it had been. Flint told me he remembered years of nightmares, and waking up, screaming and swearing with horror. The burnt cities and crushed men were hard to live with, but then those eight months – looming so large in the past – were hard to live without. Audie Murphy told his doctor, shortly before he died in 1971, that Alsace had been with him all his life, and that every night since he'd slept with a pistol under his pillow. 'How does a soldier survive the war?' he was once asked.

'I don't think they ever do,' he replied.

159

My last day, Flint appeared with two rifles.

'I forgot to show you these,' he said.

The first was the *Wehrmacht* sniper rifle.

'A terrible thing,' said Flint. 'Look at this, a hair trigger.'

I brushed a finger over the curl of metal, and – click! – the bolt sprang back into place. Flint tapped it thoughtfully. 'I guess it made killing easier. Relieved the psychological pressure . . .'

The other gun was the *Drilling* that had belonged to the Austrian assassin.

'See what I mean? An exquisite thing to be killed by?'

I agreed: it would've been like being shot with a beautiful clock.

Flint patted it affectionately. 'Damn near took my head off.'

'Would have made my life easier,' I said.

Flint grinned. 'Yep. A lot of things would've been different . . .'

'I wouldn't have had to chase you over those hills . . .'

'. . . there'd be no farmhouse . . .'

'. . . no automatic batter mixers . . .'

'. . . no viscosity controllers for McDonald's . . .'

'They'd have to find some other way to get breadcrumbs on their nuggets!'

Flint was laughing so much he could hardly find the catch on the stock.

'This,' he said, through his sobs, 'is the bullet compartment.'

With a tiny, silky click, the cover popped open. Inside were four slots, each designed for a round. In the fourth slot was an old yellowy cartridge, but the other three were empty. Presumably, the assassin had loosed off two at the wildlife before trying to pop the third into Flint. This, one of the last shots of the war in the Tyrol, had cost the marksman his life.

'And you've never felt tempted to fire the fourth bullet?' I asked.

Flint paused, running his finger around the edge of the fatal slot.

'No,' he said. 'That was enough. The war ended here.'

Afterword

NANCY WAKE thrives, and has just celebrated her 95th birthday in the company of her friends, the aging saboteurs.

Air Chief Marshal Sir LEWIS HODGES, the pilot who escaped from occupied France in 1941, died in January 2007.

CHARLIE KENNEDY died suddenly in November 2007. Amongst the many hundreds of messages of sympathy was one from the French government, which still regards him as one of its own, a hero of *la Libération*.

Almost nothing remains of the 824th TDB. Like every other tank destroyer battalion, it was disbanded in 1945. The last reunion was held over ten years ago, in Hicksville, New York, and since then its members have dispersed.

GEORGE NOWICKI, Flint's brilliant gunner, was last heard of in California, where he resumed his trade as a furniture restorer. 'I'd love to see him if he's still alive,' said Flint, 'but you get kind of scared nowadays making enquiries as to who's around.'

In September 2007, Flint's daughter, KITTY BARTLEY, died after a long battle with cancer. For him, her life had always had a special poignancy. She was born on the third day of the German's devastating counter-offensive, at a time when her father was immersed in the utter devastation of war. Despite all he's experienced, he now says that the death of his daughter was the hardest thing he'd ever been through.

The BAADER-MEINHOF GANG resurfaced briefly in 2007. After twenty-four years in jail, one of the Second Generation guerrillas, Brigitte Mohnhaupt, sought parole. Convicted of five murders, including that of Schleyer, she was once described as 'the most evil and dangerous woman in Germany'. Despite her lack of remorse – and a massive public outcry – it was felt that enough was enough, and she was finally released.

There are 3.2 million SECOND WORLD WAR VETERANS living in the USA. They are now dying off at the rate of several thousand a week, and the time will soon come when the story that only they can truly tell will disappear for good.

Bibliography

France (General)

Adamson Taylor, Sally, *Culture Shock! France* (Graphic Arts Centre Publishing, Oregon, 1990)

Barnes, Julian, *Something to Declare* (Macmillan, London, 2002)

Black, Jeremy, *The Grand Tour in the Eighteenth Century* (Sutton, Stroud, 1992)

Boswell, James, *Boswell on Grand Tour*, McGraw-Hill, ed. F.A. Pottle (London and New York, 1952)

Coryat, Thomas, *Coryat's Crudities* (London, 1611)

Hazlitt, William, *Notes on a Journey through France and Italy* (London, 1856)

Hudson, Roger, *The Grand Tour* (Folio, London, 1993)

Moryson, Fynes, *An Itinerary Containing his Ten Yeeres Travell* (London, 1617)

The Rough Guide to France (Rough Guides, London, 2003)

Young, Arthur, *Travels in France* (London, 1792)

France: Resistance and Liberation

Allcorn, William, *The Maginot Line 1928–45* (Osprey Publications, Oxford, 2003)

Braddon, Russell, *Nancy Wake* (Cassell, London, 1956)

Hohnadel, Alain, *Le Simserhof: Découverte d'un Ouvrage Maginot du Pays de Bitche* (Conseil Général de la Moselle)

Keegan, John, *Six Armies in Normandy* (Jonathan Cape, London, 1982)
Kladstrup, Don and Petie, *Wine and War* (Broadway Books, New York, 2001)
Koestler, Arthur, *Scum of the Earth* (Jonathan Cape, London, 1941)
Leslie, Anita, *A Story Half Told* (Hutchinson, London, 1983)
Thompson, R.W., *The Devil at My Heels* (MacDonald, London, 1947)
Wake, Nancy, *The White Mouse* (Sun Books, Melbourne, 1986)

The US Army in Western Europe

Ambrose, Stephen, *Citizen Soldiers* (Touchstone, New York, 1998)
Bass, Michael, *The Story of the Century* (The Century Association, Paducah, Kentucky, 1946)
Fussell, Paul, *The Boy's Crusade* (Weidenfeld and Nicolson, London, 2004)
Henry, Mark, *The US Army in World War II Northeast Europe* (Osprey Publications, Oxford, 2001)
Murphy, Audie, *To Hell and Back* (Corgi, London, 1950)
Vonnegut, Kurt, *Slaughterhouse-Five* (Delacorte Press, New York, 1994)
Zaloga, Stephen, *M18 Hellcat Tank Destroyer 1943–47* (Osprey Publications, Oxford, 2004)
The 103rd Infantry Division (Turner Publishing, Kentucky, 1996)
The 100th Infantry Division (Turner Publishing, Kentucky, 1996)

Battalion Records: 824th Tank Destroyers

National Archives, College Park Maryland, ref. RG 407 Entry 427

Marseille and the Rhône

Baillie, Kate, *Provence and the Côte d'Azur* (Rough Guides, London, 1996)
Evelyn, John, *The Diary of John Evelyn* (London, 1906)
Fortescue, Lady, *Perfume from Provence* (William Blackwood, London, 1945)
Huddleston, Sisley, *Mediterranean Blue* (Evans, London, 1948)
Jankowski, Paul, *Communism and Collaboration: Simon Sabiani and Politics in Marseille, 1919–1944* (Yale University Press, New Haven, 1989)

Klarsfeld, Serge, *Marseille 1942–1944 Der Blick des Besatzers* (Temmen, Bremen, 1999)

Roth, Joseph, *The White Cities: Reports from France 1925–39* (Granta Books, London, 2004)

Smollett, Tobias, *Travels through France and Italy* (London, 1766)

Sterne, Laurence, *A Sentimental Journey* (London, 1768)

Thicknesse, Philip, *A Year's Journey through France and Part of Spain* (Dublin, 1777)

Tixier, Jean-Max and Cres, Christian, *Marseille vous souhaite la bienvenue* (EEMP, 1998)

Williams, Roger, *Provence and the Côte d'Azur* (Eyewitness Travel Guides, London, 1995)

Young, John, *The French Foreign Legion* (Thames & Hudson, London, 1984)

Alsace and Lorraine

Comité National de Struthof, *Concentration Camp Natzwiller Struthof* (Nancy, 1990)

Elsy, Mary and Norman, Jill, *Travels in Alsace and Lorraine* (Merehurst, London, 1989)

Gosse, Jeanne, *Alsatian Vignettes* (Geoffrey Bles, London, 1946)

The Green Guide: Alsace Lorraine Champagne (Michelin, Watford, 2004)

Menkes-Ivry, Vivienne, *Alsace, the Complete Guide* (Simon & Schuster, London, 1991)

Newman, Bernard, *The Sisters Alsace-Lorraine* (Herbert Jenkins, London, 1950)

Townroe, B.S., *A Wayfarer in Alsace* (Methuen, London, 1926)

Whiting, Charles, *Operation Northwind: The Other Battle of the Bulge* (Spellmount, Staplehurst, 1986)

Paris

Baxter, John, *We'll Always Have a Paris* (Doubleday, London, 2005)

Beach, Sylvia, *Shakespeare and Company* (Harcourt, Brace, New York, 1959)

Beevor, Antony and Cooper, Artemis, *Paris after the Liberation 1944–1949* (Penguin, London, 2004)

Bourget, Pierre, *Paris 1940–1944* (Plon, Paris, 1979)

Clark, Val, *The Parisian Café: A Literary Companion* (Universe, New York, 2002)

Hemingway, Ernest, *A Moveable Feast* (Jonathan Cape, London, 1964)

Hemingway, Mary Welsh, *How It Was* (Knopf, New York, 1976)

Izbicki, John, *The Naked Heroine* (Spearman, London, 1963)

James, Clive, *Flying Visits* (Jonathan Cape, London, 1984)

Jamet, Fabienne, *Palace of Sweet Sin* (W.H. Allen, London, 1977)

Malraux, André, *Anti-Memoirs* (Bantam, New York, 1970)

Miller, Arthur, *Timebends* (Methuen, London, 1987)

Morris, Jan, *Locations* (OUP, Oxford, 1992)

Palin, Michael, *Hemingway Adventure* (Weidenfeld & Nicolson, London, 1999)

Paris Occupé, Paris Liberé (Arcadia, Paris, 2004)

Paul, Elliot, *The Last Time I Saw Paris* (Random House, New York, 1942)

Sawyer-Lauçanno, Christopher, *The Continual Pilgrimage: American Writers in Paris 1944–60* (Bloomsbury, London, 1992)

Stein, Gertrude, *The Selected Writings of Gertrude Stein* (Random House, New York, 1962)

Stearns, Harold, *The Street I Know*, (Lee Furman, Inc., New York 1935)

Toklas, Alice, *The Alice B. Toklas Cookbook* (Michael Joseph, London, 1964)

Germany

Ardagh, John, *Germany and the Germans* (Penguin, London, 1991)

Germany (Time-Life Books, Amsterdam, 1984)

Gibbon, Monk, *Western Germany* (Batsford, London, 1955)

Leigh Fermor, Patrick, *A Time of Gifts* (John Murray, London, 1977)

Prinzhorn, Hans, *The Artistry of the Mentally Ill* (Springer Verlag, New York, 1972)

The Rough Guide to Germany (Rough Guides, London, 2004)

Tacitus, *The Agricole and The Germania*, trans. S.A Handford and H. Mattingly (Penguin Classics, London, 1971)

Twain, Mark, *A Tramp Abroad* (American Publishing Company of Hartford, Connecticut, 1880)

The Battle for Germany

Baccque, James, *Other Losses* (Stoddart, Toronto, 1989)

Burleigh, Michael, *The Third Reich: A New History* (New York, Hill & Wang, 2000)

Cross, Robin, *VE Day: Victory in Europe 1945* (Guild Publishing, London, 1985)

Hastings, Max, *Armageddon: The Battle for Germany 1944–45* (Macmillan, London, 2004)

Irving, David, *The Trail of the Fox* (Weidenfeld & Nicolson, London, 1977)

Liddell-Hart, B.H., *The Rommel Papers* (Collins, London, 1952)

Minott, Rodney G., *The Fortress that Never Was: The Myth of the Nazi Alpine Redoubt* (Longmans, London, 1965)

Moorehead, Alan, *Eclipse* (Granta, London, 2000)

Read, Anthony, *The Devil's Disciples: The Lives of Hitler's Inner Circle* (Pimlico, London, 2004)

Russell, Lord, *The Scourge of the Swastika* (Cassell, London, 1954)

Short, Neil, *Germany's West Wall: The Siegfried Line* (Osprey Publications, Oxford, 2004)

Trevor-Roper, H.R., *The Last Days of Hitler* (Macmillan, London, 1947)

Whiting, Charles, *Paths of Death and Glory: The Last Days of the Third Reich* (Spellmount, Staplehurst, 1997)

Young, Desmond, *Rommel* (Collins, London, 1950)

Swabia and Bavaria

Bechert, Tilmann, *The Heidelberg Student Prison* (Translated by Peter Johannsen, Landsmannschaft Zaringia im CC, Heidelberg, 1996)

Insight Pocket Guide to Bavaria (APA Publications, Singapore, 2001)

McIntosh, Christopher, *The Swan King: Ludwig II of Bavaria* (Tauris Parke, London, 1982)

Austria and the Tyrol

Auer, Alfred and others, *Ambras Castle* (Electra Art Guides, Milan, 2000)

Hubatschek, Erika, *Vom Leben am Steilhang* (Innsbruck, 2003)

Montagu, Lady Mary Wortley, *The Letters and Works of Lady Mary Wortley Montagu* (London, 1837)

Morrow, Ian, *The Austrian Tyrol* (Faber & Faber, London, 1931)

Pick, Hella, *Guilty Victim: Austria from the Holocaust to Haider* (I.B. Tauris, London, 2000)

Romilly, G. and Alexander, M. *The Privileged Nightmare* (Weidenfeld &
Nicolson, London, 1954)
The Rough Guide to Austria (Rough Guides, London, 2005)

Boston and the USA

Ellis, James, *The Rough Guide to Boston* (Rough Guides, London, 2005)
Seitz, Raymond, *Over Here* (Weidenfeld & Nicolson, London, 1998)

Index